May It Please the Court!

May It Please the Court!

From Auto Accidents to Agent Orange: Building a Storefront Law Practice into America's Largest Suburban Law Firm

Leonard Rivkin
with
Jeffrey Silberfeld

Carolina Academic Press
Durham, North Carolina

ISBN 0-89089-915-0
LCCN 99-069959

Carolina Academic Press
700 Kent Street
Durham, North Carolina 27701
Telephone (919) 489-7486
Fax (919) 493-5668
E-mail: cap@cap-press.com
www.cap-press.com

Printed in the United States of America.

Contents

Introduction   3

Part One — The Early Years

Chapter One
But Dad, I Don't Want to Be a Doctor   11

Chapter Two
Leonard L. Rivkin: Attorney-at-Law   23

Chapter Three
*The Tote Board, Life with Johnny, and
Other Early Tales*   41

Chapter Four
The Judicial Inquiry   55

Chapter Five
Crossing the Street: Representing Defendants   71

Part Two — Major Clients, Major Cases

Chapter Six
The First Dow Case   89

Chapter Seven
The Staten Island Gas Tank Disaster   99

Chapter Eight
Franklin National Bank   141

Part Three — Agent Orange

Chapter Nine
Not Your Typical Garden Variety Lawsuit   203

Chapter Ten
Litigation Strategy   233

Chapter Eleven
Litigation Chronology   247

Chapter Twelve
Settlement   303

Part Four — New Partners, New Offices

Chapter Thirteen
*Garden City: Transformation, Emergence,
and Growth*   347

Chapter Fourteen
Chicago and Washington   391

Chapter Fifteen
EAB Plaza   407

Sources and Footnotes   417

Index   429

May It Please the Court!

Introduction

In March of 1950, less than two years after graduating from the University of Virginia Law School, I opened a one man law practice in the back of an insurance brokerage office in the quiet, mostly residential village of Freeport, Long Island. My clients were relatives, friends, and neighbors. I wrote wills, handled real estate closings, and litigated relatively uncomplicated automobile accident and slip and fall cases. My first partner, who joined me in 1953, was my landlord's brother.

Thirty-five years later, I was the senior partner of Rivkin, Radler, Dunne & Bayh, a nationally prominent law firm employing nearly two hundred fifty attorneys in five offices in three states and the District of Columbia. Our main office occupied three entire floors, more than ninety thousand square feet, at EAB Plaza, Long Island's most prestigious business address. We also occupied smaller but no less impressive quarters on Madison Avenue in New York City, "I" Street in Washington, D.C., LaSalle Street in Chicago, and in Century City in Los Angeles. My clients included Fortune 500 corporations and insurance companies embroiled in complex, multi-million dollar litigation. I defended Dow Chemical in the Agent Orange case, one of the largest products liability class actions in American legal history; Fireman's Fund Insurance Company in the Franklin National Bank case, which involved the largest bank failure in United States history; Pittsburgh Corning Corporation in asbestos litigation, involving one of the most lethal products in American legal history; and AEGIS Insurance Company in the Texas Eastern interstate pipeline litigation, which resulted in one of the costliest environmental cleanups in United States history. My partners included state legislators, a future New York State Supreme Court judge, a former law school dean, the future Chief of the Civil Rights Division of the United States Department of Justice, and even a former United States Senator who twice sought his party's nomination for President.

What a long and improbable journey! From solo practitioner to senior partner. From auto accidents to Agent Orange. From Village

Court in Freeport to federal courts throughout the country to the Supreme Court of the United States.

How did I do it?

How did I build a small, storefront law practice into the largest suburban law firm in the country?

How did I successfully litigate not just headline grabbing, precedent setting cases but routine matters as well?

With a lot of hard work.

With a little bit of luck.

With a lot of help from family, friends, partners, and clients.

With a uniquely aggressive and creative approach to business development and litigation strategy.

The essence of that approach: take the initiative.

In other words, do not sit on your hands waiting for something to happen; make it happen. Do not react to your adversary; make him react to you. Even when representing a defendant, do not be lulled into doing nothing more than responding to plaintiff's claims and parrying his thrusts. Instead, take the initiative. Wrest control of the case from the plaintiff, for example, by aggressively pursuing affirmative defenses and third-party claims.

Take the initiative. This approach is not just a litigation tactic; it is a surefire way to develop and expand a law practice. Clients do not materialize in an attorney's office out of thin air. They will not find you unless you find them first. This requires you to market yourself and your talents. Join professional associations. Attend seminars. Publish articles. Make inquiries. Write letters. Use the telephone. Circulate.

Take the initiative.

* * *

This book is my professional autobiography. Organized chronologically, it tells the story of how I became an attorney, started and developed my practice, and litigated my cases, taking the initiative every step of the way.

Part One, "The Early Years," covers my childhood, education, military service, and the first twenty years of my legal career: working at my first job at a two man firm in Brooklyn, going out on my own in Freeport, developing an expertise representing plaintiffs in personal injury litigation, acquiring my first insurance company clients, and shifting the emphasis of my practice from plaintiff's work to defense. The focus of this section is on practice development; during this period, I aggressively sought new business and succeeded in expanding the size of my law firm from one attorney to ten.

Part Two, "Major Clients, Major Cases," covers my entry into the arena of big time clients and big time litigation. After describing how I acquired The Dow Chemical Company and the Home Office of Fireman's Fund Insurance Company as clients, this section discusses at length my involvement on behalf of Dow and Fireman's Fund in a series of increasingly complex lawsuits, including the Staten Island natural gas tank explosion and Franklin National Bank. Unlike Part One, which focuses on practice development, this section focuses on litigation skills, tactics, and strategy. But there is a marketing lesson in this section as well; writing letters and making telephone calls may open doors for you, but don't count on attracting many new clients unless you can demonstrate that you achieved great results for your old ones.

Part Three, "Agent Orange," chronicles my involvement on behalf of Dow Chemical in one of the most extraordinary cases of our time. Broken down into four chapters, this section details the unprecedented size and scope of the litigation, discusses our litigation strategy, presents a litigation chronology, and describes the intense, round-the-clock, last minute settlement negotiations. As the section makes clear, Agent Orange is a case that contains a lifetime of litigation experiences and is one that refuses to go away. The first Agent Orange lawsuit was filed in 1978; as this book goes to press, my firm is still litigating Agent Orange matters. Without a doubt, the Agent Orange litigation was the highlight of my legal career. It's a safe bet that every one of the dozens of lead attorneys who worked on the case would undoubtedly say the same thing.

Part Four, "New Partners, New Offices," describes the explosive growth of my firm from ten to 250 lawyers and its transformation from local to national prominence. Here, as in Part One, although there are brief discussions of important clients and case, the focus is on practice development. I have always believed that big firms should market themselves as aggressively as sole practitioners; this section describes efforts by me and my partners to maintain our existing clients and attract new ones.

Although the four sections of the book cover different time frames and different subjects, they have much in common. Each contains episodes of aggressive and creative lawyering. Each describes innovative and resourceful methods of attracting and keeping clients. Thus, the book should prove to be a valuable reference tool for young lawyers starting out on their own looking to develop their litigation and marketing skills.

But this is more than a "how to" book for young lawyers. It describes the extraordinary transformation and growth of a law practice. It peeks behind the scenes at Agent Orange, Franklin National Bank, and other compelling cases. It paints a vivid picture of what it's like to litigate routine traffic accident cases and headline-grabbing class actions: the pressure, the suspense, the unexpected twists, the humor, the elation, and the despair. It takes you into the conference room, not just the courtroom. It gives you the reasons, not just the results. I would think, therefore, that this is a book that will entertain and enlighten both lawyers and non-lawyers alike.

* * *

Before I begin, I must include a word of acknowledgment to the family, friends, partners, and clients who helped me along the way. Obviously, I couldn't have done it alone and owe a debt of gratitude to many people. The following deserve special mention:

My parents, especially my father, who may have been chagrined by his son's decision to become a lawyer but ultimately took great pride in his son's achievements.

Lenore, my first wife of thirty-seven years, who encouraged me through the lean years and shared in my later success. Lenore was a loving and supportive wife and mother who was equally at home helping our children with their homework and socializing with an important client. The whole family suffered a great loss when Lenore died of cancer after a long and courageous struggle.

Betty, my second wife, whom I married in 1987. I had known Betty for nearly fifty years; her late first husband was Lenore's first cousin. Betty was born wise, gentle, and insightful. She has complimented me in every way that matters. She brought balance, strength, and happiness to my life at a time when I most needed it.

My children, John and Janet, who endured the demands of my profession when they were growing up and have always brought great joy to me. John became a lawyer like his father and is now a senior partner at the firm. Janet became a lawyer to please her father but is now a practicing clinical psychologist.

My partners: Victor Leff, Stu Sherman, Phil Weinberg, John Dunne, Jeff Silberfeld, Bill Savino, Warren Radler, Bruce Drucker, Ed Hart, and Birch Bayh.

And my clients: Bob Buell of Fireman's Fund; Don Frayer, Charley Carey, Wayne Hancock, and Keith McKennon of Dow; and Bill Bailey and Dick Jordan of Commercial Union.

* * *

Finally, a quick word about the title: *May It Please the Court!*

As a neophyte attorney, I litigated my first cases in Freeport Village Court, gradually moving my way up to the local county, state, and federal courts on Long Island and in Brooklyn and Manhattan. Later, as my firm expanded and developed a national presence, I litigated cases in state and federal courts around the country, some quite well known, and certainly not because of me or any of my cases: the state courthouse in New Jersey where the Lindbergh kidnapping case was tried; the federal courthouse in Oklahoma City that was tragically bombed in 1995; the state courthouse in San Rafael, California, designed by Frank Lloyd Wright; and, of course, the most famous courthouse of them all, the United States Supreme Court.

Almost from day one, whenever I appeared in court, no matter where and no matter what the occasion, I always began my presentation with the same words: "May it please the court." When I was a young attorney practicing on Long Island, it seemed to me that all of the prominent local trial and appellate lawyers did the same thing. It sounded dignified and professional, so I followed suit. Later on, as a younger generation of trial attorneys came onto the scene, many of them adopted a more informal style. They began their presentations with a simple "Good Morning, Your Honor" or something very similar. Sometimes they just started right in on their argument. But I never changed my style. I was saying "May it please the court" in 1950 and was still saying it forty years later.

PART ONE

The Early Years

Chapter One

But Dad, I Don't Want to Be a Doctor

One cold winter evening in 1946, six months short of my twenty first birthday, three weeks into my third semester as an undergraduate student at the University of Virginia, I walked briskly across the campus, hands in my pockets, head down, deep in thought. To me, the University of Virginia was and still is the most beautiful college campus imaginable. The famous Rotunda, the school's administration building, with its imposing dome, pillars, and steps, was designed and built by Thomas Jefferson, as was the "Grounds," the University's original campus, with its tree-lined walkways crisscrossing an expanse of lawns dotted with classrooms and dormitories. But that night, I was oblivious to my surroundings, because I was too busy preparing myself for the most difficult task that I have ever faced in my entire life.

More difficult than dodging bullets in Europe as a combat infantryman during World War II.

More difficult than summing up a hopeless case before a hostile jury.

I was about to telephone my father, the man I most loved, admired, and respected in the whole world, to tell him that I did not want to go to medical school and become a doctor.

* * *

His name was Hyman Rivkin. Dr. Hyman Rivkin. His specialty was radiology, and in 1924, when he opened his office in Far Rockaway, New York, he was the only radiologist in private practice between Brooklyn and Montauk Point—a distance of 130 miles—with his own x-ray equipment. Ultimately, he became the Director of Radiology at Rockaway Beach, now known as Peninsula, and Long Beach Hospitals.

Solidly built but only five feet five inches tall, my father was not an overpowering physical presence. Nevertheless, he commanded respect by his quiet but forceful personality and clean cut, formal appearance. He always wore a suit and tie, whether at home, in the office, or at the hospital. In fact, he didn't even own a sports jacket until he retired to Florida in his mid-70s. He was a loving and devoted family man but was not an overtly emotional person; a pat on the back from him was like a hug and kiss from anybody else. He didn't smile easily, but when he did, you knew he meant it. He was sincere and honest; he believed that if you worked hard, did the right thing, and had integrity, you would lead a successful life.

My father practiced medicine at a time when society bestowed upon physicians an extraordinarily high level of prestige and status. This was particularly true in Far Rockaway, where my father was known, respected, and admired by the entire community. The prevailing view there was that doctors were saints unto themselves. Well educated, well trained, and totally dedicated to their fellow man, they could do no wrong. You trusted your doctor implicitly. If he told you to do something, you did it without hesitation. Malpractice lawsuits were virtually non-existent. You didn't sue your doctor because you couldn't imagine your doctor making a mistake.

My father shared this attitude about physicians and then some. To him, medicine was not just the noblest and most honorable profession, it was the only profession. Of course, there may have been one or two bad apples, but my father's view was that the vast majority of doctors occupied a level far above everybody else on the evolutionary scale. My father never told me why he felt as deeply about medicine as he did. Perhaps it was because his immigrant father, a good and decent man who struggled for years in the garment business to support his family, never came close to gaining the status and respect that my father enjoyed as a practicing physician.

With that attitude, it is not surprising that all of my father's friends were doctors. He wouldn't think of socializing with a non-physician. For example, for twenty years my father held a weekly bridge game at our house. All of the participants were physicians. There were usually five in the group, with one man sitting out each week. The games lasted several hours, and the only topics of discussion during the games were medicine (the latest news at the hospital) and bridge (the last bungled hand). If, for some reason, only three members of the group were available, they would try to find another doctor to fill in. If they couldn't find a fourth doctor, they simply wouldn't play.

My mother, Nettie Rivkin, was the opposite of my father in certain respects. He was quiet and reserved; she was loquacious, friendly, and outgoing. Because my father's friends were all physicians, most of my mother's friends were physicians' wives. But she also had many friends from our community who were not married to doctors. She felt comfortable and at home with just about everybody. Nevertheless, she loved being a doctor's wife and was proud of her life as "Mrs. Dr. Rivkin," which is how people greeted her as she strolled down Central Avenue in Far Rockaway in the 1920s and 1930s wearing an outfit typical of the times, which always included white gloves and a parasol.

My parents had two children. I was born in 1925, the year after my father opened up his practice. My sister Judy, who was a child prodigy on the piano, was born six years later.

Unlike my sister, who played as a guest artist with the Long Island Symphony and at Town Hall in New York City and who later won a scholarship to the Juilliard School, I possessed no extraordinary abilities as a youngster. Much to my parents' chagrin, I did as little schoolwork as I could get away with. Much to their puzzlement, I spent most of my free time playing whatever sport was in season—baseball, football, or basketball. There were lots of children in my neighborhood and we always had enough for a game. Most of the time we played in the street alongside our house. My father was not the type to roll up his sleeves and play catch with me after work. In all fairness, however, not many of the doctors on our block played ball with their sons. Later, when I played on the high school team, my father was a frequent spectator.

At the time, I never gave much thought to what I would do when I grew up. That's because there was nothing to think about. From the day I was born, my future was carved in stone. Like my father, I would practice medicine.

What choice did I have? I was raised in medicine. I could read x-rays when I was in grammar school. I knew what an articular fracture was before I could roller skate. Around the dinner table, we had conversations about doctors and their families, not merchants or manufacturers. All of our neighbors were doctors, and my friends were their sons. We lived in a nice neighborhood and didn't want for anything. But most significantly, I idolized my father and knew what he wanted for me: to be as well educated and highly esteemed as he was. Only by practicing medicine could I aspire to that same level. I couldn't imagine disappointing him. Moreover, as I was growing up in Far Rockaway watching him live the good life, becoming a doctor didn't seem like all that bad an idea.

Many times my father told me that there were two kinds of people in the world that he did not trust: lawyers and orthopedists. He didn't trust lawyers because "they never tell the truth," and he didn't trust orthopedists because "they're putting X-ray machines in their offices," thus hurting his business. Ultimately, not only did his only son become a lawyer, but also his only daughter married an orthopedist. Similarly, my son and daughter—his grandchildren—both became lawyers, and my daughter married an orthopedist. Talk about bad luck! Nevertheless, my father accepted all of this with grace, although I don't know if he was ever really happy about it.

*   *   *

My Mother Takes the Initiative

I applied to the University of Virginia during my senior year at Woodmere Academy, a small, co-educational prep school fifteen minutes from my home via the Long Island Railroad. I had no burning desire to go to college, but I was going to be a doctor, so I had no choice. College first, then medical school. End of discussion.

I chose the University of Virginia simply because one of my father's good friends (a doctor, of course) recommended it on the basis of its "absolutely fantastic" medical school. Since I applied to no other college, luckily I was accepted.

But as much as U. Va. may have wanted me, Uncle Sam wanted me even more. When I graduated from high school in June 1943, World War II was in full swing. I expected to receive my draft notice before the end of the summer. Without question I was going to serve in the military. The 1940s were not like the 1970s. There were no anti-war movements of any consequence. Virtually the entire country opposed Hitler and supported the war effort. The attitude among draft age men in those days was that if you were healthy, you did your duty, and I was no exception. Under the circumstances, it appeared that college and medical school might have to wait.

Nevertheless, my mother urged me to start college immediately (U. Va. offered a summer session which began in early July) and go for as long as possible until I was drafted. She predicted that when the War was over, all of the young men returning home from the front would inundate the colleges with applications for admission. Her "motherly wisdom" told her those who had started college before going into the service would have an advantage over those who had not.

That argument made sense to me, but I hesitated going all the way to Charlottesville knowing that I was likely to be drafted before the end of my first semester. I preferred to hang around the beaches of Far Rockaway. But my mother did some research and learned of an Army program called the Enlisted Reserve Corps ("ERC"), which offered potential draftees the option of enlisting in the Army with a guarantee that they could complete one semester of college before going on active duty.

That settled that. I enlisted in the ERC, enrolled at U. Va. as a premed student, finished one uneventful summer semester, and entered the Army in October of 1943. I was 18 years old.

*   *   *

Dodging Bullets

After enduring more than nine months of basic training in Georgia, Louisiana, and California, I shipped off to Europe in the fall of 1944 as a member of the 86th Infantry Division, known as the Black Hawks. We landed at Le Havre, France, a harbor town under the control of the Allies. From Le Havre, we moved eastward across France, Belgium, and Germany. We marched, sat in the back of trucks, and rode on trains through bombed out cities and small towns and villages, over hills, and across open fields and farmland. In Cologne, Germany, every building in the center of the city had been leveled by Allied bombs except for the majestic cathedral, which was untouched. In Belgium, we entered an industrial town which had been completely flattened. We had an unobstructed view from one end of town to the other over the rubble.

At first, I served as a light machine gun operator. Later, I became a machine gun squad leader. I saw plenty of action, but often didn't even see the enemy. We had what were called "firefights." For example, approaching a hill or a town, we would be fired upon by the enemy. We would scatter and fire back. Then we would call for a mortar barrage. Afterward, when it was quiet, we would advance. Usually, by that time, the enemy was gone.

I was awarded two Purple Hearts for wounds I received in the line of duty. The first time I was wounded a piece of shrapnel hit me in the ankle. The second time a German thrown concussion grenade exploded near my gun emplacement shattering my left eardrum and dislocating both of my shoulders.

I was also awarded a Silver Star for capturing eighty German soldiers in Rarin, Germany, a rural village that consisted of one street and less than a dozen small buildings. I was riding in the back of an open truck with other troops hand carrying my light machine gun. We were part of a column of approximately forty vehicles. As we approached the town, the Germans began firing at us from roadside buildings. We returned the fire and then jumped off the truck and scattered for cover. As I was setting up my machine gun, the Germans began firing at us from the crest of a hill. Once again, we returned the fire. Then I got up and, carrying my machine gun, began to run across an open field toward the hill, stopping periodically along the way to lie down and return the fire. As I approached the hill, I was able to come around from the side and pretty much surprise the German soldiers who were shooting two 88 mm guns at our troops. As they were reloading, I began to fire at them from their flank. Suddenly, they all jumped out from behind their guns with their hands up. My squad and some other men from our outfit were moving up behind me at that moment, so I marched the Germans, who were bunched up in front of me, down the road to meet our troops.

During that entire episode, and whenever I was engaged in combat, I performed entirely without thinking. My actions were essentially reactions. I was trained to set up, camouflage, and shoot my weapon whenever somebody shot at me, which I did. When the Germans opened fire at us in Rarin, I didn't think about what my options were or how risky it would be for me to run across the open field. I just did it.

*　*　*

The episode that most accurately captures my wartime experience was not the incident at Rarin but one that occurred at the army hospital where I was recuperating from my wounds. As I lay in bed one afternoon, a group of doctors and nurses urgently wheeled a gurney into the area next to my bed. It was obvious, from all the excitement and commotion, that the soldier on the gurney was hurt quite badly. Suddenly, one of the nurses came over to my bed and asked me to help out. Although my ankle and both of my shoulders were bandaged, the nurse helped me up, walked me gingerly over to the gurney, and handed me an intravenous line.

"Just hold this steady for us please," she said, which I did for less than two minutes, not in any pain, curious about what was going on but too squeamish to look or ask.

Then the nurse took the line away from me.

Then I did what any seasoned combat veteran would have done under the circumstances.

I fainted.

* * *

My Mother Takes the Initiative Again

I served in the Army for nineteen months. Following my discharge, in May of 1945, I re-enrolled at the University of Virginia for the summer session. This was near the end of the War, and many other returning veterans were seeking admission to college. But just as my mother had predicted, the University welcomed me back with open arms and could not have been nicer and more accommodating. Who knows if I would have received the same red-carpet treatment if I hadn't followed my mother's good advice and completed that one semester before entering the service?

Returning to college after my discharge from the Army was one thing; staying in college was quite another. After my wartime experiences, I began to have some problems. I had no trouble sitting in class listening to my professors, but I found it very difficult to concentrate when attempting to wade through lengthy reading assignments in densely written textbooks on history, economics, sociology, and the like. It was even more difficult for me to stay focused when attempting to write papers. I was also having a rough time sleeping. When I was in the army hospital in Europe, with my arm in a sling and my leg in a cast, I couldn't sleep, so they gave me sleeping pills. After I was discharged, I stopped using the pills, and I guess my body needed some time to readjust. It wasn't that my injuries were bothering me. It must have been the abrupt change from life in combat to life in college, which occurred in less than two months and apparently was just too much for me at the time.

So I telephoned my parents and discussed my problems with them. They immediately suggested that I pack up and come home. I went to see the Dean of Students, and he also advised me to consider taking some time off. He suggested that I try to relax both physically and psychologically and then consider returning to school. He assured me that the University's doors would always be open to me.

In those days, it wasn't as acceptable as it later became to see a psychologist or a psychiatrist for problems like the ones I was having at college. But my mother in her wisdom had an idea, which sounded terrific to me, for treating my lack of concentration and inability to sleep. She wanted to pack me off to Grossinger's, which, at the time, was New York's premier resort hotel. It featured the finest accommodations, the best food, the most complete athletic facilities, and the most attractive young women that the Catskill Mountains had to offer. My father opposed the idea; I guess he thought that living at home in Far Rockaway was better therapy than frolicking at a resort hotel in the Catskills. But my mother prevailed, and off I went. I stayed for one month. Every day I ate three sumptuous meals, stuffing myself to the point where I had difficulty getting up from the table. During the day I swam and played basketball, and at night I went to the night club and did what any twenty-year-old just home from combat would do: I drank and chased women, who weren't that interested in me when I was dressed in civilian clothes but were most responsive when I wore my Army uniform bedecked with three rows of ribbons. My month of carousing passed very quickly, and at the end of my stay, it turned out that Dr. Mom, once again, was right on the money. I was cured. I felt relaxed and healthy and had no difficulty reading a newspaper or book. I could sleep through the night. I was not as short-tempered with people as I had been when I first returned from overseas. At the end of the summer, I decided, with the full support of my parents, to return to Virginia for the September term.

* * *

I headed south driving an old rattletrap of a Buick that my father had purchased for me following my discharge from the Army. But I didn't quite make it as far as Charlottesville. On route, my Buick blew a rod, and when we learned that repairing the car would cost more than it was worth, I junked it. My father said he would spring for another car for me if I could find one, which was very difficult in 1945. Because of wartime shortages, private citizens could not buy new cars unless they were disabled. So I went to a local Ford dealership in Charlottesville and, for the first time, used advocacy skills that I didn't know I had. I told the dealer about my war record. I said that although I was not technically "disabled," I did suffer wounds, which were still bothering me, to my ankle and shoulders. A car, I explained, would make it much easier for me to get around. I was up front and honest with the dealer, who seemed to like me, listened attentively, and promised to get back to me shortly. Surprisingly, about two weeks later, he called to say that he had a new car for me if I was still interested. It was a brand new 1945 two-door Ford. I'll never forget the color: Tucson Tan. It was a real beauty; to me it was as glamorous as a Rolls Royce. I immediately called my parents to tell them of my good fortune. They were as shocked as I was that I was able to find a car so quickly. My father gladly paid for it, so there I was, at the University of Virginia with the a brand new Tucson Tan Ford, and the world awaited me.

* * *

But Dad, I Don't Want to Be a Doctor

When school started in September, I enrolled in my first two pre-med science courses: chemistry and biology. I was less than enthralled with both. To me, chemistry was boring: nothing more than the straight memorization of formulas and symbols. When I had first come back from the War, I had difficulty falling asleep; in Chemistry class, I had difficulty staying awake. In biology, my problem was not staying awake, it was how to keep from losing my lunch. I was rather squeamish when it came to dissecting worms, frogs, and fish.

To my horror, I was developing a real distaste for science, which caused me to seriously consider for the first time what I wanted, as opposed to what my parents wanted for me. The more I pondered, the more I began to think the unthinkable: maybe I didn't want to spend another four or five years studying science and medicine; maybe I didn't want to go to medical school. This period of reflection, which began in the fall of 1945 and lasted into early 1946, caused me great anguish. I felt that by rejecting a career in medicine, I would be rejecting my family and the only way of life I had ever known. Moreover, I idolized my father, desperately wanted to please him, and was certain that it would break his heart if he knew that I was considering going into some other field.

But I finally reached the point where I knew that I did not want to become a doctor and had to tell my parents. Nothing that I have ever experienced before or since made me as apprehensive as I felt walking into the fraternity house where I lived to make the call. There was a telephone in the back of the house on the first floor, in a closet-like room where you could have a degree of privacy. To add insult to injury, I even called collect. My father answered the phone; when he recognized my voice, he called for my mother to pick up the extension. With my heart pounding, I started with some small talk—hello, how are you—and then, in spite of myself, blurted out exactly how I felt.

"I don't know what I want to do," I told them, "except I want to stay in college but not continue in pre-med or go on to medical school." After a silence that seemed to last forever, my father's response was that I was old enough and mature enough to make my own decisions. He couldn't hide the disappointment in his voice. Later in the conversation, when he questioned me about other careers I may have been considering, he sounded almost defiant. It was almost, "I dare you to tell me something else." My mother, always supportive, told me that she was disappointed by my decision to quit pre-med but pleased that at least I was going to finish college. There was nothing left to speak about, so we said our good-byes and hung up. At that moment, I felt as if the weight of the world had been lifted off my shoulders. I had finally told my father. I also felt that both my parents belonged on a higher pedestal than ever before because of the manner in which they had handled the horrible news I had just given them, which was basically that since I was not going to be a doctor, I was going to be a bum —there was no middle ground.

*   *   *

Maybe I Should Have Been an Architect

Early in 1946, although I knew what I didn't want, I had no idea what I wanted. Here's how I chose law school.

When walking around the campus, I always admired the Law School building, known then as Clark Memorial Hall. I had walked inside once or twice and was greatly impressed by the "main" or "central" hall, which contained huge oil paintings of well known legal scholars. I was also in awe of the law students I saw in the building, thinking that they were going to be our future lawyers, judges, senators, governors, and maybe even a President or two. While I had no abiding love of the law or drive to be an attorney, I did want to have a profession and believed that law provided a solid basis for many career options. I suppose that my admiration of the law school building could just as easily influenced me to become an architect, but for some reason I leaned toward practicing law.

With that degree of enthusiasm, I went to the law school building one wintry afternoon to inquire if there were any undergraduate course requirements. They told me no, just take general courses, maybe some political science would be good. I then decided that I would go to school during the summer semester so that I could graduate early and make up some of the time I lost in the service. I enrolled in courses in political science, logic, philosophy, and economics, courses that would look good on my law school application. My grades when I was pre-med were less than average, but I found the pre-law courses much more interesting and actually made the Dean's List for the summer semester. When the semester ended, I went back to the law school and asked for an application. I filled it out, submitted it, and in about two weeks (there were no LSAT's in those days) they notified me that I was accepted into the Law School starting in October 1946.

I began law school after only two years in college, which was not unusual in those days, and then took two more years, including summers, to finish law school. That's a lot different from the way it is today for most aspiring lawyers, who usually complete four years of college and three years of law school. I suppose this extra schooling may make for better lawyers, but many attorneys from my generation who finished school in less than seven years have done quite nicely.

In law school, the work load was heavy but not difficult. However, I actually flunked a course for the first and only time: first year torts. Our entire grade was based on one final examination, an essay test given at the end of the semester. There were no right or wrong answers; you had to discuss theories of law and apply those theories to a set of facts. After getting my F, I was devastated and began to wonder whether I had made the correct career choice. Then I overheard some upperclassmen in the law school talking about first year torts. They said that the professor always flunks the same number of students each semester, and when the flunking students take the course a second time, they always get a B. So I repeated the course and sure enough got a B.

Ironically, one of my specialties as an attorney has been torts, and I think maybe I became a successful torts lawyer because I took the course twice.

I graduated from the law school with the Class of 1948. My section finished up in October; the formal graduation ceremony had occurred the previous June. But I didn't need the ceremony, I was happy just to have the diploma. When it finally arrived in the mail about a month after classes ended, I stuffed my belongings into my Tucson Tan Ford, sold my books to the local bookstore, and headed home to Far Rockaway to begin the pursuit of my chosen profession.

CHAPTER TWO

Leonard L. Rivkin:
Attorney-at-Law

Actually, when I first got back to Far Rockaway, getting a job as a lawyer was the furthest thing from my mind. My father allowed me to live at home rent free, the government was sending me a small monthly disability pension because of my wounds, so I was content to hang around Far Rockaway reacquainting myself with friends that I hadn't seen since high school. Some were just getting out of the Army; others were home on furlough. It was a pleasure to have some free time with a few dollars in my pocket.

After a while, I began to prepare a resume. Most of my classmates from U. Va. were applying for jobs at elite Wall Street law firms, but I had no desire to work in Manhattan, and at the time the prestigious downtown law firms were not hiring Jews. So I confined my job hunting to the Far Rockaway area.

I managed to land a job doing clerical work for a local practitioner named William Katz. I did menial tasks for Mr. Katz, such as filling out forms for people trying to collect money from foreign governments for property illegally seized during the war. Many of the jobs I performed for Mr. Katz were not even remotely associated with the law. The job lasted only a few months because he barely had enough business to sustain himself, let alone me.

Thereafter, several other local attorneys agreed to interview me mostly as a favor to my father. Although these lawyers had prosperous practices, in the 1940s single practitioners in the suburbs simply didn't hire law clerks. That was a luxury that even the most successful single practitioners could not really afford.

Then I began to look for opportunities on my own. My main source of leads was the Help Wanted section of the New York Law Journal. After answering ads for about six months, I received a call from a lawyer named Irving D. Josefsberg, whose offices were on Clinton

Street in Brooklyn. I scheduled an appointment to meet with Mr. Josefsberg the very next day.

*   *   *

The King of Brooklyn City Court

Irving Josefsberg was a successful trial lawyer whose specialty was personal injury. His typical case involved an automobile accident, a slip and fall, or a defective product. He always represented the plaintiff, that is, the person who was injured. Since his clients often suffered relatively minor injuries, Irving litigated many cases in Brooklyn City Court, where jurisdiction was limited to claims of three thousand dollars or less. In fact, he tried so many cases in that forum that he became known as "The King of Brooklyn City Court."

But Irving also tried his share of major personal injury cases where the damage claims were far in excess of three thousand dollars. He litigated those cases in the New York State Supreme Court not only in Brooklyn but throughout the metropolitan area.

Irving was about forty years old when I first met him. He was tall and heavy set, always puffing on a big, black cigar. He smiled and made friends easily and was very charming and eloquent. As a result, juries loved him.

The local judges loved him, too. Like Irving, most of them were from Brooklyn. He knew them all on a first name basis.

Irving's practice was a two-man operation. Irving handled all court appearances, and his associate did everything else, which included pleadings, motions, and examinations before trial.

At my interview, Irving told me that he had received dozens of responses to his ad, that he was looking for a clerk to do his "gofer" work, that I was one of several candidates being interviewed, and that one of the candidates was his own nephew.

Much to my surprise, Irving called me about a week after my interview to offer me the job. I wondered what had happened to the nephew, or whether there even was a nephew, but didn't bother to ask. The job paid twenty-five dollars per week, a decent wage in those days. I wasn't sure that I wanted to be a plaintiff's personal injury lawyer, but it was a job, so I took it. I started in the spring of 1949.

*   *   *

The Education of a Trial Lawyer

Irving Josefsberg ran a typical plaintiff's personal injury practice, although his firm was unique in one respect. Unlike most of his contemporaries, who relied primarily on clients, former clients, friends, and relatives to refer cases to them, almost ninety percent of Irving's referrals came from other lawyers. We called this "Of Counsel" work. For example, there would be a lawyer in Manhattan, Brooklyn, Queens, or even Nassau County who did commercial work, real estate, or wills and trusts, but not personal injury litigation. One day, one of his clients would get injured in an accident. The client would then go to the lawyer and sign a retainer, and the lawyer would refer the case to Irving. Irving's office would issue the summons and complaint, do all of the paperwork and pretrial discovery, and, if necessary, the trial itself.

The defendants in Irving's cases were usually represented by lawyers selected and paid for by the defendant's liability insurance company. The insurance company was not actually a named defendant. In automobile accident cases, for example, the named defendant was the owner of the vehicle or the driver; in slip and fall cases, the named defendant was the owner of the property, or the tenant, or the person otherwise responsible for the condition that caused the accident. But the standard automobile or homeowner's insurance policy, then as now, usually obligated the defendant's liability insurer to pay defense costs in any suit against the insured as well as the amount of any judgment or settlement. Thus, the insurance company hired and controlled the defense attorneys and had ultimate settlement authority. We dealt with insurance adjusters more frequently than we did with other law offices.

Irving was in court almost every day, arguing a motion, attending a conference, selecting a jury, or conducting a trial. He started as many as two trials per week. Some he tried all the way to verdict; others he managed to settle while the trial was in progress.

Every day that Irving went to court, I went with him. Since court usually convened at 10:00 a.m., we would meet in his office at 8:00 a.m., prepare the necessary files, and then walk or ride to the courthouse. I watched him select dozens of juries, attend dozens of settlement conferences, argue dozens of motions, and try dozens of cases. I watched him make opening and closing statements, conduct direct and cross examinations, and make objections. When Irving sat at counsel table, I sat next to him. When he met with the Judge in chambers, I was there. When he prepared his witnesses, I was there. I watched him work against different defense attorneys before different judges in different courts in Brooklyn, Manhattan, Queens, and the Bronx.

It is impossible to overstate how much I learned from Irving Josefsberg about trial work: how to conduct a smooth, compelling direct examination; how, on cross-examination, to create doubts about an adverse witness's testimony; how to read a judge or a jury; how to tell if an insurance adjuster's "last" offer really is just that. It is also impossible to imagine any other scenario where I could have learned all of these things more quickly. Remember that I was in court almost every day watching an experienced and highly skilled trial lawyer ply his craft. Had I been working for a Wall Street firm, I wouldn't have seen the inside of a courtroom for years. Had I been working on my own, quite possibly I wouldn't have had any clients for years.

But I learned far more from Irving than the "how to's" of trying a case; I learned about the exhilaration and excitement that is an inevitable part of the life of a trial attorney. I entered law school almost on a whim not knowing what direction my professional life would take. Working for Irving Josefsberg, I discovered the answer.

*   *   *

On My Own

When I was growing up, I often heard my mother say that no matter what you do for a living, they can never fire you if you are your own boss. I took those words to heart and left Irving's office after working there for about one year. I decided that the time had come for me to go out and try things on my own.

While working for Irving, I had managed to squeeze in the time to take bar review courses and ultimately sat for and passed the New York State Bar Examination. It was shortly after I was sworn in as a member of the New York Bar, which occurred in March of 1950, that I told Irving of my intention to leave. He wished me well and off I went.

I opened my first office in the Village of Freeport in Nassau County on Long Island. I had never been to Freeport and didn't know anything about it. I wish I could say that I did a complete and scientific feasibility study regarding the prospects for a young lawyer in that community, but I did not. Instead, I landed in Freeport solely because the woman I was about to marry suggested, on a whim, that I speak to her father.

The woman was Lenore Friedman, whom I met during my last year at U. Va. She had attended Ohio State University and ultimately graduated from Adelphi. After college, she worked for an engineering firm in New York City. My cousin, who roomed with Lenore in Ohio, introduced us. After a brief courtship, we became engaged and were married in October of 1950. After our honeymoon, we moved to the Village of Hewlett into a house built and paid for by my father and her father. Some wedding present! I was a young lawyer newly out on my own, about to start a family, in the enviable position of owning a house with no mortgage. Lenore and I lived in that house for almost thirty-five years, until her death from cancer in 1985.

Anyway, while I was considering where to open my practice, Lenore suggested that I speak to her father, who knew a lot of people. He referred me to his brother, Lenore's uncle, who knew a man from Freeport named Jack Leff. Jack had a son, Paul Leff, who was a successful insurance broker in Freeport. Apparently, Paul was looking to sublet the back one-third of his storefront office. According to Paul, an ambitious young lawyer such as myself would be an ideal tenant.

Paul's office was located at 35 West Merrick Road, one of two major east-west thoroughfares running through the bedroom communities of southern Nassau County and into Suffolk. It was part of a block-long row of stores set back along the sidewalk in a two story building with walkup apartments on the second floor. Behind a solid glass front and door the office measured about fourteen feet wide by sixty feet deep. The front two-thirds, where Paul ran his insurance business, contained three desks along the right wall, one behind the other, facing front: Paul himself worked at the first desk; his father, an insurance company appraiser, worked at the second; the third was vacant. At the rear of Paul's portion of the office was a partition, the top half of which was glass. A swinging door on the partition led to a back room, about ten feet deep, containing a desk and two chairs. At the rear of this back room was another door, leading to a restroom and storage closet.

I liked both Paul and his father. Paul's insurance business seemed to be doing quite well. They both knew a lot of people in the area. The office was located in a bustling part of the community. Overall, I felt quite comfortable and optimistic about the possibilities. On that basis, I agreed to become Paul's tenant.

*   *   *

I rented Paul Leff's back room, with its desk and two chairs, for twenty-five dollars per month. I signed the lease during the summer of 1950 and moved in at the end of the year. My lease gave me the right to put my name on the front window of the office — "Leonard L. Rivkin, Attorney-at-Law" — and also a sign saying that I was a notary. Incidentally, for the first three months of my practice I made more money as a notary than I did as a lawyer. I received twenty-five cents per document, which in those days was more than adequate for lunch money.

Business may have been slow at first, but it certainly appeared that I was very busy, and not just because of all the notarizing I was doing. Just about every customer who entered Paul Leff's thriving insurance brokerage office made his or her way through the revolving door of the partition into my office. Unfortunately, those customers didn't stop to do business with me; they were merely on their way to the restroom in the rear.

My very first clients came to me even before I moved into my new quarters. Jack Leff recommended me to an accident victim. When a local merchant filed an automobile claim with Paul Leff, Paul recommended me to handle the personal injury suit on behalf of the merchant's wife. Another local merchant needed advice regarding his will. One matter led to another, and by the time I had physically moved into my new digs, I had between six and one dozen files.

After I moved in, more clients trickled my way. Most of the business came from relatives, friends, and neighbors. A cousin retained me for the sale of his house. A neighbor of mine in Hewlett owned a company that built kitchen cabinets. The early 1950s was a perfect time to be in that particular business on Long Island because of the phenomenal home building boom. As my neighbor's business increased, so did the number and amount of unpaid bills. I was retained to do his collection work.

In addition, a lot of the business came from the Leffs, who were well known in Freeport. Jack Leff referred a landlord who was having problems with his insurer. Paul Leff referred a police officer whose girlfriend had been hit by a car. The couple retained me to represent the young woman in her dealings with the driver's insurance company.

Many days during that first year I was hard at work. However, there were also many days when I sat in my office with nothing to do but twiddle my thumbs. Occasionally, I would sneak away from the office to spend the afternoon at the local movie house.

* * *

My first "big" client was Jerry Weiss, an old classmate of mine from Woodmere Academy. Jerry and his father owned a construction company, Cedarpoint Realty, which was building new homes in an area called Woodmere Park, which, like a lot of property along the south shore of Long Island, was an old swamp area filled in for residential real estate construction. The homes ranged in price from twenty-five to thirty-five thousand dollars; in the early 1950s, that was a lot of money. Most of the homes were built on slabs or half cellars and were selling quite well. Cedarpoint Realty drew up the contracts for the sale of the new homes, but Jerry needed a lawyer to handle the closings. He came to me. The closings were held at the offices of the Dime Savings Bank in downtown Brooklyn, near Borough Hall. I negotiated a deal with Jerry in which he agreed to pay me $18.75 per closing, provided I was assigned a minimum of three closings at a time. Thus, I would drive to Brooklyn at 1 p.m. with three files next to me on the front seat. We then finalized the closing of the building loans, converted those loans into mortgages, and closed title on the houses. I returned home that evening, usually before 6 p.m., with $56.25 in my pocket, quite pleased with myself for having earned a substantial fee for a solid day's work.

* * *

My First Trial

My very first trial was a case I handled for Cedarpoint Realty early in 1951. I had been eager to try cases and was thrilled when an opportunity arose to do so. As a neophyte attorney, I don't know why but I had absolutely no fear of courtrooms or trials, in contrast to most young lawyers I have met. Perhaps it was the training I received while working for Irving Josefsberg. In my view, nothing could happen to me in court that I hadn't already seen. I probably had more confidence in myself than was warranted at the time, but I wasn't overconfident to the point where I overlooked one of the most important aspects of successful trial work: preparation. I would never even think of going to a meeting, a closing, a conference with another lawyer, or most particularly a courthouse to try a case unless I had worked the previous day, night, or weekend preparing every aspect of what I was to do, hear, or say.

Anyway, a buyer of one of the homes in Woodmere Park sued Cedarpoint Realty claiming a defect in the heating system. The buyer commenced his action in the Nassau County District Court located in the Village of Lawrence. I was happy that the buyer had selected that forum, which handled only non-jury trials, because under the circumstances a jury trial was the last thing I wanted. My view, shared by many attorneys at the time, was that many Long Island residents were new homeowners, that no matter how well a new home had been built the buyer always had a complaint or two against the builder, and that a jury composed of disgruntled home buyers was not likely to look favorably upon a builder no matter how honest and competent.

Upon reviewing the facts of the case, I found evidence that the heating system in the house may have been defective. I advised my client that, under these circumstances, a judge could easily rule in favor of the purchaser. But I did see a potential defense based upon a technicality. (Lawyers are routinely condemned by everyone except their clients when cases are won on a so-called "technicality.") I thought we had a reasonable argument that the buyer did not give the builder adequate notice of the alleged defect nor a reasonable opportunity to come in and make any necessary repairs.

After all these years, I still have a copy of the decision by the Honorable George S. Johnson, Judge, District Court of Nassau County. The decision tells us that the testimony was "highly conflicting." The buyer claimed that he notified Cedarpoint by registered mail that the heating system was defective and that a consultant retained by the buyer estimated that repairs would cost almost five hundred dollars. Cedarpoint Realty claimed that it never received a registered letter from the buyer (the buyer could not produce a copy), that the defect was minor and could be repaired for approximately $125, and that, once notified, it sent workers to the home on repeated occasions for the purpose of making the necessary repairs but they were refused admittance.

The court weighed all of this conflicting evidence and then stated its conclusion: "The defendant was not duly notified of any alleged imperfections of the heating system...and was not admitted to the premises in order to correct or improve the system..." I couldn't believe it! We won on the very technicality I had suggested to my client! He thought I was a brilliant attorney; I thought I was one lucky s.o.b.

The decision concluded with the four words that every lawyer who ever represented a defendant in any type of trial loves to hear: "The complaint is dismissed."

* * *

I Begin to Take the Initiative

By the end of 1951, after one year on my own, I had built up a decent, well-rounded, local practice typical of what you might expect from a young lawyer fresh out of school. I did closings. I wrote some wills. I did collection work for a company that installed stone facades on homes in place of aluminum siding. I incorporated a company for a friend who decided to start a business selling and renting uniforms to hospitals.

But the largest single category of cases that I handled at that time consisted of accident cases, and at that stage of my career I represented only plaintiffs, that is, the injured party or parties claiming damages against the defendant or the defendant's insurance company. To the extent that I was beginning to make any sort of a local name for myself, it was in this practice area, which was okay by me. I enjoyed accident cases because they offered me the opportunity very early on in my career to try cases on my own. Moreover, my background in medicine and training under Irving Josefsberg provided me with the necessary skills and tools.

At the time, relatives, friends, and neighbors were my main sources of business, including personal injury cases. Then, one afternoon, I ran into Irving Josefsberg in the Nassau Supreme Court building in Mineola. Irving was there to try one of his "of counsel" accident cases that had been referred to him by a local Nassau County attorney. This was common practice among the members of the local bar, who usually would try to settle their accident cases but, if they couldn't, they would bring in a hot shot lawyer from Manhattan or Brooklyn, such as Irving, for the trial. There were few, if any, high profile attorneys on Long Island willing to try accident cases on behalf of injured plaintiffs. I began to wonder: why go all the way to Brooklyn to find a trial lawyer? Wouldn't it make more sense for a Nassau County attorney to refer his cases to another Nassau County attorney? Like me? I certainly thought so. The problem was how to inform my fellow practitioners that a top young trial lawyer — at least in my opinion — was right in their own backyard.

Then, along came the South Nassau Lawyer's Association ("SNLA"). The SNLA had been organized by young attorneys practicing on the south shore of Long Island as a protest against the well-established Nassau County Bar Association ("NCBA"). The young lawyers felt that the older, more established practitioners unfairly controlled the NCBA. In the early 1950s, you had to be sponsored by a member in order to be invited to join the NCBA; the young lawyers felt that membership should be open to all practicing attorneys in the area. Such membership offered certain distinct benefits, such as added stature and professional prestige and opportunities to attend continuing legal education seminars and conferences.

Basically, the SNLA was a social organization. Looking back, I guess it is fair to say that it was really kind of a wild group. We held monthly dinners at McCluskey's, a prominent steak house in Bellmore. Although we usually invited a speaker of local interest, the focus of these dinners was the food, the drink, and the opportunity to mingle with fellow practitioners. Very often the dinners lasted until closing time. The SNLA also organized an annual vacation trip, typically a Caribbean cruise, which involved some sort of seminar so it would be tax deductible but which, like the monthly dinners, focused on the food, the drink, and the camaraderie.

The monthly SNLA dinner meetings at McCluskey's provided me the very opportunity that I was looking for. At these dinners, lawyers would be sitting at the bar discussing their cases, and there would always be one or two of them with an accident case they didn't want to try. They would mention the name of one attorney in Brooklyn and another in Manhattan. At that point in the discussion, as subtly as I could I let it be known I was available to do this "of counsel" work. I held myself out as a specialist in this area and asked why send a client all the way to Brooklyn or Manhattan when you could send him just down the road to Freeport.

I may have been a young lawyer at the time, but, as indicated earlier, my experience working for Irving Josefsberg had given me an enormous amount of self-confidence when it came to trial work, and it must have appeared that I knew what I was talking about because slowly but surely attorneys from the SNLA began sending me cases. I remember coming home from the dinners thrilled that I had picked up two or three files from a lawyer I had previously known or one file from a lawyer I had met for the first time that very night.

Within a year, thanks mainly to the "of counsel" work my SNLA colleagues were sending me, my practice had grown to the point where

I was taking in new accident cases at the rate of nearly one every two weeks. Together with the rest of my caseload, this was a bit overwhelming for a young lawyer who was handling not only the legal work but the filing and hunt-and-peck typing as well. To ease my burden, I hired a part-time secretary. Remember that there were three desks in Paul Leff's portion of the office, but only two of them were in use. So I made a deal with Paul to have my part-time secretary use his third desk on a part-time basis. For this I paid Paul an extra ten dollars per month. By the end of 1952, I was busy enough to require a full time secretary, who utilized Paul's third desk for the entire week.

* * *

My First Partner

Then I met Victor Leff.

Victor was my landlord's brother. He had just graduated from the University of Miami Law School, Class of 1953, and returned home to Freeport looking for a job with a local attorney. I figured that the Leffs figured that Victor would team up with me. The Leffs had referred a lot of business to me during my first years in practice and had introduced me to many local residents, merchants, and businessmen. I felt that if I didn't do something for Victor, it would not be the best thing I could do for my relationship with the Leff family.

I spent some time with Victor, whom I didn't really know, gave the matter a great deal of thought, and ultimately decided to bring him in as a fifty-fifty partner.

Now the question is, why would a thriving attorney in practice for nearly four years go into a fifty-fifty partnership with a lawyer fresh out of law school? For one reason, to keep his landlord and best source of business happy. For another, after spending one day with Victor, I was hooked, not so much by his legal skills but by his personality. I was convinced that Victor was a born rainmaker and that, together, we could develop the busiest plaintiff's personal injury practice in all of Nassau County.

Victor made friends more easily than anybody I have ever known. He was about my age, single (although he later married), and very handsome. He had a warmth that was infectious. He could walk into a bank, where no one was talking above a whisper, laugh, and instantly everyone in the bank — employees and customers — would be laughing with him. In a restaurant, he could start a conversation with a guy at the next table, within minutes the guy would be Victor's best friend, and the next night the guy would be over at Victor's house for dinner.

He was spontaneous, whimsical, high-spirited, almost child-like. Once, as a hurricane approached, he sailed his boat, a small sloop, out into the Atlantic, just to see what it was like. In the fall, when his neighbors had raked the fallen leaves into neat little piles on the side of the road, Victor would race his MG convertible down the block, zig-zagging from side to side, through the piles, leaves scattering in his wake. He enjoyed skiing and outfitted one of his ski poles with a movie camera with a trigger. He would ski down a mountain right at a tree with the camera going, stop the camera, ski around the tree, and then restart the camera. On film, in looked like he skied right through the tree.

People not only instantly liked Victor, they trusted him. He could walk into a store to buy something, with no intention of looking for new business, and then next thing he knew the store owner would be pouring his heart out to Victor and begging him to take his case.

Victor and I became partners around October of 1953. The first thing we did was move me out of his brother's office on West Merrick Road. The area behind the partition was barely big enough for me, let alone me and Victor. Instead, we moved into a bigger office at 11 West Sunrise Highway, still in Freeport. We rented space on the second floor above an automobile supply store. The space consisted of two offices and a reception room. My office was long and narrow, approximately twelve feet by twenty feet, and doubled as our library. One of my walls contained a built in floor to ceiling bookshelf containing used editions of New York statutes, case reporters, and other research tools. Victor's office was approximately twelve feet by twelve feet — after all, he was the junior partner. Our full-time secretary sat in the reception room. I forget what we were paying her at the time, but I do remember that the rent at our new quarters was a whopping fifty dollars per month — quite an increase, but we felt we could handle it.

Almost immediately, my partnership with Victor was a stunning success. We called our firm Rivkin & Leff. I handled most of the legal work. Victor concentrated on being Victor: meeting new people and making new friends, more often than not without any notion that new business would result, but it invariably did.

As I had envisioned, we were especially successful in expanding our plaintiff's personal injury practice. Victor's many friends and acquaintances proved to be an excellent source of new cases, but our "of counsel" referral business, which I had been cultivating at SNLA dinner meetings, was also growing. Victor began to attend these meetings with me and was a great help. Like just about everybody else, other lawyers loved Victor and couldn't give him new cases quickly enough. But it certainly benefitted our referral business that I was appearing in court frequently, generally getting good results, and becoming reasonably well known in the area.

Just to provide some idea of the growth Victor and I experienced in this field, in 1954, our first full year together, we were getting new accident cases at the rate of approximately one per week. We doubled that rate one year later.

*   *   *

My membership in the SNLA helped Victor and me increase our case load; it also enabled me to meet a significant number of people who became lifelong friends. Perhaps the most important friendship that blossomed during that time was with a young attorney named Edward J. Hart. We began in the 1950s as adversaries and ended up in the 1980s as partners! Ed, who until his recent death was a judge in the Appellate Division of the New York State Supreme Court in Brooklyn, graduated from St. John's Law School in 1951. After a stint as an Assistant General Counsel for Ohio Farmers Insurance Company, he joined with another local attorney to from a partnership called Curtis & Hart. Where my specialty was representing injured plaintiffs, Ed's was representing insured defendants. In those days, it was quite unusual for attorneys working different sides of the street to become friends. In fact, our friendship was generally looked down upon by Ed's fellow practitioners. Many times Ed would be asked, "What kind of defense attorney are you? You're friends with Len Rivkin!" But despite the differing nature of our respective clientele and the reaction of Ed's peers, our friendship survived because we had much in common. We both were veterans; we both were perceived by our elders as rather eager pursuers of new business; and we both had a burning desire to become successful trial attorneys.

There was also Nat Rudes, who was the Village Attorney and an Associate Police Justice in Lynbrook, several towns west of Freeport along Sunrise Highway. I passed Nat's office every day on my drive home. He had a successful general practice and, before meeting me, referred his litigation to an attorney in Mineola whom he never saw. I guess he decided that it made more sense to send his litigation to a lawyer who could conveniently drop in for a visit from time to time.

And Al Hauft, who lived in Suffolk County but practiced in Freeport. Neither Al nor his partner, both of whom did a lot of commercial and real estate work, enjoyed going to court and were eager to find a nearby attorney — my office was almost right next door to theirs — to handle their trial work.

And Noah Richman, who practiced in Lawrence. Noah's brother was a doctor in Far Rockaway who was friendly with my father. Noah referred his trial work to me and, during the course of our relationship, introduced me to Nick Calabria, who owned one of the largest insurance brokerage houses in Inwood. When one of Nick's customers needed a lawyer, Nick often sent him to me.

*   *   *

By late 1954 or early 1955, Victor and I had become so busy that we decided to hire some part time help. We placed an ad in *Newsday* and, after interviewing several candidates, hired Stuart Sherman, a graduate of the Wharton School at the University of Pennsylvania and a second year student at Brooklyn Law School. Stu was a veteran, but his military experience was quite different from mine; while in the army, he ran a nightclub in Trieste. He had just gotten married and was living in a furnished basement in East Meadow, a ten minute drive from our office.

Stu and I had an instant rapport. Fitting together like the pieces of a puzzle, we typified the old adage that "opposites attract." Stu was tall and thin; like my father, I was short and stocky. Stu was laid back, I was intense. Stu was thoughtful, I was impetuous. Stu spoke softly and slowly, I spoke loudly and rapidly, even more so once I got going on an argument or a summation. After only a few short weeks, it seemed like we had been working together for years. Stu knew what I wanted done without me saying a word. When one of us started a sentence, the other finished it.

After graduating from Brooklyn, Stu worked for us full time. Ultimately, he became my partner, and we practiced together throughout the period of the firm's most rapid growth, and through four moves, from Freeport to Garden City to Uniondale, until he retired in 1985.

*   *   *

Stu's ambition, when he first came to work for me, was to become a trial lawyer. Even though he was only in his second year of law school at the time, he had already developed excellent trial skills, having completed courses in Evidence, Trial Practice, and other pertinent subjects.

Almost immediately, we called upon Stu to utilize his incipient trial talents.

Victor Leff would have been the first to admit that his forte was not trying cases. He was affable and glib, but not in court. He just didn't have the instincts. Some trial lawyers make objections intellectually; others make them viscerally. Victor could do neither.

Unfortunately for Victor, we were becoming so busy that we had no choice but to send him to court. Stu went with him. Together, they devised a system whereby Stu would signal to Victor when to make an objection. Stu would tap his pencil on the table to get Victor's attention. Then, if the pencil was pointed up, Victor would object on substantive grounds; if the pencil lay flat on the table, Victor would object as to form.

Their first case together was a paternity suit. Stu, who was very nervous, sat next to Victor at counsel table. As their adversary called his first witness and asked his first question, Stu began to fidget. Inadvertently, he tapped his pencil on the table. Immediately, Victor jumped up and screamed, "I object!"

Everyone in the courtroom froze and stared at Victor. The attorney had asked the witness to "state your name."

"Objection, counselor?" asked the judge, peering down at Victor over his glasses. "On what grounds?"

Victor looked at Stu, who had placed the pencil in his suit pocket and slouched down in his chair. Victor looked back at the judge, shuffled his feet for an instant, and then shouted: "It's against my client's interests."

Victor and Stu had other misadventures in court, including a criminal case where Victor was the defendant. Late one afternoon, Victor was motoring his boat in Reynolds Channel, near Long Beach, at an excessive speed. With sirens blasting, the local marine patrol drew up alongside of Victor and ordered him to pull over.

"We're boarding you," shouted the marine constable.

Victor drew himself up to his full height, put his hand inside his shirt like Captain Bligh, and said, "I am the captain of this ship. No one boards without my permission."

After Stu bailed Victor out of jail, Victor, who was only charged with speeding, vowed to take his case all the way to the Supreme Court. He assigned the matter to Stu, who did some legal research and prepared a sixty-page brief arguing that the case against Victor had to be dismissed on constitutional grounds. According to Stu's brief, since ocean going oil tankers used Reynolds Channel, under the Constitution only the federal government, and not any state or local authority, could police its waters.

Victor and Stu appeared in court to contest the case. The judge read the briefs, listened to argument, seemed convinced, but then hesitated.

"My son is a constitutional lawyer," the judge said. "Let me call him to see what he thinks."

The judge then went into his chambers and Victor and Stu went outside the building for a smoke. Just as they lit up, the clerk came outside and told them the judge had a question for them. Victor and Stu went back into the courtroom, where of course smoking was prohibited. But Victor kept his lighted cigarette cupped in his hand behind his back. Victor and Stu stood up before the judge, who was asking his question, but suddenly he stopped and glared at Victor.

"Counselor," he said gravely. "You'd better be on fire, because if that smoke rising up above your head is coming from a cigarette, you're in a lot of trouble."

In spite of Victor's nicotine habit, he ultimately won the case. The judge bought Stu's constitutional argument but didn't want to anger the local authorities by taking away their power to police Reynolds Channel. Instead, he dismissed the case on a technicality.

Incidentally, shortly after Victor's speeding trial I had a case in front of the same judge. I kept objecting to my adversary's questions, and the judge kept ruling against me. Finally, in my frustration, I threw my pencil into the air.

"Counselor," the judge said gravely, "if that pencil comes down, you're in contempt."

*   *   *

Stu Sherman, Victor Leff, and I had fun working together and building a practice for about two years.

But then, Victor went to sleep on January 1, 1957, and never woke up. He died leaving a wife and young daughter. He was only thirty-two years old. The cause of death was a heart attack; Victor had had some coronary problems over the years I never knew about. Coincidentally, six months earlier we had taken out partnership insurance policies on one another. Victor's wife received the proceeds of his policy, and I became the sole owner of the thriving law firm of Rivkin & Leff. I kept Victor's name in the firm name out of respect for him; it wasn't until 1985, when we had close to two hundred lawyers and former United States Senator Birch Bayh joined the firm as a partner, that Victor's name was replaced.

Victor's death came as quite a shock to me, and the thought of continuing the practice without him was a bit daunting. But Stu Sherman had recently passed the bar and been formally admitted to practice. With Stu by my side, the next phase of my legal career was about to begin.

Chapter Three

The Tote Board, Life with Johnny, and Other Early Tales

Stu and I did quite well together after Victor died, getting much of our new business from the same old sources: local attorneys, the well-connected Leff family, relatives, friends, and neighbors. But we also began to acquire a lot of business from an entirely new source: satisfied clients. In our field, personal injury, satisfied clients can generate new business for an attorney at an astounding rate. At the time, we had a base of existing and past clients of well over five hundred people. If just twenty-five of them, five percent, each referred two people to our firm, we would have fifty new clients. Those numbers are actually quite conservative. We satisfied far more than five percent, and a satisfied client was likely to recommend us to two, three, or more people.

Again, just to provide some numbers to illustrate our growth, from 1954 to 1955 we doubled the rate of new plaintiff's cases coming into the office. That rate stayed the same in 1956. In 1957, the year after Victor died, it increased by twenty percent. In 1958, once again it doubled.

And remember, I'm only talking about the rate of new accident cases. That was our specialty, but we also handled a wide variety of other matters: commercial litigation, real estate transactions, wills and trusts, even some criminal cases. Basically, we accepted whatever came our way.

By early 1959, so much had come our way that Stu and I were swamped. To help ease the burden, we hired first one lawyer and then another. Suddenly, with four lawyers and one full time secretary, we had outgrown our small three room office at 11 West Sunrise Highway. So we rented some additional space on the same floor, just down the hall. Then, in mid-1959, we moved into larger quarters directly across the street at 16 West Sunrise Highway. We occupied the entire second floor over yet another automotive supply store. I recall that, in our new space, we had six private offices, a reception room, and a small combination conference room/library.

We stayed at 16 West Sunrise for nearly seven years. During that time, I had as many as four lawyers working for me, six secretaries, and even an occasional law clerk. Stu Sherman tried some cases but had become my primary "inside man," drafting pleadings, discovery demands, affidavits, and briefs. Herb Burdow, a law school friend of mine, handled whatever real estate and commercial matters came our way. Stu Davis, a young Brooklyn Law School graduate, helped Stu Sherman with the inside work and argued some motions. Frank Bunting did legal research and helped Stu Sherman write briefs. I handled the bulk of the actual in-court trial work.

Incidentally, Frank Bunting, who was with me for only a few years, moved to Vermont, his wife's home state, where he later became a prominent state senator. And one of the clerks who worked for me for a short time at 16 West Sunrise was Norman Levy, who later became a distinguished state senator in New York.

*   *   *

Managing My Growing Firm

During this period of early growth, I spent most of my time in court and hardly any time in the office supervising my staff of young attorneys. This situation did not bother me in the least until late one afternoon, when a client phoned regarding a problem that had arisen in his case. It was something that never should have happened but was easily corrected. Afterwards, I wondered whether there were other problems in other cases that I did not know about.

I decided to investigate. Accordingly, I began to take files home at night and on the weekend. After reviewing those files, I determined that more supervision and involvement by me was, in fact, necessary.

In some instances, my office was not moving the cases quickly enough. It may be okay to foot-drag if you're representing the defendant, to put off the date of any adverse judgment for as long as possible. But since we were representing mostly plaintiffs in those days, my goal was to get the case to trial at the earliest possible date, for two reasons. First, I wanted my clients to get their money sooner rather than later. And second, I was handling most of my plaintiff's work on a contingent fee basis — my fee was a percentage of the amount of the judgment or settlement in favor of my client; if we lost the case I got nothing. Under those circumstances, the sooner my client got his money, the sooner I got mine.

In other cases, I was concerned about the quality of the work being done. Maybe the complaint alleged two causes of action when it should have alleged three. Maybe the discovery requests were not sufficiently thorough. Maybe the examination-before-trial should have developed better testimony. Maybe somebody made an unwise strategic decision.

To alleviate my concerns, I implemented two office procedures. First, I installed a "tote board" on one of the walls in the room that doubled as our conference room and library. Remember, I'm talking about a small suburban law firm, not a huge downtown legal factory. My conference room/library was less than twenty feet by twenty feet in total area. There was a small table in the center with four chairs used for closings or legal research. Along two walls were bookshelves containing only the most basic research tools: statutes, reported decisions, digests, and forms. We hung the tote board between two windows on the outside wall.

The board was four feet wide by five feet high. It was constructed of white printing board with a thin glass cover. The board was lined both horizontally and vertically, into columns, like a giant page from an accountant's entry book. Each of the columns contained a heading: Name of Case, Summons and Complaint, Answer, Demand for Bill of Particulars, Bill of Particulars, Depositions, Jury Demand, Note of Issue, etc. The name of each case was entered under the "Name of Case" column. Then, under each of the other columns, the date that the particular item was served or received was entered.

Simply by glancing at the tote board, I could immediately tell whether a particular case was proceeding at an acceptable pace.

When we first installed the tote board, there were maybe 150 cases entered on it. But the board had room for upwards of five hundred cases, and in what seemed like a very short period of time it was completely full.

There was always a lot of activity going on around the tote board, with attorneys or secretaries adding new case names and pleading dates. I even had a platform installed on which someone could stand in order to reach the top of the tote board, to make it easier to enter the necessary information. Surveying the scene one afternoon, my friend Ed Hart, recalling an incident during his youth when he inadvertently stumbled into the back room of a candy store, commented, "Len, this reminds me of a bookmaker's place."

The second procedure I implemented was that I would review all incoming mail before it was distributed to the attorneys working on the various cases. Reviewing the incoming mail gave me a very good idea of how competently the attorneys in my office were handling their caseloads. For example, if a letter came in on a particularly heavy case suggesting that there were problems, I could immediately review the file or speak with the attorney in my office in charge of that case to make sure that the problems were solved. In addition, if an adversary made an important or complicated motion in a case, I could monitor our response.

Reviewing the incoming mail also enabled me to monitor the relationship between the attorneys in my office and our clients, opposing counsel, and the attorneys who were referring us business. These three areas required very close scrutiny on my part. We certainly didn't want any problems with our clients; if a letter from a client suggested that one of the attorneys in my office was not returning phone calls or otherwise not responding promptly to the needs and desires of that client, I would be on that attorney's case in an instant. Nor did I want problems with opposing counsel. Litigation is difficult enough; treating your adversary with courtesy and respect helps to keep those difficulties to a minimum. Finally, I certainly did not want any problems between my office and the attorneys who were sending us business. You could be the best lawyer in the world, but nobody would know it unless you had the cases to prove it.

Since I was in court most mornings, the mail would generally sit on my desk until I got back to the office at around 4:30 p.m. Then I would review and distribute it. If one of the lawyers in my office was expecting an important letter or document and needed to see it first thing in the morning, my secretary would get it for him but also make a copy and leave the copy on my desk. If, for some reason I couldn't get to the mail (if I was in stuck in court or on vacation), then Stu Sherman would cover for me.

*   *   *

With four lawyers and six secretaries on the payroll, I also needed constant reassurance that I could handle my overhead. One way to do this, of course, was to monitor the firm's cash flow. But all that told me was how I did during a particular month. I needed some way to make sure that my future income would be sufficient to meet my growing expenses.

In order to do this, I began to keep close track of our new business. To that end, I created a "New Case Book." Every new matter that came into the office was entered into this book: the date we received it; the name of the referring attorney; the name of the lawyer in my office I assigned it to; and the type of case it was (for example, personal injury, commercial, real estate closing, etc.). To me, this was the best way of monitoring the firm's finances. Current income was important, but it was more important to keep up a steady and even increasing flow of new cases. I was happy as long as the graph charting the number of new cases every month read like the graph charting the Dow Jones Industrial Averages: there could be peaks and valleys, but over time the general direction had to be up.

I don't remember the exact number of new cases per month that I felt we needed when we first moved to 16 West Sunrise, but I think the number was somewhere around twenty.

*   *   *

As our personal injury caseload was growing, I began to appreciate all the time my father had spent talking to me about medicine. My knowledge of medical terminology, my ability to read x-rays, and my familiarity with methods of treatment were invaluable. I could understand a doctor's report and probe him for more details. I could ask the right questions when interviewing an injured client or cross examining an insurance company physician.

But I also knew that I had a lot to learn about the medical aspects of personal injury litigation. So I enrolled in just about every continuing legal education course I could find dealing with this topic. These courses, sponsored by groups such as the Practicing Law Institute, ordinarily met one evening each week over a period of two to three months in New York City. Whenever I had a class, I would first put in a full day in court or at the office, drive or take the train into the city, grab a quick bite, and then sit for two hours listening to doctors and lawyers lecture on a wide variety of personal injury related topics.

I learned a great deal from these lectures which helped me become a better lawyer. Among other things, I learned that no matter how smart you think you are and how many years you've been in practice, you can never get enough continuing legal education. In fact, throughout my career, as the nature of my practice changed, as the cases became more complex, as I expanded into unfamiliar subject matters, I never hesitated to enroll in a continuing legal education program that was pertinent to what I was doing at the time: from representing an injured plaintiff to defending a nationwide class action to suing the United States government.

But there was also an ancillary benefit to my ongoing legal education. In class I met lots of lawyers, doctors, businessmen, insurance executives, and other potential sources of new business for my firm. Very often, I walked away from a course not only with new knowledge but also with a new client.

*   *   *

I dabbled in politics when I first started practicing on Long Island. In the early 1950s, I became a Republican Committeeman for my home district in Hewlett. The Executive Committeeman who offered me the position was a doctor from Far Rockaway who had known my family for years and had recently moved into my neighborhood. As a Committeeman, I was responsible for drumming up support for the Republican candidates and encouraging registered party members to get out and vote. I attended strategy meetings and recruited people to make phone calls and hand out fliers.

I never had long or even short range political aspirations. I entered politics simply to meet new people and get my name better known in the community. In other words, to help my practice.

My friend Ed Hart was also involved in politics but, at the time, he was a Democrat. In fact, he was the Vice Chairman of the statewide Young Democrats organization. The Young Democrats were all followers of Adlai Stevenson. On Long Island, their mission was to wrest control of the party from the older Democrats, who apparently no longer had the heart to do battle in Nassau County, which was so heavily Republican.

In 1958, the local Democratic party asked Ed to run for district court judge. Shortly thereafter, he dropped by my office and asked me to take a walk with him along Sunrise Highway.

"Len," he said, "I'd like you to run my campaign." His thinking was that I would carry out that task with the same zeal and energy that I practiced law; if so, he would make quite a run.

I was flattered. Ed was a respected local attorney, a frequent adversary, and a friend from the SNLA. He knew a lot about me, but apparently not everything.

"I'd love to," I replied, "because I think you would make a great judge." I hesitated. "But I don't think I can."

"Why not?"

"Because I'm the Republican Committeeman from Hewlett. I don't think my bosses in the party would like it."

We both had a good laugh. Ed ran anyway and went on to finish first among the Democrats, which was good but not good enough to win him a seat.

* * *

During the 1950s, an important source of business for me was the Freeport Police Department. When I had been practicing by myself in the back of Paul Leff's office, his father Jack had recommended me to a friend of his, a Lieutenant Arthur Wolff, who at the time was the number three man in the Department. A friend of Lt. Wolff had been hit by a Bee Line bus. I handled the case and got a very good result. The accident victim was very happy, and so was the Lieutenant. As a result, word spread around the Department that there was this new young lawyer in town who could really do a good job for you. As you would imagine, the Department was a close-knit group, as are most small town police departments, and slowly but surely policemen would come to me with their legal problems or would recommend me to their friends. By the time I had set up shop at 16 West Sunrise, I was getting maybe two or three cases a month from my various police sources. Right around that time, I became counsel to the Village of Freeport PBA. I represented the PBA for more than ten years at no charge because I made some really good friends there and, as I envisioned, it turned out to be an excellent business move.

* * *

Other cases, clients, and characters from those years stand out in my mind.

I assigned Stu Sherman his first solo trial the day after he was sworn in as a member of the bar. He arrived at the office expecting festive balloons and a cake. Instead, I greeted him in our reception room holding a three foot stack of files.

"Stu," I said, "don't take off your coat. You're on your way to Supreme Nassau to select a jury."

Stu turned as pale as a sheet and almost fainted.

"Don't worry," I told him, "this is an ideal case for a first trial. Our client is one of ten defendants. You have nothing to lose because we're expected to lose, and it doesn't matter if we lose because our client has no money and no insurance. He can't pay any judgment. So you can say anything you want, nobody's gonna pay any attention. And if that's not enough, our client is a deaf mute, so he won't even hear you."

My pep talk didn't seem to help Stu at all; beads of sweat had formed on his forehead. Nevertheless, I handed him the files, gave him a reassuring pat, and pushed him back out the door.

The case involved a fire at a boat yard that destroyed four boats. Our client started the fire while removing paint from one of the boats with a blowtorch. The boat owners were suing for their damages. The other defendants included the yard owner and the manufacturer of the blow torch. Our client was the only defendant without assets.

When he got to court, Stu fully expected to sit around for a couple of days reading the file until a courtroom opened up for jury selection. Instead, when the assignment judge saw that the case involved ten defendants, he somehow found a vacant courtroom and ordered the attorneys to begin jury selection immediately.

Stu panicked. Fortunately, he did not have to go first. So he sat and watched some of the other defense attorneys as the questioned prospective jurors. Then, it was his turn. He stood up, faced the jury box, opened his mouth, and nothing came out. Not a peep. He wanted to cry. At that moment, he happened to glance over at a woman juror, who apparently knew exactly what Stu was going through because she looked like she wanted to cry.

Ultimately, Stu found his voice and tried the case. Believe it or not, he got a hung jury. He was convinced that he had stumbled upon a foolproof trial strategy: look so helpless and inept that the jury finds in your favor out of pity.

*   *   *

A few years later, Stu handled another matter for the office that made the boat yard fire case seem like a cakewalk. The matter was pending in the New York Court of Appeals, the highest court in the state. We represented a little girl who was suing a summer camp for injuries sustained when she fell off a horse. The appeal involved a very narrow issue — whether to enforce an indemnity agreement between the girl's parents and the camp. Our position was that the agreement was invalid; if we were wrong, then for all practical purposes the little girl's claim would be worthless.

From the outset, Stu felt that we had two chances of winning: slim and none. The reason: the playing field wasn't level; a flyweight was entering the ring to fight the heavyweight champion. Don't get me wrong; Stu had quickly become a skilled litigator, but he was only five years out of law school. In contrast, the attorney representing the camp, Stu's adversary, was almost forty years out of law school; he was a senior partner at one of the largest, most prestigious New York City law firms; and, if all that wasn't bad enough, he was the President of the American Bar Association, recognized and respected by lawyers and judges not just in New York but throughout the country.

If you think our chances in this case couldn't have gotten any slimmer, you'd be wrong. On the morning of oral argument, Stu, an experienced pilot, was flying to Albany as a passenger on a commercial airline. There were only five other people on the flight. Shortly after takeoff, Stu was reading a magazine and drinking a cup of coffee. Sitting across the aisle to his right was a distinguished elderly gentleman. As the plane was flying over Long Island Sound, Stu looked out the window and saw some ominous looking storm clouds, which he knew were close enough to cause a rather bumpy flight. Not wanting to spill coffee on his suit, Stu held the cup in his right hand and extended his right arm out over the aisle.

Suddenly, the plane hit an air pocket and bounced severely. The cup stayed in Stu's hand but the coffee flew across the aisle and landed squarely in the elderly gentleman's lap. Not one drop landed on Stu. The man looked at Stu, who pretended to be wiping coffee from his sleeve. Stu apologized meekly. Nothing else was said.

When Stu finally arrived in court, he took a seat in the front row. As he was reviewing his notes, the seven judges filed solemnly in. Stu looked up and noticed that the second judge from the left was the elderly gentleman from the flight. The judge glared down at Stu and shook his head. Stu thought: "Oh, shit."

If you think that our chances in this case were now as slim as they could possibly be, you'd be wrong again. The Court listened to oral argument in three or four other matters. Then, Stu's case was called. As he and his adversary, the President of the American Bar Association, approached the bench, another one of the judges leaned forward and spoke quietly to Stu's opponent, calling him by his first name.

"Our wives will arrive at the restaurant first to get us a table," whispered the judge. "We'll meet them there later."

"Oh, shit," Stu thought again.

But then a funny thing happened. Figuring he had no chance at all, Stu relaxed and argued brilliantly and convincingly. He won a unanimous decision. Even the judge with coffee stains on his lap voted in Stu's favor.

* * *

Neither of our two offices on Sunrise Highway had a coffee machine, so Stu and I took our breaks at a small coffee shop on the corner. At the coffee shop, we met a man who was reputed to be a Mafia boss on the south shore. Let's call him Johnny.

Johnny was a bookmaker and ran the numbers game. He spent a lot of time at the coffee shop and enjoyed chatting with Stu and me whenever he saw us. In fact, he took a real liking to Stu and sort of adopted him. Stu became Johnny's buddy.

One night, Stu was working very late in the office on a brief. At ten o'clock, the phone rang. It was Johnny. He wanted to know why the lights were on, what was going on.

"Nothing is going on," Stu told him. "I'm working on a brief. I don't have time to talk." He hung up.

Thirty minutes later, Stu heard someone banging on the office door. He walked downstairs, opened the door, and there stood a girl, very blonde, very young, very innocent looking.

"Johnny sent me," she said. "He thinks you're working too hard and need a break."

"Thank you, no," Stu replied. "I'm a happily married man."

The girl frowned. "Hey, you have to let me in. If I don't go upstairs with you, Johnny would be very disturbed."

Not wanting to offend Johnny, Stu brought the girl upstairs, where she sat and watched him work on his brief for about an hour. Then she left. Stu never saw her again.

Another time, Johnny dropped by the office for a visit. He walked into Stu's office while Stu was on the phone with another attorney discussing a real estate deal. The conversation began pleasantly enough but soon turned nasty. Stu tried to stay calm but lost his cool and started yelling into the phone. Finally, Stu shouted, "I'll see you in court," and slammed the receiver down.

Johnny was just sitting there, holding a pen and pad in his hand, poised to begin writing. "Gimme his name," he said.

"Whose name?" asked Stu.

"The guy on the phone," said Johnny. "You want us to go pay him a visit?"

Johnny rarely sought legal advice from us. He just liked to chat. But one day he came to us because he was having a labor problem with a company in upstate New York. He told us the facts, and Stu began some legal research.

A few days later, Johnny returned to our office.

"Forget about upstate New York," he said. "It's all taken care of."

"What happened?"

"I put sugar and steel wool filings in every gas tank of every truck in the company's fleet."

Not exactly what they teach in law school, but that's one way to avoid a lengthy and expensive lawsuit.

*   *   *

I represented a man named Gilbert Lee Beckley on minor gambling charges in City Court in Long Beach. I had heard rumors that Beckley was a big time bookmaker, but I didn't learn how big until several years later, when the Nassau County District Attorney's office arrested and charged him with over one hundred counts of conspiracy and felony bookmaking. According to a newspaper account of the arrest, Beckley was reputed to be the "kingpin" of a nationwide bookmaking operation whose annual take, in the New York metropolitan area alone, was supposedly over $100 million. The newspaper article contained other juicy allegations: Beckley was a close associate of the famous gangster Meyer Lansky; his little black book of names included Frank Sinatra and H. L. Hunt; a famous college football coach was overheard on a taped phone conversation placing a ten-thousand-dollar bet on his own team. Unfortunately for the District Attorney, much of the evidence against Beckley was suppressed because of illegal wiretaps. As a result, the one hundred felony gambling charges had to be reduced to one charge of disorderly conduct, a misdemeanor. Unfortunately for Beckley, he never showed up in court to plead guilty to that reduced charge. In fact, he never showed up anywhere. He simply vanished, just like Jimmy Hoffa.

Beckley did show up for our earlier court appearance in Long Beach. He picked me up at my office in a limousine wearing a custom made suit. An attractive young woman sat with us in the back seat. The bar in the limo was stocked with the finest vodka, gin, and scotch. In court, I moved to dismiss the charges against Beckley because of a defect in the search warrant. The motion was granted. The next day, *Newsday* published a picture of Beckley and me leaving the courthouse.

I was pleased; a lawyer likes to see his name in the paper and, assuming that he's not in handcuffs, loves to see his photograph.

My mother-in-law's reaction:

"You look more like a gangster than he does."

*   *   *

One of my cases ended in real tragedy. It involved a love triangle. My client, who owned a bar, was having an affair with his bartender, who happened to be married. One day, my client told me that the woman's husband, claiming she was suicidal, had committed her to a psychiatric hospital. My client insisted that the woman was not suicidal; he claimed that the husband was getting back at her for leaving him. He wanted me to see if I could get her released.

We commenced an action in county court. At the hearing, our psychiatrist, who examined the woman on several occasions, testified that she was not suicidal. He explained that her three suicide attempts were nothing more than calls for help because each time she purportedly tried to commit suicide she immediately phoned for an ambulance. The court also heard testimony from a hospital psychiatrist supporting the woman's confinement but ultimately believed our doctor and ordered the woman's release.

One week later, the woman killed herself.

As an attorney, you try not to become emotionally involved with your client or your client's position, so as not to cloud your judgment. Nevertheless, the woman's suicide was quite a jolt. It brought home something that a lot of lawyers frequently lose sight of. For us, win or lose, life goes on. For our clients, the stakes can be significantly higher.

*   *   *

Other Early Marketing Strategies

In my early years practicing law, I was concerned with becoming as good an attorney as I possibly could and was equally concerned with expanding my practice. I was always thinking of ways to attract new clients and cement my relationship with old ones.

After we moved the practice to 16 West Sunrise, I initiated my annual custom of sending out holiday greeting cards at Christmas/New Year's. Our list of names ran into the thousands. The list consisted of clients, opposing attorneys, referring attorneys, local merchants, neighbors, members of associations or organizations we represented, etc. We were constantly adding names. I selected cards that were on the humorous side and insisted that we write (not type) the addresses on the envelopes and sign (not stamp) the signature on the cards. The task of addressing the envelopes and signing the cards kept most of my secretarial help busy for much of the month of December. (I admit that

I did not personally sign every card!) At the end of January, when I checked the New Case Book, I was amazed at the number of new cases. In fact, January always seemed to be our busiest month. I believe this was because of our holiday greeting cards, which had the effect of placing my name freshly in the minds of existing and prospective clients.

Looking back, perhaps I should have sent greeting cards out at other times of the year: Thanksgiving, Easter/Passover, Groundhog Day, etc.

Another one of my practices was to personally handle the task of communicating to the client the final settlement offer from the insurance company, in other words, the offer that I was going to recommend that the client accept. I always handled this meeting in person rather than over the phone. I would explain to the client why the offer was fair, why I felt we should accept it, and why I believed we would not do any better — and quite possibly would do a lot worse — if we took the case to trial. I felt that I could handle these discussions, which could be quite delicate and emotional, better than my associates.

Usually during this meeting the client brought up the subject of my fees. In the typical personal injury/accident case, my fee would be anywhere from one-third to one-half of the amount of the settlement. Usually, there was no problem, but sometimes I could sense that a client was not comfortable with the fee. In those instances, I would reduce it. Although every lawyer wants a fair fee for his services, I had no problem reducing what I considered a fair fee if the end result was a satisfied client. I always used to tell clients, "No matter what I charge you — five hundred or five thousand dollars — I'm going to end up making ten times that amount." They would do double takes and ask for an explanation. "Easy," I would say. "If you're happy with the result we obtained, including the amount of my fee, you're going to recommend me to all of your friends."

I also used to personally handle the final meeting with the client, after we had finalized the settlement agreement, signed the release, and received the check from the insurance company. Nothing makes a client happier than when he finally gets the money he believes he is entitled to, and I wanted to be the one to hand him that money. This also gave me one last chance to make sure that our client was satisfied with our services so that he would, in fact, recommend us to his friends.

*   *   *

By the end of 1965, we had outgrown our space at 16 West Sunrise. Once again, it was time to move. I looked all around the area but thought it best to stay in Freeport. I had been in practice there nearly fifteen years, was happy with our growth, and figured there was no reason why it couldn't continue.

I found an ideal piece of vacant land on North Ocean Avenue, and one block north of Sunrise Highway. The land was directly opposite the Freeport Village Hall, which was adjacent to several municipal parking lots. This particular section of Ocean Avenue was a combination residential/professional street, with small office buildings and apartment houses on both sides.

I purchased the land and contacted a friend of mine named Howard Rose, a well known commercial builder in the area. We had grown up together in Far Rockaway. We hired an architect, who drew up a set of plans for a two story building with five thousand square feet of space on each floor. Howard then prepared a construction contract (I think it was for about ninety-eight thousand dollars), which I signed, and we were all ready to go, or so I thought. Two weeks later Howard came to me and said that his partner didn't think I was paying Howard enough money. "No problem," I told him, and added another five thousand dollars to the contract. That was the way we did business in those days. So Howard went to work and finished my building in about four months.

There were two offices on the ground floor; I rented one to a dentist and the other to a pediatrician whose father-in-law happened to be a New York State Supreme Court Justice.

We occupied the entire second floor. My office was in the front of the building, overlooking the street; Stu Sherman's was in the back. That way, between the two of us, we could see everything that was going on in the office at all times.

We ended up staying at 55 North Ocean Avenue for ten years. When we first moved in, I fully expected that the firm would continue its uninterrupted flow of prosperity and growth. Little did I realize that my worst nightmare lay just ahead of me.

CHAPTER FOUR

The Judicial Inquiry

The Origins of the Judicial Inquiry

Ambulance chaser.

In the 1950s and 1960s, you could not call an attorney a dirtier name. The term refers to the unethical solicitation of cases by plaintiff's personal injury attorneys. It conjures up images of an ambulance speeding toward the hospital bearing the dying victim of an automobile accident with a lawyer racing his car in hot pursuit, holding his business card out the window.

A good example of ambulance chasing occurs in the beginning of the movie "The Verdict," where a down and out lawyer played by Paul Newman reads the obituaries, appears at the funeral of a man he never met who died in an accident, offers his sympathy to the man's widow, and says, while pressing his business card into her hand, "Let me know if there's anything I can do."

In real life, I have heard stories about lawyers in Nassau County, where I lived and worked, who supposedly disguised themselves as doctors — white coats, stethoscopes, charts — and wandered around inside a hospital looking for clients. I have also heard stories about lawyers who paid tow truck operators, automobile repairmen, service station owners, and even doctors to refer clients.

In the late 1950s, there were enough of these stories floating around to prompt the Grievance Committee of the Nassau County Bar Association to thoroughly examine court records for evidence of ambulance chasing. Among the Committee's findings: several plaintiff's attorneys in Nassau County had acquired an extraordinary number of new clients considering their relative lack of experience. One firm in particular, which included two partners admitted to practice for less than ten years, had acquired 471 new clients in 1957 and 395 new clients in 1956, compared to none at all in 1955. Another attorney admitted to practice for less than five years had acquired nearly three hundred new clients in 1957; his records indicated that almost all of them were referred to him by "previous clients." Still another attorney had received dozens of referrals from the same person. And several attorneys had filed dozens of lawsuits in Nassau County on behalf of persons who resided outside of the County or where the accident occurred outside of the County.

The Bar Association reported these and other findings in a letter to the Appellate Division of the New York State Supreme Court, Second Department, the state court with supervisory and disciplinary authority over attorneys in Nassau County, Suffolk, Queens, and Brooklyn. In that same letter, the Association characterized the Grievance Committee's findings as "strong evidence of improper solicitation of negligence cases by some lawyers in our County" and asked the court "to appoint a Justice of the Supreme Court to conduct an investigation into this matter."

In response to the Bar Association's letter, the Second Department issued a series of orders establishing the "Judicial Inquiry on Professional Conduct" in Nassau County. The pertinent order, for purposes of this discussion, was issued on December 19, 1962. In that order, the Second Department empowered the Judicial Inquiry to investigate ambulance chasing, that is, "any corrupt and unethical practices...[by plaintiff's personal injury lawyers]...in the solicitation of retainers..." But the court also directed the Judicial Inquiry to go well beyond ambulance chasing and investigate any improper and unethical conduct by plaintiff's attorneys "in the subsequent prosecution and disposition of claims and actions, and in any other matters..." The court designated the Honorable Frank A. Gulotta, a Justice of the State Supreme Court in Nassau County, to preside over the investigation.

* * *

I Become a Target

Early in 1963, I was contacted by a man named William F. Hanrahan, a local attorney who identified himself as an Assistant Counsel to the Judicial Inquiry. Mr. Hanrahan advised me that the Judicial Inquiry wanted to review some of my plaintiff's personal injury files and asked me to please produce those files at his office in Garden City.

Mr. Hanrahan's request caught me completely by surprise. I knew that I had done nothing wrong and that no one had recently filed a complaint against me with the local bar association. In fact, as of this writing, no one — no unhappy client, no disgruntled adversary, no opposing attorney, no judge — has ever filed a complaint against me with any court or grievance committee. So after recovering from my initial shock at hearing Mr. Hanrahan's request, I asked him why the Judicial Inquiry had decided to investigate me.

The answer was quite simple. Every time a plaintiff's personal injury attorney acquired a new client, the law required the attorney to file a copy of the retainer agreement in the Second Department. Mr. Hanrahan told me that the Judicial Inquiry had decided to automatically review the case files of every attorney who had filed more than fifty retainer agreements in any one year. In my case, I had filed thirty-seven retainers in 1952, the second full year I had been in practice by myself in Freeport. In 1953, I filed thirty-nine. In 1954, Victor Leff's first full year with me, we hit the jackpot, filing fifty retainers. In 1955, we filed ninety-one; in 1956, we filed ninety-six. From 1957, the year after Victor died, through 1962, I filed as many as 223 and as few as 121.

Based on these numbers, the Judicial Inquiry ultimately reviewed every one of my case files opened from 1956 through 1960.

*   *   *

An Early Setback

I produced my files, in waves, at the Judicial Inquiry's office in Garden City. They would review a batch, call me down to answer questions about why certain things had been done, where was the backup for certain allegations, and then they would request more files and call me down to answer more questions. During our discussions, I willingly told them everything they wanted to know, and they were courteous and respectful and always seemed satisfied with my explanations. My only concern during this phase of the investigation was that I was losing valuable time I could otherwise have devoted to my practice.

This went on for nearly two and one-half years. Then, in early 1965, Judge Gulotta listened to some testimony and reviewed some documents relating to my cases. The proceedings before Judge Gulotta were informal and non-adversarial. Once again, everyone involved was courteous and respectful. Maybe I wasn't as perceptive as I should have been, but nothing happened during the course of these proceedings that caused me to be the least bit concerned.

On June 28, 1965, Judge Gulotta submitted a confidential report to the Second Department that contained his findings and recommendations. Even though I wasn't given a copy, I fully expected, based upon all that had transpired, that Judge Gulotta's report would quickly bring the matter to a close.

Imagine my shock when three weeks later, on July 19, 1965, the Second Department issued an order directing Samuel Greason, a retired trial court judge who was Chief Counsel to the Judicial Inquiry, to institute formal disciplinary proceedings against me. What a bombshell! I had always thought that if a client, or an adversary, or a judge filed a grievance against you, then there might be a need for formal disciplinary proceedings. In my case, there were no such grievances, and for good reason: I had never done anything unethical or improper. Nevertheless, to my horror, I was about to become embroiled as a defendant in a proceeding that could conceivably result in a letter of admonishment from the Bar Association, my suspension from the practice of law, or, even worse, my disbarment.

Suddenly, my attitude changed dramatically. Until then, I was more or less acting as my own attorney as I cooperated with the Judicial Inquiry's investigation, in violation of the adage that a lawyer who represents himself has a fool for a client. But no longer. I immediately hired William Beasley, one of the finest civil trial lawyers I have known in nearly fifty years of practice, to handle my defense.

*   *   *

The Charges

The Second Department's July 19 order directed the Judicial Inquiry to institute proceedings against me; that order did not specify the charges. For three months, I was in the dark. How could I begin to defend myself if I didn't even know what I had done wrong?

Finally, on October 20, Judge Greason filed a petition with the Second Department that set forth the exact nature of the charges against me. Ironically, those charges did not include ambulance chasing, which was what the Bar Association had been so worked up about back in the late 1950s and was the main reason for the creation of the Judicial Inquiry in the first place. Instead, after a thorough review of hundreds of my files which produced no evidence that I had improperly solicited new clients, Judge Greason nevertheless charged that I had committed roughly one hundred acts of professional misconduct while litigating thirty-four of my cases. In almost every instance, the essence of the charge was that I exaggerated the amount of my client's medical expenses and the extent of his injuries in a court document known as a bill of particulars.

*   *   *

The Facts

For those of you unfamiliar with the term, a bill of particulars is technically not a pleading but is used to amplify a pleading. For example, frequently the allegations of a pleading, such as a complaint or an answer, are broadly drawn. In a personal injury action, plaintiff's complaint may choose to allege only that the defendant was negligent and that the plaintiff suffered bodily injury. In such a case, the defendant would demand from the plaintiff a bill of particulars, which would require plaintiff to set forth the details of his claim, including the manner in which the defendant was negligent, the exact nature of the injuries sustained, and the amount of medical expenses incurred.[1]

Sounds simple enough, but back in the 1950s it really wasn't. Back then, as now, bills of particulars served two very specific purposes: to prevent surprise at the time of trial and to limit the scope of plaintiff's proof. In other words, if you didn't put it in your bill of particulars, you couldn't try to prove it at the trial. Moreover, until 1979, when the law was amended,[2] once you filed your bill of particulars, you couldn't supplement it to include newly documented injuries or medical expenses without leave of the court, which was not routinely given. Under those circumstances, it was imperative for you to draw your bill of particulars as broadly as possible in order to fully protect your client's rights. Your worst nightmare would have been to have a compelling piece of evidence excluded from the trial because the claim it supported wasn't in your bill.

To guard against that nightmare, I drew my bills of particulars broadly. For example, in a case where medical bills in the file totaled $385, my bill of particulars stated that medical expenses were "approximately" $425. I added forty dollars to the amount in the file because I estimated the cost of future x-rays and medical supplies. In another case, where medical bills in the file totaled $156, my bill of particulars stated that medical expenses were "approximately" two hundred dollars. I added forty-four dollars to the amount in the file because I estimated the cost of future physiotherapy treatments and prescription drugs.

For these and other similar acts, the Judicial Inquiry charged me with professional misconduct. Forty dollars here, forty-four dollars there. Always preceded by the term "approximately." Always an amount that I could justify or explain. Always to make sure that my client's rights were fully protected.

Some exaggeration.

That's how I handled medical expenses in bills of particulars; what about injury claims? Here's one example: my bill of particulars stated that plaintiff's injuries included a "possible" cerebral concussion and post-concussion syndrome. No such diagnosis was contained in the medical reports in the file, but those reports did specify that plaintiff was suffering from headaches, dizziness, and nausea.

Professional misconduct? Hardly. My statement about plaintiff's injuries in this case and every case was always preceded by the word "possible" or "probable." It was entirely consistent with what every doctor knows, what is written in every medical textbook, and what I knew based upon my background, training, continuing legal education, and fifteen years of experience. As before, all I was doing was protecting my clients' rights at the time of trial to offer the broadest possible proof.

*   *   *

The Trial

I may have thought that the Judicial Inquiry's charges against me were groundless, but they obviously had a different view, and it soon became quite clear that they fully intended to prosecute. On November 29, 1965, the Second Department designated the Honorable William R. Brennan, Jr., a Justice of the New York State Supreme Court in Nassau County, to preside over the proceedings. Shortly thereafter, Judge Brennan assigned us a February 1966 trial date.

As the trial date approached, Bill Beasley, Stu Sherman, and I spent many a long afternoon and evening poring through files, doing intense legal research, and otherwise preparing our defense, which we believed was airtight. Quite simply, we decided that there was no point in disputing the facts. Documents in our office files plainly established that we had done just about everything they accused us of doing. Instead, we would argue that, under applicable legal principles, nothing that we had done was even remotely unethical or improper.

*   *   *

The trial lasted eight days, longer than many murder trials. Judge Brennan heard testimony from nine witnesses. The transcript of the proceedings was 951 pages. The two sides submitted a total of 208 documentary exhibits. It was an excruciating experience. I felt as if the Judicial Inquiry was dissecting my whole life, and not just thirty-four of my files. When it was over, my belief in my own integrity hadn't wavered. Nevertheless, I was more than a little nervous as I awaited Judge Brennan's decision.

*   *   *

The Decision

On July 18, 1966, Judge Brennan released a fifty-two page report containing his findings of fact and conclusions of law. If, the next day, someone had nominated me for sainthood, on the strength of Judge Brennan's report I probably would have been elected in a landslide.

After a meticulous examination of each alleged act of misconduct, Judge Brennan concluded that I had done nothing improper by approximating my clients' medical expenses:

> It is the finding of the undersigned that in the vast majority of cases it is practically an impossibility for a plaintiff's attorney at the time of serving his bill of particulars to set forth all medical expenses with exactitude. The attorney is under a duty to prosecute his case with alacrity. The bill of particulars is frequently served at a time when the client is still under treatment. Due to delay or lack of cooperation, it is frequently difficult to obtain a current or complete medical bill from a physician prior to serving the bill of particulars, and it is next to impossible to obtain an accurate cost of medicines and drugs without reliance upon the oral word of the client.

He also determined, with a few minor exceptions not worth noting, that I had done nothing improper in my handling of my clients' personal injury claims:

> A perusal of the various medical reports in this case, in addition to the over-all familiarity of the undersigned with medical reports in injury cases, demonstrates conclusively that certain

physicians are notoriously cryptic while others are notoriously verbose. The same considerations demonstrate that certain doctors are liberal in their diagnoses while others are conservative and, aside from liberality and conservatism, there are definitely differing medical schools of thought upon giving different diagnoses based upon the same underlying facts and complaints. To require the attorney to parrot an incomplete, cryptic, conservative report of a treating physician would be to deprive him of properly presenting his client's case.

I stated earlier in this discussion that "in almost every instance" the charges against me related to my handling of bills of particulars. What about those instances where the charges involved something else? I haven't addressed those charges yet for the sake of simplicity and brevity. I will address them now for the sake of completeness. In some cases, Judge Brennan concluded that the acts in question were "inadvertent oversights." In others, he concluded that there was no evidence to support the charges. And in still others, he found that the evidence against me was "woefully inadequate."

All very well and good, but the best was yet to come. After completing his analysis of each of the underlying charges, Judge Brennan concluded his report with a brief but glowing evaluation of my professional reputation, character, and fitness as an attorney. This evaluation was based on the testimony of people who knew me and knew my work. These witnesses, all of whom appeared voluntarily, included the Honorable Bernard S. Meyer, who at the time was a Justice of the New York State Supreme Court and who later served with distinction on the New York State Court of Appeals; the Honorable Cortland A. Johnson, also a Justice of the New York State Supreme Court; Peter T. Affatato, Esq., and Frederic Montfort, Esq., both of whom were prominent attorneys in Nassau County who specialized in personal injury defense work and were frequent adversaries of mine; and four physicians who were frequently employed by insurance companies to examine my clients.

After considering the testimony of the above witnesses and all of the other evidence in the record, Judge Brennan concluded that "the one thing which clearly emerges from this hearing" is that Leonard Rivkin "is possessed of high professional ability and [an] excellent reputation for character and morality." He commended my efforts to keep up to date in my practice areas through frequent participation in continuing legal education; my active involvement in professional associations; my free representation of indigent defendants; my involvement in charitable and civic activities; and my war record. He trivialized the charges against me:

> The petition in this case...is significant not only in what it charges as evidence of professional misconduct, but also in what it fails to charge. There is no charge that the respondent ever defrauded a client. There is no charge that he ever permitted a lay person to obtain signed retainers or aid in the settlement of cases. There is no charge that he ever submitted false statements pertaining to loss of time or loss or earnings. There is no charge that he ever loaned or paid moneys to clients or others to obtain or retain any client, case or action. There is no charge that any complaint was ever made against the respondent by any person, client, firm or court.

Judge Brennan's final assessment: "He is a capable, aggressive advocate."

* * *

The Low Point

Before I even knew of Judge Brennan's decision, I received a telephone call from William Hanrahan, the attorney for the Judicial Inquiry who had first contacted me to review my files. Mr. Hanrahan told me that the decision was on route and was favorable to me. In fact, I'll never forget his words: "It looks like an article sponsoring you for a judgeship."

After receiving and reviewing a copy of Judge Brennan's report, I had to agree. I felt totally vindicated. At the office, we all heaved a collective sigh of relief. Thank heaven this was behind us. I don't think we got any work done that afternoon. Christmas had come in the middle of July, and we celebrated long into the evening.

But then, another bombshell. Apparently, whoever was calling the shots at the Judicial Inquiry did not agree with William Hanrahan that I was fit to be a judge, because on October 14, 1966, the Judicial Inquiry submitted a 170-page brief to the Second Department asking the court for a determination, based on the evidence submitted to Judge Brennan, that I was guilty of more than one hundred acts of professional misconduct. This was so unexpected that it was almost comical. Judge Brennan's decision couldn't have been more complimentary to me than if I had written it myself. Didn't the person in charge of the Judicial Inquiry even bother to read it?

We filed our answering brief and then waited. Nothing happened for four months. The longer we waited, the more apprehensive I became. It made no sense that the Second Department was taking so long to affirm my innocence.

Then, in the middle of a wintry February afternoon, I received a telephone call from a reporter from *Newsday*. He wanted me to comment on the decision of the Second Department to suspend me from the practice of law for six months.

Imagine that. I learned of the Second Department's decision to suspend me from a reporter. I just sat at my desk, holding the phone to my ear, unable to speak. Even today, I am unable to put my feelings about the Second Department's decision into words. All I can say is that no one loved or respected the practice of law more than I did, and still do. To be told that my efforts to fully protect the rights and interests of my clients amounted to professional misconduct was totally shattering.

"Mr. Rivkin?" the reporter repeated several times when I did not respond. Finally, I told him that I had no comment and hung up.

The next morning, I picked up a copy of *Newsday* on my way to the office. It didn't take long for me to find what I was looking for. The story appeared under a two column headline in the middle of page six. To my chagrin, *Newsday* reported all of the gory details.

That same morning, a copy of the Second Department's decision arrived in the mail. We read it, but we didn't believe it. They spelled my name correctly, but that was about it.

For example, they condemned my practice of estimating the amount of plaintiff's medical expenses in bills of particulars "without even stating that [the amounts] are estimates."[3] Didn't they read the record? The evidence established, and Judge Brennan found, that I always preceded any estimated medical expenses with the word "approximately."

The court also condemned me for including claims in bills of particulars for injuries I "could not hope to prove."[4] In other words, where plaintiff complained of headaches, dizziness, and nausea, the court concluded that I "could not hope to prove" a cerebral concussion, even though, as reflected in the record, every medical textbook and every practicing physician would flatly disagree.

All of our arguments similarly fell on deaf ears. In fact, considering how unsympathetic the court was to our position, I guess I should have felt lucky that they only wanted to suspend me for six months and not disbar me. Though I viewed the court's punishment as draconian, they thought they were letting me off easy, saying:

> In considering the nature and extent of the discipline to be imposed, we have taken cognizance of several factors in mitigation, including the absence of complaints by clients, the absence of evidence of fraud upon clients, the fact that respondent co-operated fully and completely with the Judicial Inquiry and evidence as to respondent's integrity and capabilities.[5]

To this day, I believe that I was not judged by an impartial panel but by one with an agenda of some sort. Maybe the Second Department, which created the Judicial Inquiry, felt compelled to justify its existence by disciplining anyone and everyone that came under its microscope.

*   *   *

Fighting Back

Clearly, the Second Department had made a mistake. The question became: what should we do about it.

Of course, one of my options was to take it easy for six months. After all, I had worked my tail off building my practice; why not relax for a while. I was entitled. Then, after I served my suspension, I could return to work with a renewed determination to rebuild my practice and resurrect my good name.

To those who knew me, however, that option was out of the question. It's not in my nature to give up, particularly when I think I have been wronged. I'm a fighter to the very end; in fact, the more hopeless the situation, the harder I battle. I was not about to let a bunch of expletives deleted take my livelihood away from me, not for six months, not for one day.

We retained the services of Edmund B. Hennefeld, an experienced appellate lawyer in New York City, to spearhead an effort to get a stay of the Second Department's decision and then appeal that decision to the New York Court of Appeals, the highest court in the state.

Before we could even think about winning in the Court of Appeals, however, we had to find a way to get our case heard in that Court.

The Second Department's decision was not appealable as of right; we needed permission to appeal, which could be obtained either from the Second Department or the Court of Appeals itself. Neither option looked very inviting. We believed that the Second Department was not likely to grant us leave to appeal in light of their hostile attitude toward me as reflected in its order of suspension. Similarly, we believed that the Court of Appeals was not likely to grant us leave because we perceived a reluctance on its part to get involved in disciplinary matters. It seemed as if we were caught between a rock and a hard place, but ultimately decided that aloof was better than hostile, so we bypassed the Second Department and made our motion for leave to appeal directly in the Court of Appeals. We coupled our motion for leave to appeal with a motion to stay the order of suspension pending the Court's decision.

Once again, we waited. Nothing happened for two months. During that period, at the suggestion of my old friend Irving Josefsberg, I threw myself into my work, arguing motions, selecting juries, trying cases. But it wasn't easy. The order of suspension, which had not taken effect because of our motion to stay, was a monumental distraction. It hung over my head like the blade of a guillotine.

Then, on May 18, 1967, we got the good news. The Court of Appeals had stayed the order of suspension and granted our motion to appeal.[6] At this point, our spirits soared. We knew the Second Department's decision was grievously wrong and unfair. By agreeing to hear our case, the Court of Appeals may have been suggesting that it agreed with us.

Both sides submitted briefs to the Court of Appeals that basically repeated the arguments previously made before Judge Brennan. The focus was on my practices regarding bills of particulars. I argued that approximating medical expenses and drawing my own conclusions about possible injuries was entirely proper; the Judicial Inquiry argued that I could only set forth exact, documented medical expenses and only those injuries expressly identified in written medical report.

While Mr. Hennefeld's appellate briefs were superb, we received some unexpected help. Both the New York State Association of Trial Lawyers and the Nassau County Bar Association filed amicus curiae briefs in support of my position.

The involvement of the Nassau County Bar Association was particularly surprising for two reasons: first, to my knowledge, the Bar Association had never before filed an amicus brief in a disciplinary proceeding; and second, the Bar Association's petition to the Second

Department back in 1958 had led to the creation of the Judicial Inquiry in the first place.

At any rate, both the Nassau County Bar Association and the New York State Association of Trial Lawyers vigorously supported my view of what an attorney could reasonably include in plaintiff's bill of particulars. The Bar Association pointed out, among other things, that it was common practice among plaintiff's personal injury lawyers to estimate medical expenses in bills of particulars and describe plaintiff's injuries as broadly as possible. The suggestion was why discipline Len Rivkin for something that all plaintiff's attorneys routinely do. The Trial Lawyers Association asserted that any attorney who included less than I did in his bill of particulars "would...fail in his ethical duty" to protect his client's rights at the time of trial. Moreover, the Association even went so far as to argue that the Second Department's decision raised "grave constitutional issues of freedom of expression and the right to counsel." The Association explained:

> This must include the right of counsel to properly protect his client's interests without fear of condemnation because of vague and amorphous charges of "exaggeration" of claims in a pleading. An attorney should not be penalized for refusing to emasculate himself by divesting his learning and experience gained by dint of hard work. The subjective expertise and legitimate resourcefulness of one in drawing papers should not be gauged by the subjective criteria of another...

The Court of Appeals heard oral argument on our appeal and then reserved decision. Again, we waited. Again, I threw myself into my work. Again, it wasn't easy. In fact, this was perhaps the most difficult time of the entire ordeal, since I knew it was about to end. The Court of Appeals was my court of last resort. One way or the other, that Court was going to bring this matter to its conclusion. I felt powerless, yet hopeful.

Finally, on December 29, 1967, the Court of Appeals issued its decision. After a five year investigation, after a thorough review of nearly every file in my office, after an eight day trial which produced a 951-page transcript, after a fifty-two-page report which painstakingly analyzed every one of alleged acts of misconduct, after nearly five hundred pages of briefs which advanced every conceivable legal and factual argument both for and against me, after a roller coaster ride the likes of which I wouldn't wish on my worst enemy, the Court of Appeals disposed of the matter in two sentences. I never read past the first: "Order reversed and charges dismissed."[7]

The battle was finally over; I was clearly and unambiguously the winner.

* * *

The Aftermath

After breathing a huge sigh of relief and celebrating with Stu Sherman long into the evening, I breathed another huge sigh of relief and celebrated with Stu long into the next evening. Fortunately, the office was closed on New Year's Day, so we had all morning and most of the afternoon to sleep off our revelry.

When the office reopened, many friends and colleagues called to congratulate me and pump me with questions, which of course was gratifying but also frustrating. At that point, the last thing in the world I wanted to talk about was the Judicial Inquiry. Gradually, the number of calls declined and ultimately stopped. At last, I was able to focus all of my attention on my clients' problems instead of my own.

Then, one morning shortly after the Court of Appeals decision, I was sitting at my desk when the phone rang. I picked it up and immediately recognized the caller's voice. It was William Hanrahan, the Assistant Counsel to the Judicial Inquiry who was heavily involved in prosecuting the charges against me.

Oh no, I thought. Won't this matter ever go away?

But Mr. Hanrahan was not calling on Judicial Inquiry business. He was a local attorney whose position with the Judicial Inquiry was part-time; his call was about matters relating to his private practice.

"Len," he said. "I have two very heavy plaintiff's cases I'd like you to try."

I was stunned. Here was the man who had just investigated me for five years asking me to try his cases for him. I asked him the same question that I had asked when he first wanted to review my files:

"Why me?"

He told me that he had never seen files prepared any better than mine or work done any more competently.

Quite a compliment, considering the source.

* * *

Finally, I could not tell the story of my involvement with the Judicial Inquiry without singling out one person for his help and assistance during the entire five year period of the investigation: Stu Sherman, my young associate who later became my partner and remained my partner until he retired from the firm in 1985.

Stu labored tirelessly on my behalf. He reviewed files, collected and marshaled evidence, prepared precise documentation and support for every challenged item on every disputed bill of particulars, researched the law, and worked with my two lawyers — William Beasley and Ed Hennefeld — on trial and appellate strategy and tactics. During the appellate process in particular, I remember many days where Stu left the office at 6:00 p.m. after a full day on the job, drove into Manhattan, grabbed a quick dinner with Ed Hennefeld, and then worked with Ed until two the morning.

Stu's help was invaluable, and for that help I will be eternally grateful.

CHAPTER FIVE

Crossing the Street: Representing Defendants

Early in 1968, as far as my law practice was concerned, things were definitely looking up.

Invigorated by my victory in the Court of Appeals, I could hardly wait to arrive at the office each morning. I was usually the last to go home at night.

Fortunately, there was plenty for me to do. Notwithstanding the negative press I received during the Judicial Inquiry, new cases were teeming into the office at a faster rate than ever before. I have no explanation as to why this was happening, except to suggest that the people who knew me, both personally and professionally, must have had faith in me.

As thrilled as I was about how busy we were, I was even more excited about the changing nature of our practice and client base. Although I was still best known as a plaintiff's personal injury attorney, I was now doing defense work on a regular basis in automobile accident cases assigned to me by Allstate, Fireman's Fund, and other insurance companies that traditionally had been my adversaries but recently had become my clients.

I acquired my insurance company clients partly by luck and partly by design. Little did I realize at the time where my budding relationship with the insurance industry would lead. It would expand my practice far beyond my wildest expectations and place me front and center in the arena of big time civil litigation.

* * *

Early Defense Work

Early in my career, beginning in the late 1950s, I did a small amount of defense work in cases referred to me by the New York State Medical Society. This was an association of doctors that was similar in structure and function to the New York State Bar Association. It lobbied, sponsored seminars, and published a professional journal. It also recommended defense attorneys to its member physicians sued for malpractice and also to the insurance companies that provided malpractice coverage.

My father, a member of the Society, had a longstanding friendship with its Executive Director, whom I had met on numerous occasions. After I had been in practice in Freeport for ten years, the Executive Director introduced me to Dick Byrnes, the Society's General Counsel. Dick and I hit it off quite well, and after a while he began to recommend me for malpractice defense work. I did not receive a lot of cases as a result of Dick's recommendations, but there was a steady flow.

I had taken and was continuing to take continuing legal education courses focusing on the medical aspects of personal injury litigation, and the malpractice work was a perfect fit. In fact, I enjoyed defending doctors so much that I usually did all of the work on each case myself, even the paperwork. The typical malpractice case ordinarily required me to closely review my client's diagnosis and treatment and to explore the question of causation, that is, did my client's treatment (or lack of treatment) cause the plaintiff's injuries. I held lengthy meetings with my client as well as with other physicians who acted as expert witnesses. I became familiar with the leading medical texts and treatises on whatever aspect of medicine the particular case involved. Although I never became the doctor that my father envisioned, at least I reached the point, thanks to my malpractice defense work, where I could discuss various medical topics with my father on a reasonably intelligent basis.

* * *

The MVAIC

In the early 1960s, I began receiving automobile accident defense work from the Motor Vehicle Accident Indemnification Corporation ("MVAIC").

The MVAIC was a government corporation funded by insurance companies and run by present and former insurance company executives and employees. Created by the legislature in 1959, its purpose was to provide a mechanism for compensating the many victims of automobile accidents caused by hit-and-run or uninsured drivers.[1]

And there were many such victims. Hit-and-run accidents were an every day occurrence. And even though New York State required its residents to carry automobile insurance, so, too, were accidents involving uninsured drivers.

How could the driver have no insurance if the law required it? In some cases, the policy had lapsed. In others, the insurance company disclaimed or denied coverage on the ground that the defendant failed to provide timely notice of the accident, or because the defendant was driving a stolen car or was otherwise driving the car without the consent of its owner. In still others, the defendant resided in a state that did not require its citizens to have automobile insurance.

At any rate, the MVAIC afforded the possibility of compensation to accident victims who otherwise had no viable remedy. Prior to 1959, a person injured by an uninsured driver could sue the driver but was not likely to recover anything, since an uninsured driver probably didn't have the financial resources to pay an adverse judgment. A person injured in a hit-and-run accident didn't even have anybody he could sue.

The compensation available from the MVAIC was minimal, but it was better than nothing. The maximum recovery under the statute was ten thousand dollars per person and twenty thousand dollars per accident.

The statutory scheme establishing the procedures for making a claim against the MVAIC was somewhat complex. For present purposes, I will overgeneralize for the sake of clarity and simplicity. The MVAIC created two categories of eligible claimants. An "insured" claimant, for the most part, was the driver or any occupant of an insured car involved in an accident caused by an uninsured or hit-and-run motorist. His sole remedy under the statute was an arbitration claim against the MVAIC. A "qualified" claimant, for the most part, was a pedestrian with no automobile insurance applicable to the accident who was injured by an uninsured or hit-and-run motorist. His remedy against the MVAIC was a lawsuit.

When the MVAIC was first formed, I represented a fair number of "insured" claimants in arbitration proceedings against the MVAIC and got some very good results. It was unusual to recover the

MVAIC's full statutory limit of liability in any one case, but I recall doing so two or three times.

How did I go from making claims against the MVAIC to defending it? Pure happenstance. I was in court one morning in Manhattan for a conference. We finished before 11:00 a.m. In the elevator, I wondered if there was something else I could get done in the city before heading back to Freeport. Then I remembered that I had an arbitration claim pending against the MVAIC that I had been trying to settle. Their office was nearby, so I hopped into a cab. Luckily, the supervisor in charge of the claim was free and agreed to meet with me. As we were discussing the matter, Tom O'Boyle, the head of the MVAIC's New York City office, just happened to stop at the supervisor's desk with a question. Tom was a good looking, heavyset Irish-American who knew everybody in politics and the insurance industry. Over the years he had worked for several insurance companies and was appointed to the MVAIC by the Governor. The supervisor introduced us, saying, "Tom, this is Len Rivkin, the lawyer from Freeport who nailed us a couple of times this year." At my suggestion, the three of us ended up going out to lunch.

At lunch, Tom remarked that the MVAIC had been assigning all of its work, even cases in Nassau and Suffolk, to attorneys in New York City, and that he had been looking for Long Island counsel. I told him I would be very interested in representing the MVAIC and reminded him that I was more than qualified to do so, in light of my recent success representing claimants against the MVAIC. He agreed, we shook hands, and that very month I received my first MVAIC files.

*   *   *

I personally handled the first few arbitration files we received from the MVAIC. But the typical case was not that complicated and did not require the hands-on attention of a senior trial attorney, so I soon began to assign the work to Stu Sherman and the junior associates in the office. They got some good results, and the number of cases I was receiving gradually started to increase.

As this was happening, I grew to appreciate one particular aspect of working for the MVAIC: the matter of our legal fees. The practice of law is a profession, but it is also a business. At the time, the firm was located at 16 West Sunrise Highway. Our rent had nearly doubled. I had four lawyers working for me, six secretaries, and an occasional law clerk. Representing plaintiffs, we worked on a contingent fee basis. We received nothing unless and until our client won a judgment or settlement. This made for a very uneven cash flow. Some months we did very well and could easily meet our expenses; others we earned nothing at all. In contrast, the MVAIC paid us every month. We earned a flat fee for each arbitration file they sent us and an hourly fee if we had to go to court. This was a new experience for me. Cash flow was becoming less of a problem. With enough MVAIC business, I could eliminate that problem altogether.

For that reason, I began to explore whether there was something I could do to increase my MVAIC business. Then I remembered a person from my past who may have been in a position to help. Back in the 1940s, I dated a girl who had a ubiquitous little brother. It got to the point where I had to pay him twenty-five cents to leave the room so I could be alone with his sister after coming back from a date. The little brother ultimately went to law school and opted for a career in politics. His name was Philip Weinberg, and in the early 1960s he was working for Governor Rockefeller as his Appointments Secretary. Although I hadn't seen either Phil or his sister in almost twenty years, I called Phil in Albany. He was surprised and delighted to hear from me. We had a long conversation reminiscing about old times. Then I mentioned my relationship with the MVAIC and interest in expanding that relationship.

Sure enough, Phil knew Tom O'Boyle, so he called Tom to make some inquiries. Tom gave my office good reviews and, as a result of his conversation with Phil, began to send me upwards of ten to fifteen cases per month.

Incidentally, Phil and I renewed our friendship as a result of my phone call to him. After serving as Governor Rockefeller's Appointments Secretary, he held the same position under Governor Malcolm Wilson. When the Democrats finally managed to elect a Democratic Governor in 1974, and Phil found himself out of a job, I offered him a partnership, which he accepted. He was instrumental in the firm's growth throughout the 1970s and 80s, opening many doors, in particular in the banking and real estate fields. Phil ultimately served as managing partner of the firm at a time when we had more than two hundred lawyers.

But as much as I valued Phil professionally, I valued him personally even more. Here was a man who wielded an enormous amount of political power when he worked in the Governor's office, and afterward the extent of his contacts never ceased to amaze me, but there was not an ounce of pretension about him. He never had an unkind word for anyone. He treated everyone he met with the same dignity and respect.

Phil's untimely death, late in 1987, was a shock to us all and a great personal and professional loss.

* * *

The Typical MVAIC Case

As suggested earlier, most of the work we handled for the MVAIC was not all that complicated. In the typical case, we defended the MVAIC in an arbitration proceeding, where the procedures were much simpler and the pace much faster than in regular courtroom litigation. In response to the claimant's demand for arbitration, we filed an answer denying the claim and then examined the claimant under oath for details about the accident and his injuries. Shortly thereafter, a hearing took place at the office of the American Arbitration Association on Madison Avenue. The hearing addressed two issues: whether the accident was caused by the negligence of the uninsured or hit-and-run driver, and the extent of the claimant's damages. The claimant testified at the hearing, and each side ordinarily offered the testimony of a physician or, since the rules of evidence did not apply, a physician's letter. Occasionally, if there was some question as to how the accident happened, either or both sides offered the testimony of an eyewitness or the police report. The hearing rarely lasted more than two or three hours; Stu Sherman often traveled to Manhattan to defend one arbitration in the morning and a second in the afternoon. We usually had a decision from the hearing officer within one week.

* * *

Some Not-So-Typical Cases

But the work did have its moments. For example, in order to qualify for arbitration under the statute as the victim of a hit-and-run, a claimant must have been injured as a result of actual physical contact between his vehicle and the hit-and-run vehicle. In other words, you couldn't have a hit-and-run without the "hit." Whenever we handled an arbitration where we suspected that there had been no "hit," we took the initiative by moving in court for a stay of arbitration pending a jury trial on the issue of whether contact between vehicles had, in fact, taken place. One common scenario involved injuries sustained by the claimant when he swerved to avoid an oncoming car and slammed into a tree or other obstacle. Under those circumstances, the claimant would not be entitled to arbitrate his claim against the MVAIC, and the court would dismiss his arbitration demand. Sounds pretty harsh, but if the legislature didn't like this result, the simple solution was to amend the statute.

There were other situations where we took the initiative and sought a court order staying the proceedings. For example, in order to qualify for arbitration, a claimant's injuries must have been caused by accident. I can recall one case where we obtained a stay of arbitration on the grounds that claimant's injuries may have been deliberate. In that case, the injured claimant was a passenger in an insured vehicle driven by her boyfriend. We alleged that the claimant's former boyfriend, "a jilted lover," was following the claimant in an uninsured vehicle. We further alleged that the former boyfriend "intentionally ran his car into the [claimant's] vehicle, forced it off the road into a telephone pole, and proceeded to back up and then ram into it once again."[2]

Still another prerequisite for arbitration under the statute was that the claimant had to be an "innocent victim" of the accident. We had a case where the claimant was injured while a passenger in a stolen vehicle being pursued by the police. We took the initiative in that case and moved for a stay, which the court granted. In that case, we alleged that the claimant had knowledge that the car was stolen and therefore was not an innocent victim.[3]

*   *   *

My First Insurance Company

In 1965, the legislature amended the law applicable to uninsured and hit-and-run motorists in a way that substantially reduced the role of the MVAIC. Under the amendment, the MVAIC would continue to handle only those infrequent claims filed by "qualified" claimants, that is, pedestrians injured by uninsured or hit-and-run motorists. "Insured" claimants, however, who comprised the great bulk of the MVAIC's pre-amendment caseload, no longer had any right to proceed against the MVAIC. Instead, the new law required "insured" claimants to file their arbitration claims directly against their own insurance companies. In other words, if the driver or passenger in a car insured by Allstate was injured in an accident caused by an uninsured or hit-and-run driver, the injured party would file an arbitration claim directly against Allstate. Other than shifting the burden of investigating and paying arbitration claims directly to the insurance companies, the new statute left the arbitration procedures essentially the same.[4]

At the time of the amendment, my office had been representing the MVAIC for nearly five years. We must have been doing something right, because every year our business with them increased. The amendment changed all that rather quickly. Before the amendment, the MVAIC assigned us as many as twenty cases per month. After the amendment, since the MVAIC no longer handled claims by "insured" claimants, if they assigned us one case every two months, that was a lot.

I needed to replace this lost business, and the logical place to look was to the insurance companies that were now obligated under the new statute to handle claims by "insured" claimants. I knew that I had the expertise, as a result of my work for the MVAIC, to do this arbitration work for any number of insurance companies. Unfortunately, I couldn't think of anyone who could open that first insurance company door for me. Nevertheless, I managed to open that door myself through initiative and good fortune. Here's how it happened.

I was handling an auto accident case on behalf of a seriously injured plaintiff, a young woman, where the defendant's insurance company was Allstate. The woman had a fractured skull with brain damage and was hospitalized for an extended period. Allstate was obligated to pay the woman's medical bills under the "Medical Payments" coverage of the defendant's policy. At the time, however, Allstate had an internal rule that it would make payments under this coverage only after all treatment was completed. In this case, medical bills were already quite substantial and there was no end in sight to the young woman's treatment. Since her parents could not afford to pay those bills, I wrote to Allstate explaining the situation and asked them to break their rule in this one case to ease the burden on the suffering family. To my surprise, shortly thereafter I received a telephone call from an Allstate supervisor who told me that they thought my request was reasonable and they would immediately start to pay plaintiff's medical expenses.

Seizing the moment, I ascertained the identity of the person in charge of that particular Allstate office, which I believe was in Freeport, and wrote him a letter thanking the company and commending the supervisor for his decision to help my client. As luck would have it, a vice president of Allstate, who was visiting the office at the time, happened to see my letter. He called me to thank me for writing it, and the next thing he knew I was inviting him to lunch and he was accepting.

At lunch, I described for the vice president my experience representing the MVAIC and suggested that I could do just as well for Allstate under the new law. I told him to feel free to contact Tom O'Boyle as a reference. The vice president was impressed; he told me that he would call a man named Ben Purvin, who was the head of Allstate's Legal Department on Long Island, to advise him of my interest. Shortly thereafter, Mr. Purvin invited me to his office to discuss the possibility of giving me work. He, too, must have been impressed; within one week he began sending me Allstate arbitration cases.

Talk about culture shock. Here was Len Rivkin, one of Nassau County's leading plaintiff's attorneys, representing the Allstate Insurance Company, a frequent adversary. Our newly formed relationship started very slowly; I guess it took a while for us to get accustomed to putting our heads together instead of butting heads. But once we got to know each other, we actually liked each other. By the end of the 1960s, not only was Allstate sending me a steady stream of arbitrations arising under the company's uninsured motorists endorsement, they were also sending me lawsuits to defend. In the typical case, the victim of an auto accident would start a lawsuit against a driver insured by Allstate; Allstate would then hire us to represent and defend the driver in court. Later, when no fault was enacted in New York in 1973, I got no-fault work from Allstate as well. During the peak years, Allstate was sending my office as many as twenty new cases per month. Even as the firm grew and entered the arena of complex, big time litigation, we continued to do liability defense work for Allstate and also became one of its national counsel in the important area of environmental insurance coverage. Our relationship has endured, uninterrupted, for upwards of thirty years.

*   *   *

My Second Insurance Company, and My Third, and My Fourth

Soon after landing the Allstate account, we began to get unsolicited calls from other insurance companies that weren't looking to hire us but instead were looking to pick our brains. These companies either knew that we had represented the MVAIC on Long Island or else had

called the MVAIC for a recommendation. Apparently, they were overwhelmed by their uninsured motorists caseload, not because of the
complexity but because of the sheer volume. The cases went every
which way and were difficult to reconcile. They were hoping that we
could provide some free advice and guidance.

We were happy to oblige. We weren't in the habit of giving away
our services, especially to those who could afford to pay us, but we
recognized the value of some positive public relations. We answered
their questions. Stu Sherman lectured their adjusters. He even prepared a pamphlet for them on how to handle uninsured motorists and
hit-and-run arbitration claims.

All the while, we never missed an opportunity to advise our callers
that we were available to do their work. These suggestions did not fall
on deaf ears; several insurance companies soon began sending us
work. We got some good results, so they increased the number of
cases they assigned to us each month. Within two years, we were getting enough arbitration work to keep two attorneys busy full time.

*   *   *

The Decision to Cross the Street

With our insurance business surging, I recognized that the firm had
reached a crossroads. We had moved into the new building at 55
North Ocean Avenue two years earlier and had already outgrown it; I
now had seven lawyers working for me and an equal number of secretaries. This growth delighted me, and I wanted it to continue.

I believed, however, that to achieve that goal I had to choose between two mutually exclusive paths. Even though we had been doing
automobile accident defense work for upwards of seven years, we
were still more widely known as a plaintiff's firm. Therefore, I could
continue to hold myself out as a specialist in plaintiff's work and expand on that basis, taking only whatever defense work happened to
come my way but not actively seeking it. Or I could try to cross the
street, that is, shift my emphasis away from doing plaintiff's work and
actively seek to expand my newly acquired defense practice. I figured
that I couldn't have it both ways: insurance companies were not likely
to send me much more business if I was perceived primarily as a plaintiff's attorney; and plaintiffs were not likely to come flocking to my
door if I was perceived primarily as an attorney for the insurance industry.

After considering my options, I concluded that emphasizing plaintiff's work was not the way to go. One problem that limited my ability to further expand in this area was that virtually every client, regardless of how seriously injured, wanted me to personally handle his or her case. While many of my clients were content to let my associates handle the paperwork and even perhaps the examinations before trial, at the very least they all wanted me to conduct the trial. This was good for my ego but bad for business. There were only so many hours in the day; I could only handle a certain caseload; if I couldn't guarantee a potential client that I would try his case, that client was likely to take his business elsewhere.

A second problem was cash flow. As I mentioned earlier, like every plaintiff's firm we had good months and bad months. As the number of my employees and therefore my expenses increased, I concluded that I would feel more comfortable in a situation where my monthly income was relatively consistent.

Defense work, on the other hand, suffered from neither of these problems. First, insurance companies were well versed in the realities of personal injury litigation and knew that they didn't need a top trial attorney for every case but only for those involving the most serious injuries. Therefore, a company could comfortably assign a firm as many as ten or fifteen cases per month, expecting that maybe only one or two would require the senior partner's personal attention. And second, cash flow would be less of a concern because most insurance companies paid their legal bills on a regular basis, usually every month.

In addition, defense work seemed to offer more immediate opportunities for growth. At the time, I only had four insurance company clients; I saw no reason why I couldn't double or triple that number, which could conceivably double or triple the flow of new cases into the office. In addition, my insurance company clients were only sending me uninsured motorists and hit-and-run arbitration claims; I saw no reason why I couldn't expand my defense practice into other insurance-related areas, which could have a similarly dramatic impact on my business. In contrast, new plaintiff's cases came into the office on a one-at-a-time basis; expansion was possible, but likely not as rapid.

These practical considerations were important to my thought process, but the deciding factor was an emotional one. Simply put, I enjoyed being a counter puncher. A good defense attorney doesn't just defend; he looks for ways to take the initiative, go on the offensive, and wrest control from the plaintiff of the pace, scope, and direction of the lawsuit. Even though the arbitration defense work I was doing at the time was relatively unsophisticated, you still had to be a good counter puncher in order to succeed. For example, every time we moved in court for an order to stay the arbitration, either because there was no "hit" in the hit-and-run, or no accident, or no innocent victim, we were counter punching, taking the offensive. It was challenging, it was fun, we were successful, our clients appreciated it, and our business grew. What more could any attorney reasonably want?

So I made a decision. I certainly wouldn't turn away any potentially lucrative plaintiff's case, but I would no longer accept everything that was offered. Instead, I would focus my energies on insurance defense work. That would be the best way of assuring that my firm would continue to grow and prosper and that I would continue to get satisfaction and enjoyment out of my profession. While hindsight is always 20/20, I can safely say that my decision on this issue was certainly a wise one.

*   *   *

Having made my decision, I proceeded to do whatever I could to get more business from my existing insurance company clients and new business from other insurers. I wrote letters, made phone calls, met with people, asked for favors, and looked for any excuse to stop by an insurance company office just to say hello. Stu Sherman, who became my partner in 1968, supported my efforts and played a vital role. He had obtained his pilot's license in 1963; insurance adjusters were thrilled when Stu invited them to fly to Southampton, Hartford, or Provincetown for lunch. Stu did a lot of flying to help the firm, and even more eating. When he first came to work for me in the mid-1950s, he weighed 165 pounds. During his peak flying, wining, and dining years, he ballooned up to 225.

*   *   *

Stu and I were tireless, persistent, and relentless in our efforts to get more insurance company business, and ultimately successful. By the early 1970s, we were receiving a substantial stream of business from Allstate, Fireman's Fund, GEICO, General Accident, and several other smaller insurers. At first, each company limited our assignments to uninsured motorists and hit-and-run arbitrations, which had become our specialty. We routinely won cases the carrier expected to lose; when we lost, the arbitrator's award was routinely less than the carrier expected to pay. Having defended arbitrations to the client's satisfaction, Stu and I would then suggest that we could do just as well defending lawsuits. We talked, the carriers listened. Soon, all of my insurance company clients were assigning to my office not only automobile accident litigation but also other types of personal injury defense work, such as slip and fall cases, landlord and tenant matters, construction site accidents, and even some products liability work. Getting this business was an enormously significant step for us. As rapidly as our caseload grew when we were doing arbitrations, it grew even more rapidly after we started defending automobile accident and other personal injury lawsuits. By December 1973, Stu and I had eight other lawyers on the payroll; we were getting as many as forty new defense files every month.

*   *   *

Not all of my dealings with insurance companies during this period ended on a high note.

In the early 1970s, Stu and I often used each other's car, depending on the circumstances. I drove a Cadillac El Dorado; Stu had an Oldsmobile Cutlass. (Remember, I was the senior partner.) During office hours, we parked our cars in a lot adjacent to the office. If one of us had to go to court, he ordinarily took Stu's car. If one of us was entertaining a client, he ordinarily used mine.

Thinking that nothing could happen to cars parked across the street from the Village Police Headquarters, neither one of us kept his car locked. I even went so far as to keep my wallet and credit cards in the glove compartment.

One afternoon, I walked downstairs, out of the building, and into the parking lot. Five minutes later, I was back in the office.

"Stu," I yelled. "Where'd you park my car?"

"I haven't used your car all week," he replied.

"Anybody else use it today?"

Silence.

"Well, it's gone."

Stu came out of his office. "Think, Len. Where'd you park it?"

"Right outside the door."

We went downstairs. It was nowhere to be found. We concluded that it must have been stolen.

I was furious; my money, driver's license, and credit cards were in the glove compartment. Stu and I walked across the street to the police station. Remember, I was counsel to the PBA; I kept a Nassau Police Conference badge on the dashboard and a Freeport Police shield on the rear bumper. We told them the problem. They thought it was hilarious but promised to get right on it.

About ten days later, I was out of the office, so a call for me was directed to Stu. A man with a deep southern accent identified himself as an FBI agent in Atlanta.

"Mr. Sherman, y'all are Mr. Rivkin's partna?"

"That's correct."

"Well, suh, Ah have a question that's a little delicate. Do y'all mind if Ah ask ya straight out?"

"Go right ahead."

"Well, suh, is Mr. Rivkin a gentleman of color?"

"Is he what?"

"Is he a black man?"

Stu was flabbergasted. "No he isn't. Why do you ask?"

"Well, suh, we got us a black gentleman down here drivin' Mr. Rivkin's Cadillac, usin' his credit cards, buyin' himself all sorts of items, claimin' he's the attorney for the local police up there, he's even flashin' a badge. He says he's gonna sue our asses if we don't let him go immediately. We were just about ready to believe that son-of-a-gun. Ah think we're gonna go have another talk with the man."

If you're wondering where the insurance company comes in, when my car was found in Atlanta, the company wanted me to go down there and get it myself. I insisted that they had to get it, and although this is no way to treat a potential client, I threatened to sue them if they didn't.

Well, they finally agreed to bring me my car. Several days later, when I arrived at the office, my car was parked right in front of the entrance. I was satisfied until I discovered that the company had gotten the last laugh. They locked the keys in the trunk.

*   *   *

Of all the insurance companies that referred business to me in the late 1960s and early 1970s, none proved more important to me than Fireman's Fund.

When I represented the MVAIC, I frequently worked with an employee named Vivian Nelson, who, unbeknownst to me, knew a lot of people at Fireman's Fund. I continued to work with Ms. Nelson even after the legislature passed the amendment that drastically reduced the MVAIC's powers. One afternoon, we were having a conversation, and she mentioned that she'd heard I was getting a lot of arbitration work from Allstate. I told her yes, that's true, and that I was looking to develop arbitration business from other insurance companies. That's when she told me she knew a lot of people at Fireman's Fund. At my request, she agreed to contact some people there and recommend us for their arbitration work. A few weeks later, a man named Joe Quinn, who was the Claims Manager of the New York City office of Fireman's Fund, contacted me about the possibility of giving us work in Queens and Nassau. I told him I was available, so he put me in touch with Ralph O'Reagan, who ran the Legal Department at the Long Island office of Fireman's Fund. Mr. O'Reagan immediately began assigning arbitrations to my office.

* * *

My relationship with Fireman's Fund progressed much like my relationship with the other insurers: arbitration work first, followed by automobile accident and other personal injury litigation. However, there was one major difference. My representation of Fireman's Fund ultimately went far beyond the relatively simple and straightforward personal injury case. In the 1970s and 1980s, I represented The Dow Chemical Company, a Fireman's Fund insured, in increasingly complex products liability litigation that culminated in Agent Orange. In addition, in the 1970s I represented Fireman's Fund in the Franklin National Bank litigation, my first complex insurance coverage case. But for my early days doing automobile defense work for Fireman's Fund, my involvement front and center in these and other complex, precedent setting lawsuits might never have occurred.

PART TWO

Major Clients, Major Cases

CHAPTER SIX

The First Dow Case

I was sitting in my office just back from court late on a Tuesday afternoon in March of 1972 when the telephone rang. I picked it up. The caller identified himself as Don Koehlinger, an attorney employed by The Dow Chemical Company in its drug division in Zionsville, Indiana, outside of Indianapolis. After some initial pleasantries, Mr. Koehlinger informed me that Dow was a defendant in a serious drug case that had been pending for nearly four years in federal court in Brooklyn.

"We have decided to reassign the case to a new attorney," Mr. Koehlinger continued. "Would you be interested in meeting with us to discuss the possibility of taking over our defense?"

At the time, my caseload consisted of automobile accident cases, other types of general liability matters, medical malpractice cases, and a smattering of products liability suits. My clients were individuals who drove cars, owned homes, or practiced medicine. I represented a few local businesses, but nothing even remotely close to Dow Chemical in terms of size and stature.

"I certainly would," I replied quickly and was about to add that I'd be on the next plane to Indianapolis when Mr. Koehlinger cut me off.

"We'd like to meet with you at your office in New York. Are you free this Friday?"

I didn't even bother to check my calendar. "I think I can squeeze you in," I said.

"Great. We're looking forward to it."

I hung up the phone and sat back in my chair. I could hardly believe what had just taken place. Dow Chemical had called, looking for a lawyer for a "serious" drug case. Why me? Where on earth did Dow get my name?

I found out on Friday, when Koehlinger came to my office with another man named Don Frayer. At the time, Frayer worked for Fireman's Fund in Detroit. Fireman's Fund was Dow's general liability insurer. When Koehlinger decided to replace Dow's attorney in the

Brooklyn case, he called Frayer for a recommendation. Frayer, who didn't know me from Adam, found my name on a list of approved attorneys generated by Fireman's Fund's New York office. He called that office, someone must have said some nice things about me, so he gave my name to Koehlinger, who also didn't know me from Adam but called me anyway, and the next thing the three of us knew they were in Freeport giving me the once over while I tried my best to act as if a visit from a Fortune 500 company was an every day occurrence.

Koehlinger and Frayer spent the entire afternoon with me, and then I drove them back to the airport. I fretted all weekend wondering if I had made a good impression. I considered calling one of them on Monday, just to follow up, but never got the chance. Koehlinger called me at about 10 a.m.

"We'd like you to be our attorney," he said.

"My pleasure."

*   *   *

This case was the first of many Dow cases that I worked on with Don Frayer. When I first met Don, he was employed by Fireman's Fund in Detroit as head of the company's Large Risk Unit. Basically, his job was to investigate and supervise the handling of all liability claims against Dow Chemical, one of Fireman's Fund's largest accounts. As a result, he spent about twenty-five percent of his time at Dow's home office in Midland, where he developed a first name relationship with everyone he met, from the Chairman of the Board on down. He did his job on Dow's behalf so well that in 1975 the company created a new position and hired Don to fill it. His new job was to develop systems and procedures for allowing Dow to go self insured. But he also continued to investigate and supervise liability claims, most notably the Staten Island natural gas tank explosion and Agent Orange.

Don made invaluable contributions every time we worked together on a case. He had a photographic memory for everything from chemical formulae to earned run averages, a meticulous eye for detail, and an uncanny ability to analyze and solve the most vexing problems.

This was my very first Dow case, and I wanted to make a good impression. With Don Frayer as my guide, I couldn't have been in better hands.

*   *   *

Ezagui v. Dow: The Facts

The name of the matter was *Ezagui v. Dow*. It was a truly tragic case. Early in 1961, Mark Ezagui (pronounced "A *zow* ee"), a normal, healthy, three-month-old baby, had been inoculated with a vaccine designed to provide immunization from four diseases: diphtheria, tetanus, pertussis (whooping cough), and polio. Five days later, Mark's mother found him lying flushed and motionless in his crib. She took his temperature; it was 108°. She immediately telephoned her pediatrician, who instructed her to rush Mark to the hospital, where doctors determined that he was suffering from a devastating illness known as post-vaccinal encephalopathy. His symptoms included high fever, convulsions, partial paralysis, and irreversible blindness, deafness, and brain damage. Mark's prognosis was grim, and he required constant care and treatment. To get that treatment, Mark and his family endured a nightmarish series of hospitalizations at four different hospitals that lasted from September 1961 until April 1970, when Mark died. He was nine years old.

At the time of Mark's inoculation in 1961, four-in-one vaccinations were relatively new. Three-in-one vaccines against diphtheria, tetanus, and pertussis had been widely used since the early 1940s. In the mid 1950s, after Dr. Salk had developed his polio vaccine, Parke-Davis Company decided to produce a four-in-one product. That product, known as Quadrigen, became available in 1959.[1] Dow's four-in-one product, known as Compligen, became available one year later. Quadrigen and Compligen were used for the same purposes but were not identical. For present purposes, it is sufficient for me to state that there were slight but significant differences in their composition and production.

In 1969, shortly before Mark died, his mother started a lawsuit against the doctor who administered the vaccine, the first hospital where Mark was treated, and Dow. Mrs. Ezagui sued Dow, and not Parke-Davis, presumably because, at the time, she believed that Mark had been injected with Dow's product Compligen. In fact, there was evidence to support that belief, including letters written by Mark's doctor and shipping receipts produced by the doctor's supplier. But there was equally persuasive evidence, including hospital records, which indicated that Mark had been injected with Quadrigen.

When we took over Dow's defense in 1972, we decided to vigorously pursue a defense based upon product identification. That is, we intended to persuade the jury that Dow could not be held responsible in this case because Mark Ezagui had been injected with Quadrigen, Parke-Davis's product. The more we learned about the facts of the case and the two drugs in question, the stronger that defense became.

For example, even though Mark's doctor had written letters stating that he had injected Mark with Dow's product Compligen, in those same letters the doctor specified that the dosage of the injection was ½ cc. According to package inserts, the recommended dosage for Quadrigen was ½ cc; for Compligen, it was 1 cc, or twice that amount.

Similarly, even though the supplier's shipping receipts stated that Compligen was delivered to Mark's doctor three days before the injection and on the date of the injection, the supplier admitted that, in spite of differences between Compligen and Quadrigen, he used the two products interchangeably and the two shipments could have been Quadrigen.

But the most dramatic support for our product identification defense was provided by two appellate court decisions in cases where infant plaintiffs who were injected with the Parke-Davis vaccine suffered injuries remarkably similar to those sustained by Mark Ezagui. One case, *Tinnerholm v. Parke, Davis & Co.,*[2] was decided by the United States Court of Appeals for the Second Circuit in New York. The other, *Parke-Davis and Company v. Stromsodt,*[3] was decided by the United States Court of Appeals for the Eighth Circuit in St. Louis. In both cases, a three month old boy was injected with Quadrigen. Shortly after the injection, both children developed a high fever and suffered seizures. Ultimately, both became partially paralyzed, sustained irreversible brain damage, and required constant care and treatment. Both cases went to trial. In *Tinnerholm,* plaintiff won a judgment against Parke-Davis of $650,000; In *Stromsodt,* plaintiff won a judgment against Parke-Davis of $500,000. Both judgments were affirmed on appeal. After considering the evidence, both appellate courts ruled that Quadrigen was a defective drug and that the defect in Quadrigen was the cause of plaintiff's injuries.

Incredible. What better proof could we possibly hope to find? Two appellate courts had determined that an injection of Quadrigen had caused high fever, seizures, paralysis, and brain damage. In contrast, there were no cases in which such serious injuries had followed an injection of Compligen. In fact, the only reports Dow had ever received regarding reactions to Compligen mentioned incidents of "high fever," but never as high as 108°, and never was there any mention of convulsions, paralysis, brain damage, blindness, deafness, or death.

* * *

To Sue or Not to Sue: That Is the Question

So it was now clear, at least to us, that Mark Ezagui had been injected with Quadrigen. We therefore had a very important strategic decision to make. Even though plaintiff had chosen not to sue Parke-Davis, we fully intended to point the finger at Parke-Davis as part of our defense at trial. The question thus became: do we bring Parke-Davis into the lawsuit and point the finger at them as a co-defendant, or do we leave them out of the lawsuit and point the finger at the so-called "empty chair."

Don Koehlinger, Don Frayer, and I debated this issue at a meeting in Zionsville. Incidentally, I made dozens of trips to Indiana during the course of the litigation not only to discuss strategy, but also to meet with Dow experts and otherwise prepare for trial. To someone whose longest previous business trip was to Staten Island, the flights to Indianapolis were as glamorous and exciting as flights to Paris or Rome. Later on in my career, of course, business travel lost much of its luster. But in those early years it was a welcome break from my day-to-day office routine.

At any rate, Koehlinger, Frayer, and I analyzed the "empty chair" issue from every possible angle. There were many arguments in favor of bringing Parke-Davis in. First, the case involved a very sympathetic plaintiff, and we feared that the jury might be reluctant to let Dow off the hook if, as a consequence, plaintiff would recover nothing. (We believed that plaintiff was not likely to prevail on her claims against the doctor and the hospital because this was not a case of medical malpractice. At the time of Mark Ezagui's vaccination, neither the doctor nor the hospital had any reason to suspect that the drug may have been defective.) But if Parke-Davis were a party, the jury would not have that dilemma; it could buy Dow's defense and, at the same time, hold Parke-Davis liable for plaintiff's damages. Second, we believed that the jury would be more likely to accept the proposition that Mark Ezagui was injected with Quadrigen if plaintiff were making that argument against Parke-Davis as opposed to Dow making that argument against the plaintiff. Third, if Parke-Davis were a party, the battle lines would be redrawn. As the case presently stood, it was plaintiff against Dow; if Parke-Davis were a party, it would essentially be plaintiff and Dow against Parke-Davis. Finally, primarily because of the *Tinnerholm* and *Stromsodt* decisions, the Ezagui's case against Parke-Davis was very much stronger than their case against Dow. Expert testimony in those cases was sufficient to establish that Quadrigen was a defective drug. Those same experts were available to testify in the *Ezagui* case. In fact, the possibility existed that Mrs. Ezagui wouldn't even need those experts to prove her case against Parke-Davis. Instead, she could argue that, under the legal doctrine known as collateral estoppel, *Tinnerholm* and *Stromsodt* required the court to enter a ruling against Parke-Davis that Quadrigen was defective.

About the only argument we could think of for not bringing Parke-Davis into the lawsuit was that they would likely be a formidable adversary. We would point the finger at them; they would most definitely point the finger right back at us.

Nevertheless, at the end of our discussion, even though we all agreed that Dow would be much better off if Parke-Davis were a party, Don Koehlinger reluctantly informed us that we could not sue them. He was vague about his reasons. My feeling is that Dow may have had an unwritten business policy that it would not sue another drug company. Professional courtesy, or something like that. Thus, even though it was probably the right strategic move, Dow said no.

*   *   *

Taking the Initiative

But that did not put the matter to rest. We could not bring Parke-Davis into the lawsuit; maybe there was something we could do to convince plaintiff to do so. Indeed, we were baffled as to why she had not yet sued Parke-Davis on her own. She obviously needed a little push. Here's what we did.

I returned to Freeport and drafted a motion for permission to file a third-party complaint against Parke-Davis. A third-party complaint is a pleading in which the defendant asserts claims against someone who is not already a party to the proceedings. Upon service of the third-party complaint, the non-party enters the litigation as a third-party defendant. The typical third-party complaint alleges that the defendant is not liable to the plaintiff, but if the defendant is found liable, he is entitled to recover some or all of the judgment from the third-party defendant.

My motion, which I had no intention of filing since Dow would not allow me to sue Parke-Davis, contained allegations about the defective nature of Quadrigen, the differences between Quadrigen and Compligen, the evidence suggesting that the doctor had injected Mark Ezagui with Quadrigen, and, most importantly, the findings against Parke-Davis in the *Tinnerholm* and *Stromsodt* cases.

Then I sent a copy of the motion to plaintiff's attorney. I wrote in my cover letter that I was sending the enclosed papers as a courtesy and would welcome any comments and suggestions.

The motion must have been thorough and persuasive, because the next thing we knew plaintiff filed an amended complaint that included claims against Parke-Davis. After all of that discussion, we succeeded in achieving through the back door what we could not achieve through the front.

*   *   *

Problems for the Plaintiff

After Parke-Davis became a party in 1972, pretrial discovery dragged on at a snail's pace for an unusually long time, nearly six years, until the case finally went to trial in January 1978. Although many defense lawyers are known procrastinators, in this case it was plaintiff's attorney, for reasons of his own, who requested and received numerous extensions and adjournments. But in spite of plaintiff's foot-dragging, during this six year period we conducted and attended dozens of depositions, produced and reviewed box loads of documents, interviewed experts, examined medical records, answered interrogatories, and otherwise investigated the merits of plaintiff's claims. I also made a concerted effort to thoroughly educate myself about vaccinations in general and Quadrigen and Compligen in particular. With the help of Dow scientists, Don Koehlinger, who was a licensed pharmacist as well as an attorney, and Don Frayer, I actually sounded like I knew what I was talking about when discussing the differences between the preservatives merthiolate and benzethonium chloride, not to mention the "phemerol causes leakage" theory.

Plaintiff's strategy during discovery was to focus on Parke-Davis, just as we had hoped she would. Moreover, as discovery progressed, it appeared that her attorney, slowly but surely, was developing a very solid case that Quadrigen was the cause of Mark Ezagui's damages.

Then, as far as plaintiff was concerned, the roof fell in.

First, in July 1977, the trial judge denied plaintiff's motion to apply the doctrine of collateral estoppel against Parke-Davis on the question of product defect. The court recognized that two previous appellate court decisions—*Tinnerholm* and *Stromsodt*—had determined that Quadrigen was defective, but refused to follow those decisions because new scientific evidence had cast doubt on the validity of those earlier findings.

Second, later that same month, the judge dismissed plaintiff's claims against the hospital that had first treated Mark Ezagui after the injection. Since that hospital was owned by the county, plaintiff was required by law to file a notice of claim prior to instituting suit. The purpose of the notice was to give the county the opportunity to investigate and settle plaintiff's claims. The court ruled that plaintiff had failed to file the requisite notice within the prescribed time limit.

Third, in January 1978, during the trial itself, the judge entered an order drastically curtailing plaintiff's use of expert testimony. Earlier, in May 1977, the court had entered a pretrial order governing the presentation of evidence at trial. Among other things, to simplify the proceedings and make it easier for the jury to grasp complex scientific issues, the order provided that all direct expert testimony would be prepared in advance in the form of written statements to be read aloud to the jury during the trial. The order further established a deadline for each party to submit his experts' written statements to all other parties and the court. Perhaps because of the complexity of the issues, ambiguity in the court's pretrial order, or some other reason, plaintiff's attorney had failed to submit properly drawn written statements from two of his key experts, even though the court had extended his deadline twice. As a consequence, when plaintiff attempted to offer the testimony of those two witnesses at the trial, the court ruled that one could offer only the most cursory testimony and the other could not testify at all.

Fourth, and most devastating, in March 1978, at the close of plaintiff's case, even before any of the defendants had called their first witnesses, the court dismissed all claims against all remaining defendants: Dow, Parke-Davis, and the doctor who administered the vaccine. After two months of testimony, the judge dismissed the case without even giving the jury a chance to assess the evidence and render a verdict.[4]

Quite honestly, it came as no surprise that the court dismissed all claims against Dow and the doctor, since plaintiff had offered very little proof against either of those defendants.

In contrast, we were shocked by the court's dismissal of Parke-Davis. Notwithstanding the court's earlier orders adverse to plaintiff's case, her attorney had presented what appeared to be compelling evidence in support of her claims against that company. For example, hospital records, letters from the doctor regarding the dosage of the inoculation, and testimony from the supplier all tended to establish that mark Ezagui had been injected with Quadrigen. In addition, letters, internal Parke-Davis memoranda, and expert testimony taken in the *Tinnerholm* case all tended to establish that Quadrigen was defective. There were reports of frequent and severe "febrile" and "systemic" reactions to Quadrigen, including one incident where a five month contracted encephalopathy following the injection and later died. There were also reports, including several from the Department of Health, Education, and Welfare, that batches of Quadrigen were "substandard" and "unstable," that other batches had failed toxicity tests, and that doctors were refusing to administer the drug. Finally, the physician who administered the injection to Mark Ezagui and other treating physicians uniformly testified that Quadrigen was the cause of Mark's encephalopathy and ultimate death.

* * *

Plaintiff's Second Chance

Naturally, plaintiff appealed. The matter was heard by the United States Court of Appeals for the Second Circuit, the same court that decided *Tinnerholm*. In April 1979, the Second Circuit affirmed the judgment in favor of Dow and the hospital, but reversed the judgment in favor of Parke-Davis and the doctor and ordered a new trial against only those two defendants.[5] With respect to Parke-Davis, the court ruled that the trial judge erred in refusing to apply the doctrine of collateral estoppel, not to establish that Quadrigen was defective but instead to establish that Parke-Davis failed to provide treating physicians with adequate warnings about known risks associated with the use of that drug. The court also ruled that the trial judge should have allowed the jury to resolve plaintiff's claims case against Parke-Davis regarding defect and causation. With respect to the doctor, the court ruled that the plaintiff's malpractice claims also raised jury questions.

That ended Dow's involvement in *Ezagui*, but the Second Circuit had given Mrs. Ezagui a second chance against Parke-Davis and the doctor. Her case against those two defendants dragged on for another two years. Then, in April 1981, after a second two month trial, the jury dismissed Mrs. Ezagui's claims against the doctor but returned a verdict in her favor against Parke-Davis for $100,000. That was a lot of money in 1981, but not all of it went to the plaintiff. In May, the court entered an order, with plaintiff's consent, dividing the proceeds of the judgment as follows: forty thousand dollars to plaintiff's attorney for expenses and disbursements; twenty-four thousand dollars to her attorney for legal fees; and thirty-six thousand dollars to plaintiff.[6]

Mark Ezagui had been injected with Quadrigen in 1961; he suffered for nine years before he died in 1970; his mother started her lawsuit shortly before Mark's death; finally, in 1981, twenty years after the injection and eleven years after Mark's death, Mrs. Ezagui pocketed thirty-six thousand dollars, a mere pittance considering the half-million-dollar judgments entered against Parke-Davis in *Tinnerholm* and *Stromsodt* twelve years earlier. Was justice done in this case? From Dow's standpoint it was; no court has ever ruled that Compligen was a defective product. But what about from plaintiff's standpoint? Today, we often hear loud complaints about extraordinarily high jury awards for seemingly minor injuries. In Mrs. Ezagui's case, however, I think even the most hardened defense attorney would agree that the verdict was inadequate.

CHAPTER SEVEN

The Staten Island Gas Tank Disaster

Early on a frigid February afternoon in 1973, a work crew returned from its lunch break and descended to the bottom of an immense, empty fuel tank, the largest liquified natural gas storage tank in the world. Made of concrete reinforced with steel cable, the tank, a hollow cylinder, measured 272 feet in diameter, stood nearly seven stories high, and was capable of holding 600,000 barrels of liquified natural gas. A reinforced concrete dome the size of a football field rested on top of the tank like a lid on a giant saucepan. The floor of the tank, its walls, and the dome were two feet thick. Outside the tank, a gently sloping earthen berm extended one hundred feet up from the ground to the base of the dome, making it appear that the tank had been submerged in a huge artificial hill.

The tank was located in an industrial section of Staten Island, New York, known as Bloomfield, one-mile south of the Goethals Bridge and one hundred yards east of the Arthur Kill, the body of water separating Staten Island from New Jersey. The area consisted of other fuel tanks and barren fields.

The work crew was repairing holes in a paper thin plastic membrane that covered the tank's insulation. The insulation, a rigid polyurethane foam eight inches thick, lined the inside of the tank's walls, floor, and dome. This particular insulation was chosen for the tank because of its thermal properties; the temperature inside the tank, when in use, had to be maintained at 260° below zero, the point at which natural gas liquifies. It was also chosen because it was labeled "non-burning" in accordance with tests conducted by the American Society for Testing and Materials, an organization which devised widely-accepted standards for hundreds of industrial products.

There was approximately 250,000 cubic feet of "non-burning" polyurethane foam insulation inside the tank, all of it manufactured by The Dow Chemical Company.

Shortly after 1 p.m., fire broke out near the bottom of the tank. At that moment, forty-two men were working inside the tank: forty on the floor and two on a scaffold hanging twenty feet below the base of the dome. When the two men on the scaffold saw the fire below them, they quickly climbed up a ladder and escaped through an opening in the dome. Thick black smoke poured out of the opening behind them. The two men later reported that just as they reached the opening in the dome, they heard a sound described as a "whoosh" and observed the plastic membrane "billowing crazily."[1] Seconds after they escaped, there was an explosion. The force lifted the huge dome, which then fell back into the tank. A workman outside the tank later stated that when the dome was lifted, he got hit by a gust of wind "like a hurricane."[2] Another workman heard a "booming noise" when the dome collapsed. After the explosion, flames shot out of the opening at the top of the tank. Although the Fire Department arrived within minutes and sprayed thousands of gallons of water into the tank, the fire burned for six hours in the bitter cold, sending up an enormous column of smoke visible from miles around.

Tragically, all forty men working on the floor of the tank were killed. The badly burned bodies of the victims were found caked in ice beneath tons of reinforced concrete debris. The coroner's report concluded that in all but one case the cause of death was asphyxiation.

Virtually all of Dow's "non-burning" polyurethane insulation was consumed in the fire.

* * *

Even the most hardened defense attorney, myself included, would have been greatly moved by the Staten Island tragedy. By focusing in this chapter on the litigation, I certainly do not intend to minimize the human suffering that resulted from the explosion nor my own feelings of sympathy for the victims and their families.

* * *

Major Litigation

The Staten Island gas tank disaster generated what I call "major litigation," which differs from routine litigation in several respects, some obvious, some subtle:

Number of Parties: The typical automobile accident case ordinarily involves one injured plaintiff, maybe two, and the same number of defendants. Even in cases involving multi-car accidents, there are, at most, ten parties. In contrast, as a result of the Staten Island gas tank disaster, forty parties commenced wrongful death actions and two commenced personal injury actions. The plaintiffs sued a total of ten defendants, including Texas Eastern Transmission Corporation, the owner and operator of the tank; Battelle Memorial Institute, which researched the tank's design; Brown & Root, Inc., which built the tank; Sinapp Company of Staten Island, the employer of the work crew; Sheldahl, Inc., the manufacturer of the plastic membrane; and Dow Chemical, the manufacturer of the polyurethane foam.

Identity of the Client: In the typical automobile accident case, the client is usually an individual, such as an injured passenger or a negligent driver. In the Staten Island gas tank cases, my client was Dow Chemical, a Fortune 500 corporation with an international reputation and worldwide business interests.

I had been representing Dow for about one year in *Ezagui* when the Staten Island explosion occurred, and my handling of *Ezagui* landed me the Staten Island assignment. Don Koehlinger recommended me, as did several people at Fireman's Fund, including Don Frayer.

Just after I was retained, I met with three representatives of Fireman's Fund in that company's Garden City, Long Island, office. We discussed various aspects of the case, and the consensus among the Fireman's Fund people was that Dow's prospects were not good. In fact, a Fireman's Fund Vice President told me at that meeting that he would be happy if I could keep Dow's share of any judgment or settlement under fifty percent.

"49.9 percent?" I asked.

"49.9 percent would be fine."

Number of Forums: The typical automobile accident case gives rise to one lawsuit in one forum. In contrast, the survivors of some of the victims of the Staten Island gas tank disaster chose to assert their claims in federal court in Brooklyn; others chose federal court in Manhattan; still others chose federal court in New Jersey; and one selected state court in Brooklyn. Ultimately, all of these cases were consolidated in Brooklyn federal court.

In addition to the New York wrongful death and personal injury actions, Texas Eastern brought an action against Dow for property damage and loss of use of the tank in yet another forum, state court in Texas.

Dollar Value: Since the typical automobile accident case involves one plaintiff, the value of the case is limited to the value of that one party's claim. In a death case in the early 1970s, that value could have been as high as $1 million or more. The Staten Island disaster involved forty death claims with a combined value of as much as $40 million or more. In addition, Texas Eastern's lawsuit against Dow for property damage and loss of use of the tank sought $130 million in damages, including punitive damages.

Related Proceedings and Investigations: There were approximately one dozen criminal, administrative, or legislative proceedings and investigations generated by the Staten Island disaster or were otherwise pertinent. We carefully monitored every such proceeding and investigation for information, ideas, witnesses, and leads. The effort was well worth it. For example:

Criminal: A grand jury in Staten Island conducted an investigation into the explosion that resulted in an indictment charging Texas Eastern with forty counts of criminally negligent homicide. Ultimately, the indictment was dismissed. In order to charge a corporation with a crime, there must be evidence that corporate officers had knowledge of the allegedly wrongful acts committed by corporate employees. Here, the court ruled that the District Attorney had failed to establish the requisite level of corporate knowledge.

Even though the indictment was dismissed, the grand jury investigation bolstered one of Dow's most important defenses in the wrongful death and personal injury actions. That defense asserted that one of the primary causes of the gas tank disaster was the negligence of Texas Eastern in failing to adopt and enforce adequate fire prevention measures. The indictment supported that defense by charging that officials of Texas Eastern negligently allowed the repair crew to use non-spark proof appliances, such as irons and vacuum cleaners, even though Texas Eastern knew that sparks from those appliances could ignite pockets of combustible gases that had formed in the tank during the repair process. The indictment may have been dismissed, but there was nothing to prevent Dow from questioning grand jury witnesses, pursuing grand jury leads, and otherwise developing proof to support the grand jury's charges of Texas Eastern culpability.

Administrative/OSHA: The Occupational Health and Safety Administration ("OSHA"), a division of the United States Department of Labor, conducted an investigation into the cause of the Staten Island incident. At the conclusion of its investigation, OSHA issued a citation charging that Texas Eastern had violated numerous federal job safety standards in connection with the repair of the tank. OSHA charged that Texas Eastern failed to develop and maintain an adequate fire detection and prevention program; failed to instruct the repair crew on fire prevention; failed to require the use of properly certified spark proof repair equipment; failed to require the crew members to wear protective clothing to guard against static electricity; failed to provide an adequate number of emergency exits; failed to conduct emergency fire drills; and failed to promptly reset fire alarms after testing.

Like the grand jury indictment, the OSHA citation was ultimately dismissed. A federal court ruled that the Department of Transportation, and not the Department of Labor, had jurisdiction over the incident. Nevertheless, OSHA's findings provided Dow with additional evidence and leads in support of its theory that a primary cause of the gas tank disaster was Texas Eastern's negligence.

* * *

Administrative/The FTC: At the time of the Staten Island explosion, the Federal Trade Commission ("FTC") was in the midst of an investigation into the flammability of polyurethane and other plastics used in construction and home furnishings. The FTC investigation was in response to a series of reports in the media about catastrophic fires in buildings containing polyurethane or similar products.

Shortly after the explosion, the FTC issued an administrative complaint against twenty six chemical companies, including Dow, charging the companies with false advertising regarding the flammability of polyurethane. In its complaint, the FTC alleged that the companies knew as early as 1967 that their products presented serious fire hazards but failed to disclose those hazards to the general public; that polyurethane burned more rapidly and produced more toxic gases than conventional building materials; and that the flammability standards utilized by the American Society for Testing and Materials were unreliable.

One year later, while the wrongful death and personal injury actions were still pending, Dow signed an FTC Consent Decree that obligated Dow to warn past and future purchasers of the fire hazards associated with the use of polyurethane. Dow warned past purchasers by publishing notices in trade journals and general circulation magazines such as *Popular Mechanics* and *Better Homes & Gardens*. Dow warned future purchasers by attaching labels to its polyurethane products stating that the products were "highly flammable and may constitute a severe fire hazard."

The FTC Consent Decree generated an enormous amount of adverse publicity for Dow, which had previously labeled as "non-burning" many of its polyurethane products, including the foam insulation used in the Staten Island tank. Now, in the Consent Decree, which received front page coverage in newspapers throughout the country, Dow appeared to be acknowledging that its "non-burning" products were actually "highly flammable."

We were monitoring the FTC proceedings and, when we first learned that Dow was negotiating a Consent Decree, advised Dow that our adversaries in the Staten Island litigation might attempt to use the Consent Decree against Dow as an admission of liability. Since Dow did not want to do anything to prejudice its defense of the Staten Island cases, they authorized us to research the question of whether administrative consent decrees are admissible evidence against a signatory in civil litigation. We did the research and concluded that administrative consent decrees were not admissible evidence. Dow executed the FTC Consent Decree only after studying our research and reaching the same conclusion.

* * *

During settlement negotiations of the Staten Island wrongful death and personal injury actions, Texas Eastern initially offered to pay one-third of whatever figure plaintiffs would agree to and doggedly tried to persuade Dow to pay the same percentage. Just as doggedly, Dow resisted, arguing that Texas Eastern's share should be substantially greater. When Dow signed the FTC Consent Decree, Texas Eastern, as expected, took this as a sign of Dow's capitulation.

"How could you possibly go to trial now?" they asked us. "The Consent Decree is an admission of liability. You'll end up paying half of any judgment, maybe more."

"You're mistaken," we countered. "If we go to trial, the jury will never see the Consent Decree. It's not admissible."

Texas Eastern disagreed, but that was an argument I'm certain we would have won. In fact, ten years later, in another polyurethane fire case, a state appellate court in Louisiana ruled that the FTC Consent Decree was not admissible evidence.[3] The court reasoned that consent decrees were compromises, not admissions of liability, and that it would be unfair to allow a stranger to the decree to enforce it. What the court did not mention is the public policy consideration favoring our position. If consent decrees were admissible evidence, no one would ever sign them, and the administrative enforcement process would grind to a halt.

* * *

Administrative/The Bureau of Mines: The Bureau of Mines, a division of the United States Department of the Interior, conducted an investigation into the cause of the incident and published its findings. The Bureau of Mines report described the "most likely sequence of events" as follows: first, there was an "outgassing" from the polyurethane insulation as the plastic membrane was raised for repair purposes. In other words, when the plastic membrane was lifted, a pocket of liquified gas trapped in the polyurethane became exposed to the air and immediately vaporized. Second, the hydrocarbon (gas) vapors were ignited by one of several possible sources: an overheated iron, a spark, or even an open flame. Third, the resultant "flash fire" vaporized additional pockets of liquified gas, which also ignited. Fourth, the burning gas ultimately ignited the plastic membrane and the insulation. Finally, the fire increased the air pressure in the tank, which caused the roof to rise and then collapse.

During settlement negotiations, Texas Eastern and Dow advocated dramatically different theories on the immediate cause of the fire in attempting to resolve their respective settlement percentages. According to Texas Eastern, the fire started as a polyurethane fire. According to Dow, the fire started as a gas fire. Texas Eastern argued that Dow's "non-burning" polyurethane insulation was ignited by a spark of unknown origin. Dow acknowledged that the polyurethane burned but argued that ignition required far more than an isolated spark. Instead, ignition of the insulation required a significant flame front, such as the front provided by a rapidly expanding gas fire.

It certainly didn't hinder Dow's negotiating position that its theory was consistent with findings compiled by an impartial governmental investigatory body.

*   *   *

Texas Eastern and Dow debated the immediate cause of the fire for two and one-half years, throughout the entire course of the lawsuit. To convince us that a spark could have ignited Dow's foam insulation without first igniting a gas fire, Texas Eastern conducted tests and gave us the results, showed us films, allowed us to interview their expert witnesses, and made written and oral presentations to us and to the court. Notwithstanding Texas Eastern's persistence, I don't believe I ever wavered in my thinking that Dow's theory that the insulation could have been ignited only by a significant gas fire was the correct one.

Don Frayer, who was supervising the case on behalf of Fireman's Fund, later told me that he sensed otherwise. Don's perception was not that I was working any less vigorously on Dow's behalf but that I was beginning to have my doubts. In his mind, I was becoming increasingly suspicious that maybe the insulation was more flammable than Dow was willing to admit.

In mid-August of 1974, about eighteen months after the incident, Don and I attended a meeting at Dow's home office in Midland, Michigan, along with Dick Darger, the no-nonsense Dow in-house attorney in charge of the case, and several Dow scientists. The purpose of the meeting was to bring everyone up to date on recent developments and discuss future strategy. When the meeting broke up early in the afternoon, Don asked the Dow scientists to set up an experiment that he believed would end my uncertainty once and for all.

We retired to a lab, where the Dow scientists placed a four feet by two feet slab of polyurethane insulation inside a hooded oven. The insulation was identical to that used in the Staten Island tank. When the insulation was in place, Don Frayer handed me a propane torch.

"Len began to cautiously play with the torch," Frayer recently reported, "touching the insulation with the flame and then removing it. The only thing that happened was that the insulation began to melt. I challenged Len to try to ignite it. He held the flame closer and for a longer amount of time but couldn't do it. All that happened was more melting. He then began to move the torch in what appeared to be a circular pattern. Still no fire. Finally, he removed the torch. To our surprise, he had used it to carve his initials into the polyurethane slab!

"Having watched Len's confidence in the product slowly deteriorate, I now watched it soar in a matter of minutes. He was smiling and defiant again. I knew we were back on track."

*   *   *

Legislative: Five months after the incident, a Special Subcommittee on Investigations of the House Committee on Interstate and Foreign Commerce held three days of hearings to determine whether legislative action was necessary to assure the implementation of adequate safety rules at liquified natural gas storage tanks. One of the witnesses who testified was one of the two scientists who had authored the Bureau of Mines report so favorable to Dow's position. We were so impressed with his presentation that we later retained him to advise us on the scientific and technical aspects of the case and testify on Dow's behalf at the time of trial.

A Vice President of Texas Eastern also testified at the hearings. In a prepared statement, he outlined his company's position that the tragedy was caused by a polyurethane fire and not a gas fire. He then introduced to the Subcommittee a scientist identified as Texas Eastern's "expert," who showed two films purporting to support Texas Eastern's theory and presented additional supporting evidence. The testimony of the Texas Eastern Vice President and his expert gave us tremendous insight into what Texas Eastern would attempt to prove in the civil litigation.

* * *

One of the members of the House Subcommittee was Congressman Norman Lent from Long Island. Congressman Lent and I had been friends for twenty years. Prior to the hearings, my office had sent Congressman Lent a list of suggested questions. During the hearings, members of the Subcommittee asked many of those questions.

In addition, the chief investigator for the House Subcommittee was a man I had known for approximately twelve years.

One afternoon when the hearings were in session, during the lunch break, I was relaxing in an easy chair in Congressman Lent's office with my feet on his coffee table when the Congressman's secretary escorted one of Texas Eastern's attorneys into the room. I assume that the attorney had a list of questions for the Subcommittee. When he saw me chatting casually with Congressman Lent and the investigator, his jaw dropped. It dropped even further when the investigator and I excused ourselves to grab a quick sandwich.

* * *

Free Time (or lack thereof): When I was trying automobile accident cases, I had my evenings free and never worked weekends unless I was in the midst of a heavy trial. In contrast, the Staten Island cases were all consuming. I worked most evenings and weekends. When not working, I thought about the cases. When asleep, I dreamt about them. Many times I awoke in the middle of the night, grabbed a pencil and notepad I kept on my night stand, and wrote myself a note. Once or twice, the note even made sense.

This frenetic pace was not something I eased into. It began from day one. The day after the case was assigned to me, I met for nearly four hours with three Fireman's Fund representatives in their Garden City office. They gave me a pile of material which I studied that afternoon and evening. The next morning I reviewed a report I received in the mail regarding the history and construction of liquified natural gas tanks. That afternoon, I met in Manhattan with Phil Weinberg, at the time Governor Wilson's Appointments Secretary, to try to get a lead on what city and state agencies were investigating the incident. I returned to the office at around four p.m., cleared off my desk, and grabbed a cab to LaGuardia for a flight to Midland. I studied more case-related material on the plane, arrived at the hotel in Midland at around ten fifteen, read till midnight, and then went to sleep.

The next morning, I met Don Frayer, who had flown in from Detroit, in the hotel lobby at around eight o'clock. Fifteen minutes later, we joined Dick Darger, the in-house Dow attorney in charge of the case, for breakfast. I had never met Darger before, and he knew nothing about me. He agreed to utilize me on the case only after receiving strong recommendations from Frayer, Don Koehlinger, and possibly other Dow or Fireman's Fund people. Breakfast resembled a job interview with me as the applicant.

We then drove to Dow headquarters, where I met all day with Frayer, Darger, three Dow engineers, and a Dow public relations man. The purpose of the meeting was to educate me about the Dow product and the incident. I had to be alert and on my toes for six hours while, one at the time, each Dow person lectured me about his particular area of expertise. Then the group fired questions at me regarding legal issues and strategy. Having been on the case for only three days, I struggled to come up with meaningful answers.

With my head spinning and two litigation bags brimming with documents, I accepted Don Frayer's offer of a ride to the airport. My flight was delayed, I missed my connection, and did not get home until just before midnight. I reviewed documents on the plane and then spent the entire weekend collecting my thoughts, reviewing more documents, and planning my next moves.

When I arrived at the office first thing Monday morning, I was exhausted but elated. I couldn't imagine a more thrilling or challenging assignment.

*   *   *

Travel: The only traveling I did trying automobile accident cases was to and from the courthouse. The Staten Island cases involved extensive travel to Midland, Michigan, to meet with the client; to Washington, D.C., to monitor House subcommittee hearings; to Houston, Texas, to monitor and assist Dow's defense of Texas Eastern's action in state court for property damage to the tank; to Shreveport, Louisiana, where Texas Eastern produced its documents for purposes of discovery; to Columbus, Ohio, to meet with representatives of Battelle Institute, a co-defendant and the designer of the tank; to San Francisco, California, to the meet with Robert Buell, the Fireman's Fund Vice President in the home office monitoring the case; and to Los Angeles, Pittsburgh, and other cities to track down witnesses and evidence.

Fortunately, the firm's travel agent had the foresight to enroll me in a frequent flier's club.

* * *

Teamwork: I could prepare and try an automobile accident case all by myself. I needed and was backed up in the Staten Island cases by a superb support team, which included attorneys and paralegals from my office, Dow scientists and engineers, Dick Darger, Bob Buell, and Don Frayer.

Don Frayer, as always, made many instrumental contributions to our efforts. Once, late in 1974, we attended a settlement conference in court. To our surprise, the Texas Eastern attorney brought along his "expert," the same expert who had appeared on behalf of Texas Eastern at the House Subcommittee hearings one year earlier. Prior to the conference, Texas Eastern had distributed a lengthy memorandum outlining its position that Dow and Texas Eastern should contribute an equal amount to any settlement package. Don and I sat thumbing the memorandum waiting for the clerk to call our case.

Suddenly, Don's eye lit up. On page seventeen of the Texas Eastern memorandum, Texas Eastern claimed that flames from burning polyurethane would reach the top of the tank, a height of approximately sixty feet, in ten to fifteen seconds. When Don read that statement, his photographic memory sprang into action. He recalled reading in the Congressional Record several months earlier that the Texas Eastern expert had testified before the House Subcommittee that polyurethane would burn to a level of eight feet in approximately one minute. Quite a discrepancy: sixty feet in fifteen seconds as opposed to eight feet in sixty seconds. Since the amount of time the fire burned before the dome collapsed was a key issue in the case, we made certain that we pointed out this discrepancy to the judge as soon as Texas Eastern began its presentation. Needless to say, our point was well taken.

* * *

Report Letters: In the typical automobile accident case, I prepared report letters for the client or the insurance company maybe three times during the course of the litigation: after our initial evaluation, after the depositions, and after the trial.

In the Staten Island litigation, I must have prepared for Dow and Fireman's Fund two hundred report letters in three years.

They wanted me to report on everything: court appearances, hearings, depositions, settlement meetings, meetings with expert witnesses, meetings with the client, meetings with adversaries or co-defendants, phone calls from the judge's law clerk, the receipt of a pleading or motion, the receipt of an important report or document.

I did as instructed. They wanted details; I gave them details. For example, after I attended three days of subcommittee hearings in Washington, I prepared a ten-page letter in which I gave my overall impressions of the hearings and their potential impact on the litigation, identified the committee members, identified the witnesses, summarized their testimony, and even described my encounter with the attorney for Texas Eastern in Congressman Lent's office.

I addressed my report letters to Dick Darger at Dow headquarters in Midland and sent copies to Sam D'Anna at the local Fireman's Fund branch office in Garden City, Don Frayer at the Fireman's Fund office in Detroit, and Bob Buell at the home office in San Francisco. For nearly three years, I prepared as many as two report letters per week. The average length was around five pages. Frequently I enclosed items such as a deposition or court transcript, documents obtained in discovery, the report of an administrative agency, pleadings, motions, scientific studies, or expert reports. Sometimes the stack of enclosures reached a height of twelve inches. All four recipients of the letter received copies of all the enclosures.

* * *

Discovery: In the typical automobile accident case, discovery is quick and easy. Plaintiff provides a copy of his medical records, the police provide a copy of the accident report, and the parties conduct usually no more than five routine depositions, each one lasting less than one day: plaintiff, defendant, one or two physicians, maybe a witness.

In the Staten Island litigation, discovery was extensive, complicated, and contentious.

Document Production: More documents were produced during discovery in the Staten Island litigation than in all the other cases in my office combined.

Texas Eastern served Dow with a document production notice asking, in essence, for every document in Dow's possession that had anything to do with Dow's polyurethane insulation products, the flammability of polyurethane, the Staten Island tank, or dealings between Dow and any of Dow's co-defendants relating to the tank. In response to that notice, Dow searched its entire corporate archive and ultimately collected enough documents to fill thirty filing cabinets. Dow produced those documents in a conference room at a hotel in Westbury, a ten minute drive from my office.

In response to an equally broad discovery notice served by Dow, Texas Eastern produced documents filling more than fifty filing cabinets at a warehouse in Shreveport, Louisiana.

In addition, other co-defendants, including Battelle Institute, which designed the tank, and Brown & Root, Inc., which built it, produced cartons of documents. Dow also obtained a substantial number of documents from non-parties, most notably the House subcommittee and the various federal and state agencies that had investigated the incident.

Interrogatories: Dow served Texas Eastern with a lengthy set of interrogatories that was nearly one hundred and fifty pages long and contained nearly four hundred separately numbered questions, some with sub-parts. In those interrogatories, Dow asked Texas Eastern to identify witnesses, employees, and documents and to provide factual and legal support for its various claims and defenses.

About one week after we had served Dow's interrogatories, I received a telephone call from the attorney representing one of the minor defendants. He wanted to compliment us on how thoroughly we had covered all of the bases but also wanted to chide us because of a slight mistake he had discovered: the interrogatory on page 117 was numbered 320; the very next interrogatory on page 118 was numbered 330.

*   *   *

Dow's interrogatories precipitated a heated discovery dispute over the timing of Texas Eastern's answers.

I wanted Texas Eastern to answer Dow's interrogatories before we commenced deposing Texas Eastern witnesses. Dow's interrogatories required Texas Eastern to name names, identify documents, and explain and support its legal and factual contentions. Having that information in advance would help us prioritize the witnesses, locate important documents, and focus our questions on the key areas of dispute.

Texas Eastern wanted to postpone answering Dow's interrogatories until some unspecified future date.

Shortly after I served Dow's interrogatories, the judge requested that the parties submit proposed orders setting forth discovery procedures and timetables. We submitted an order on behalf of Dow, as did the attorneys for Texas Eastern and the attorneys for the plaintiffs. Ours was the only order that required Texas Eastern to answer Dow's interrogatories before producing witnesses for depositions.

In response, the judge convened a pretrial conference in an attempt to reconcile all of the differences in the three proposed orders. That conference was a raucous affair; for more than an hour the parties argued back and forth, making petty points, hurling accusations. Plaintiffs accused the defendants of stalling; Texas Eastern charged that Dow's interrogatories were vexatious and burdensome; Dow complained that Texas Eastern was holding back information. Finally, the judge threw up his hands and indicated that he was not going to make any ruling other than to set a date certain by which all discovery had to be completed. He directed the parties to resolve their remaining differences on their own time.

I could have left it at that. Having Texas Eastern's answers in advance would have been helpful, but it was not essential. Nevertheless, I decided to go to the mat on this relatively unimportant issue for three reasons: first, because I thought we were right; second, because I felt we had to demonstrate to the court and the parties that we were not afraid to stand up for our client's rights; and third, because I wanted to generate some positive momentum, which is vitally important in major litigation. I expected that the case would take years to litigate and believed that every victory along the way, even the minor ones, would keep the client happy, boost attorney morale, and otherwise increase the odds of a successful disposition.

So I made a motion to compel Texas Eastern to answer Dow's interrogatories, and one week after the judge had stated that he was not going to make any discovery rulings we were back in court asking him to make a discovery ruling.

Needless to say, the judge was not happy. At first, he took out his displeasure on me, the moving party. "Mr. Rivkin," he fumed, "I thought I said no more motions." Very respectfully, I asked to be heard. The judge sighed but allowed me to proceed. I made a brief presentation, stressing that the relief I was seeking was reasonable and not likely to cause significant delay. After I finished, Texas Eastern's attorney spoke briefly in opposition to my motion. After he finished, the judge looked sternly at both of us.

"All right," he snapped, "I'm granting Mr. Rivkin's motion. Texas Eastern must serve its answers to Dow's interrogatories on February 14; depositions of Texas Eastern employees will commence two weeks later."

* * *

Depositions: At the start of the litigation, we anticipated conducting more than one hundred depositions. Texas Eastern had identified more than thirty Dow employees they wanted to depose. We had identified an equal number of Texas Eastern employees. We had only just begun to focus on the other co-defendants. There would have been depositions of each party's expert witnesses. There would have been depositions of non-parties.

It is likely that many of the depositions would have lasted significantly longer than one day. For example, the first Texas Eastern employee we deposed was its chief engineer at the time of the incident. His deposition lasted six weeks. I questioned him for nine days.

During that deposition, Texas Eastern's attorney constantly interrupted the examination to object to a question or clarify an answer. If one of the other attorneys present disagreed with the objection or clarification, which was usually the case, the two attorneys debated the point. Sometimes the debate escalated into an argument and even a screaming match (sometimes the loudest screamer was me), all of which was transcribed by the court reporter. This delayed the proceedings, increased everyone's expenses, and muddled the record.

If I had been Texas Eastern's attorney, I may have done the exact same thing. That particular witness had much to say that was damaging to Texas Eastern's position, and his attorney was not about to hand that information to his adversaries. He was going to make them work for it.

But I was Dow's attorney, not Texas Eastern's. I wanted testimony, not shouting matches. I also wanted the Texas Eastern attorney to understand that some of his adversaries may have been willing to endure his obstructionist tactics, but I was not. Accordingly, I moved the court for the appointment of a Special Master to preside over all future depositions of Texas Eastern employees. Over Texas Eastern's strenuous objection, the court granted my motion and appointed as Special Master a retired New York State Appellate Division judge. Thereafter, while I would hardly characterize the atmosphere at depositions as cordial, there were fewer objections and even fewer fights. Moreover, while the first Texas Eastern employee required nine days for his deposition, subsequent Texas Eastern employees with just as much to say required no more than one week.

* * *

During settlement negotiations, Texas Eastern insisted that Dow had blatantly misrepresented the flammability of its polyurethane foam insulation prior to selling that insulation to Texas Eastern for use in the tank. According to Texas Eastern, Dow had represented that the insulation was "non-burning" when in fact it was highly flammable. Moreover, Texas Eastern denied having any knowledge regarding the true burning characteristics of the product.

Prior to deposing an important Texas Eastern witness, we received a telephone call from the attorney representing Battelle Institute, the designer of the tank. His message was brief and to the point: Texas Eastern was lying when it said it didn't know that the insulation in the tank was flammable. Moreover, he told us that he had documents that supported his contention.

We met with the attorney shortly thereafter. According to the documents he showed us, when the tank was under repair Texas Eastern purchased additional insulation from Dow to replace some of the original insulation that had been ripped out. Texas Eastern then sent a sample of this "replacement" insulation to Battelle and asked Battelle to determine whether the replacement insulation burned the same as the original. After running some tests, Battelle reported to Texas Eastern that the burning qualities of the original and replacement insulation were the same.

Armed with this information, I confronted the Texas Eastern witness during his deposition. I asked him general questions regarding whether he or anyone at Texas Eastern had any knowledge that the Dow insulation may have been flammable. He said no. I then asked him whether Battelle Institute had ever advised him or anyone at Texas Eastern that the Dow insulation was flammable. He categorically denied that Battelle had ever provided Texas Eastern with any such information.

At that moment, the attorney for Battelle angrily stated "on the record" that Battelle had, in fact, advised Texas Eastern that the insulation was flammable and that he was prepared to offer proof in support of that contention "at any time."

Thus, with the help of Battelle's attorney, I had driven a wedge between Texas Eastern and Battelle that I was certain would ultimately enure to Dow's benefit. Subsequent events proved me one hundred percent correct.

*   *   *

Procedural Issues: In the typical automobile accident case, most procedural issues are straightforward and relatively inconsequential. In the Staten Island litigation, procedural issues were hugely significant.

Order of Depositions: I believed that it was vitally important for us to depose Texas Eastern's witnesses before Texas Eastern deposed Dow's witnesses, for two reasons. First, I wanted the opportunity to chip away at Texas Eastern's defenses before they had the opportunity to chip away at mine; and second, I could better prepare the Dow witnesses for their depositions if the Texas Eastern witnesses had already testified.

Unfortunately, there was no legal authority I could cite to the court in support of a request for an order directing Texas Eastern to produce its witnesses first. The recently amended Federal Rules of Civil Procedure made no provision for bestowing deposition priority on any party and in fact contemplated that the parties could conduct depositions of each other simultaneously.

Nevertheless, I wrote a letter to the court in which I observed that several deposition notices had already been served and that an order regarding deposition priority would resolve any potential scheduling conflicts. I suggested that the court direct that the defendants be deposed in the order in which they were named in the caption of the lawsuit. Not coincidentally, the first named defendant was Texas Eastern; the fifth named was Dow.

To my surprise, the court granted my request. Shortly thereafter, the parties began deposing Texas Eastern witnesses. Almost immediately, the benefits to Dow were nearly incalculable.

Before the depositions started, almost all of the defendants had supported Texas Eastern's efforts to convince Dow that Dow should contribute a major share to any settlement package. During the depositions, the Texas Eastern witnesses tried to pin the blame not just on Dow but on nearly everyone else except, of course, Texas Eastern. As a result, after the depositions most of the defendants were lined up against Texas Eastern, not with them.

Moreover, even though the Texas Eastern witnesses tried to point the finger at the other defendants, the witnesses actually pointed the finger right back at Texas Eastern. Their testimony tended to establish that Texas Eastern was grossly negligent in failing to implement adequate fire prevention measures while the tank was under repair. Their testimony also tended to establish that it was a gas fire, and not a polyurethane fire, which caused the explosion at the tank.

This was not just my opinion; the attorneys for the remaining defendants had the same reaction to the testimony. In fact, the consensus among the group was that with each passing day of testimony Texas Eastern's position was getting weaker and weaker.

*   *   *

Texas State Court: Early in 1975, just as discovery proceedings were heating up in the wrongful death actions in federal court in New York, Texas Eastern commenced an action against Dow in state court in Houston, Texas, for property damage to the tank and loss of use. The state court complaint sought to recover $130 million in compensatory and punitive damages.

Instituting the Texas state court action at that time was an excellent strategic move on Texas Eastern's part, for at least three reasons:

First, New York did not appear to be a favorable jurisdiction for Texas Eastern to litigate the question of what caused the fire and explosion in the tank. There had been much public opposition on Staten Island when Texas Eastern first announced its plans to build the tank. Moreover, after the incident Texas Eastern received a great deal of unfavorable publicity in the local media. Perhaps the most damaging stories were those regarding the indictment charging Texas Eastern with forty counts of criminally negligent homicide. In addition, the judge had made several pretrial rulings that were unfavorable to Texas Eastern; the most obvious one was his order regarding deposition priority. Finally, plaintiffs' attorneys had made clear that they intended to focus most of their energies against Texas Eastern.

In contrast, Texas Eastern's prospects in Texas state court before a Texas judge and a Texas jury had to be better.

The second strategic reason for the Texas state court action was to put settlement pressure on Dow. Indeed, Texas Eastern's Texas lawyer told Dow's Texas lawyer that this was the primary reason for instituting the Texas lawsuit. Texas Eastern had complained loudly and repeatedly about Dow's hard line position on settlement; their thinking must have been that they could use the Texas action to induce Dow to contribute a greater percentage of the New York settlement package.

The third strategic reason for the Texas action was to give Texas Eastern a more immediate opportunity to depose Dow witnesses. Because of the order regarding deposition priority, Texas Eastern would most likely have to wait for months before deposing any Dow witnesses in New York. The state court judge in Texas most likely would not place Texas Eastern under a similar restraint.

We reacted quickly and decisively to Texas Eastern's Texas strategy. In New York, we filed a motion in the wrongful death actions for a federal court order staying the Texas state court case. Federal courts rarely grant such relief, but we felt we had a reasonable argument. Specifically, we contended that we were entitled to a stay order because the proceedings in Texas would interfere with the proceedings in New York by requiring the parties to litigate virtually identical claims on two fronts at the same time. In Texas, Dow's attorneys moved to dismiss the state court action on the grounds of forum non conveniens. The argument there was that Texas state court was neither an appropriate nor convenient forum for litigating property damage claims arising from an explosion on Staten Island.

Perhaps giving an indication of where his sympathies lay, the judge in Texas summarily denied Dow's forum non conveniens motion. Then, while our motion for a stay was still pending in New York, the Texas judge entered an order directing Dow to produce documents in Texas and three witnesses for deposition. The judge issued that order "ex parte," meaning that he granted Texas Eastern's application for the order without giving Dow any opportunity to be heard in opposition.

That order actually strengthened our motion in New York for an order staying the Texas proceedings. The three witnesses whose depositions were ordered in Texas were vital to our trial preparation efforts in New York. Moreover, the documents we were ordered to produce in Texas were at that moment being readied for production in a hotel room on Long Island. Thus, it was no longer a possibility that the Texas state court action would interfere with the New York wrongful death actions, it was a reality.

During oral argument in support of our motion, the judge appeared to favor Dow's position but requested that Dow and Texas Eastern first attempt to work out a procedural compromise. After negotiating with Texas Eastern's attorney for nearly three hours, we reached an agreement quite favorable to Dow. The agreement, which was ultimately embodied in a court order, provided that the timing of Texas discovery would depend upon the timing of the trial in New York. Specifically, the New York trial was scheduled to begin in late spring. If the trial went off as planned, depositions in Texas would take place after the trial was completed; if the trial date was adjourned, depositions in Texas would take place after depositions in New York were completed.

Thus, luckily, we dodged a rather menacing bullet. Our agreement with Texas Eastern's counsel placed the Texas state court action firmly on the back burner, eased whatever settlement pressure that action created, and preserved the current deposition schedule, which required Texas Eastern to produce its witnesses first.

*   *   *

Substantive Issues: Although automobile accident cases are fun to try, they involve an every day occurrence and typically raise relatively simple issues: how fast was the defendant driving? Which car had the right of way at the intersection? Was the owner of the car legally responsible for the driver's negligence?

In contrast, the Staten Island litigation involved a compelling, once-in-a-lifetime event and raised legal and factual questions that were complex and intricate.

Misrepresentation: Perhaps the most important issue bearing on Dow's alleged liability for the gas tank tragedy was whether Dow misrepresented to Texas Eastern the flammability of the polyurethane insulation used in the tank.

Non-Burning: Dow represented on product labels and in promotional literature that its polyurethane insulation was "non-burning" in accordance with American Society for Testing and Materials ("ASTM") standards. Yet there is no doubt that the product burned. Nearly all of the insulation inside the tank was consumed in the fire. Moreover, the Staten Island fire was one of hundreds of building fires involving polyurethane that occurred in the United States in the early and mid-1970s. Indeed, in March of 1976, an article in *Business Week* magazine reported that there were at least one hundred polyurethane fire cases pending in federal courts throughout the country seeking more than $200 million in damages. According to the article, polyurethane insulation was not merely flammable, it was "fast burning." The article described the typical case as involving a "small fire, often set off by a welder's torch, [which] suddenly demolishes a structure."

Thus, at first blush it appeared that Dow did, in fact, materially misrepresent the flammability of its polyurethane insulation. That was certainly Texas Eastern's position. At settlement talks and in open court, Texas Eastern's attorneys relentlessly argued that Dow's liability in the litigation was based primarily on the fact that "Dow told us the product wouldn't burn but it did."

But Dow never said that the product "wouldn't burn." It said that the product was "non-burning." To the layman, that may have been a distinction without a difference. To experts in the field, however, the distinction was crucial. To product manufacturers, architects, designers, engineers, consultants, builders, contractors, and site owners, the term "non-burning" was simply an ASTM classification that reflected how a product performed on certain flammability tests devised and administered by the ASTM. It was not a representation that the product would not ignite.

ASTM Tests and Standards: Founded in the early 1900s, the ASTM was an independent organization that devised tests and standards for hundreds of industrial products, including flammability tests and standards relating to polyurethane and other materials used in building construction.

The flammability tests applied to Dow's polyurethane insulation were so-called "small scale" tests, one of which involved a strip of insulation six inches long by two inches wide by one-half of an inch thick. The strip was marked into three equal sections and suspended horizontally. A Bunsen burner flame was placed under one end of the strip and held there for sixty seconds. After the flame was removed, the extent to which the strip continued to burn was monitored. If the strip did not burn past the first mark, it was rated "non-burning." If it burned past the first mark but not past the second, it was rated "self-extinguishing." If it burned past the second mark, it was not rated.

When tested, strips of Dow's polyurethane insulation did not burn past the first mark. Dow's representations that the product was "non-burning" reflected this fact and nothing more.

Significantly, ASTM standards, which were published and widely circulated, specifically stated that the small scale burning tests could not be applied to products that did not burn. The standards also stated that the purpose of the small scale tests was to establish relative burning characteristics and that they were not to be used as criteria for evaluating fire hazards.

Texas Eastern was a sophisticated and experienced user of building materials. The tank was constructed after eleven years of study. The design specifications for the tank, prepared by Battelle Institute and approved by Texas Eastern, required the use of "non-burning" insulation. Texas Eastern's corporate records, produced during discovery, included a substantial stack of letters between Texas Eastern, Battelle, and Dow regarding the ASTM tests and the rating assigned to Dow's polyurethane insulation. Under these circumstances, Texas Eastern could hardly be expected to claim that it misunderstood the limited significance of the small scale burning tests and the resulting product ratings. Yet that is exactly what Texas Eastern did. Even after we learned through discovery that a Texas Eastern employee was a member of the ASTM committee responsible for the flammability tests and standards and confronted Texas Eastern with this fact, they persisted with the argument that Dow's representations were misleading.

*   *   *

Knowledge: A second significant issue was whether Texas Eastern, apart from Dow's representations regarding flammability, had independent knowledge that polyurethane insulation would burn. If so, then Dow's representations would be irrelevant.

Texas Eastern denied having such knowledge and, at first, we had difficulty finding evidence suggesting otherwise. Articles had appeared in the scientific literature discussing the flammable nature of polyurethane, and we speculated that employees of Texas Eastern must have read these articles but could not prove it. Then, we got a huge break when Battelle's attorney produced witnesses and documents establishing that Battelle had advised Texas Eastern well before the incident that the polyurethane insulation was flammable.

How the Fire Started: Texas Eastern argued that the fire started when a spark of unknown origin ignited Dow's polyurethane insulation. Dow argued that the fire started when a spark of unknown origin ignited a pocket of gas, which ignited more gas, which ignited the plastic membrane, which ultimately ignited the polyurethane insulation. Both sides had retained experts with impeccable credentials prepared to offer supporting testimony. I believed Dow's version of the facts, but recognized that combustion was a complex subject and was not about to bet the ranch that a jury would resolve the issue in our favor.

What Caused the Dome to Collapse: Texas Eastern argued that the dome collapsed because a rapidly burning polyurethane fire caused the air pressure inside the tank to rise enough to lift the dome, which then fell back and shattered. Dow argued that the dome collapsed because a rapidly burning gas fire caused the rise in air pressure and that the polyurethane did not begin to burn to any significant degree until after the collapse.

The timing of the incident was an important factor in resolving this dispute. Both sides agreed that the dome would have lifted in one minute or less after first ignition in a gas fire (Dow's position) and closer to three minutes after first ignition in a polyurethane fire (Texas Eastern's position).

At one point during settlement negotiations, Texas Eastern submitted a lengthy memorandum to the court which, among other things, attempted to refute Dow's position that the fire burned for one minute or less before the dome lifted. The centerpiece of Texas Eastern's argument on this point was the testimony of a crane operator at the site at the time of the incident. Texas Eastern quoted from that testimony at length. According to the operator, he was seated in his car just after lunch when a car horn called his attention to white vapor blowing out of an opening at the top of the tank. The operator then drove his car approximately three hundred feet, stopped, and looked back at the tank. When he saw smoke coming from the opening, he realized that the tank was on fire. He then drove another five hundred feet to the main gate of the plant but had difficulty opening the gate because it was electronically controlled. Again, he looked back at the tank and saw fire all around the perimeter of the dome and blowing out of the opening. The flames appeared to be thirty to forty feet high. Having finally managed to open the main gate, he drove outside the plant property to a fire alarm box. He then heard a booming noise, which apparently indicated that the dome had just collapsed.

"It is difficult to imagine," Texas Eastern wrote, "that [the crane operator] could have accomplished his separate observations, driving with two intermediate stops across the property, and then fumbling in efforts to open the gate, all within a period of less than a minute."

I had to admit that the crane operator's testimony, as presented by Texas Eastern, almost convinced me that the amount of time involved suggested a polyurethane fire. Don Frayer's reaction was the same as mine, except that Don, a natural born skeptic, decided to look up the crane operator's testimony in the record just to make certain that Texas Eastern had quoted him accurately. Don found the passage in question, compared it to the excerpt in Texas Eastern's memorandum, and found them to be identical.

Except that Texas Eastern had omitted the last sentence of the crane operator's statement.

After describing how he drove from here to there, stopping twice to look back at the tank, fumbling with the lock on the gate, and finally setting off the fire alarm, the crane operator concluded his statement by saying:

"I smelled gas."

* * *

Negligent Design: Dow claimed that the tank was negligently designed by Battelle and Texas Eastern because polyurethane insulation was utilized inside the tank in close proximity to highly flammable materials, including the thin plastic membrane that covered the insulation and, of course, natural gas.

Negligent Fire Prevention Measures: Dow also claimed that the entire repair operation was negligently conceived, undertaken, and supervised by Texas Eastern.

After the tank had been in operation for less than one year, Texas Eastern discovered leaks in the plastic membrane. Nevertheless, the tank remained in operation for approximately four months. Finally, Texas Eastern emptied the tank and hired Sinapp Company, a Staten Island contractor, for the repair project.

Even though Texas Eastern took many precautions to assure that all liquid gas had been removed from the tank and that no gas vapors remained inside, Dow contended that Texas Eastern had not done enough. Specifically, we alleged that before the tank was shut down gas had seeped through tears in the plastic membrane, saturating the insulation; that gas had even seeped through the insulation and concrete walls of the tank into the earthen berm; and that after the tank was shut down pockets of liquid gas had remained trapped inside the tank behind the insulation and plastic membrane. We further alleged that Texas Eastern was aware of the presence of this highly flammable gas in and around the tank during the repair operation, which involved the use of several different kinds of electrical appliances, but negligently failed to implement and enforce adequate fire prevention and detection programs.

Significantly, the Staten Island grand jury indictment and OSHA civil citation, both of which were issued after thorough investigations, contained many of the same allegations regarding Texas Eastern negligence.

* * *

Settlement: Automobile accident cases are relatively easy to settle. Even in cases involving multiple defendants and hotly contested issues of liability and damages, the parties can usually hash out a settlement after a few phone calls and one or two meetings.

In the Staten Island litigation, Texas Eastern began settlement negotiations even before the first lawsuit had been filed, and these negotiations continued for nearly two and one-half years.

* * *

The **"Dole Doctrine"**: Dow heard from Texas Eastern for the first time shortly after the incident. Texas Eastern's New York City lawyers called to request a meeting. Don Frayer attended on behalf of Fireman's Fund along with a supervisor from Dow's in-house insurance department. They met with Texas Eastern's lawyers in a plush, dimly lit conference room at the firm's typically swank downtown offices.

One of the firm's senior partners, a professorial type, hosted the meeting. He began by condescendingly noting that since the Dow people were from the mid-west, they probably were not aware of a recent change in New York law. He then proceeded to lecture Frayer and his companion on the "Dole doctrine." He must have used the term "Dole doctrine" at least twenty times. According to the attorney, Dow's potential exposure in the case was much greater under the "Dole doctrine" than under prior New York law. He regaled his guests with stories about the generosity of New York juries. He warned that even a small percentage of a verdict in this case, which involved forty deaths, would be a huge sum of money. And every time he mentioned the "Dole doctrine," his tone suggested that he was certain that his guests had never heard of it.

When the attorney finished his presentation, Don Frayer innocently asked the attorney if he could provide the full name of the case upon which the "Dole doctrine" was based. The attorney frowned and muttered to himself: "Dole versus, Dole versus..." Suddenly, a light bulb went off.

"Dole versus Dow Chemical," he said.

Silence.

Finally, Frayer spoke. "In case you may have forgotten," he said, "we are Dow Chemical, and I personally supervised the *Dole* case for Fireman's Fund."

After that, there was not much left to say. Frayer stated that he was not aware of any information suggesting that Dow was in any way responsible for the accident. He offered to consider any information that Texas Eastern might want to provide. Then he said good-bye, and he and his companion flew back to Midland.

* * *

Battle Lines: Texas Eastern settled the first wrongful death case by itself, without any contribution from the other defendants, in July 1973, five months after the accident. They settled a second case in December of that same year.

But then Texas Eastern decided not to settle any more cases on its own. Instead, they wanted to work out a global settlement of all of the cases, with each defendant paying its fair share.

The problem was that, from the outset, Texas Eastern and Dow did not see eye to eye on what Dow's fair share should be. Texas Eastern considered Dow one of three major players, along with itself and Battelle, and insisted that each of them should pay an equal share of any settlement package. Depending upon how much the "minor" defendants were willing to contribute, the share of each of the major players could be as much as one third. In contrast, Dow viewed itself as a minor player and for nearly two and one-half years made no settlement offer at all. Finally, in August of 1975, Dow offered ten percent.

Texas Eastern tried everything to convince Dow that the two companies faced the same potential liability. They invited us to a meeting where one of their expert witnesses made a detailed presentation that purported to establish that the dome was raised by a polyurethane fire and not a gas fire. When he finished his presentation, Texas Eastern's attorneys refused to allow him to answer our questions.

They invited the judge to participate in the discussions. During one court settlement conference, they argued that prior to the accident an independent engineering firm had conducted flammability tests on a batch of the Dow polyurethane that indicated a "flame spread rate" above the maximum rate allowed for a product to be classified as "non-burning." According to Texas Eastern, Dow never notified Texas Eastern about the higher flame spread rate. Their attorney was indignant. "No mention of this test," he scoffed. "No mention that its product was other than non-burning. Delivery of the batch was in April and thereafter silence, silence, silence to the date of the accident."

We responded by producing a letter from Dow to Texas Eastern four months before the accident forwarding a copy of the engineering firm's report in its entirety.

At that same conference, Texas Eastern showed two films. One, a documentary called "Fire" produced by ABC News, purported to demonstrate that the Dow insulation was highly flammable and primarily responsible for the damage at the site. The film was an indictment not only of Dow but of the entire plastics industry and the ASTM. The second film, produced by experts retained by Texas Eastern, depicted flammability tests that the experts conducted on the Dow polyurethane. These tests purported to demonstrate that polyurethane saturated with natural gas burned no more readily than dry polyurethane and that the ASTM "small scale" burning tests were misleading and inaccurate.

We had nothing to equal the dramatic impact made by the films, particularly the ABC documentary. But with Don Frayer's help we prepared and submitted a short memorandum rebutting the points made in the film produced by the Texas Eastern experts. For example, the experts conducted a test to demonstrate that the polyurethane insulation burned in an irregular manner. To establish this fact, they ignited the left side of a piece of insulation. The flamed extinguished itself. Then they ignited the right side of the insulation, which burned until the entire piece was completely consumed. In our memorandum, we pointed out that the insulation contained a fire retardant that is emitted in the presence of heat. Thus, the retardant was present to extinguish the flame when the left side of the insulation was ignited but was no longer present when the right side was ignited.

We thought our memorandum was quite convincing, but Texas Eastern was not impressed. They submitted a thirty-seven-page brief, with supporting exhibits, "as a final effort to underline the wasteful and egregious lack of realism in which Dow is engaging in refusing to acknowledge that the principal issues in this case inevitably expose Dow to liability equal to or greater than that of any other defendant." That was the memorandum in which Texas Eastern accurately quoted the testimony of the crane operator but omitted his last three words: "I smelled gas."

Nothing Texas Eastern tried worked. Their experts told them it was a polyurethane fire; ours told us it was a gas fire. They charged that Dow's misrepresentations were the major cause of the accident; we charged that the major cause was Texas Eastern's negligence. They wanted our settlement share to be the same as theirs; we stuck to our guns at ten percent and refused to offer one penny more.

*   *   *

The Pressure Graphs: In November 1974, Dow learned for the first time of the existence of two graphs that had recorded the air pressure inside the tank at the time of the fire. These graphs were not mentioned at the congressional hearings or in the Bureau of Mines report. We speculated that the graphs had been in the possession of the Staten Island grand jury and just recently released.

According to Texas Eastern, the graphs demonstrated that the air pressure within the tank rose for between two and three minutes before the dome was raised and that this time frame was consistent with a polyurethane fire and not a gas fire. At Texas Eastern's request, we met with one of their expert witnesses who explained the system that had created the graphs and exactly what the graphs signified. In response to our questions, the expert admitted that the system and the graphs suffered from certain technical deficiencies. He insisted, however, that notwithstanding these deficiencies the graphs indicated with a reasonable degree of scientific certainty that the dome was raised by burning polyurethane.

Although our expert witness maintained that the graphs were ambiguous, we fully appreciated their potential impact. They were generated at the time of the incident and contained data that was arguably consistent with Texas Eastern's theory. They were the next best thing to eyewitness testimony. In explaining the graphs to us, Texas Eastern's expert had made an impressive, convincing presentation. We had to assume that he would be just as impressive and convincing in front of a jury.

Naturally, Texas Eastern's attorneys were present when we met with their expert. Just as the meeting was breaking up, the attorneys advised us that, in their view, the graphs unequivocally established that Dow was, in fact, a major player in the litigation. They asked us to get back to them as soon as possible with a concrete settlement proposal from Dow, either in terms of dollars or a percentage. They indicated that they fully expected that Dow's offer would be a substantial one.

Don Frayer, Dick Darger, Bob Buell, and I debated how to respond to Texas Eastern's request for an offer in a series of conference telephone calls. There was a strong difference of opinion among the group regarding the significance of the graphs: Dick Darger and I did not think they were all that damaging to our position, but Buell and Frayer thought otherwise. Notwithstanding these differences, we all agreed on what our response should be. Bob Buell best expressed it as follows: "If we have been injured, now is not the time to let them know it."

Accordingly, I telephoned Texas Eastern's lawyer and told him that we were not persuaded by the graphs, that they suffered from technical difficulties that created doubts about their reliability, and that after examining them our expert had concluded that they did not establish a time frame consistent with a polyurethane fire.

"What are you telling me?" the attorney asked.

"I'm telling you that we still consider ourselves a minor player and are prepared to negotiate with you on that basis. At this time, however, we do not have a specific proposal."

* * *

The Turning Point: The negotiations continued. More often than not, whenever we met with Texas Eastern's attorneys, they talked about the graphs. We needed something—anything—to focus their attention elsewhere.

The turning point came when the attorney for Battelle Institute provided us with evidence, discussed earlier, that notwithstanding Texas Eastern's statements to the contrary, Texas Eastern had full knowledge prior to the incident that the Dow insulation was flammable.

The Battelle evidence compelled Texas Eastern to do a remarkable about face. For two years they had insisted that they had no knowledge that Dow's insulation would burn. Then, after we confronted them with the Battelle evidence, they told us that they knew the insulation would burn, "but not so ferociously."

That might have been a reasonable position had Texas Eastern taken it from day one. But after uttering so many denials during so many settlement meetings and court appearances, Texas Eastern's new position hardly rang true. Their credibility had taken a serious hit.

* * *

Shortly thereafter, Texas Eastern blinked. They circulated a settlement proposal requiring a $2 million contribution from Texas Eastern and a $1 million contribution from Dow. After nearly two years of intransigence, Texas Eastern had finally retreated from its position that their share of any settlement and Dow's share had to be the same.

The Battelle evidence was probably one of several factors that caused Texas Eastern to soften its settlement stance. Others included the ongoing depositions of Texas Eastern employees, which produced much testimony damaging to Texas Eastern's various defenses; the unfavorable procedural rulings handed down by the court, which, among other things, stalled Texas Eastern's discovery efforts against Dow in both New York and Texas; and the financial pressure on Texas Eastern caused by the fact that the tank could not be repaired and reopened until all of the litigation arising from the explosion had been concluded.

* * *

Texas Eastern's proposal went nowhere, so one month later they circulated another proposal in which they offered to contribute $5 million and asked for $2 million from Dow. Dow rejected that proposal but for the first time responded with one of its own. Dow's offer was to pay ten percent of the total settlement package.

That was the beginning of the end. All that remained was to negotiate final figures with the plaintiffs. Within weeks, an agreement was reached. The package totaled approximately $13 million dollars. Texas Eastern's share was approximately $7 million. Dow's share was $1.5 million. Battelle's paid $2 million, and four other defendants contributed the balance.

* * *

Dow and Fireman's Fund were thrilled that I had kept Dow's share of the total settlement package to just under twelve percent. (In contrast, Texas Eastern's share was approximately fifty four percent.) I was thrilled that my first venture into the arena of big time litigation had been a smashing success.

Looking back, I do have one regret.

During the many settlement meetings I attended with the attorneys for Texas Eastern, I did not buy a single one of their arguments that Dow was a major player facing the same potential liability in the wrongful death cases as Texas Eastern and Battelle. Not one. Their arguments, for the most part, were well reasoned and well presented, but I steadfastly stuck to my guns.

My stubbornness exasperated Texas Eastern's attorneys to no end, and occasionally their frustration showed. Once, after a court appearance in which I had summarized for the umpteenth time Dow's assessment of the case, one of Texas Eastern's attorneys cornered me in the corridor and began to grill me about Dow's insurance coverage. I told him that Dow's insurance coverage was none of his business. For some reason, this prompted him to state rather snidely, in a voice loud enough for other attorneys on the case to hear, that he would be willing to bet that Dow ended up paying as much as Texas Eastern and Battelle.

"How about a steak dinner?" I quickly replied.

He looked startled but agreed to the wager.

Twenty months later, when the cases settled, and Dow contributed $1.5 million, and Texas Eastern contributed more than four times that amount, I never got my steak dinner.

Maybe I should have included an appropriate provision in the final settlement papers.

Me in Far Rockaway in 1930.   With my mother.

My father (center) with his doctor friends and their children attending the Penn Relays. That's me in front holding the "Relays" program.

My parents, my sister Judy, and me in 1944.

My father and me in 1944.

elh/McM/1000

AGPD-R 201 Rivkin, Leonard L.
(8 Aug 45) 12 225 585

8 December 1945

Mr. Leonard L. Rivkin
918 Cornaga Avenue
Far Rockaway, New York

Dear Mr. Rivkin:

Further reference is made to my letter of 8 August 1945, concerning the award of the Silver Star and Combat Infantryman Badge to you.

I have the honor to inform you that by direction of the President, you have been awarded the Silver Star and the Combat Infantryman Badge. The citations are as follows:

SILVER STAR

"For gallantry in action against the enemy inRarin, Germany on 14 April 1945. A column of forty vehicles was moving forward when suddenly two enemy 88 mm. guns, situated on the crest of a hill, fired upon the road. While the troops scattered for cover in nearby fields, Private First Class Rivkin, disregarding the fact that the enemy positions were protected by machine gun fire and by a prepared mortar barrage, dashed forward four hundred yards across an open field and, without regard for his own personal safety, single-handedly set up his light machine gun and prepared to rake the enemy strong point. Private First Class Rivkin, together with two officers, then boldly advanced across the open field toward the enemy guns and captured eighty prisoners of war. The valor and magnificent courage displayed by Private First Class Rivkin were a distinct inspiration to his comrades and reflect high credit upon himself and the armed forces of the United States."
(Authority: GO#20, 86th Inf Div., 2 May 1945, Pfc., Inf, Co L, ***Inf Regt.)

COMBAT INFANTRYMAN BADGE

"For satisfactory performance of duty in ground combat against the enemy in Germany."
(Authority: GO#37, 343rd Inf., 3 October 1945, PFC, Infantry)

My Silver Star citation from the War Department.

On a South Nassau Lawyer's Association cruise in 1955. Left to right: me, my late first wife Lenore, Victor Leff, and Victor's wife Barbara.

With Lenore enjoying that same cruise.

At my desk in Freeport in 1960.

Receiving an honorarium from the president of the Freeport PBA in 1967.

My first office, now a candy store, at 35 West Merrick Road in Freeport.

The first office of the law firm of Rivkin and Leff at 11 West Sunrise Highway in Freeport. Our second office, across the street at 16 West Sunrise Highway, is now a vacant lot.

The office we built for the firm on Ocean Avenue in Freeport.

The firm's office at 100 Garden City Plaza in Westbury, adjacent to the site from which Charles Lindbergh took off on his famous solo flight across the Atlantic.

The firm's current office at EAB Plaza in Uniondale.

At the firm retreat on Montauk Point with Stu Sherman (right) in 1983.

A partnership meeting in 1985, featuring on the left side of the table Ed Hart, Phil Weinberg, Bill Savino, Don MacMillan, Warren Radler (partially hidden), and Bruce Drucker. That's Jeff Silberfeld on the right with the beard. That's me on the right side down at the end. John Dunne took the picture.

Receiving an honorary degree from Hofstra Law School in 1989.

Birch Bayh (left) making a presentation in 1989. The late State Senator Norman Levy looks on.

Receiving a Community Service award presented by my son John.

The firm's 40th anniversary party. That's me cutting the cake, with Warren Radler, Stu Sherman, John Dunne, Ed Hart, and Jerry Kremer.

With my present wife Betty in 1996.

My sister Judy and her husband, Dr. Ted Feldman.

Now that I'm retired, this is how I spend my spare time in Jupiter, Florida.

My 70th birthday party. Left to right or right to left, children, spouses, and grandchildren.

Chapter Eight

Franklin National Bank

On October 9, 1974, I began my workday, as usual, sitting at my desk reading the New York *Times*. That morning, a front page head-line reported that the Comptroller of the Currency had declared Franklin National Bank insolvent. In those days, bank failures were not uncommon; Franklin was the fifty-fifth federally insured bank to collapse between 1965 and 1974. Nor was Franklin's failure totally unexpected; rumors about the bank's deteriorating condition had been circulating for years. Nevertheless, Franklin's collapse made headlines not only in New York but around the country because it was the largest bank failure in American history. On the date of its insolvency, Franklin ranked twentieth among the nation's banks, with assets total-ing $4.5 billion. Although best known as the preeminent bank on Long Island, where it had maintained more than fifty branches in Nas-sau and Suffolk counties, it had recently opened twenty-five branches in New York City and an important overseas branch in London.

The article mentioned some of the reasons for Franklin's demise: bad management, poor earnings, huge losses in foreign currency trad-ing, a missed dividend payment, a run on deposits, and the $1.77 bil-lion Franklin owed to the Federal Reserve. The article also reported that European American Bank had reached an agreement with the Federal Deposit Insurance Corporation to take over the failed bank. Remarkably, the morning after Franklin's insolvency all of its branches reopened as branches of European American, there were no interrup-tions of service, and none of Franklin's 600,000 depositors suffered any loss.

Later that day, I met with Stu Sherman to discuss firm business. "Too bad about the Lollipop Bank," he said.

"What are you talking about?" I asked.

"Franklin. They used to call it the Lollipop Bank. Whenever a kid opened an account there, they gave him a lollipop."

That evening, returning home from work, I drove past one of the bank's branches. "Franklin National Bank," proclaimed the lettering on the door. "European American Bank," announced a hand painted sign in the window.

Then I arrived home, ate dinner, and didn't give Franklin National Bank another thought. Little did I realize that the time would soon come when I would think of little else.

*   *   *

Leaving Freeport

The firm business that Stu Sherman and I discussed on the day after Franklin's insolvency, and on many other days late in 1974 and into 1975, was our growing concern over office space. In 1966, when we moved to Ocean Avenue, the firm consisted of five attorneys. There were rooms on our floor of the building we did not even use. By the end of 1974, five had grown to twelve; by mid-1975, twelve had grown to fifteen. As many as three attorneys shared offices barely big enough for one. Secretaries sat crammed up against the wall in the hallway.

It was obvious we had to move, so Stu and I began to search for another location in Freeport. I had been practicing there for twenty-five years with great success, the people in the village had been very good to me, and at first the thought of moving elsewhere never entered my mind. But nothing in Freeport appealed to us, which forced us to reconsider. Upon reflection, I realized that it was no longer important for us to stay in Freeport for business purposes. When I first started out I survived on walk-in clients, but by 1974 virtually all of the firm's clients were referred to us by insurance companies or other attorneys. To them, our location in Freeport was irrelevant. I also realized that most of the lawyers in the firm went to court almost every day, usually in Nassau County, so it made sense to relocate closer to the court complex in Mineola.

Ultimately, we found an impressive five story building at 100 Garden City Plaza in Garden City, adjacent to the famous Roosevelt Field Shopping Center, which occupied the very spot from which Charles Lindbergh took off in 1927 on his solo flight across the Atlantic. Coincidentally, this was also the very spot where I landed in 1945 aboard an army hospital plane returning me home from the War. The firm rented most of the top floor of the building; most of the ground floor was occupied by the brokerage firm Paine Webber, whom we soundly defeated in softball at least twice each summer.

In Garden City, each attorney had his own office with huge floor to ceiling windows. Each secretary occupied her own cubby. There was a spacious conference room with a long, rectangular, cherry wood table and even a separate albeit modest legal library.

About the only downside to our new quarters was that, as a result of the move, my commuting time doubled, from fifteen minutes to thirty.

*   *   *

Bob Buell Takes the Initiative

We moved into our new quarters on October 1, 1975, just as the Staten Island explosion case was beginning to wind down. I had thoroughly enjoyed my first experience litigating a major case and was hoping for another such opportunity.

Later that month, I received a telephone call from Bob Buell, the Fireman's Fund Vice President at the home office in San Francisco who was supervising the Staten Island case. I had never worked with Bob before Staten Island, but during the case we developed a strong rapport. Moreover, although I had frequently represented individuals and corporations insured by Fireman's Fund, and had also represented local Fireman's Fund branches, I had never worked directly for the corporate home office.

Never one to beat around the bush, Bob got right to the point.

"Len, what do you know about Franklin National Bank?" he asked.

"Just what I read in the papers."

"Did you know that Fireman's Fund wrote the bank's primary fidelity coverage?"

"Bob, I'll take the case."

He laughed. "I figured you would. Don't you want to hear what it's about first?"

"So tell me."

"When Franklin went under, the FDIC acquired the right to seek insurance coverage for the bank's losses. Five months ago, the FDIC submitted two claims for $15 million each under the bank's fidelity policies. The essence of the claims is that the bank's losses in foreign exchange were caused by fraudulent and dishonest acts by the bank's foreign currency traders. We want you to represent Fireman's Fund, investigate the claims, give us an opinion as to whether we owe any coverage, and defend us if they start a lawsuit."

I was flabbergasted. Bob knew that I had never done any fidelity or surety work, which at the time was a highly specialized field. The claims involved multi-million-dollar losses and complex facts. It was a high profile matter that would be closely followed by the insurance industry. Under these circumstances, the safe choice for Bob would have been to hire an experienced, well established fidelity and surety lawyer to represent Fireman's Fund's interests.

But Bob chose instead to take a risk. In his view, most if not all of the old line fidelity and surety lawyers were too conservative. For this case, he wanted an aggressive attorney who paid careful attention to background and details but was not averse to going out on an occasional limb. He saw how that approach had worked for me in Staten Island and other personal injury cases and concluded that it could be just as successful in the fidelity and surety arena.

*   *   *

I first met Bob Buell through our membership in the Federation of Insurance Counsel. At the time, he had been with Fireman's Fund for nearly twenty years. He had a broad range of claims experience, including general liability, automobile coverage, ocean marine matters, libel and slander, and fidelity and surety. He even spent some time underwriting motion picture cast insurance. He became a Vice President of Claims in 1970. In 1977, during the pendency of the Franklin case, he was promoted to Senior Vice President.

Bob and I hit it off immediately. We saw each other at FIC meetings and spoke occasionally on the telephone. Never one to be a shrinking violet, I soon began to explore, as tactfully as possible, the prospects of getting business from him. But before I got anywhere on that front, Dow and the New York office of Fireman's Fund selected me to represent Dow in the Staten Island explosion case. Imagine my surprise when I discovered that my contact at the Fireman's Fund Home Office would be none other than Bob Buell himself!

Working with Bob was an enormous challenge. To this day, I believe that he had the brightest mind for litigation of any person I have ever met. A graduate of Harvard Law School, he knew the law; many times he had to explain difficult legal concepts to me! He could also breeze through a lengthy memorandum and immediately separate what was important from what was not. He had a way of asking you a question that made you feel that you better come up with the right answer, even if it was one that he didn't want to hear. No doubt about it, I became a better lawyer as a result of our relationship.

Not only that, but Bob was responsible, more than anyone else, for my firm's involvement in our two biggest cases: Franklin National Bank and Agent Orange. He alone made the courageous decision to assign me the Franklin case even though, at the time, I had no experience litigating fidelity insurance claims. Then, following our success in Franklin, he enthusiastically recommended me to Dow to handle Agent Orange.

Obviously, many of my partners were instrumental in the development and growth of my practice. But you also need clients, and Bob was my most significant client by far. I owe much of my success to his trust, loyalty, and friendship.

* * *

And I Thought Staten Island Was Major Litigation

The Franklin National Bank litigation consumed more than four years of my life. I ended up defending not one but two lawsuits in federal court in Brooklyn seeking insurance coverage under the Fireman's Fund fidelity policies, one by the FDIC and another by the Trustee in Bankruptcy of Franklin New York Corporation, the holding company that had owned virtually all of the bank's stock. In these actions, the FDIC and the Trustee alleged that the bank and the holding company had suffered combined losses of more than $100 million as a result of fraudulent and dishonest acts committed by bank employees not only in the foreign exchange department but also in the investment department, where United States corporate and government bonds were traded and maintained. Also named as defendants by the FDIC and the Trustee were Aetna Casualty and Surety Company and Insurance Company of North America ("INA"), the bank's excess fidelity insurers. These two actions were consolidated into one court proceeding along with more than one dozen other cases, including a class action, all arising from the bank's collapse. In these actions, the FDIC, the Trustee in Bankruptcy, and the class plaintiffs sued the bank's former officers and directors, the bank's outside auditing firm, and other banks that had done business with Franklin, including Continental Bank of Illinois and Manufacturer's Hanover Trust in New York. The FDIC and the Trustee also sued each other. In addition to defending the lawsuits by the FDIC and the Trustee, Fireman's Fund, Aetna, and

INA asserted claims against the bank's officers and directors, the outside auditing firm, and Continental Bank. The insurers and the bank's outside auditors also sued the United States government, claiming negligent bank regulation by the Office of the Comptroller of the Currency.

During discovery in the consolidated litigation, the FDIC produced more than 50 million documents and stored them in a warehouse in Manhattan. The parties deposed close to two hundred witnesses at 630 separate sessions generating seventy-five thousand pages of transcripts.

In addition to the consolidated civil litigation, there was a criminal investigation by the United States Attorney's Office in Manhattan. That investigation resulted in more than one dozen indictments of former Franklin directors, officers, and employees. All either pleaded guilty or were convicted after trial.

On the administrative side, the Securities and Exchange Commission investigated Franklin's collapse. On the legislative side, at least three committees and subcommittees of the House and Senate held hearings relating to bank regulation in general or Franklin in particular.

*   *   *

Let's Not Kill All the Lawyers

Not surprisingly, with so many parties to so many lawsuits asserting so many claims for so much money, the Franklin case involved lawyers. Lots of them. More than forty firms appeared in the consolidated civil proceedings, including some of the most elite names in Manhattan, and not just one attorney from each firm. Senior partners handled court appearances. Junior partners and senior associates handled depositions. Junior associates reviewed documents and prepared briefs, discovery requests, and other legal documents. A few of the firms had as many as eight attorneys involved in the case at the same time.

In most instances, the lawyers who occupied center stage were superb litigators. Indeed, at a court hearing on December 1, 1978, the judge presiding over the Franklin case stated as much on the record:

> I do want to add one personal note....I have really enjoyed working with all of you. You have exemplified to me the highest and best that the bar in this city can offer. You have been prompt, you have been courteous, and you have cooperated with the Court in a way that a judge rarely gets to see on such a consistent basis.

Not the least bit daunted by the prominence of my opposing counsel, and steadfast in my determination to totally justify Bob Buell's faith in me, I entered the fray the only way I knew how: by taking the initiative.

*   *   *

Getting Started

My first endeavor was to learn as much as possible as quickly as possible about Franklin National Bank. Recognizing that the project was far too big to handle alone, I hired Jeff Silberfeld, a recent law school graduate, to assist me. Together we reviewed material in Fireman's Fund's files that had been provided by Franklin and, after the insolvency, the FDIC. We met with Aetna's attorneys, who had been investigating Franklin's insurance claims for nearly one year. We began a systematic review of the millions upon millions of documents in the FDIC warehouse in Manhattan. We collected and reviewed newspaper and magazine articles about the bank going back to 1965. We monitored criminal proceedings in federal court in Manhattan against former employees of the bank's foreign exchange department. We met with the Assistant United States Attorney in charge of those proceedings. We met with attorneys representing the holding company's shareholders in class actions against the bank's directors and outside auditors. We hired a foreign currency trader recently retired from a major New York City bank to educate us about foreign exchange in general and Franklin's foreign exchange department in particular. We met privately with several of the bank's former directors and their attorneys. We met privately with one of the bank's former foreign currency traders. We monitored civil lawsuits in federal court in Manhattan and Brooklyn arising from the bank's failure. We met privately with the author of an article in Fortune Magazine about the bank's demise. We issued subpoenas for the production of documents to the United States Attorney's Office in Manhattan and the FDIC and the Comptroller of the Currency in Washington. We monitored subcommittee hearings in Washington.

Since this was my first fidelity insurance matter, I also undertook to learn as much as I could as quickly as I could about fidelity and surety law. To that end, Jeff and I met several times with in-house Fireman's Fund attorneys, who gave us a crash course, we studied articles on fidelity law in law reviews and professional journals, and Jeff collected and analyzed all of the relevant precedent.

Almost immediately, our two major strategies began to take shape: the so-called "alter ego" defense, and our claim of negligent bank regulation.

Alter Ego: The "alter ego" defense is based on the premise that an insured may not profit from its own wrongdoing. Thus, the Fireman's Fund fidelity policies provided coverage for loss sustained by Franklin as a result of dishonest or fraudulent acts committed by the bank's employees, but not if the bank authorized, had knowledge of, or participated in the alleged dishonesty or fraud.

The defense is relatively easy to articulate, but extremely difficult to apply, especially in cases where the insured, like Franklin, is a corporation. The problem is: how does one establish that a corporation authorized, had knowledge of, or participated in the fraud or dishonesty of a corporate employee? It is not enough to prove one officer's knowledge or participation, or one director's. Rather, the only way to do so is to prove knowledge or participation by the corporation's "alter ego," that is, by the people (officers, directors, or otherwise) who exercise total and complete control over all corporate affairs and business.[1]

The proofs of loss submitted by the FDIC in support of its insurance claims for Franklin's losses alleged that dishonest and fraudulent acts had been committed by low level employees in the bank's foreign exchange and investment departments. The alleged misdeeds by foreign exchange department employees fell into three categories: traders had concealed foreign exchange contracts by hiding them in their desks instead of entering those contracts in the bank's books and records; traders had entered into foreign exchange contracts in violation of the bank's written trading limits; and traders and record keepers had made false entries in the bank's books and records. The alleged misdeeds by investment department employees fell into two categories: traders of government and corporate securities had made false entries in the bank's books and records; and traders had purchased and held securities and transferred them from the bank's trading account to its portfolio account, or vice versa, in violation of the bank's written guidelines and limitations.

Before long, however, it became apparent that participation in the alleged wrongs was not limited to mere low level foreign currency and securities traders and may have included those persons in actual control of the bank. In December 1975, Franklin's Executive Vice President, who was also a member of the bank's Board of Directors, pleaded guilty in federal court in Manhattan to charges of misapplication of bank funds, making false entries in bank records, filing false statements with federal regulatory agencies, and conspiring to defraud the United States. By pleading guilty, the Executive Vice President acknowledged his involvement in all of the alleged misconduct by the bank's foreign currency traders. This senior manager had been personally recruited to run Franklin's foreign exchange department by Michele Sindona, an Italian financier who in 1972 paid $40 million for 21.6 percent of the shares of Franklin's holding company, which was considered a "controlling interest" in the bank by federal regulators. Upon acquiring his stock in Franklin, Sindona stated: "I'm going to make most of my money in foreign exchange. That's the way I do it in my Italian banks."[2] Although Sindona, a foreign national, was barred by law from sitting on the bank's board, he was able to influence Franklin's business as a member of the holding company's board and as Chairman of the holding company's International Executive Committee. Indeed, early in 1974, both the Comptroller of the Currency and the Federal Reserve Board concluded that Sindona "completely dominated Franklin's affairs."

If this was not enough to raise a red flag, our initial investigation disclosed that by early 1973 Franklin was in serious financial trouble. To keep the bank afloat and save his investment, Sindona suggested a merger between Franklin and Talcott National, a finance and factoring company also controlled by Sindona. In order to obtain regulatory approval for the merger and to secure financing, Franklin had to show that it was a viable, profitable institution when, in fact, it was not. All of the fraudulent and dishonest acts alleged by the FDIC and Trustee were intended either to generate profits for the bank or hide losses, and thus bring about the proposed consolidation. These circumstances clearly suggested, at least to us, a grand scheme orchestrated from the highest levels of executive power within the bank.

Years later, Bob Buell told me that, in his view, an old line fidelity and surety lawyer would have quickly concluded that the above evidence was rather flimsy and the " alter ego" defense was not worth pursuing. But with Bob's full support and encouragement, we vigorously developed the defense to the point where we felt we could implicate the bank's controlling stockholder, Chairman, President, Vice-Chairman, and Senior Executive Vice President in all of the foreign exchange and investment department frauds claimed by the FDIC. "I have no doubt," Bob said recently, "that the alter ego defense was a factor of considerable significance in the ultimate disposition of the case."

Negligent Bank Regulation: Almost everywhere we looked, we saw signs that something was not right in the relationship between Franklin and federal bank regulators. For example, the Office of the Comptroller of the Currency had conducted three national bank examinations of Franklin between December 1972 and November 1973. Each examination involved a thorough review of virtually all aspects of the bank's operation. Examining teams consisted of as many as forty persons. The examinations lasted for as long as three months. Under these circumstances, the examiners must have detected at least some of the conduct by foreign currency and domestic securities traders later claimed by Franklin and the FDIC to be fraudulent and dishonest. If so, what steps, if any, did the examiners take to stop that conduct? If not, why not?

Another example: early in 1974, Manufacturers Hanover Trust Company, a major New York City bank, was negotiating to merge with Franklin as a means of rescuing Franklin from its impending insolvency. Even after Franklin's foreign exchange losses were announced in May, Manufacturers Hanover continued to express an interest in the proposed deal. But Sindona, Franklin's controlling stockholder who stood to lose the most from that merger or any merger, managed to quash it. Somehow, he arranged a high level meeting with representatives of the Federal Reserve, the Comptroller's office, and the Securities and Exchange Commission and persuaded them to agree to a proposal that would save Franklin, and Sindona's investment, by raising millions of dollars in additional capital from the bank's shareholders. With his poor track record at Franklin, how did Sindona ever manage to convince the regulators to leave him in control? What else did Sindona do in 1973 and 1974 to get the regulators to look the other way as Franklin slid closer and closer to its demise?

We were not alone in our suspicions. Early in 1975, two subcommittees of the United States House of Representatives conducted hearings on national bank regulation. One hearing specifically addressed the Comptroller's regulation of Franklin, and subcommittee staff members provided us with many of our early leads.

But did any of this information give rise to a claim for damages against the various banking agencies? There was no easy answer to this question. In San Diego, a claim against the Comptroller's office arising from the recent failure of the United States National Bank had been dismissed by the trial court, but the facts of that case differed significantly from our facts, and at any rate the decision was on appeal. Two other similar cases were pending in Los Angeles, but there had not yet been any rulings. Other cases against the government not involving bank regulation but which laid down general principles of law did not provide a definitive answer. In effect, we would be trying something brand new; we would be writing on a clean slate.

Eventually, after many hours of research and much internal debate, we decided to proceed. As it turned out, our damage claims against the government turned out to be one of the most hotly contested aspect of the entire Franklin dispute.

*   *   *

Face-to-Face Discussions

Three months into my investigation, I received a telephone call from Bill Purcell, one of the lead attorneys for the Trustee in Bankruptcy. Bill called to invite me and the attorneys for Aetna and INA to a meeting with him and Bill Kelly, the attorney for the FDIC. "We want to bring the insurers up-to-date on the status of our settlement negotiations with the bank's former officers and directors," he explained.

Although I had previously spoken on the telephone with the Bill Purcell and Bill Kelly, I had never met either of them in person. Therefore, I prepared for the meeting all the preceding day and late into the evening.

At the meeting, Bill Purcell advised us that prospects for a settlement between the Trustee and the officers and directors looked promising. Apparently, Lloyd's of London, which insured the officers and directors, was considering offering just under the $7.5 million policy limit. "Since I would have to execute a release as a condition to the settlement," Bill explained, "I would need the fidelity insurers' consent."

From his tone, Bill's obvious expectation was that the fidelity insurers would have no objection to any settlement with Lloyd's. He seemed a bit surprised as I rattled off my concerns.

"We'll only consent if the settlement is reasonable," I began. "So we would need to see some sort of evidentiary basis. I also think that Lloyd's may be obligated to pay more than one policy limit. Have you looked into this? And we would have to know how the settlement money was credited. To foreign exchange? To the Investment department? Or to some other aspect of the bank's operation? And what about the fact that the coverage provided by the Lloyd's policies and the fidelity policies overlap to some extent. Have you considered that problem?"

Bill was reluctant to discuss any of my concerns in depth. Ultimately, all we could agree upon was that he should continue his discussions with Lloyd's, and we would attempt to resolve my concerns if and when a settlement was reached.

Not surprisingly, after discussing his case against the officers and directors, Bill steered the conversation in the direction of the fidelity claims. He addressed his first questions to me, as counsel to the primary insurance carrier.

"What's your position on coverage?" he asked me.

"I don't have one yet."

"When will we get an answer?"

His question seemed harmless enough, but I did not want to get pinned down to anything, even a matter of timing, so early in the game.

"There's so much material to review," I replied, "that all I can say is that in two months I should know how much longer it will take before I can intelligently discuss my client's position."

Realizing that he was getting nowhere with me, Bill turned to Martin London, Aetna's lead counsel and a partner at Paul, Weiss, Rifkind, Wharton & Garrison. Aetna's policies were excess to Fireman's Fund's, which meant that Aetna was not obligated to make any payments until the applicable limits of the Fireman's Fund policies were exhausted.

"What about your client?" Bill asked.

"I don't know," Martin answered lazily. "We're so far up the pole I've hardly thought about this case at all."

*   *   *

Grand Jury Secrecy

In addition to Franklin's Executive Vice President, six former low level employees of the bank's foreign exchange department pleaded guilty in December 1975 and January 1976 to federal charges of misapplication of bank funds. The Vice President and all six employees had previously testified behind closed doors before the grand jury investigating Franklin's collapse. My chances of obtaining copies of the minutes of that testimony were slim, in light of the long standing policy in favor of grand jury secrecy. But I was always looking for ways to take the initiative and thought I could make a decent argument that we had a compelling need for the transcripts. Therefore, as part of my early investigative efforts, I made a motion in federal court in Manhattan for an order directing the United States Attorney to produce the pertinent material.

The judge began oral argument by stating that he was going to deny my motion. When he gave his reasons, I requested an opportunity to be heard. He allowed me to speak for a few minutes and then tried to cut me off. I stood my ground, determined to have my say:

THE COURT: No, I am going to —

MR. RIVKIN: Would you just bear with me a second, sir, and hear me?

THE COURT: Yes.

MR. RIVKIN: I am sorry, I don't mean to push, but I have a client to represent.

THE COURT: I know.

MR. RIVKIN: And I believe sincerely in my cause. You might rule me wrong and I will respect you for it, but I won't necessarily agree. So please bear with me, sir.

I stated my case but was unable to change the court's mind. The judge did throw me a bone, however, stating that I could renew my motion when the grand jury ceased its investigation or when the witnesses in question testified at any trial against my client.

*   *   *

See You in Court

In March 1976, in the midst of my investigation into Franklin's alleged fidelity losses, the FDIC and the Trustee each filed a lawsuit against Fireman's Fund, Aetna, and INA in federal court in Brooklyn. The FDIC's action sought to recover $45 million in losses allegedly sustained by the bank as a result of employee fraud and dishonesty in the bank's foreign exchange and investment departments. The Trustee's action sought to recover more than $60 million in foreign exchange and investment department losses allegedly sustained by the holding company. Both the bank and the holding company had been named insureds on the Fireman's Fund, Aetna, and INA policies.

In addition to asserting claims against the fidelity insurers, the FDIC's complaint asserted a claim directly against the Trustee. In that claim, the FDIC alleged that the Trustee and the FDIC were suing to recover the exact same losses and sought a declaration that the Trustee had no right to recover any portion of those losses under the fidelity policies.

*　*　*

Motion Denied

After studying the two complaints, I arranged a series of meetings with the attorneys for our co-defendants, Aetna and INA, to discuss the possibility of a coordinated response. Among other things, we all agreed on the following important propositions: the FDIC and the Trustee were, in fact, suing to recover the exact same losses, as alleged in the FDIC's complaint; the FDIC or the Trustee, but not both, was entitled to maintain an action to recover those losses; and the FDIC and the Trustee, by instituting separate actions for the alleged losses, had created the risk of a double recovery.

To eliminate this risk, I suggested that the insurance companies file an immediate motion asking the court to determine as early in the litigation as possible which plaintiff had the right to proceed. Counsel for Aetna and INA preferred to take some discovery first and then attack plaintiffs' complaints.

Although outvoted two to one, I elected to file an immediate motion. One reason that I bucked the majority was that the Fireman's Fund policies were primary and the Aetna and INA policies were excess. Together, the three companies provided $15 million in coverage per claim. As the primary carrier, Fireman's Fund owed the first $6 million of every covered loss. As the first layer excess carrier, Aetna owed the next $4 million. As the third layer excess carrier, INA paid the last $5 million. Since Fireman's Fund's exposure was greater and more immediate, I believed that Fireman's Fund should have the most say regarding the defense of the lawsuits.

Another reason I bucked the majority was that as a matter of style I always preferred to act rather than wait. Moreover, Bob Buell had hired me to handle the Franklin case because of my willingness to go out on an occasional limb, and I did not want to disappoint him.

The precise course of action I chose for Fireman's Fund was a motion to stay all claims in both the FDIC's and the Trustee's complaints except for the FDIC's declaratory judgment claim against the Trustee. The issue raised by that claim was the very issue we wanted resolved first: was the FDIC or the Trustee the proper party to proceed against the fidelity insurers. We argued that, by resolving that issue at the outset, the court would eliminate duplication, streamline the litigation, and simplify the proceedings.

Although I believed our motion was well conceived and quite persuasive, the one person who mattered, the judge, whose name was Orrin Judd, thought otherwise. Before I could even open my mouth at oral argument, Judge Judd said:

> THE COURT: I really don't see the purpose of your motion. Come and try to explain it to me. You were saying somebody doesn't have the right to sue under our American System?
>
> MR. RIVKIN: I said one party has the right to sue, the other doesn't.
>
> THE COURT: They both have the right to sue....There are two claims. One may be a good claim and one may be a bad claim. Why can't you defend both?

I tried to answer the judge's question but got nowhere. Judge Judd listened to me rather impatiently for a few minutes and then curtly rendered his decision:

> THE COURT: Motion for a stay is denied.

*   *   *

Strike Two

During oral argument on our motion to stay, Judge Judd planted in my mind the seeds of our next plan of attack.

> MR. RIVKIN: Why must we proceed against two adversaries...when we know one claim must fall?
>
> THE COURT: You haven't made a motion to dismiss.

We caucused with our co-defendants and decided to accept what appeared to be an invitation by the judge to move to dismiss the

Trustee's claims. In support of the motion, we advanced a rather technical legal argument. Simply put, our contention was that the proper party to seek insurance coverage for Franklin's foreign exchange and investment department losses was the FDIC, suing on behalf of the insolvent bank; New York law did not recognize an action to recover those losses by the Trustee, suing on behalf of the bankrupt holding company.

Shortly before oral argument, Judge Judd died suddenly, and the case was reassigned to Judge Thomas Platt, a federal judge who also sat in Brooklyn. We argued the motion to dismiss before Judge Platt and left court feeling cautiously optimistic. At one point, Judge Platt asked us whether the holding company had paid any extra premium when it was added as an insured on the bank's policies. We told him no, and he nodded his head accordingly.

But then, about three months later, Judge Platt not only ruled against us, he hammered us. His ruling on the merits was simple enough: since the holding company was a named insured, the Trustee had standing to assert claims against the fidelity insurers for the holding company's alleged losses. But Judge Platt did not confine his remarks to the merits of the case. Commenting on the fact that each of the three fidelity insurers had submitted lengthy briefs and affidavits in support of the motion to dismiss, he accused us of

> operating under the mistaken assumption that a torrent of words and paper will either overwhelm the Court or somehow otherwise do away with [the fidelity insurers'] obligation to defend on the merits lawsuits brought against them by their insured.[3]

In addition, commenting on the fact that we had first moved for a stay and then to dismiss, he accused us of "foot dragging."[4] Finally, in response to statements suggesting that we planned additional motions, he told us not to bother until after the completion of all discovery and ordered us to file answers to the FDIC's and the Trustee's complaints.[5]

In light of Judge Platt's decidedly negative attitude toward the fidelity insurers, one would think that we came away from the court's ruling with our tail between our legs. Not so. In fact, in one respect we had gained a hugely important victory.

As I mentioned earlier, one of our main concerns from the outset was that, by instituting separate lawsuits, the FDIC and the Trustee were trying to achieve a double recovery. The FDIC would recoup the bank's losses and the Trustee would recoup the holding company's losses as if they were separate from and additional to the bank's losses when in fact they were one and the same. But in denying our motion to dismiss, Judge Platt gave its assurance that this would not happen:

> It should be noted that both the Trustee and the FDIC have agreed that defendants' liability will not be increased by the fact that two, rather than one, of the insureds claim coverage. Thus, there will be only one recovery...and the allocation of that recovery will be determined if, when and after defendants' liability is determined.[6]

Thus, the Trustee may have won the right to proceed with his lawsuit, but not much else.

*   *   *

Answering the Complaints

As ordered, we filed answers to the complaints of the FDIC and the Trustee ten days after the court denied our motion to dismiss. Our answer to the FDIC's complaint contained twenty five affirmative defenses and seven counterclaims. Our answer to the Trustee's complaint contained twenty six affirmative defenses and one counterclaim.

One of our key affirmative defenses was the "alter ego" theory. There were others. Both the FDIC and the Trustee alleged that they were entitled to recover two separate $15 million foreign exchange losses and an additional $15 million investment department loss, for a total of $45 million. We alleged that the maximum recovery under the fidelity policies for all of the bank's losses was $15 million. We also alleged, among other things, that the acts complained of by the FDIC and Trustee were not fraudulent or dishonest within the meaning of the fidelity policies and were not the cause of any covered loss; that coverage had lapsed with respect to one of the bank's foreign currency traders because the bank had withheld from the fidelity insurers that this particular trader had committed prior fraudulent acts; and that the FDIC and the Trustee had failed to comply with policy provisions requiring timely and adequate notices of loss and supporting proofs.

One of our key counterclaims alleged that the FDIC had knowingly submitted false statements to the fidelity insurers in support of its claims for coverage.

*   *   *

Third-Party Actions

In addition to filing answers to the complaints of the FDIC and the Trustee, we also filed four third-party complaints: one against the bank's former directors; one against the bank's former outside accountants; one against Continental Bank of Illinois; and one against the United States of America.

We filed these third-party complaints to enforce Fireman's Fund's right of subrogation. Our theory was as follows: the Fireman's Fund policies did not cover Franklin's alleged foreign exchange and investment department losses, but if the court were to rule otherwise, then Fireman's Fund would be entitled to recoup its insurance payments from the person or persons responsible for those losses.

Franklin's former directors were responsible, we alleged, because they mismanaged the bank.

Franklin's former outside accountants were responsible because they negligently audited the bank's books and records.

Continental Bank was responsible because it negligently withheld information from Franklin that one of its foreign currency traders had committed fraudulent and dishonest acts during his previous employment at Continental.

The United States of America was responsible because of negligent regulation and supervision of Franklin by the FDIC, the Federal Reserve, and the Comptroller of the Currency.

*   *   *

Our third-party complaint against the United States was forty-eight pages long, probably four times the length of the typical third-party complaint. The reason: we took the unusual step of including dozens of very detailed factual allegations regarding specific acts of negligence by federal bank regulators. Our purpose was to focus the court's attention away from the legal basis for our claims against the United States, which was uncertain at best, and toward the factual basis for those claims, which was quite compelling.

At one point, we sent a detailed draft of the third-party complaint to a Fireman's Fund officer in New York City. Shortly thereafter, an article appeared in the Newark *Star Ledger* reporting on the failure of federal bank regulators to effectively respond to Franklin's growing problems in the early 1970s. The article repeated many of the charges against the regulatory agencies that we had itemized in our draft pleading. This thrilled the Fireman's Fund officer to no end.

"You know," he told us, "it's like they read our gosh darn draft complaint before they printed the gosh darn article!"

*   *   *

Enter the Government

We served our third-party complaint against the United States on January 1, 1977. The next day, we served a notice to take the depositions of ten present and former employees of the Office of the Comptroller of the Currency. We also served a demand upon the Comptroller's Office to produce all of its records for the period 1970 through 1977 pertaining to Franklin National Bank.

The government's response was to make a motion to stay this discovery to give the government the opportunity to make a motion to dismiss Fireman's Fund's third-party complaint. The government argued that the requested discovery was inordinately burdensome, that its motion to dismiss would almost certainly be granted, and that following the dismissal of Fireman's Fund's third-party complaint the need for that discovery would no longer exist.

In opposition, we argued that the government's motion to dismiss would almost certainly be denied and that, even if granted, we would nevertheless be entitled to the requested discovery as part of our defense of the actions by the FDIC and Trustee.

This time, Judge Platt agreed with us. At oral argument, he told the government's attorney, "I don't really see any advantage in waiting until your motion to dismiss is decided. You are going to be examined even if I dismiss against you."

Then Judge Platt made a remark that nearly knocked me out of my chair: "The government is in this case up to its ears."

In court, I always looked for signals, subtle or otherwise, from the judge about his attitude toward the parties, the claims, the defenses, and the issues. I could not have gotten a more positive signal regarding the merits of our third-party claims against the government if I had written it myself.

*   *   *

Like Pulling Teeth

We now had the green light to pursue discovery against the government. In my wildest dreams I never imagined the difficulties we would encounter.

Our deposition notice requested the Comptroller's Office to produce its first witness on March 8, 1977. The Comptroller did not produce his first witness until mid-July.

Our deposition notice requested the Comptroller's Office to produce ten witnesses by name, one after another, beginning on March 8. By the end of the year, the Comptroller had produced only three of them.

Our document production notice requested the Comptroller's Office to produce "all" of its documents relating to Franklin National Bank on March 8. Although we were advised that the documents filled fifty cubic feet of space, by the end of March the comptroller had produced a stack of documents no more than eight inches high.

Moreover, the documents produced by the Comptroller in March were copies, not originals, as required by the Federal Rules of Discovery.

In addition, the Comptroller had improperly deleted portions of the documents with no explanation.

Ultimately, the Comptroller's Office produced documents in waves but did not finish producing documents, originals not copies, until October, six months later. Along the way, they missed deadlines, requested adjournments and modifications, and committed "inadvertent" omissions.

But even in October they did not make "all" of their Franklin Documents available to the parties. They withheld production of thousands of pages, claiming various governmental privileges. The government's attorneys prepared a thick two volume index identifying the allegedly privileged documents by date, author, and subject and submitted to the court a lengthy memorandum of law supporting the privilege claims. Several parties submitted opposing memoranda. Thereafter, after finishing his business on other cases, Judge Platt sat in court in the afternoon for weeks on end, listened to argument from the parties, looked at each document claimed to be privileged, and issued rulings one document at a time.

Along the way, I wrote many letters and appeared in court many times to complain about the government's lack of cooperation. At one hearing, I got a little carried away:

MR. RIVKIN: A number of things have occurred since our last court appearance which I think must be brought to the court's attention. I would like to make an orderly presentation but I think I might get a little emotional because of what's been going on....

The government is refusing to abide by Your Honor's order that we proceed expeditiously with discovery, they are refusing to cooperate with the parties, and I submit they have a game plan. They are stalling and frustrating discovery until they can make their motion to dismiss our third-party complaint, which they seem to think they might win and thus limit their disclosure obligations. I would further submit, and I don't think the Court needs to see documentation for this, but I have it in front of me, that this game plan is country wide. There is a motion for sanctions against the Comptroller in California this very day, in federal court, because a bunch of lawyers from the west coast flew to Washington for a deposition of an employee of the Comptroller's Office and then the Comptroller did not allow the deposition to go forward.

It's a plan, Judge. I believe it's a plan so they can try to get out of the case and avoid discovery. What should be done?

At another hearing, Judge Platt became so enraged when the government missed yet another discovery deadline that he threatened to fine the government's attorneys one thousand dollars per day for each day past the deadline that production was incomplete.

Ultimately, we obtained from the Comptroller's Office just about everything we wanted, but it did not happen overnight and was not easy. In fact, as I stated in a report letter to Bob Buell, "It was like pulling teeth."

*   *   *

The government's foot-dragging aggravated me but should not have surprised me. When we first began to research the possibility of suing the government, we contacted two law firms on the west coast who were involved in litigation against the United States based upon negligent bank regulation to pick their brains and share information and theories. Among other things, both firms warned us that the government was not a willing participant in the discovery process.

*   *   *

The Government's Motion to Dismiss

The government served its motion to dismiss shortly after the court denied its motion to stay discovery. The motion to dismiss raised complex and intriguing legal and factual issues that the parties probed in painstaking detail in hundreds of pages of law review quality supporting and opposing briefs. Did the federal statutes empowering the Comptroller's Office, the FDIC, and the Federal Reserve to examine and monitor national banks create or contemplate a cause of action for negligent bank regulation? If so, did the court have jurisdiction over claims of negligent bank regulation under the Federal Tort Claims Act ("FTCA")?[7] Were those claims barred by the "discretionary function" exception to FTCA jurisdiction? By the "misrepresentation" exception? By the "regulation of the monetary system" exception? By the Statute of Limitations?

On most of these issues, the case law tended to support the government's position. Moreover, the government needed only to prevail on one of its arguments for the court to dismiss all of our third-party claims. Under these circumstances, the odds against our defeating the government's motion were formidable.

But not hopeless, primarily because we had devised a novel but persuasive argument in opposition to the government's motion based upon a relatively simple but well established legal doctrine: the so-called "Good Samaritan" theory. Very briefly, under the Good Samaritan theory, when a party assumes an obligation to exercise due care where none otherwise exists, he is liable for damages if he breaches that assumed duty. The elements of the theory are conduct, reliance, and negligence. In the famous *Indian Towing*[8] case, the Supreme Court held the United States liable as a Good Samaritan for conduct (operating a lighthouse to guide ships), reliance (by the ships), and negligence (allowing the light to go out). In our briefs, we had argued that the government should be liable in the Franklin case as a Good Samaritan for conduct (bank examinations, orders, directives, suggestions, and follow-up), reliance (by the bank's management) and negligence (failing to detect and prevent the bank's losses).

On June 17, 1977, twenty two attorneys entered formal appearances to hear oral argument, and dozens more sat at counsel table, in the section of the court reserved for spectators, and even in the jury box.

Joan Bernott, an attorney from the Justice Department in Washington, appeared for the United States in support of the motion. I argued in opposition, as did Martin London, Aetna's lead attorney, and Dan Kolb, a partner at Davis, Polk & Wardwell, the attorney for the bank's outside auditors.

Although the attorneys spent considerable time at oral argument rehashing some rather abstruse legal contentions, the most revealing exchanges dealt with the Good Samaritan theory. Joan Bernott mentioned it first and tried to distinguish it:

> MS. BERNOTT: In *Indian Towing*, the government undertook the physical operation of a lighthouse beacon. This is not analogous to the government's role in relation to the banking system and member banks. Clearly, the government did not operate Franklin National Bank. I do not understand any of the pleadings to contend that. The government did not control the day-to-day activities of Franklin National Bank.

When it was my turn to argue, Judge Platt interrupted my discussion of the *Indian Towing* case to question me about Joan Bernott's remarks:

> MR. RIVKIN: The *Indian Towing* case, which counsel for the government referred to, is directly on point. If I may, Your Honor, in that case...
>
> THE COURT: Is that the lighthouse case?
>
> MR. RIVKIN: Yes, Your Honor. In that case, just like here, the government contended that they owed no duty of care. If the light went out, and all the ships at sea went down, the government's position was...
>
> THE COURT: But Ms. Bernott's argument, Mr. Rivkin, is that the government was operating the lighthouse. If the situation were comparable, the government would have been operating the bank. Is that what you're suggesting?

Nowhere in any of our pleadings or briefs did we explicitly state that the government had been "operating" Franklin National Bank. But by alleging that the government had examined the bank, met with the bank's senior management, issued and followed up on orders, directives, and suggestions, and participated in the bank's decision making process, we were certainly suggesting it. Moreover, as I pondered the judge's question, it seemed to me that I had better suggest it again if we were to have any chance of defeating the government's motion:

> MR. RIVKIN: Yes I am. Your Honor, there was no decision of any consequence made by the Franklin National Bank in the

last five years, according to a report issued by a Congressional subcommittee, that the Comptroller of the Currency did not take part in or even make. Take branch banking. They opened seventeen branch banks during this period. They could not open any of them unless the Comptroller examined their books and gave them permission. And that's only one example.

Later, Martin London, Aetna's attorney, made the very same point:

> MR. LONDON: I suggest, Your Honor, that the facts will show that long before October 1974 the government was perhaps even managing this bank. You asked before if they operated the bank, and counsel for the government said no, but I think the facts will show that the answer to that question is yes.

*   *   *

Seven months to the day after hearing oral argument, Judge Platt handed down a thunderbolt of a decision denying the government's motion to dismiss,[9] thus becoming the first and to this day the only judge to sustain the legal sufficiency of claims alleging that federal bank regulators acted negligently. Although the judge considered all of the issues raised by the government's motion, the key portion of his thirty-seven-page opinion focused on the Good Samaritan theory. After acknowledging that the government could not be liable under the FTCA for mere negligent bank regulation, the judge ruled, citing *Indian Towing*, that the government could be liable under the FTCA as a Good Samaritan if it "goes beyond its normal regulatory activities and substitutes its decisions for those of the bank's officers and directors."[10] In other words, the government could be liable if, as we had contended, it operated or managed Franklin.

This was an enormous victory for Fireman's Fund and strengthened our position in the litigation almost beyond measure. First, it gave us momentum. In major litigation, there are many interim decisions leading up to the final disposition. Some you win, others you lose. The wins propel you forward, boost your morale, and keep you going. Second, it put us in a position to control the pace of the litigation. No longer would we simply respond to the plaintiffs' claims against us; we could take the initiative by aggressively pursuing our claims against the United States. Third, it guaranteed us full disclosure from the government. Now that the court had confirmed the government's status as a party to the proceedings, as opposed to merely a non-party witness, the government would be hard pressed to argue that its obligation to produce witnesses and documents should be curtailed or limited to any significant degree. Fourth, it created the very real possibility that the government would end up paying for some or all of the bank's alleged losses, either through judgment or settlement. The case was all about money, and every dollar paid by the government might mean one less dollar paid by Fireman's Fund. And fifth, it strengthened our bargaining position. The parties had recently initiated settlement discussions but had gotten virtually nowhere, in large part due to the hard line position taken by the FDIC against the fidelity insurers. However, the government as a third-party defendant now faced enormous litigation expenses in addition to its potential liability. Accordingly, we envisioned a scenario whereby the government would exert pressure on the FDIC to temper its settlement demands in order to bring the litigation to a rapid and inexpensive conclusion.

The court's decision was also an enormous victory for my firm. Early on in the litigation, while we were vigorously advocating the idea of suing the United States, firms representing other parties were recommending against it. While Bob Buell enthusiastically supported our proposal, others inside Fireman's Fund were skeptical. While others doubted that claims against the government would survive a motion to dismiss, we worked hard to collect evidence and develop legal arguments. While we did not defeat the government's motion alone, we played a major role. The court's decision vindicated our strategy and hard work. It demonstrated that we could litigate as equals with and against the biggest and best firms in New York City. And it established our reputation as expert Federal Tort Claims Act litigators, thus leading to our subsequent involvement in other important cases against the government, including Agent Orange and asbestos.

*   *   *

If at First You Don't Succeed

The government refused to take no for an answer.

Shortly after Judge Platt denied its motion to dismiss, the government made a motion for reconsideration in which it asked the court to dismiss our third-party claims on the grounds that those claims were barred by the statute of limitations. In other words, the government argued that the fidelity insurers had failed to commence their third-party action against the United States within the prescribed statutory time limit.

Since the government had advanced this very same argument in its original motion to dismiss, which was denied, not surprisingly its motion for reconsideration met the same fate.[11]

Then, two months later, the government filed a second motion to dismiss. Although not specifically asking the court to reconsider its earlier decisions, the government's second motion essentially rehashed many of the same legal arguments previously rejected by the court. But the second motion also asserted, for the first time, public policy arguments regarding the alleged "chilling effect" that the court's earlier denial was having on the government's continuing obligation to regulate national banks.

Joan Bernott, representing the government, elaborated on that "chilling effect" at oral argument:

> MS. BERNOTT: This is an important case. The stakes are very high indeed. More than money is involved here. The failure of the 20th largest bank in the United States is important to every citizen of this country. And the operation of the bank regulatory agencies is equally important to them and to the future of our national as well as international economy. This court's decision nine months ago set a precedent in bank law in this country because it set sail in American Jurisprudence a theory by which the United States can be liable under the Federal Tort Claims Act from regulating or attempting to regulate a bank that fails.

> The fact of the matter, Your Honor, is that there are bank examiners all over this country in banks and they are trying to do their job. And it is hard for me to imagine that there doesn't come a time, especially when they are dealing with problem banks, that they start wondering exactly what is going on in Franklin and what they have the authority to do and what they don't have the authority to do.

> Congress has made its feelings on this crystal clear. Two years ago it published a report regarding Franklin which concluded that perhaps there was too little action by the Comptroller, too passive regulation, too lax supervision. So Congress gave the Comptroller the authority to pursue more aggressive action.

> But what does the examiner do when he is considering aggressive action in Ohio but the Comptroller is embroiled in expensive and protracted litigation in Brooklyn? How does the

Comptroller know what he can do without exposing the Government to enormous potential liability?

THE COURT: The trouble, counselor, is that I wrestled very long and hard over my decision to deny your first motion to dismiss. I think I am right. You think I am wrong. Everybody in the government, I am sure, thinks I am wrong. If you do think I'm wrong, your proper interim solution is to mandamus me to the Court of Appeals or ask me to certify the question for appellate review. But it really does no good to keep coming back and telling me I made a mistake.

MS. BERNOTT: Does this mean, Your Honor, that for time immemorial the United States is going to be a defendant in every bank failure case?

THE COURT: I don't think so. Look, I can tell you right now that when Judgment Day comes, if they can't come up and lay some facts before me which support their position, you are going to walk out of here with a little halo around your head, so stop worrying.

MS. BERNOTT: I'm afraid the United States may be walking out of actions like this for the next 20 or 30 years.

Judge Platt attempted to allay the government's fears with a little humor at my expense:

THE COURT: After they try a few times their clients will realize that this may be a futile thing. After all, the Government is paying for this but just think of what the insurance companies are paying Mr. Rivkin.

MS. BERNOTT: The stakes in this action are so high, Your Honor, that even Mr. Rivkin's salary can't make much of a dent in them.

THE COURT: Oh?

MR. RIVKIN: I haven't opened my mouth, Your Honor.

Those were my only words during oral argument on the government's second motion to dismiss. At the conclusion the government's presentation, Judge Platt denied the motion from the bench.

*   *   *

Still not satisfied, the government asked the court to certify its decision for immediate appellate review. This was necessary because, under applicable law, the government could not appeal the decision as of right. Once again, the court denied the government's motion, reasoning that an immediate appeal would further delay a lawsuit that was already nearly four years old.

*   *   *

In the midst of the government's repeated efforts to obtain a dismissal of the fidelity insurers' third-party complaints, the United States Court of Appeals for the Ninth Circuit scheduled oral argument on an appeal from a decision dismissing claims against the United States based upon negligent bank regulation. With Fireman's Fund's blessing, I flew to Seattle to attend the argument, which lasted less than one hour. I wanted to see for myself how the judges reacted to the various arguments for and against the disputed claims.

*   *   *

For Your Amusement

Also in the midst of the government's efforts to obtain a dismissal, the government was producing waves of documents in response to the parties' numerous discovery notices. One such document was a 1977 letter from an attorney for the Federal Reserve Bank of New York to the attorney for the FDIC forwarding a copy of one of the fidelity insurer's third-party complaints against the government. The Federal Reserve attorney wrote that he was forwarding the third-party complaint to his colleague "for your amusement."

We first saw that letter late in 1978, after the court had denied the government's second motion to dismiss, and wondered if the two attorneys were still laughing.

*   *   *

Light Moments

The Franklin case was serious business, but after appearing before Judge Platt dozens of times we were able to share an occasional light moment.

On July 1, 1977, a Friday, about twenty lawyers appeared before the judge to discuss the status of discovery, which was about twenty-five percent complete. Twenty jaws dropped when the judge began the proceedings as follows:

THE COURT: All right. We are here to find out when you fellows can go to trial. How about Monday?

THE CLERK: Monday is the 4th, Your Honor.

THE COURT: That shouldn't matter to anybody.

Later during that same hearing, the parties were discussing the issue of whether to try each of the consolidated cases separately or all together in one massive proceeding. Bill Kelly, representing the FDIC, and I were standing at the podium talking about the case against the fidelity insurers. Out of the blue, Bill mentioned his case against the bank's outside auditors. When that happened, Dan Kolb, the lead attorney for the auditors, stood up and approached the Bench:

MR. KELLY: I might point out, Your Honor, we haven't even discussed the case against the auditors. We are just getting started with that case. It may take three or four years just to get the discovery.

THE COURT: Mr. Kolb just stepped up here. I didn't want him here.

MR. KELLY: I saw him coming out of the corner of my eye.

THE COURT: He will complicate things. Don't go away, Mr. Rivkin. Mr. Kolb wasn't invited up here. He just came up here.

MR. RIVKIN: He's on my side, though, Judge.

MR. KOLB: May I be up here, Your Honor?

THE COURT: Why do you have to come up here and confuse us any more than we already are? We don't need you.

MR. KOLB: Your Honor, I wonder if you don't.

Dan then made an impressive presentation regarding how much more discovery was needed and how fast and expeditiously the parties were proceeding and concluded:

MR. KOLB: I might say I think all the defendants have been committed to the diligent prosecution of the case. We are proceeding under discovery schedules which are at least as fast, if not faster, than the FDIC's schedule, so that the matter can be disposed of in much less than fifteen years, as Your Honor alluded to earlier.

MR. RIVKIN: We're shooting for ten, Judge.

* * *

The FDIC and Trustee Take the Initiative

In April 1978, two years into the lawsuit, the FDIC and the Trustee took the initiative by making a motion for a separate trial of their claims against the fidelity insurers beginning in September. As envisioned by the FDIC and Trustee, the September trial would include only their claims against the fidelity insurers and not any of the fidelity insurers' third-party claims against the government, the bank's outside auditors, the bank's directors, and Continental Bank. Those claims would be severed and tried, if necessary, at an unspecified later date.

The FDIC and the Trustee would have gained a significant upper hand in their dispute with the fidelity insurers had the court ordered a separate September trial. For one thing, the FDIC and the Trustee were fully prepared to try the case in September, since they had already completed virtually all of the discovery they needed relating to insurance coverage issues. In contrast, it would have been next to impossible for the fidelity insurers to fully prepare for a September trial, since their discovery needs were much broader than those of their adversaries and no way could the insurers have completed that discovery in just six months. For another, the FDIC and Trustee apparently preferred to resolve the various Franklin lawsuits in a series of proceedings, each one focusing on a particular defendant or group of defendants. In contrast, the fidelity insurers wanted to pay their attorneys to try the case only once. Were they to lose to the FDIC and Trustee, they would face the prospect of paying their lawyers for a second, nearly identical trial against the third-party defendants.

* * *

We Respond in Kind

Since it was vitally important for us to defeat the FDIC's and Trustee's motion, not only did we submit an opposing affidavit and memorandum of law in which we forcefully argued against the proposed September trial date and the severance of our third-party claims, but also we attempted to retake the initiative by making our own motion that sought affirmative relief that was diametrically opposed to the relief sought by the FDIC and the Trustee.

For years, we had been attempting to depose certain key members of Franklin's senior management, including the bank's Chairman, President, Vice Chairman, Executive Vice President, Vice Chairman of the International Executive Committee, and Mr. Sindona himself, who was the bank's controlling shareholder and the Chairman of the International Executive Committee. We needed this testimony to bolster our "alter ego" defense. Each of these individuals, however, had either been indicted or named as an unindicted co-conspirator on charges relating to Franklin's collapse. Two of them had already pleaded guilty to Franklin related charges but had not yet been sentenced. Accordingly, all of them refused to testify at depositions in the civil Franklin litigation, claiming their 5th Amendment privilege against self- incrimination.

In our motion, we reported these facts to the court and requested an order stating that no trial date in any of the Franklin civil cases would be set and no ruling on severance would be made until such time as the criminal investigation of Franklin was over and the crucial testimony of the bank's controlling officers and directors became available.

I did not expect to win this motion. Instead, I made it to give Judge Platt a way out in our favor. This judge frequently looked to take the middle road. My hope was that, in this instance, taking the middle road meant that the judge would deny both motions. That would not guarantee my obtaining the directors' crucial testimony, but it would eliminate the specter of a separate September trial.

Aside from offering the judge a middle road solution to the question of whether to sever our third-party claims and order a separate September trial, our motion served a second extremely important strategic purpose.

For years, the FDIC and the Trustee had been bombarding the judge with papers describing the allegedly dishonest and fraudulent acts committed by low level employees in the bank's foreign exchange and investment departments. According to these papers, the employees had violated bank rules and regulations, entered into unauthorized foreign exchange and securities transactions, falsified bank records, committed crimes, been indicted, pled guilty, and served jail time. The papers also described the huge foreign exchange and investment department losses suffered by the bank. Reading these papers, the judge very well may have wondered what possible defenses could the insurance companies have to such seemingly airtight fidelity claims.

In our motion, we provided the judge with factual and legal support for just such a defense: the "alter ego" theory. We did not just mention that defense by name, we cited and explained the cases that supported it. We did not just mention the names of the bank's senior managers whose testimony was relevant to that defense, we explained what we expected them to say and what others had said that tended to establish it. Reading our papers, the judge very well may have wondered why the FDIC and Trustee were so eager for a trial date on claims that the insurance companies were likely to defeat.

*   *   *

The Decision

Judge Platt listened to oral argument on the severance/trial date motions three times over the course of five months before issuing his decision.

The first time the motions were argued, Judge Platt stated right at the outset that he was inclined to grant severance because the issues were too numerous and too complex for the entire case to be tried at one time before one jury. So I stood up and explained to the judge why severance was not the answer. The main reason was that the same witnesses and the same documentary evidence would be utilized by the insurers in defense of the FDIC's and Trustee's coverage claims and in the prosecution of the insurers' third-party claims. Therefore, severance could conceivably result in two or more lengthy, virtually identical trials, grinding the court's other business to a halt and creating the possibility of inconsistent verdicts. I must have said something right, because at the close of argument Judge Platt said: "Well, I thought this would be an easy one to decide. Now I guess I'll have to go and read the briefs and affidavits."

By the date of the last oral argument, which happened to take place in September, Judge Platt had done a complete about face. He began by stating that he was not inclined to order an immediate trial date or rule on the severance issue at that time. Thus, the judge had decided, at least for the moment, to take the exact middle road we envisioned when we filed our "alter ego" motion.

Several minutes into the judge's opening remarks, I stood up to say something, but the judge cut me off: "Mr. Rivkin, you know, when you're ahead and the judge is arguing for you, you don't really have to say anything."

Bill Purcell, the Trustee's attorney, then attempted to change the court's mind. But Judge Platt stood firm:

> THE COURT: The more I have thought about it, and believe me I have thought about it, right into the wee hours of the morning, I've become convinced that the only solution to this problem is to deny severance and try this case non-jury. I just don't see how I can, consistent with my obligations to the rest of the court, try this case in successive jury actions. It is just an impossible thought....To try and retry the issues in separate jury trials would bring everything in this court to a shrieking halt.

I would have been happy if the proceedings had ended at that moment, but Judge Platt then made some observations about the alter ego defense indicating that our strategy of educating him about that theory may have paid off.

> THE COURT: Does it make sense to force people on to trial when perhaps by virtue of testimony that they would eventually get they are going to establish a defense?
>
> COUNSEL FOR THE FDIC: Here is where I hate to get into the merits of it, Your Honor. We don't think it will establish a defense.
>
> THE COURT: Suppose the bank's chairman knew about unrecorded foreign exchange contracts.
>
> COUNSEL FOR THE FDIC: We say it wouldn't be a defense.
>
> THE COURT: And directed the traders.
>
> COUNSEL FOR THE FDIC: No defense. The entire Board of Directors has to know and authorize it.
>
> THE COURT: Let us assume that the Chairman—I am talking like Rivkin now —
>
> MR. RIVKIN: Thank you for that, Judge.
>
> THE COURT: Let us assume...
>
> MR. RIVKIN: Brilliant comments coming from the bench....
>
> THE COURT: Let us assume that the Chairman brought it up at every board meeting. He told all the directors this was going on and it was going on at the direction of Mr. Sindona and the bank had to do it for these various reasons to survive and so forth.

In litigation, there are few things a lawyer likes better than when the judge argues the case on the lawyer's behalf.

* * *

Making Headlines: Grand Jury Leaks

In the spring of 1978, during discovery, we learned that FBI agents who were assisting the ongoing criminal investigation into Franklin's collapse may have violated the rule of grand jury secrecy by disseminating reports about matters that had transpired before the grand jury to the Comptroller's Office, the Federal Reserve, and the FDIC.

Three years earlier, Judge Platt had observed that "the government is involved in this case up to its ears." Suddenly, those words took on a very ominous tone. The judge was referring to the FDIC, the Comptroller, and the Federal Reserve. But was the FBI also involved? Was the FBI "leaking" secret grand jury information to the banking agencies to assist them in their civil lawsuit? What other illegal acts had the FBI or the United States Attorney's Office in Manhattan or the Justice Department in Washington committed to further the banking agencies' position?

Since one of federal agencies that may have benefitted from the FBI's largesse was suing my client for upwards of $45 million, we felt we were entitled to answers and satisfaction. Accordingly, we made a motion seeking a wide variety of relief, some of it rather drastic and unprecedented. We requested an evidentiary hearing to determine the number and nature of grand jury violations; an order prohibiting the FDIC was utilizing the services of a foreign exchange expert who had also assisted the grand jury and was privy to confidential grand jury information; an order directing the production to Fireman's Fund of all grand jury material and transcripts; and, if the violations proved sufficiently serious, an order dismissing the FDIC's complaint.

To my surprise, reporters from three New York newspapers, including the *Times*, were among the people who crowded into the packed court room for oral argument, where I charged that the FBI reports in question could very well be "the tip of the iceberg." I also observed that the days of "Ellsberg, Watergate, the whole thing" were apparently not behind us.

The next morning, the normally staid *Times* reported that FBI agents had distributed the reports "in violation of the law and against specific orders of federal prosecutors" and that the dissemination comes on the heels of the indictment of L. Patrick Gray 3d, former acting F.B.I. director, and two other former top bureau officials, last April, on charges that they had authorized burglaries and illegal searches, and of disclosures of a pattern of illegal wiretaps, break-ins, mail-opening and harassment of political dissidents by F.B.I. agents.

The article also reported that the White House had been contacted about the distribution of the FBI reports and had "no comment."[12]

Ultimately, however, no scandal materialized. After reviewing the disputed documents *in camera* and speaking privately with the Assistant United States Attorney in charge of the grand jury, Judge Platt determined that the dissemination had been inadvertent and inconsequential and denied my motion in its entirety.

* * *

More Headlines: Indictments and Trials

The criminal investigation of Franklin made more headlines in July 1978, following an announcement by the United States Attorney's Office in Manhattan that Franklin's former Chairman of the Board, President, and Senior Vice President had been indicted by the grand jury. The indictment charged the three officers with falsifying bank records to conceal more than $5 million in losses in the bank's foreign exchange and investment departments. The indictment also named Michele Sindona, the bank's largest single shareholder, as an unindicted co-conspirator, along with three other former bank officers and directors, including its Vice Chairman and Executive Vice Chairman, both of whom had previously pleaded guilty to similar charges.

When I heard the news, I telephoned Bob Buell in San Francisco immediately. "It's a whole new ball game!" I shouted. He probably would have heard me if I had just yelled out of my open window.

The reason for my excitement was that these latest criminal charges promised to provide us with overwhelming support for our two key affirmative defenses to the FDIC's and Trustee's insurance coverage claims.

Pursuant to the "alter ego" defense, we alleged that the officers, directors, and stockholders who exercised total and complete control over the bank's affairs participated in or had knowledge of the allegedly dishonest and fraudulent acts. Thanks to the indictment, we could now reasonably expect to implicate or involve the bank's controlling stockholder, Chairman of the Board, President, Executive Vice Chairman, Vice Chairman, and Senior Vice President.

"Even a small time country lawyer from Garden City ought to be able to convince a jury that this group exercised total and complete control over Franklin's affairs," I told Bob.

Pursuant to our "one claim" defense, we alleged that regardless of the number of separate foreign exchange and investment department losses claimed by the FDIC and Trustee, their combined total recovery was limited to one claim, that is, one policy limit of $15 million. This defense was based upon language in the policies that, in effect, limited coverage to $15 million for all losses in which the same person or persons were "concerned or implicated." Before the indictment, all we had was evidence that one group of low-level bank employees were "concerned or implicated" in the foreign exchange losses and a second group of low-level employees were "concerned or implicated" in the investment department losses. Under that scenario, the fidelity insurers' maximum exposure was two policy limits, or $30 million. Now, thanks to the indictment, we could reasonably expect to "concern or implicate" six members of the bank's senior management in both the foreign exchange and investment department losses, thus cutting the fidelity insurers' maximum exposure in half.

*　*　*

The criminal case against Franklin's former Chairman, President, and Senior Vice President made more headlines when it went to trial in December.

Some of the testimony from that trial was spellbinding. Regarding Sindona's ability to control Franklin's affairs, one former director testified:

Q. To your knowledge, sir, did Mr. Sindona utilize large sums of money to bribe people to assist him in his various activities?

A. Yes.

Q. Including, for example, Franklin's Executive Vice President?

A. Yes, sir.

Q. To your knowledge he bribed Franklin's Executive Vice President?

A. Yes, Sir.

Q. We're talking about the $476,000?

A. Yes, sir.

Q. Which you and Mr. Sindona caused to be placed in the Executive Vice President's secret bank account?

A. Yes, sir.

Q. You participated in that, didn't you?

A. Yes.

Q. And that was done to influence the Executive Vice President?

A. Yes, sir.

Q. To do what Mr. Sindona wanted him to do?

A. Yes, sir.

Regarding Sindona's knowledge of and participation the foreign exchange frauds, the bank's former Executive Vice President testified:

Q. In May of 1972, did you participate in a phony foreign exchange transaction?

A. Yes, sir.

Q. Did that come about at the instance of Mr. Sindona?

A. Indirectly, yes.

Q. Did you speak to Sindona about that at that time?

A. I did.

Q. Had you previously informed Mr. Sindona that there was going to be a loss in foreign exchange at Franklin for the month of May, 1973?

A. I did.

Q. Did he then say to you "speak with my associate on the board of the holding company, he will take your losses and we can have some gains?"

A. That's correct.

Q. Did you then speak with Mr. Sindona's associate?

A. I did. I made a deal with him to pass a loss position off Franklin's books on to the books of Bank Unione [an Italian bank owned by Sindona].

Q. That was a non-arms length transaction, was it not?

A. That's correct.

Q. That was a transaction not at the prevailing rates for foreign exchange?

A. That's correct.

Q. That was a phony transaction.

A. That's correct.

That same Executive Vice President also implicated that bank's former Chairman of the Board in the foreign exchange fraud:

A. I went to the Chairman's office. Sindona's associate who was a director of the holding company was in there. I said to the Chairman, "You will get your $700,000. Sindona's associate has arranged it." Then the Chairman looked at his watch and it was obviously time for the International Executive Committee meeting. So the Chairman picked up his books, walked to the door, the door between his office and the committee meeting, and as he was passing through the door, I said, "I am not sure that it is legal, you know," and as he went out he said, "Then don't discuss it."

The former director who testified about Sindona's bribes also implicated the Chairman in the foreign exchange losses:

A. What I mean to say is that I asked the Chairman what the problem was, and he answered that he had been informed that the foreign exchange department of Franklin National Bank would show a loss at the end of that month, that is, March 1974, and that something had to be done, I had to help him, because otherwise he was to be a ruined man and he would have to resign because of this, because the bank, the corporation, would have no money to pay dividends to the shareholders.

Finally, the bank's former Vice Chairman implicated both the Chairman and the President in the investment department losses:

A. The bank's President told me in substance that if the outside auditors could be convinced that he had instructed me to transfer the $100 million of government securities from the trading account to the portfolio, if he had told me this on March 8, the auditors might agree to valuing those securities as of the next business day, which would have been March 11.

Q. Did anyone join that meeting during the conversation or at any point in the conversation?

A. Yes. As I was leaving the President's office, I remember the Chairman being present.

Q. Do you know if the Chairman's office adjoins the President's?

A. It did. There was a passageway between.

Q. Was there any further conversation after the Chairman arrived?

A. As I was leaving the office the President said to me, "I am sorry to have to ask you to do this, but there are some things that we have to do for the good of the bank," and I remember the Chairman being there, putting his hand on my shoulder and saying, "Good luck."

* * *

The obvious result of Franklin's collapse was the loss of huge sums of money. But, sadly, the bank's demise permanently altered and even ruined the lives of men who, prior to the collapse, had been respected New York bankers. Although steadfastly maintaining their innocence throughout the trial, the Chairman, President, and Senior Vice President were all found guilty as charged. After noting his "firm conviction" that the verdicts were amply supported by the evidence and that a "significant penalty" was required to deter future misconduct, the judge sentenced the Chairman and President to three years in jail and the Senior Vice President to one year.

The Chairman's remarks at his sentencing hearing were particularly poignant:

THE DEFENDANT: Being sentenced as a Federal felon is an unbelievably sad time for me and my family. But I do not stand here with any guilt in my heart or mind. I know I am innocent of the charges and I rest easy that in God's eyes I am innocent. I never knew that Franklin National Bank issued false statements. I was just another one of Mr. Sindona's victims.

* * *

Recusal

On December 1, 1978, Judge Platt unexpectedly recused himself from the Franklin litigation. All of the cases were thereafter reassigned to Judge Jack B. Weinstein.

The incident leading to Judge Platt's recusal occurred in open court on Halloween day, October 31, 1979. As subsequently reported in The New York *Times*, Judge Platt began a pretrial conference that afternoon by reading a parody of the Franklin case prepared by his deputy court clerk. Since Judge Platt later placed all copies of the clerk's parody under seal, and since the seal remains in effect to this day, I cannot discuss what the clerk wrote or what Judge Platt said, except to say that the *Times* characterized the parody "as a spoof involving numerous participants in the litigation, including a number of prominent law firms and even Judge Platt." The *Times* also reported that the parody made Sindona the butt of a joke.[13]

A few days later, the law firm representing Sindona in the civil litigation wrote a letter to Judge Platt "formally and strenuously" objecting to the parody and asking Judge Platt "to consider recusal from any further matters in which Mr. Sindona is involved."

To no one's surprise, Judge Platt refused to disqualify himself from the litigation because of his reading of the parody, which virtually all of us considered harmless fun. But to everyone's surprise, Judge Platt disqualified himself anyway. The reason, as reported in the *Times*: Judge Platt's son, a law student, had accepted a summer job at one of the firms involved in the Franklin case.

*   *   *

Judge Weinstein Takes the Initiative

Early in March of 1979, Judge Weinstein scheduled his first status conference.

At the time, Judge Weinstein had a well-earned reputation as a mover and shaker. He liked to get his cases resolved as quickly as possible. He considered himself a trial judge, not a motion or discovery judge. I was concerned about how he would react to a case that had been pending for nearly four years.

"Good afternoon, everybody," Judge Weinstein greeted the more than forty lawyers who attended. "I understand that I now have the case. Ready or not. This is kind of an informal briefing session, as I understand it, that counsel thought would be useful. So I'll listen."

The conference lasted about one hour. The parties addressed many topics but made little headway.

"Anything else?" Judge Weinstein asked as he rose to leave the bench. "Well, shall we adjourn this unproductive session? All right."

One week later, Judge Weinstein held another hearing at which he acted more like himself. He began to probe and push. He asked a lot of questions. When he was not happy with an answer, he let us know it:

THE COURT: What is the outside risk you face?

COUNSEL FOR THE AUDITORS: It has never been calculated. I must say that we don't think there is a tremendous amount of exposure at all here. But if you take a worst case situation, a theoretical figure, I don't know what that is. It is a lot, I suppose, if you imagine everything. But I don't know what it is.

THE COURT: It is very strange to me. Nobody knows what this case is about.

COUNSEL FOR THE AUDITORS: Well, Your Honor, if...

THE COURT: What do you tell your clients when, I don't want to pry, but what do you tell them when they ask you why you are sending them such big bills?

When he did not want a particular subject addressed, he told us in no uncertain terms:

COUNSEL FOR THE GOVERNMENT: First of all, the waiver argument. This...

THE COURT: I am not interested. Don't spend any time on it.

COUNSEL FOR THE GOVERNMENT (on another subject): If other courts had agreed with that reasoning...

THE COURT: Excuse me. I am simply not interested in what other courts have done. I have read all the cases you've given me, and they don't help me one whit.

When the parties properly placed an issue before him, such as whether the government was obligated to produce in discovery the confidential sections of examination reports of Franklin prepared by the Comptroller's Office, he resolved it quickly and completely:

THE COURT: Now, that covers all of these so-called reports of examination. Is that clear? The whole thing gets revealed. Nothing is excepted.

COUNSEL FOR THE GOVERNMENT: Yes, Your Honor.

THE COURT: That applies not only for these particular years, these critical years, but all the earlier years, up through and including 1974.

COUNSEL FOR THE GOVERNMENT: From 1962?

THE COURT: To 1974, the whole bit, so that will simplify everything. You won't have to go through it document by document.

Two weeks later, Judge Weinstein sent a memorandum to all counsel requesting suggestions for background reading about banking in general and the Franklin case in particular. Most of the lead firms responded. The suggestions included earlier written decisions in the case, court transcripts, the Purchase and Assumption Agreement between the FDIC and European American Bank, FDIC news releases, magazine and law review articles, congressional hearing reports, speeches, banking texts, and even a novel described by Martin London as "a somewhat useful, albeit fictional, introduction to the arcane world of foreign exchange trading."

Knowing Judge Weinstein, I had no doubt that he read every item, including the novel.

*   *   *

On May 1, 1979, Judge Weinstein sent another memorandum to all counsel in which he expressed his concern about "the slow pace at which these actions are progressing. They are now the oldest cases on my docket." He advised us of his intention to begin trying the cases "this summer." He requested the parties to immediately submit suggestions for how to structure and conduct the trials. He scheduled a pretrial conference for May 14.

In response to the judge's request for trial management suggestions, thirteen firms submitted separate proposals totaling nearly sixty pages containing their differing views on issues such as the status of discovery, trial dates, severance, order of trials, order of proof, jury versus non-jury trials, and the 5th Amendment.

At the conference, Judge Weinstein put on a memorable demonstration of his remarkable ability to move even the most complex matter toward a speedy resolution.

He began by urging the assembled attorneys to settle the case rather than to try it:

THE COURT: Good morning, everybody. We are here this morning, I think, essentially to try to work out a trial schedule. Assuming the case should be tried. I don't believe, myself, it should be tried, based on the preliminary reading I have done. It seems to me that there isn't that much to it. It should be settled. Some of the claims are just extravagant. But if you want a trial, I'll give it to you.

But the trial he was willing to give us was not one that any of the parties wanted: a twenty day jury trial where all of the claims by and against all of the parties would be litigated together in one proceeding, even though most of the lawyers on the case had estimated that such a trial would require from six months to one year, and where most of the evidence would be presented on paper, either documents or deposition transcripts, even though most of the lawyers preferred to try their cases using live witnesses.

THE COURT: I am going to try the whole shebang at once, in one trial, because it is going to be repetitive otherwise and I am not going to try these cases over and over again. It will be a six-person jury, with four alternates, probably, or maybe six alternates, in light of the time it will take. I am assuming about 20 trial days for the case, which means you are going to have to Xerox all your papers that are admitted into evidence. Each juror will get a full set of all your documents. Any depositions you want to put in, you can put in. They'll be Xeroxed. The jury will get them. They'll take them home with them. If you want any reports in, they'll be Xeroxed. The jury will take them home.

We will probably have to take a break in the middle of the case at various points so that the jury can work at home or come in here and work because I am not going to sit around while they read these things in court. And you will each get a certain number of days to put in your case and that will be it. You can use your time any way you want to.

After rejecting my request to postpone setting a firm trial date until after all 5th Amendment issues had been resolved, the judge scheduled jury selection for the morning of October 2. "Because this is a complex case," he told us, "jury selection should take about two hours." Most of the parties had estimated that jury selection would take at least two weeks. He scheduled opening statements for the afternoon of October 2. That came out to about fifteen minutes per attorney. He set aside only two days for summations, less than sixty minutes per side. He indicated that he would require but one hour to instruct the jury on the vast body of law relating to fidelity insurance coverage, accountant's liability, officer's and director's liability, class action stockholder derivative lawsuits, misrepresentation, and the Federal Tort Claims Act.

In light of the severe time constraints he was putting us under, Judge Weinstein suggested that we "clear out all of the peripheral junk, because if you can't tell a Brooklyn jury what your case is about in a half hour and put on all your evidence in four or five days, you can forget it." He urged us to meet to try to work out stipulations, limit issues, and reach agreements on orders of proof and allotment of trial time.

Any such meeting, of course, would have been an exercise in futility, and Judge Weinstein knew it. Thus far in the litigation, the parties had been unable to stipulate or agree to virtually anything of substance. Moreover, there was no way that the FDIC, the Trustee in Bankruptcy, the class action plaintiffs, the three fidelity insurance companies, the outside auditors, Continental Bank, the two firms representing the bank's outside directors, the seven firms representing the various inside directors, and the United States of America ever could have agreed on how to allocate twenty days of trial and two days of summation. I needed at least twenty days of trial and two days of summation just for myself, and most of the other lead attorneys in the case probably felt the same way.

But Judge Weinstein urged us to have these meetings anyway, and his purpose was clear. It was not a trial management agreement he was looking for, but a settlement agreement. Thus, when Dan Kolb, the attorney for the bank's outside auditors, complained that the FDIC was withholding certain damage information, the judge replied:

> THE COURT: I expect you to get together sensibly as attorneys and work it out. They'll get together with you.
>
> They don't want to try the case this way any more than you do.

* * *

To the extent that Judge Weinstein's plan was to nudge the parties toward settlement, it worked. Before the end of the conference, several attorneys specifically requested that the judge himself get involved in settlement efforts:

> COUNSEL FOR THE CLASS PLAINTIFFS: Your Honor, what I am trying to suggest to you is that the parties apparently on their own cannot get together for one or more reasons. What I am suggesting is that if your Honor really wants to play the role of settlement judge, that...
>
> THE COURT: I do not want to play any role. I have played whatever role counsel wants me to play. If counsel wants me

to play any role, I will be delighted to play it. But I have no desire one way or the other. I could not care less about this case or more about it. As far as I am concerned, this case has got about as much appeal as an intersection case in Bay Ridge, Brooklyn, involving a fifty thousand dollar broken leg. It does not mean anything to me. So I will do whatever I have to do with this. It is just one case like any other.

COUNSEL FOR THE CLASS PLAINTIFFS: Your Honor, I'm not suggesting that you get emotionally involved in the problem. What I am suggesting is that maybe your emotions will get less involved if we approach this thing by getting together on a specific date.

The judge agreed to do so if all of the parties wanted it. Accordingly, at the request of the attorney for the Trustee in Bankruptcy, all of the attorneys remained in the courtroom after the hearing was over to discuss the possibility of involving the judge in settlement talks.

*   *   *

Sindona Vanishes

On August 2, 1979, as discovery in the civil litigation was winding down and settlement negotiations were heating up, Michele Sindona disappeared.

The press declared that he had been kidnapped. "I fear my father is already dead," his son told reporters and the F.B.I.[14]

At the time of his disappearance, Sindona was in serious trouble. Five months earlier, he had been indicted by a federal grand jury in Manhattan on ninety-nine counts of fraud, conspiracy, and misapplication of bank funds. This same grand jury had been investigating Franklin's collapse since 1975 and had previously indicted six former directors of the bank. As Franklin's controlling shareholder, Sindona was the key to our "alter ego" defense, and the indictment supported that defense by alleging that Sindona had directed efforts by the bank's senior managers in 1973 and 1974 to fraudulently generate profits and conceal losses. The indictment also charged that Sindona had purchased his $40 million interest in Franklin with money embezzled from banks he owned in Italy and that he had stolen more than $45 million from Franklin by illegally transferring funds from Franklin to his Italian banks. If convicted, Sindona faced up to five years in prison on each count.

In addition, Sindona was embroiled in proceedings to extradite him to Italy to face criminal charges that he embezzled $300 million from two of his Italian banks. He was vigorously opposing extradition, arguing that the charges against him were politically motivated and that his life would be in danger if he were returned to his native country.

Sindona was also a defendant in more than one dozen civil lawsuits in the federal court in Brooklyn. The parties suing Sindona included the Securities and Exchange Commission, the FDIC, the Trustee in Bankruptcy, thousands of Franklin shareholders, the fidelity insurers, the bank's outside auditors, and several of Sindona's fellow former directors. The suits alleged that Sindona stole millions of dollars from Franklin and was primarily responsible for the bank's collapse. The parties sought tens of millions dollars in damages.

Apart from his legal problems, at the time of his disappearance Sindona financial empire, once estimated at $500 million, was in shambles. Franklin was the first Sindona bank to fail but not the last; at least four other banks he controlled in Italy and Switzerland were also in liquidation.

Supposedly, he was broke. He owed more than $1 million in legal fees. Nevertheless, he was living in an opulent apartment in the Hotel Pierre. He claimed he could afford the apartment only because of "the charity of friends in Italy who were sending him funds."[15]

There were also the rumors. One year before his disappearance, the FDIC had filed a civil lawsuit against the American businessman who had sold Sindona his controlling interest in Franklin. Among other things, the FDIC alleged that, prior to the sale, the businessman, as controlling shareholder, owed the bank a fiduciary duty to investigate Sindona's background and that, had he done so, he would have discovered that Sindona was not an acceptable purchaser because of his "underworld connections." The complaint contained no particulars but lead to all sorts of speculation: Sindona was a "Don" in the Sicilian Mafia; he was the mastermind behind efforts by the American Mafia to infiltrate legitimate businesses throughout the world; he was the Mafia's primary money launderer.

Then were was Sindona's Vatican connection. Supposedly, he was the "Pope's Banker," in charge of the Vatican's huge investment portfolio. According to the rumors, in the late 1960s, fearing a change in Italy's tax laws, Sindona masterminded a scheme of dubious legality to shield the Vatican's profits on the Italian stock market from the new laws utilizing a series of off-shore corporations. In other words, he laundered the Vatican's money the same way he laundered the Mafia's. But not very successfully, apparently, since at the time of his disappearance the Italian press was reporting that the Vatican's losses through its dealings with Sindona totaled nearly $100 million.

And his political connections. In the United States, his good friend was a former Secretary of the Treasury under President Richard Nixon. In Italy, his good friends were members of a group known as P-2, a Masonic Lodge which engaged in extreme right wing political activity in Italy and South America. Supposedly, Sindona had financed a P-2 plan, canceled at the last minute, for a military overthrow of the Italian government.

Under these circumstances, Sindona's disappearance, or kidnapping, was hardly a surprise.

*   *   *

Sindona reappeared three months later with a bullet wound in his leg that had been inflicted while he was under anesthesia. He later admitted that his kidnapping had been a hoax.

The criminal fraud case against Sindona went to trial in Manhattan in March 1980. During the course of the trial, allegations surfaced that Sindona had hired a man to threaten the life of the Assistant United States Attorney who was prosecuting the case. At the conclusion of the trial, the jury found Sindona guilty on all but one count of the indictment. Two days before his scheduled sentencing, he apparently attempted suicide by ingesting an overdose of a heart stimulant and slashing his wrists. Ultimately, the court sentenced Sindona to twenty five years in prison and fined him $207,000.

But Sindona did not spend his last days in an American jail. In 1984, he was extradited to Italy, where he was tried and convicted of fraud stemming from the failure of one of his Italian banks. He was sentenced to twelve years in prison.

Then, as if to lend an aura of truth to all of the sinister charges and rumors regarding the so-called "Mystery Man" of Italian finance, an Italian court convicted Sindona of murder. The victim was the government appointed liquidator of Sindona's financial interests in Italy, who was gunned down in 1979 in front of his home in Milan. Sindona was convicted of hiring the Mafia marksman who did the shooting.

Four days after receiving a life sentence for the liquidator's death, Sindona himself died under mysterious circumstances. In his Italian jail cell, even though he was heavily guarded and his food came in sealed containers, somehow he had managed to ingest a lethal dose of cyanide. Was it suicide or murder? That was the last of many questions we had asked ourselves about Sindona that never were answered.

*　　*　　*

One More Time

Just before Sindona's temporary disappearance in 1979, another Franklin litigant, the United States of America, made its fifth attempt to permanently disappear from the proceedings.

Following its motion to dismiss the fidelity insurers' third-party claims, it's motion for reconsideration, its second motion to dismiss, and its motion for certification for appellate review, all of which were denied, the government moved in the spring of 1979 for summary judgment.

In support of its motion, the government argued that in spite of generating more than 100,000 pages of deposition testimony and compelling the production of more than one million pages of documents, the parties had produced not one shred of evidence in support of their claims of governmental liability.

We, of course, thought otherwise, and submitted three volumes of exhibits to support our contention that the government had gone "beyond its normal regulatory activities and substituted its decisions for those of the bank's officers and directors."

To our shock, Judge Weinstein agreed with the government, ruling in a lengthy opinion that we had

> totally failed to establish a sufficient factual basis for...the claim that the bank regulatory agencies somehow exceeded their regulatory authority or actually managed Franklin. At their best, the third-party plaintiffs' assertions constitute only those "conclusory allegations" and "unsupportable claims" that summary judgment motions are intended to eliminate.[16]

Nevertheless, to the government's shock, Judge Weinstein denied the motion for "practical considerations." Judge Weinstein acknowledged that he was impressed by the government's "persuasive arguments for granting summary judgment" and that the "claims against the government were highly unlikely ultimately to prevail." Nevertheless, the judge explained that dismissing the government from the lawsuit would "not expedite the proceedings" or "shorten the trial"; that the issues raised by the claims against the government would be litigated even if the government were not a party;[17] that keeping the government in the case would "insure a more full and fair development of the evidence"; and that the Second Circuit, which applied notoriously stringent standards to the disposition of summary judgment motions, might reverse a decision granting the motion, thus forcing "a costly and inefficient retrial."[18]

But the most important factor in Judge Weinstein's decision, not surprisingly, was his determination to bring about a settlement:

> Extensive settlement conferences have been conducted by the Court and the parties. The Comptroller's Office is a necessary participant in any realistic appraisal of the various claims. One of the three directors of the FDIC, which has the key role in settlement discussions, is the Comptroller of the Currency. The court expects the Comptroller, among others, to utilize his knowledge and experience in discussions leading towards settlement. It is the court's view that the probabilities of settlement will be enhanced if the motion for summary judgment is not granted at this time.[19]

As the judge had explained during oral argument: "I'm trying to practically settle a litigation. I'm not developing an ethereal concept of the law."

And earlier: "I have never tried a case like this. Nobody has. Nobody tries cases like this, because most lawyers and clients are too sensible to allow a case like this to go to trial."

Clearly, Judge Weinstein was issuing a challenge to the lawyers and clients in the Franklin case. It remained to be seen whether we could meet it.

* * *

Settlement

Long before Judge Weinstein began urging the parties to negotiate rather than litigate, Bob Buell of Fireman's Fund had initiated settlement discussions with an in-house attorney employed by the FDIC. As frequently happens with aggressive litigators, the trial attorneys in the Franklin case had become so hardened in their positions that neither side was willing to make even the slightest concessions for settlement purposes. Therefore, Bill Kelly, the lead trial attorney for the FDIC, and I, as lead counsel for Fireman's Fund, agreed to let our clients speak to each other directly. Our feeling was that since the clients did not personally participate in depositions, motion practice, brief writing, and oral argument, where emotions ran the hottest, perhaps they could look at the issues a bit more dispassionately and make some inroads.

Bob Buell was bright, tough, and experienced. I had no problem with Bob carrying the ball for Fireman's Fund at these initial sessions.

*   *   *

Bob met with the FDIC attorney in San Francisco in July of 1977, but all that happened at that first meeting was a failure to communicate. At the time, the FDIC was seeking to recover a total of $45 million from the three insurance companies on the basis of two separate $15 million foreign exchange claims and one $15 million investment department claim. Bob came away from the meeting thinking that the FDIC's opening settlement demand had been $15 million but that the FDIC was willing to negotiate downward. The FDIC's attorney came away from the meeting thinking that his opening settlement demand had been $15 million but that Fireman's Fund had to be willing to negotiate upward. Talk about a difference of opinion! Each side was so indignant over what it claimed was a lack of candor by the other that it took more than fifteen months to get the parties together again.

*   *   *

Bob and the FDIC attorney ultimately scheduled their second meeting for early November 1978 at the FDIC's offices in Washington, D.C. Bob asked me to fly down the day before and stay overnight to prep him. I arrived late in the afternoon and met Bob at the hotel. After I checked in, I suggested that we meet in my rather spacious room where we could spread out our papers while we talked. When Bob entered the room, his jaw nearly hit the floor.

"How is it," he complained, "that you get to stay in a suite while I'm stuck in a broom closet? My room is smaller than your bed!"

"I did it on purpose," I explained. "We have to toughen you up for the meeting tomorrow."

Actually, what had happened was that by the time I got to the hotel that afternoon, all of the "broom closet" sized rooms, one of which I had reserved, were booked, so they gave me a suite at a bargain basement price. Fortunately, I knew Bob well enough to know that he was really not upset.

*   *   *

After working for several hours, Bob suggested that we go out for dinner.

"Let's go to this place where all the big shot politicians eat. We can see how many we recognize. It's only a ten minute walk."

"That sounds great, but let's take a cab." I hated walking anywhere with Bob. He loved to walk, was well over six feet tall, and took gigantic strides as he briskly moved along. I had to take frantic little strides, huffing and puffing all the way, just to keep up.

But Bob insisted on walking, as he always did, and I relented, as I always did, even though it was a brisk November evening and I knew it would be more than ten minutes.

When we finally arrived at the restaurant, it was deserted. No big shots, no politicians, maybe two other tables of diners. Bob was very disappointed. I was too cold and out of breath to care.

"I'm really sorry I made you walk all the way over here for nothing," said Bob.

"No problem," I panted.

We learned later that the restaurant did attract a celebrity crowd, but only for lunch.

*   *   *

After much deliberation, in my suite and over dinner, Bob and I decided that he would attend the meeting the next morning with a mind set that $15 million, that is, one policy limit, was a fair settlement figure. We arrived at that number as follows: the FDIC was seeking $45 million, that is, three policy limits, on the basis that the bank had sustained three separate losses, two in foreign exchange and one in the investment department. But the bond had a provision limiting coverage to $15 million for all losses in which the same person or persons were "concerned or implicated." It was easy to "concern or implicate" the same person or persons in the two foreign exchange losses. In our view, deposition testimony had clearly established that the bank's foreign currency traders, including the head trader, and the Executive Vice President in charge of the foreign exchange department knew about or participated in the concealment of foreign exchange contracts, which was the basis of the first foreign exchange loss, and the making of false entries in the bank's books and records, which was the basis of the second foreign exchange loss. It was a bit more problematic to "concern or implicate" the same person or persons in both the foreign exchange and investment department losses. Nevertheless, there was persuasive evidence that Sindona, who was the bank's controlling shareholder, and members of the bank's senior management, including the Chairman and President, orchestrated, authorized, had knowledge of, or at the very least acquiesced in all of the acts that formed the basis of all of the losses claimed by the FDIC: concealed foreign exchange contracts, false entries in the bank's books and records regarding foreign exchange, improper and unauthorized transactions involving domestic securities, and false entries in the bank's investment department records. The evidence suggested that these acts were all designed to generate profits and conceal losses in a desperate and ultimately unsuccessful attempt to maintain the viability of the financially beleaguered bank.

Having reduced three losses to one, we then factored in the "alter ego" defense and concluded that we had a decent chance, maybe fifty-fifty, of establishing that the FDIC was not entitled to coverage for any of the losses.

We also concluded that even if our "one loss" and "alter ego" defenses were unsuccessful, the FDIC would have difficulty proving causation. For example, the concealed foreign exchange contracts, which formed the basis of one of the foreign exchange losses, were "futures" contracts. They obligated the bank to deliver a foreign currency that it did not own for a specified price on a specified date. By entering the contract, the trader was gambling that the price of the currency would fall below the contract price before the delivery date. The trader would then buy the currency and deliver it for a profit. Unfortunately, the price of the currency rose above the contract price, forcing the bank to buy it and deliver it for a loss. The FDIC's theory of causation was that if the contract had not been concealed, the bank could have purchased the currency before the price rose above the contract price, thus avoiding the loss. Our theory was that there was no meaningful concealment and thus no causation. The bank's senior managers had encouraged the foreign currency traders to generate profits by speculating in foreign exchange. If the contracts had not been "concealed," perhaps the bank's senior managers would have covered the positions. But perhaps not. It was just as likely, maybe more likely, that they would have taken the same risk as the traders and gambled that the price of the currency would go down and not up. In that event, the losses would have occurred anyway.

But we also recognized that none of our defenses was a sure thing and that the FDIC would be entitled to a substantial award of prejudgment interest on any recovery.

On that basis, a $15 million settlement seemed more than reasonable.

*   *   *

Bob's meeting the next morning with not one but two FDIC in-house attorneys was very encouraging. He left convinced that a $15 million settlement was, in fact, attainable and agreed to meet again in January 1979 at Fireman's Fund's Manhattan office. Bob and the FDIC attorneys also agreed to invite representatives from Aetna and INA, the bank's excess insurers, as well as trial counsel for all parties.

Seventeen people attended the New York session: Bob Buell and two other representatives from Fireman's Fund; three representatives from Aetna; two from INA; two from the FDIC; the chief liquidator of Franklin National Bank; the FDIC's lead trial attorneys; Aetna's lead trial counsel; INA's lead trial counsel; and Jeff Silberfeld and me.

Bob Buell thanked everyone for coming and then turned the meeting over to Bill Kelly, the FDIC's senior trial attorney, who then stood up and proceeded to lecture the group for at least thirty minutes on why the FDIC believed that it had three valid claims for $15 million each and why none of the insurance companies' defenses had any chance of success. He concluded his speech by advising us that his firm settlement demand was $45 million. Not one penny less.

We were stunned. In Washington less than three months earlier, the FDIC in-house attorneys had given Bob Buell completely different signals.

After a brief pause, during which the silence was palpable, Bob Buell closed his briefcase, pushed his chair away from the table, and stood up.

"Before we adjourn," he said, "does anybody have anything else to say at this time, because I certainly don't." He picked up his briefcase and turned toward the door.

In an instant, the senior of the two FDIC in-house attorneys jumped up and ran to intercept Bob just as he walked into the hallway. The door closed behind them. The rest of us sat and waited. Five minutes later, Bob stuck his head into the room and asked Bill Kelly and me to join him outside. The FDIC in-house attorney, Bob told us, had made a recommendation and Bob wanted our input. The attorney was suggesting that the FDIC bring in another attorney, an expert in the field, to act as a settlement mediator. Bob and I were all for it. Bill Kelly was less than enthusiastic. Nevertheless, we all agreed that with the present cast of characters, settlement negotiations were going nowhere. Therefore, with nothing to lose, we decided to give the mediator a shot.

*   *   *

The man the FDIC recommended to mediate was Frank Skillern, one of the leading attorneys in the United States in the field of fidelity insurance. A partner at a large Dallas law firm, over the years Frank had represented the FDIC in many bank failure cases, including two, which he settled, involving the second and third largest bank failures in United States history, the United States National Bank case in San Diego and the Hamilton Bank case in Tennessee. More recently, Frank had begun to represent insurance companies in fidelity cases not involving the FDIC. Ultimately, he was elected Chairman of the American Bar Association's Committee on Fidelity and Surety Claims.

But perhaps Frank's most striking quality was his slow Texas drawl. After arguing fidelity law with fast talking New York lawyers for more than three years, it was a pleasure to sit back and listen to someone who knew as much as any of us and took his time letting us know it.

*   *   *

Frank Skillern entered the case shortly after Judge Platt had recused himself. Judge Weinstein's positive disposition toward settlement was obvious. Considering the United States National Bank and Hamilton Bank cases, which were as hotly contested as the Franklin case, Frank's settlement record was admirable. Bill Kelly, whose hawkish attitude had almost driven us away from prior settlement efforts, was relegated to the background. Under these circumstances, how could we not feel cautiously optimistic?

Things happened reasonably quickly.

At Frank Skillern's request, both the FDIC and the insurance companies prepared memos summarizing their claims and defenses.

In February 1979, the insurance company's trial attorneys met with Frank, who demonstrated that he was a quick study. In less than one month, he had become familiar with the important facts of the case and the crucial legal issues.

Following the February meeting, we prepared another memo for Frank focusing exclusively on the "alter ego" defense.

In March, the attorneys met with the Frank a second time to discuss all of our defenses. Although no specific settlement numbers were discussed, after the meeting we agreed with the attorneys for Aetna and INA that Frank seemed to be leaning toward recommending a $15 million settlement. Moreover, during the meeting Frank made a vital concession, namely, that if we reached an agreement with the FDIC, we would not have to deal with the Trustee in Bankruptcy, who was also suing to recover under the fidelity policies. Instead, the FDIC would agree to satisfy the Trustee's claims out of the settlement proceeds.

In April, Frank lectured at an ABA seminar on fidelity insurance in Boston. A Fireman's Fund Vice President attending the seminar had drinks with Frank at an afternoon cocktail party. The Vice President teased Frank about taking so long to settle the Franklin case. Based on Frank's reaction, the Vice President concluded, just as we had, that Frank was thinking in terms of one policy limit.

In May, at a pretrial conference, Judge Weinstein began in earnest to prod the parties to negotiate. Several of his statements reflected his apparent belief that the value of the FDIC's case was $15 million or less. For example, Judge Weinstein said, "Some of the claims are just extravagant." He also said, after listening to an explanation of the FDIC's claim based upon concealed foreign exchange contracts, "It seems to me you don't have that clear a case." In response to the contention that Sindona was a covered employee within the meaning of the insurance policies, the judge said, "It seems remote." Responding to an explanation of how the concealment of foreign exchange contracts caused the bank to lose money, the judge observed, "They would have suffered the losses anyway, wouldn't they?" He added:

> THE COURT: Well, it's not clear to me that you are going to be able to show loss, even though there were crimes committed. It's not clear to me that the crimes have anything to do with the loss. Basically you have a business judgment problem here, it seems to me, with this bank.

Then he said, turning his attention to the claims against the Bank's outside auditors:

> THE COURT: Supposing you get ten million from the insurance companies? What do you expect to get from the accountants?

Immediately following the conference, we forwarded to the mediator a letter setting forth verbatim all of the judge's comments regarding settlement.

On June 1, Bob Buell and representatives from Aetna and INA met with Frank Skillern without trial counsel present. For the first time, numbers were discussed. Frank admitted that he was, in fact, thinking in terms of one claim, maybe slightly more. The insurance companies responded not with a firm offer but with the suggestion that they had valued the case at approximately $10 million.

One week later, attorneys for all of the Franklin parties attended a settlement conference with Judge Weinstein, whom we brought up to date on the status of our negotiations with the Frank Skillern. At the conference, the judge asked for and received our permission to contact Frank directly.

Then, at the end of the month, Judge Weinstein heard argument on and denied the government's motion for summary judgment. One of the reasons for denying the motion was his belief that the Comptroller of the Currency, who was a member of the FDIC's Board of Directors, would be more likely to assist the settlement process if he faced the prospect of a long and expensive trial.

Needless to say, we forwarded a transcript of the court's decision to Frank Skillern the very next day.

In July, good news for Frank Skillern and bad news for us. Frank was hired by the FDIC to replace its retiring in-house General Counsel. The next day, Bill Kelly advised us he was taking over the negotiations on behalf of the FDIC and that Frank Skillern, who apparently felt he was under some sort of ethical restraint in light of his new position, would no longer be directly involved. Bill Kelly then dropped a bombshell: The FDIC's firm settlement demand was $15 million plus interest, for a total of $20 million. He also advised us that the FDIC was no longer willing to agree to share the settlement proceeds with the Trustee and that we would have to deal with the Trustee ourselves.

This was a huge step backwards and created the very real possibility that the insurance companies would walk away from the negotiating table once and for all. The only way to save the negotiations, we concluded, was to re-involve Frank Skillern, notwithstanding his new position as General Counsel. Accordingly, we contacted Judge Weinstein to advise him of what had taken place and even went so far as to suggest that the judge contact Frank Skillern and request his continued involvement.

To our relief, Judge Weinstein wrote a letter to Frank urging him to carry on, "indeed to intensify, your important and vital work to bring about a settlement of this matter." The letter continued:

> It would be a grave disservice to the banking system, the legal profession and the court were you to withdraw your skills as a negotiator at this critical juncture. Your continued participa-

tion in the Franklin National Bank case would be in the best interests of the court and all the parties, and would be consistent with the highest standards and traditions of good government, public service, and professional ethics. I look forward to your continued participation and, I hope, successful efforts.

One week later, Judge Weinstein presided over a settlement conference at which Bill Kelly represented the FDIC. At the conference, Bill did nothing more than repeat that the FDIC's settlement demand was a "firm" $20 million. He noted that he personally considered this a very low figure and characterized it as a "poverty number." At that moment, the attorney for the Trustee in Bankruptcy interjected that the Trustee would insist upon receiving one-half of the proceeds of any FDIC settlement with the insurance companies. Judge Weinstein's response to the Trustee's attorney vindicated our efforts at the outset of the litigation to dismiss the Trustee's claims: "You're not going to get it. I don't buy your theory that the Trustee has valid claims against the insurance companies."

A few days after the conference, the insurance companies responded to the FDIC's "firm" demand with a "firm" offer of $10 million, but only if that amount settled the Trustee's claims as well.

In August, Frank Skillern was back in the picture. His first act was to advise us that in light of the judge's remarks at the July settlement conference, the FDIC and the Trustee in Bankruptcy had agreed to present the insurance companies with one figure to settle all of their claims. If the figure was acceptable, the FDIC and Trustee would give the insurance companies full releases. The FDIC and Trustee would then negotiate or litigate with each other over the allocation of the settlement proceeds.

In September, Frank demanded $15 million on behalf of the FDIC and Trustee to settle both lawsuits against the insurance companies.

Then, another step backwards. The insurance companies liked the size of the demand but could not agree on each company's share. Fireman's Fund and Aetna had assumed all along that if the cases were settled for $15 million, then each company would pay one policy limit. Under that scenario, Fireman's Fund, the primary insurer, would pay $6 million; Aetna, the first level excess insurer, would pay $4 million; and INA, the second level excess insurer, would pay $5 million. But INA suddenly insisted that it should pay less than one full policy limit, and Fireman's Fund should pay more, since the insurers were settling three losses, not one. Amazingly, the negotiations had become deadlocked not because of differences between plaintiffs and defendants but because of differences among the defendants.

But the deadlock did not last long. In October, in order to accommodate INA's desire to save a little money, we presented a counter-offer to Frank Skillern for slightly less than $15 million, which he accepted.

It took four months to draft the settlement agreement and the accompanying releases. In February of 1980, the agreements were signed, the money was delivered, and the suits against the insurance companies were dismissed with prejudice.

*   *   *

Afterthoughts

After the cases were dismissed, I made a special trip to California to celebrate with Bob Buell. We both had reason to be quite happy with the result. The FDIC's and Trustee's lawsuits had originally sought a combined total of more than $100 million from the fidelity insurers. Through hard work and perseverence, we had settled both matters for less than fifteen cents on the dollar.

My one regret was that as part of the settlement, all of the insurance companies' third-party complaints, including the complaint against the government, were dismissed. Even though Judge Weinstein had commented on the weakness of our claims against the government when he denied their summary judgment motion, I believed we had a strong case and was looking forward to a rousing trial. Too bad I never got the opportunity.

Surprisingly, I learned from many well-connected sources long after the case was over that the Comptroller of the Currency, contrary to the expectations of the judge when he denied the government's summary judgment motion, put no settlement pressure at all upon the FDIC. The judge's theory was that if he forced the Comptroller to participate in the trial as a third-party defendant, the Comptroller, who sat on the FDIC's Board of Directors, would do his best to bring about a settlement of the FDIC's claims against the insurers. But this did not happen. The FDIC settled the case without any pressure from the Comptroller, the Justice Department, or any other government agency or officer.

Then why did the case settle when, at the outset, the parties were so far apart? My theory was that, thanks to Frank Skillern, cooler heads prevailed. Although Bill Kelly genuinely believed in the strength of the FDIC's case against the insurance companies, his hard line approach was not bringing the parties closer together. So Frank rejected that approach and instead engaged in the same type of analysis that Bob Buell and I had engaged in. He considered all of the factors, the claims, the defenses, the third-party claims, the complexity of the case, the legal issues, the judge, and the potential jury pool, and concluded, as we did, that $15 million was a fair and reasonable settlement figure.

Shortly after he settled the insurance cases, Frank Skillern turned his attention to the claims against Franklin's former officers and directors, the outside auditors, and Continental Bank and managed to settle those as well. Although the court ordered the parties not to release the settlement figures, the press reported that the total settlement package, including the insurance settlement, was $20.85 million. Of that amount, the FDIC's share was reportedly $16.35 million; the Trustee's share was $4.5 million.[20]

Judge Weinstein, who also played a major role in the final settlement, was so pleased with the result that he invited the lawyers into his chambers for a champagne toast. By settling three months earlier, the insurance company attorneys, including me, missed out on the judge's hospitality.

Finally, after all of the cases had settled, I turned my attention to one final critical unresolved issue. Way back in 1975, the attorneys for Aetna and I had agreed to share the cost of hiring a handwriting expert to analyze the writing on the unrecorded foreign exchange contracts to determine which trader or traders were responsible. The expert's bill was five hundred dollars, which we paid. As of February 1980, more than four years later, Aetna's attorneys still had not reimbursed us their share. So I wrote one final letter on the Franklin case to gently remind my fellow defense attorneys of their unpaid obligation.

"But Len," they protested, "we thought you were going to let us keep the $250 to thank us for helping you squeeze those last few settlement dollars out of INA."

I received their check the next day.

PART THREE

Agent Orange

CHAPTER NINE

Not Your Typical
Garden Variety Lawsuit

Early in the afternoon of April 19, 1979, I arrived at the United States Courthouse in Westbury, Long Island, for the very first pretrial conference in the Agent Orange litigation, a highly publicized, emotionally charged class action lawsuit by American, Australian, and New Zealand veterans who had served in the armed conflict in Vietnam. The suit was against the manufacturers of Agent Orange, a controversial herbicide used by the Allied Forces in Vietnam to defoliate trees and kill crops. The veterans claimed that many of them were suffering from cancer and other serious illnesses; that those that were presently healthy had an increased risk of contracting cancer in the future; that many of their wives had suffered miscarriages; and that many of their children had sustained grievous birth defects, all as a result of the veterans' exposure in Vietnam to Agent Orange. They sought billions of dollars in damages.

My client in the Agent Orange case was one of the defendants, Dow Chemical, which had manufactured more Agent Orange for use in Vietnam than any other company.

There was one item on the court's agenda that afternoon, a minor discovery matter. Something only a lawyer could get worked up about. Nevertheless, I fully expected a standing room only crowd and was not disappointed. More than one hundred people jammed their way into the courtroom, including attorneys for both sides, employees of the corporate defendants, reporters, and spectators.

Nothing to be alarmed about, except that two dozen of those spectators were Vietnam veterans dressed in full combat fatigues. They were unarmed, of course, but the presence of uniformed soldiers in a federal courthouse was startling and intimidating. All but one of the veterans sat in the gallery and listened very attentively to everything that was said. The last veteran stood at attention inside the main door to the courtroom for the entire length of the proceedings holding an American Flag.

There were dozens if not hundreds of court hearings in the Agent Orange litigation. Veterans in combat fatigues attended almost every one of the them.

*   *   *

Jump ahead four years. On a cool spring morning in 1983, I arrived at my office shortly after the crack of dawn prepared to spend another twelve hour day working on Agent Orange. I rode the elevator up to my fifth floor corner office and walked behind my desk when suddenly I stopped dead in my tracks. There was a small round hole about waist high in the floor to ceiling window directly behind my chair. Several cracks radiated outward from the hole like the spokes of a wheel. I was no expert but quickly concluded that nobody could throw such a small rock through a fifth floor window. The hole must have been made by a bullet.

*   *   *

Not counting the cracked window, I received numerous death threats during the course of the Agent Orange litigation, as did many high ranking executives at Dow's Midland, Michigan, corporate headquarters. My office and Dow's corporate headquarters also received several bomb threats. There was a bomb threat at the federal courthouse Brooklyn, after the case was reassigned there. In addition, break-ins occurred at three government offices where Agent Orange records were stored.

As the scheduled trial date approached, the number of death threats against me and Dow employees increased to the point where we felt compelled to hire a security firm to assess the situation and provide recommendations and advice. They suggested, among other things, that we install a steel door to the room where we maintained our Agent Orange files; that we change the locks at our homes and offices; that we provide them with any intelligence we might have regarding groups in Michigan and on Long Island that were interested in the case; that on weekdays security guards work two shifts, from 4 p.m. to 8 a.m., at our homes and at the temporary quarters we rented in Manhattan; that on weekends the security guards at our homes work around the clock; that we not hold any impromptu news conferences outside the courthouse; that we rent equipment for the detection of mail bombs; and that they check out the places where we planned to eat lunch during the course of the trial.

They also suggested that the attorneys who were going to try the case and the Dow employees who would be attending court on a regular basis be fitted for bullet proof vests.

Then they asked us a rather scary question: in the event of gunfire, who would be the number one individual to protect. Every lawyer on our Agent Orange defense team voted for himself.

*   *   *

Veterans in combat fatigues. Bullet holes. Bomb threats. Break-ins. Death threats. Bullet proof vests. The Agent Orange litigation was obviously not your typical, garden variety lawsuit; it was one of the most extraordinary cases in recent legal history, not just in these respects, but in many, many, more.

*   *   *

Agent What?

When Dow first approached me late in July 1978 to defend the first Agent Orange lawsuit, which Paul Reutershan, a veteran who was dying of cancer, commenced in New York state court, my reaction was, "Agent what?" Of course, I had followed the Vietnam War in the newspapers and on television and must have seen or heard the term "Agent Orange" at some point, but in 1978 I drew a complete blank.

Ultimately, I learned that Agent Orange was a phenoxy herbicide, a chemical compound that could cause leaves to fall off of trees and kill certain plants. It consisted of a fifty-fifty mixture of the n-butyl esters of herbicides known as 2,4,5-T and 2,4-D. Although Agent Orange was sold only to the military for use in Southeast Asia, and was never sold commercially, herbicides containing different esters of 2,4,5-T and 2,4-D had long histories of safe and effective agricultural and domestic uses as weed killers and plant growth regulators in the United States and around the world.

During the Vietnam War, the Allied Forces used Agent Orange and five other herbicides (Agents Blue, Green, Pink, Purple, and White) for important military purposes.[1] The military sprayed herbicides from Fairchild C-123 transport planes to defoliate the thick jungle canopy around roads, rivers, canals, railroads, and power lines, in order to reduce the potential for ambush and open those areas for aerial observation. They also aerially sprayed herbicides to defoliate more remote portions of the jungle, in order to reduce the potential for ambush, deny enemy soldiers freedom of movement and cover for their camps, and force enemy soldiers to evacuate sprayed areas. They sprayed herbicides by hand to defoliate areas around American camps and gun emplacements to protect our soldiers from surprise attacks and open our lines of fire. Finally, they aerially sprayed herbicides on rice fields and other crops to destroy the enemy's food supply.

In all, the Allied Forces sprayed between 17 and 19 million gallons of herbicides in Vietnam, including 11 million gallons of Agent Orange, more than all of the other herbicides combined. The military sprayed herbicides on 6 million acres, or ten percent, of the Vietnamese countryside. Some areas were sprayed two, three, or four times. The military sprayed at a rate of at least three gallons per acre, three times the normal commercial concentration.

The decision to use herbicides in Vietnam was made at the highest levels of government based upon nearly twenty years of testing and study by the military. President Kennedy himself personally authorized the start of the spraying operation, which was called Project Ranch Hand. The first Ranch Hand mission was flown in January 1962.

From a military standpoint, Project Ranch Hand was a huge success. The casualty level of American soldiers in Vietnam was considerably lower on a monthly basis than in Korea and World War II, a fact attributed in large part to the defoliation program. During the war, the government periodically reviewed the operation, and "the conclusions of all the evaluations prior to 1969 recognized that defoliation had reduced the incidence of ambushes, saved lives and disrupted enemy tactics."[2] The evaluations also concluded that "crop-denial efforts have made subsistence of the enemy in the field more difficult and have adversely affected his operations."[3]

At his deposition during the Agent Orange litigation, although he "did not get involved in the details" and could not remember the specific color designations of the various agents, General William Westmoreland, the Commander-in-Chief of American forces in Vietnam, testified that herbicides were an "effective weapon of war." Former Secretary of State Henry Kissinger also testified that "the military certainly felt strongly about the fact that there was a military benefit."

At first, there was virtually no public outcry against the use of herbicides in Vietnam. Then, beginning in 1964, there was a growing opposition based upon moral, environmental, ecological, and political concerns by organizations and groups such as the Washington Post, the Federation of American Scientists, the American Association for the Advancement of Science, and the Rand Corporation. The concern was that the use of herbicides amounted to chemical warfare, that peasants were starving because their crops had been destroyed, and that the spraying had killed large areas of South Vietnamese forests, the country's most viable natural resource.

The first suggestion from scientists that Agent Orange was potentially toxic to humans was made in a report prepared by the Bionetics Research Laboratory for the National Institute of Health. The Bionetics report, issued in 1969, concluded that 2,4,5-T could cause birth defects in mice when administered in high doses to the mothers during pregnancy. Later, scientists determined that the potential teratogenicity of 2,4,5-T resulted from the presence of a contaminant, known as dioxin or TCDD, produced during the manufacturing process of trichlorophenol (TCP), a necessary precursor chemical to 2,4,5-T.

Largely because of the Bionetics report, the Secretaries of Health Education and Welfare, Agriculture, and the Interior issued a joint statement on April 15, 1970, suspending virtually all commercial uses in the United States of herbicides containing 2,4,5-T.[4] That same day, the Department of Defense suspended all military uses of herbicides containing 2,4,5-T. The government continued spraying Agents White and Blue, which did not contain 2,4,5-T, until January 1971, when the last Ranch Hand mission was flown.

*   *   *

My Own Personal Dilemma

By the time I received a copy of the Reutershan complaint, I had learned enough about Agent Orange to realize that I needed to do some serious soul searching about whether to accept the assignment. As a combat veteran of World War II, I was somewhat reluctant to side against a fellow soldier who obviously had suffered greatly since his return from battle. Moreover, as uncomfortable as it may have been to defend a claim by one veteran, I fully expected that a "multitude" of veterans with similar problems would soon file suit. In fact, I wrote to Dow early in September that I was "absolutely at a loss to understand how, with all the national publicity, there can be but one claim."

But I had been representing Dow for nearly ten years in a wide range of product liability matters. I knew Dow not as a faceless corporate entity but as a group of mostly dedicated individuals who sincerely believed that Agent Orange could not possibly have caused the veterans' injuries. I was skeptical of their position at first, but it did not take long for them to convince me that they were right. The existing medical and scientific literature simply did not support the veterans' claims.

So I took the case.

Maybe the litigator in me would have taken it anyway even if Dow's position on causation did not appear so clear cut. Fortunately, I never had to face that question.

I wish I could say that I never gave the matter another thought. I second guessed myself every time I read that the Veterans Administration had rejected another claim, or attended the deposition of another dying veteran, or saw an obviously deformed child at an Agent Orange court hearing, or heard Victor Yannacone, the flamboyant, passionately dedicated lead attorney for the veterans, explain why he was spending huge sums of his own money to prosecute the lawsuit:

> MR. YANNACONE: And for the benefit of those that wonder why we're doing it, part of it is the conventional, the practice of personal injury law, and the other part is the fact that many of my colleagues who were veterans of a prior war felt somewhat of an obligation to a great many young men, many who have been unemployed, many who have been destitute, many of whom already died, and many of whom are running up seventy-eight- and eighty-thousand-dollar-a-year medical bills and who are not fully insured.[5]

Notwithstanding these conflicting feelings, I litigated the case with my usual vigor. No one was more sympathetic to the plight of the veterans than I, but I sincerely believed and still believe to this day that there was no legal or moral basis for holding Dow accountable. Subsequent decisions by the trial court, by the United States Court of Appeals for the Second Circuit, and the United States Supreme Court proved that my early instincts were not wrong.

Although I was vilified by many veterans and their sympathizers, some apparently understood my position and treated me respectfully. In fact, one gesture by a veteran's wife was perhaps the most personally moving incident of my entire legal career.

This particular young woman had been a very vocal and visible supporter of the class action. She told a group of veterans in 1979 that the use of Agent Orange in Vietnam was "corporate genocide" that "cannot be swept under a rug."[6] She and her husband testified before a congressional subcommittee about the horrendous treatment provided by the Veterans Administration in response to her husband's Agent Orange related health claims. She brought her young daughter, who was suffering from numerous crippling birth defects and was confined to a wheelchair, to nearly every court hearing in Westbury and Brooklyn.

Nevertheless, at Christmastime in 1985, seven months after my own wife Lenore had passed away from cancer, the veteran's wife put her obviously strong feelings about the case aside and wrote me a note of condolence. "For no other reason," she explained, "I'm writing to wish you a stronger, peaceful spirit at this time of year. Your loss must feel very large at this moment. I thought if you knew there were people who cared and wished you well it might help."

*   *   *

More Than a Lawsuit

The Agent Orange litigation was more than a lawsuit. It was the centerpiece of a campaign by the veterans for answers, assistance, and the same respect that the American people had bestowed upon veterans of prior wars. With "Agent Orange" as their rallying cry, the veterans waged their battle not just in the courtroom but in the press, on television and radio, in Congress, before the Veterans Administration and other federal agencies, in state legislatures around the country, and before state agencies and commissions. Their goal was not simply to obtain an award of money damages against the manufacturers of Agent Orange but also to publicize their plight, compel the VA to acknowledge and pay for Agent Orange related health claims, and secure the passage at the state and federal level of remedial legislation.

Publicity: It is impossible to fully and accurately document the extent of the media coverage of Agent Orange.

We recently searched a database containing hundreds of newspapers, magazines, and journals for articles published from 1978 through 1984 mentioning Agent Orange. The search produced 3,934 articles, approximately two articles every day for a period of six years. Only a handful of publications in the database went back that far in time, so the search probably produced just a small fraction of the total number of reports.

During the litigation, we kept copies of all articles relating to Agent Orange that appeared in major New York metropolitan area newspapers and magazines, such as The New York *Times*, The *Daily News*,

Newsday, The New York *Law Journal*, and *New York* Magazine, as well as national newspapers and magazines, such as The *Wall Street Journal*, *USA Today*, The *National Law Journal*, *Time* and *Newsweek*. In The New York *Times* alone, we counted 181 such articles, averaging out to thirty per year, one every ten days.

In addition, attorneys and other contacts from around the country and around the world routinely sent us copies of articles from their own local newspapers dealing with Agent Orange, and Dow's public relations department collected articles and sent us copies, as many as fifty in one month.

Many of the articles painted very sympathetic pictures of veterans and their family members, describing in vivid detail their illnesses and injuries. An article in the Boston *Globe* reported on the plight of eight friends from the same town who had enlisted in the marines and served together: "One has a child born with a cleft palate, deformed right arm and other defects such as deafness. Another has two young children with cancer and a wife who has suffered a miscarriage. [Another] has had five heart attacks....[Another] has had half his stomach removed....Two [suffer from] severe anxiety." A *Newsday* article reported on three veterans: one had a son who "was born with deformed genitals and hearing problems. His first child was stillborn." The second "has had hepatitis, jaundice, hypertension, severe and constant headaches and a persistent skin rash." The third "has a daughter who was born with a congenital hip deformity and a son born with an enzyme deficiency that causes mental retardation." Even the normally staid New York *Times* reported on a veteran who "wonders about his once-strong arms, now weak; about his hair that falls out in huge clumps in the shower; about the anger that overwhelms him unexpectedly; about the four children who were born dead or deformed, or lived but became emotionally disturbed."

Some of the articles were blatantly anti-Dow, like the one that appeared in a Berkeley, California newspaper under the headline: "Dow lies & spies on Vietnam vets."

Some assumed, without proof, that Agent Orange caused the veterans' health problems, like the one in an Australian newspaper that proclaimed: "Now, eleven years later, one of the most tragic results of the war is becoming apparent: the effect of the defoliant Agent Orange on soldiers who were exposed to it."

Some were just plain bizarre, like the one in the Boston *Globe* that reported that a veteran had been acquitted of a drunken driving charge based upon a defense of exposure to Agent Orange.

Even those that tried to be even-handed contained very anti-Dow sentiment. When Dow asserted the "government contract defense," *Newsday* quoted Victor Yannacone as likening Dow to Nazi war criminals: "It was not a good defense at Nuremberg," he reportedly told the *Newsday* writer, "and the veterans we represent feel it's not a good defense here in the United States." Yannacone described the assertion of the defense as "a reprehensible attempt by multinational stateless conglomerate chemical empires to further smear the memories of those men who died in Vietnam."

All of this publicity about Agent Orange was a major reason that so many veterans joined in the lawsuit and became so passionate about it. The Baltimore *Sun* did a story about a veteran whose son had learning disabilities, eye problems, and a club foot. "Why do I think it was Agent Orange?" the veteran asked. "To be honest, because of the media." And a prominent U.C.L.A. scientist testified at a California state legislative hearing that "the fear which is generated by the current publicity is very likely to be the most serious consequence of the use of Agent Orange."

Much of the publicity about Agent Orange and the lawsuit was generated by Yannacone himself. Although he boasted that in twenty years of public interest litigation he "never called a newspaper reporter, held a press conference, or issued a press release,"[7] he somehow managed to find ways to get an Agent Orange story published and himself quoted.

At first, Dow did very little to offset all of the negative publicity that the case and Yannacone were generating. The pro-veteran/anti-Dow articles were passionate and inflammatory. In contrast, statements by Dow representatives sounded almost perfunctory. For example, a Dow employee made the following statement to the media on the courthouse steps following an early pre-trial conference: "We believe that the veterans may have real problems and we support the need to determine what the causes are but based upon thirty years of safe use and over forty thousand scientific papers that support the safety of our product, we do not believe there is a causal relationship between their problems and our product."

Hardly the kind of statement that was likely to arouse a fired up public to rush to Dow's defense.

But then Dow took the initiative. At Don Frayer's suggestion, Dow began to contact journalists to educate them, to increase their objectivity, and to tell them Dow's side of the story. This strategy paid off almost immediately. As but one example, over lunch one afternoon, Don provided a *Newsday* reporter with documentation that soldiers in Vietnam were exposed not just to Agent Orange but to a host of other potentially toxic substances, including insecticides such as DDT; drugs such as dapsone, taken to prevent malaria; and known carcinogens, such as aflatoxin, which occurred naturally in the environment. Don followed up by calling the reporter periodically with more information. Ultimately, *Newsday* published an article on the subject that stated: "In the midst of the national controversy over the toxicity of Agent Orange, evidence is emerging that the veterans' ills may be related to exposure in South Vietnam to a far more complex 'toxicological cocktail,' as one scientist put it with grim whimsy."

Finally, Agent Orange received almost as much coverage on television and radio as it did in newspapers and magazines. By the end of January 1979, one month after the filing of the first class action complaint, we had become aware of more than one hundred television documentaries and news broadcasts dealing with Agent Orange. According to Victor Yannacone, the filing of that complaint triggered stories about veterans who had died of cancer or some other disease on hundreds of radio stations throughout the United States and Australia. The popular CBS news program "60 Minutes" did a show on Agent Orange. I was interviewed on CNN and National Public Radio. The Chairman of Dow's Board of Directors appeared on the CBS "Morning News." Charley Carey from Dow's Legal Department debated Victor Yannacone on Ted Koppel's "Nightline."

Congressional Hearings: Over a six year period, beginning in October 1978 through September 1984, Congress held no less than twenty-four separate hearings on the subject of Agent Orange.[8] Most were concerned either with the health risks, if any, resulting from exposure to Agent Orange or the VA's treatment of Agent Orange related health claims.

We attended the hearings whenever possible simply to monitor and observe. In contrast, many veterans and their supporters frequently attended as active participants.

VA Medical Exams: Veterans began filing Agent Orange related health claims with the VA in 1977.[9] At the time, the VA's official policy was that there was no causal connection between exposure to Agent Orange and the illnesses and conditions complained of. Therefore, any veteran complaining about Agent Orange exposure was not eligible for medical treatment at VA hospitals unless he was destitute.[10]

Beginning in 1979, as the class action lawsuit gained momentum, many veterans and their supporters began to voice their great disapproval with the VA's position. As a consequence, the VA began to receive some very unfavorable press. *Time* Magazine quoted a veteran as saying, "If you go in to a VA hospital and say you are an Agent Orange victim, they look at you as if you were nuts." The New York *Daily News* reported that the head of the VA had telephoned VA hospitals around the country, identified himself as a Vietnam veteran, and asked if his health was endangered by exposure to Agent Orange. To his chagrin, the VA head discovered that "nobody knew what he was talking about." His assistant thereafter reportedly telephoned every VA hospital in the country, telling them, "You folks better get your act together."

Congress reacted to the growing firestorm by passing a law in 1979 directing the VA to conduct an epidemiological study to determine whether there were any adverse long term health effects due to exposure to Agent Orange.[11] Incidentally, the VA was not the only federal agency to undertake an epidemiological study relating to Agent Orange. The Air Force conducted a health study of the servicemen who had participated in Project Ranch Hand. In addition, the Center for Disease Control, jointly supported by the Department of Defense, the VA, and Health and Human Services, conducted a birth defect study which included an assessment of various risk factors including exposure to Agent Orange.

In 1981, Congress passed another law authorizing the VA to provide hospital and outpatient care to veterans complaining of Agent Orange exposure.[12]

By April 30, 1984, 130,000 veterans complaining of Agent Orange exposure had gone to VA hospitals for medical checkups.[13]

VA Disability Benefits:[14] In addition to seeking medical treatment at VA hospitals, many veterans complaining of Agent Orange exposure filed claims with the VA for disability payments. The number of such claims as of May 1979 was less than five hundred. Within one year, there were five thousand. Two years later, there were fifteen thousand. By October 1984, there were 21,693.

The VA denied all but twenty five of these claims on the grounds that the injuries complained of were not "service related." The VA consistently took the position that the only disease caused by exposure to Agent Orange was chloracne, a skin condition.[15]

EPA Administrative Proceedings: These proceedings focused on the commercial uses in the United States of 2,4,5-T, one of the two herbicides used in combination to make Agent Orange.

The administrative process began in the spring of 1970 and lasted until early 1981.[16] They involved four federal agencies, including the

EPA. There were actually two separate rounds of administrative proceedings. The first was triggered by the release in 1969 of the Bionetics report, which had concluded that 2,4,5-T could cause birth defects in mice. The second was triggered by the release in 1979 of a study by Colorado State University which had concluded that there was a statistical correlation between the spraying of 2,4,5-T on forests near Alsea, Oregon, and the occurrence of spontaneous miscarriages in women residing in that area. Both resulted in orders suspending certain commercial uses of 2,4,5-T. Dow unsuccessfully challenged both orders in two separate court proceedings and was preparing to challenge them again in a hearing before the EPA when it decided to settle the matter. As part of the settlement, Dow agreed that it would no longer market or sell 2,4,5-T in the United States for any purpose. Dow's decision to settle with the EPA was one of expediency. Dow fully believed in the safety of its product but no longer wanted to fight the battle on two fronts: against the EPA on the one hand and the veterans in the Agent Orange class action on the other.

State Legislative Action: From the late 1970s through the end of the 1980s, when the Agent Orange controversy was at its peak, at least thirty states—Arizona, California, Connecticut, Delaware, Georgia, Hawaii, Illinois, Indiana, Iowa, Kansas, Kentucky, Louisiana, Maine, Michigan, Minnesota, Missouri, Montana, New Jersey, New York, Ohio, Oklahoma, Oregon, Pennsylvania, Rhode Island, South Carolina, Texas, Virginia, Washington, Wisconsin, and West Virginia—passed laws for the benefit of veterans complaining of Agent Orange exposure.[17]

Statutes of Limitations: From our standpoint, the most significant state laws were those enacted in Connecticut,[18] Delaware,[19] New York,[20] Ohio,[21] Rhode Island,[22] and West Virginia[23] extending the statute of limitations for Agent Orange lawsuits.

The New York amendment, passed in 1981, was especially important, since the Agent Orange class action was pending in that state. One of our strongest defenses at the outset of the litigation was that the claims were barred under New York's then existing statute of limitations, which applied the so-called "exposure rule." Under that provision, which many viewed as draconian, a person injured by exposure to a toxic substance had to commence his lawsuit for damages within three years of the date of that exposure, even if he did not know he was injured or even exposed! Applying that rule to the Agent Orange case would have resulted in a complete victory for the defendants, since our soldiers were out of Vietnam by 1973, the last possible exposure date, and did not commence the first lawsuit until 1978, five years later.

The New York amendment changed the statute of limitations for Agent Orange lawsuits to a "discovery rule," which provided that an Agent Orange claimant could bring his lawsuit within two years from the date he discovered or reasonably should have discovered his injury. In addition, the amendment contained a "revival" provision directed at those veterans whose claims were already time barred. The "revival" provision extended the period for those veterans to commence litigation to one year after the effective date of the amendment.

As a result of the amendment, Dow's potential statute of limitations defense was all but eliminated. We could not let this happen without a fight. Even though there was wide support for the bill throughout the state, one of our attorneys, a former law clerk to a judge on the New York State Court of Appeals, drafted a letter which Dow signed and sent to the Governor arguing that the amendment was unconstitutional. The Governor signed the bill anyway and issued a press release in which he stated, "This legislation is a major step in preserving the legal rights of veterans who may have suffered from [Agent Orange] exposure as a result of their service to our country. Such efforts are testimony to our commitment, here in New York, to honor the efforts of our veterans and to recognize our debt to them."

Agent Orange Commissions: More than twenty states passed statutes authorizing investigations into the health effects of exposure to Agent Orange. In some states, the legislature assigned responsibility for the investigation to a preexisting agency, such as the Health Department[24] or the Department of Veterans Affairs.[25] In others, the legislature created a new agency just for that purpose, such as the Vietnam Herbicides Information Commission in Connecticut,[26] the Michigan Agent Orange Commission,[27] the New York State Dioxin Commission,[28] the Agent Orange Advisory Council of Ohio,[29] the Oklahoma Agent Orange Outreach Committee,[30] and the South Carolina Agent Orange Advisory Council.[31] The statutes authorized the agencies and commissions to collect medical data from veterans, conduct epidemiological studies, compile reports, make recommendations regarding legislation and public assistance, offer genetic testing, provide referral services, assist veterans in processing Agent Orange related health claims, and provide information to the VA, state health agencies, veterans organizations, and medical associations.

*   *   *

The Agent Orange Litigation:
The Numbers Tell the Story

Even without the publicity, the legislative activity, and the administrative proceedings, the Agent Orange lawsuit gave new meaning to the term "major litigation." Although numbers do not usually tell the complete story, in this case they paint an extraordinarily vivid picture.[32]

Plaintiff Files a 163-Page 674-Paragraph Class Action Complaint: Paul Reutershan commenced the first Agent Orange lawsuit in July 1978 in state court in Manhattan. Reutershan was the only named plaintiff. He did not purport to bring a class action. His run-of-the-mill products liability complaint was six pages long. He sought $10 million in damages.

Six months later, in January 1979, Reutershan filed the first Agent Orange class action complaint in federal court in Brooklyn. The complaint was drafted by Reutershan's new attorney, Victor Yannacone, and was anything but run-of-the-mill. The complaint was 163 pages long and contained 674 paragraphs. It sought to recover declaratory, injunctive, and other equitable relief as well as money damages. It alleged violations of the United States Constitution and various federal anti-trust, unfair competition, and trademark statutes as well as traditional products liability theories of recovery. It asserted claims for money damages on behalf of the United States Department of Defense, the Veterans Administration, the Department of Health, Education and Welfare, and the Social Security Administration as well as on behalf of a class of 2.4 million former servicemen who served in Vietnam. It also sought to recover money damages on behalf of stockholders, rate payers, and subscribers of public utility companies. It contained one hundred pages and 441 paragraphs describing the history of the corporate defendants. It contained fourteen pages and fifty-seven paragraphs describing the history of phenoxy herbicides and certain of their ingredients.

Keep in mind that the Federal Rules of Civil Procedure required that the complaint contain a "short and plain statement" of the claims against the defendants.

17,500 Plaintiffs Commence One Thousand Agent Orange Lawsuits: During a court appearance on June 21, 1979, Yannacone told the judge that he intended to file a separate complaint for each and every one of his growing number of Agent Orange clients. Holding up a copy of Reutershan's class action complaint, the judge replied, "The last thing I need is a pile of complaints like this, whether it's three hundred, seven thousand, or four million."

Notwithstanding the judge's admonition, 17,500 plaintiffs ultimately commenced one thousand separate Agent Orange lawsuits in state and federal courts throughout the country. By September 1984, the class action included six hundred lawsuits with fifteen thousand named plaintiffs. In addition, 2,500 veterans who had chosen to "opt-out" of the class action had commenced four hundred lawsuits of their own.[33]

Thankfully, most of the complaints in these lawsuits were considerably shorter than Reutershan's.

One Agent Orange Judge: Remarkably, although thousands of Agent Orange plaintiffs commenced lawsuits in federal and state courts throughout the country, every one of those lawsuits was ultimately transferred to federal court in Westbury (and later Brooklyn) and assigned to the same judge.

17,500 plaintiffs, one thousand separate lawsuits, one court, one judge.

Actually, there were two Agent Orange judges. The first was Judge George C. Pratt, United States District Court, Eastern District of New York, who presided over the litigation in Westbury for more than four years beginning in May 1979. In October 1983, when Judge Pratt withdrew, the litigation was assigned to Chief Judge Jack B. Weinstein, United States District Court, Eastern District of New York, who sat in Brooklyn.

Judge Pratt withdrew because he was promoted. In June 1982, he was named to the United States Court of Appeals for the Second Circuit. Rather than withdraw from the Agent Orange case at that time, he stayed on as presiding judge by special designation, but only for another sixteen months. By October 1983, the demands on his time had simply become too great.

Coincidentally, this was the same Judge Weinstein who had taken over the Franklin National Bank litigation after that case had been pending for four years.

We accomplished this mammoth transfer and consolidation in the Agent Orange case by invoking the powers of the Judicial Panel on Multidistrict Litigation. By statute,[34] the Panel, which consisted of seven federal court judges temporarily assigned on a rotating basis, was authorized to transfer similar cases pending in different federal jurisdictions to one federal judge and consolidate those cases for all pretrial purposes, including motions and discovery, so long as the transfer and consolidation served "the convenience of parties and witnesses" and promoted "the just and efficient conduct" of the litigation. As Judge Weinstein himself observed, "The savings in time and money when many cases are investigated and prepared together for disposition [pursuant to the multidistrict statute] can be enormous."[35]

As of March 1979, Yannacone had commenced a total of thirteen Agent Orange lawsuits in federal court: five in Westbury, five in Manhattan, and three in Chicago. Recognizing the advantages to Dow of multidistrict consolidation, we knew that we would ultimately make a motion before the Panel to transfer and consolidate these 13 cases and every subsequent Agent Orange case.

Before making the motion, however, we took the initiative to increase the chances not only that the motion would be granted, but also that the cases would be consolidated right in our own backyard.

First, we approached Judge Pratt, who had been assigned to preside over the five Agent Orange cases pending in Westbury, which was a five minute drive from our office. We asked Judge Pratt if he would be interested in accepting a multidistrict assignment of all Agent Orange cases. He said yes. We asked him if the Panel was likely to contact him before assigning him the cases. He again said yes and assured us that he would tell the Panel of his willingness to accept the assignment.

Second, we approached Victor Yannacone.

"I've been thinking about multidistrict litigation for all of your Agent Orange cases," I told him.

"What's that?" he asked.

I explained and told him that Dow wanted the cases in Westbury, which would be great for both of us. "I'd like to have your support for the motion," I said.

"You got it. What do I have to do?"

"File some papers and go to St. Louis in April to appear before the Multidistrict Panel. I know a place there we can go for dinner. My treat."

Having gotten these assurances from Yannacone and Judge Pratt, we filed our motion on March 8. We specifically asked the Panel to transfer all thirteen cases to Judge Pratt in Westbury. The Panel heard oral argument on April 27. It granted our motion from the bench. The cases were assigned the caption re "Agent Orange" Products Liability Litigation

Later, as more Agent Orange cases were filed, the Panel transferred every one of them to New York for inclusion in the Agent Orange multidistrict litigation. Not a single case was excluded or overlooked. Even those cases that were commenced in state court were transferred to New York. Since the Panel had no jurisdiction over state court proceedings, we first had to remove the cases to federal court and then petition the Panel to transfer them. This was not always easy. Many plaintiffs attorneys around the country vigorously opposed our efforts to remove and transfer. "I just want my case to stay in state court in Boston," one attorney told us. "I want no part of that circus on Long Island." Another attorney argued that his case should remain in state court in Kentucky because the New York proceedings involved a lot of "sheer foolishness" and "my client wants to have his case tried during his lifetime." But this opposition was all for naught.

As a result of the complete consolidation of the Agent Orange litigation, there was no duplication of effort in different jurisdictions during the pretrial process. We produced our documents once. We deposed every witness once. We made and opposed every motion once. You did not need an accounting degree to conclude that multidistrict consolidation of the Agent Orange litigation saved Dow huge sums of money in defense costs and expenses.

2.4 Million Class Members: The fifteen thousand named plaintiffs in the Agent Orange class action were suing not only on their own behalf but also on behalf of a class, or group, defined as "those persons who were in the United States, New Zealand or Australian Armed Forces at any time from 1961 to 1972 who were injured while in or near Vietnam by exposure to Agent Orange." The class also included "spouses, parents, and children of the veterans born before January 1, 1984, directly or derivatively injured as a result of the exposure."[36]

Plaintiffs contended that all 2.4 million servicemen who served in Vietnam "had some chance of exposure to Agent Orange" and thus were class members, along with their spouses and children. Others estimated that the number of exposed servicemen was closer to 600,000.[37]

The parties and the court wrestled long and hard to arrive at a workable class definition. One issue that was potentially very troublesome was whether to include unborn children. The defendants' position was that unborn children were not injured and may never be injured and therefore had no cause of action. The court's view was that including unborn children would make the situation "almost intolerable. You'd have to have a guardian for each unborn child. We don't know what the situation will be." Plaintiff's lead trial attorney then surprised everyone by telling the court, "This may be a situation where the plaintiffs and defendants agree."

> THE COURT: All right. Then the class will exclude the unborn as of the time judgment is entered. They have to be born before the time of judgment. That simplifies that. That takes care of an infinitum of generations. This is the largest exclusionary ruling ever made in the history of the law. Billions of people.

The judge made clear that he was not disenfranchising the unborn children. He was merely excluding them from the class. "They can bring a separate suit later on their own behalf."

Incidentally, as if a class action by 2.4 million Vietnam era veterans was not enough, a second class action was commenced in Hawaii and transferred to New York on behalf of thirty-five thousand civilian residents of Hawaii who alleged that they were exposed to Agent Orange during a testing program in 1967.[38]

200,000 Class Notification Letters: The Agent Orange litigation was certified under a provision of the Federal Rules of Civil Procedure which required the court "to direct to the members of the class the best notice practicable under the circumstances [of the pendency of the action], including individual notice to all members who can be identified through reasonable effort."[39] To satisfy this requirement, the judge directed the named plaintiffs to mail notice of the class action to more than 200,000 persons, including all persons who had filed Agent Orange lawsuits, all class members represented by attorneys involved in the Agent Orange litigation, and all persons listed on the Agent Orange Registry maintained by the Veterans Administration.

Plaintiffs also mailed copies of the notice to the governors of each of the fifty states with a request that the notice be referred to all state agencies with responsibilities relating to Vietnam era veterans.

Public service announcements regarding the pendency of the class action aired on the three major television networks and on major radio stations in the one hundred largest radio markets.

Notice of the class action was published in The New York *Times, U.S.A. Today, Time* Magazine, the *American Legion* Magazine, *VFW* Magazine, *Air Force Times, Army Times, Navy Times,* and the *Leatherneck.*

Notice was also published in the ten largest circulation newspapers in Australia and the five largest in New Zealand.[40]

Multinational Stateless Conglomerate Chemical Empire Defendants: A total of twenty-four corporations participated as defendants in the Agent Orange litigation,[41] although as it turned out only seven companies manufactured Agent Orange for use in Vietnam.

Yannacone, never satisfied in court or in the press to refer to the defendants simply as "the defendants" or "the chemical companies," used far more colorful terms, such as the time he called us "multinational stateless conglomerate chemical empires,"[42] all designed to win sympathy for the veterans and create hostility toward his adversaries.

The main defendants, the manufacturers of Agent Orange, included such household names as Dow, Monsanto, Hercules, Uniroyal, and Diamond Shamrock. The combined net assets of the seven companies which manufactured Agent Orange, including insurance, was nearly $16 billion.[43]

The United States government was also a defendant and third-party defendant.

$12 Billion in Damages: From the very beginning of the Agent Orange dispute, Dow had a pretty good handle on the nature of the veterans' health complaints. Many were suffering from fatal forms of cancer; many of their children were suffering from debilitating birth defects. Other complaints included rashes, numbness, sleeplessness, irritability, frequent headaches, loss of sex drive, psychological problems, and other troublesome but not fatal or totally disabling conditions.

The cancer and birth defect claims caused the most concern. In the late 1970s, a successful plaintiff in a serious cancer or birth defect case could easily recover $1 million. If twelve thousand veterans, only one-half of one percent of the 2.4 million class members, recovered that amount, which was conceivable although not likely, damages would have totaled $12 billion.

Fifteen Thousand Plaintiffs' Attorneys: Nearly fifteen thousand law firms from all of the United States were involved to some extent representing Agent Orange plaintiffs and class members. Virtually all of the work, however, was performed by lead counsel. For the first four and one-half years, lead counsel was "Yannacone & Associates," also referred to as the "Long Island Consortium," which consisted of attorneys from eight Long Island law firms. Thereafter, lead counsel responsibility was assumed by the "Agent Orange Plaintiffs' Management Committee," which consisted of nine attorneys from firms in Chicago, Cincinnati, Houston, Philadelphia, Pittsburgh, San Francisco, and Long Island. Six law professors also made major contributions to the class plaintiffs.[44]

Hundreds of Defense Attorneys: Hundreds of attorneys participated in the litigation on behalf of the corporate defendants.

At our firm, in July 1978, when the case first began, I assigned two lawyers to assist me. Five years later, our defense team had grown from three to twelve, including five partners. In a pinch, we borrowed attorneys from other parts of the firm's practice on a temporary basis. For example, early in 1983 we assigned five lawyers to full time two week shifts to help us review documents. In May 1984, on the eve of trial, we assigned fifteen lawyers to assist us in conducting as many as two hundred depositions which would proceed simultaneously with the trial. Overall, approximately twenty-five lawyers from our firm worked full time on Agent Orange at some point between July 1978 and December 1984.

I was very fortunate to have a superb group of attorneys assisting me on the case. Those who worked the longest on the case and made the greatest contributions were Les Bennett, Steve Brock, Bill Cavanaugh, Pam Esterman, Marge Mintzer, Joe Ortego, Stan Pierce, Jim Ruger, and Jeff Silberfeld.

Les Bennett, Steve Brock, and Jeff Silberfeld were exceptional researchers and writers whose efforts, considering the amount of briefs that had to be written, were indispensable. As but one example of how highly regarded their work was, in November 1983 Morton Silberman, one of the lead attorneys for Thompson-Hayward and a former New York State Supreme Court judge, sent us a letter saying that our class action brief was a "truly excellent piece of work. It is one of the finest briefs that I have seen in this litigation."

Stan Pierce and Jim Ruger were scientists as well as lawyers. Stan had a Masters and Ph.D. in biology from New York University and was the former Acting Chairman of the Biology Department at Queen's College. Jim was a licensed pharmacist who obtained his Ph.D. in Toxicology while working on the Agent Orange case. Jim kept a jar of Agent Orange on a bookshelf in his office, which made several people in the firm who were swayed by the media coverage of the case more than a little nervous.

I doubt we would have understood the complex science of the case nearly as well as we did without having had Stan and Jim on our defense team. Moreover, aside from educating us mere mortals, Stan and Jim helped Dow's cause in other ways we never could have imagined.

For example, on a trip to London, Stan and Charley Carey of Dow met with a potential expert witness. The witness told them that he was finalizing a paper in which his conclusions regarding causation were not favorable to Dow's position. Stan scanned a draft of the paper while Charley continued the interview. "There are a lot of mistakes in here," Stan said when he was done reading and began to explain. The witness promised to hold up publication so that Stan could send him some supporting documentation, which Stan did, as soon as he got back to New York.

Another time, on trip to Australia, Stan and Charley Carey were at the home of a very impressive potential expert witness who had reluctantly agreed to the interview and showed no interest in working on Dow's behalf. The witness had a remarkable, museum like collection of archeological artifacts and sea shells on display and was giving Charley and Stan a tour. As they approached a shelf of shells, Stan bent down to look at one in particular. "Scaphopoda, genus dentalium," Stan said. The witness was stunned. "I can't believe you knew that," he said. At that moment, his whole attitude about Dow seemed to change. At the end of the interview, he agreed to become one of Dow's experts.

Believing that the Agent Orange case would involve a great deal of factual investigation, I hired Joe Ortego, a former prosecutor from the Manhattan District Attorney's Office, who showed a great deal of thoroughness and creativity in tracking down and eliciting helpful information from potential witnesses.

One time, attempting to locate witnesses who had attended certain meetings at Dow in 1964, Joe flew to Toledo to interview a dermatologist. When Joe identified himself over the telephone as an attorney for Dow, the dermatologist refused to speak with him. So Joe called the dermatologist's office and, posing as a patient, made an appointment for the next morning. Once inside the examining room, Joe revealed his true identity to the dermatologist, who was impressed by Joe's determination and agreed to an interview. During the course of the interview, the dermatologist revealed that he had boxes of old papers in his attic. That night, the dermatologist searched through those boxes and found handwritten notes he had prepared summarizing meetings at Dow. But Joe could not be sure that the notes summarized the 1964 meetings, because they were undated. After being snowbound in Toledo for two days with only the clothes on his back, Joe took the notes back to New York and contacted an old friend from the FBI, who told the Joe that FBI technicians could figure out the date of the document by examining the ink. The technicians later determined that the document was prepared in 1964.

*   *   *

In addition to the lawyers from our firm, Dow also used the services of twenty-four law firms, which we referred to as "local counsel," in twenty-five cities in twenty-one states to assist us in transferring to

New York Agent Orange cases that were commenced elsewhere. The twenty-four firms were located in Albany, Baltimore, Baton Rouge, Belleville (Ill.), Boston, Charleston (W. Va.), Chicago, Columbus, Dallas, Denver, Denville (N.J.), Detroit, Houston, Jackson (Miss.), Las Vegas, Los Angeles, Louisville, Miami, Milwaukee, Minneapolis, Nashville, Philadelphia, Portland (Ore.), Reno, and San Francisco. Dow also retained a law firm in Sydney, Australia. A lawyer from our office visited every one of Dow's local counsel in the United States at least once. We also held a meeting in Midland in May 1981, which all local counsel attended, in order to establish an "eyeball to eyeball relationship."

* * *

The lawyers from our office were also supported by a team of paralegals which grew from four when the case first began to twenty-five on the eve of trial. The paralegals took their responsibilities as seriously as the lawyers took theirs. They had input into the filing system, room assignments, and individual responsibilities. They were included in our weekly update meetings. They even graciously agreed to run an occasional personal errand for an attorney (frequently, that attorney was me), but insisted that such errands "not take precedence over our everyday duties."

Last but not least, Joanne Miele, my personal secretary for fourteen years, including the entire length of the Agent Orange litigation, worked long hours typing and then retyping my letters and memos, keeping my schedule, confirming my travel arrangements, and even balancing my checkbook. When the Dow people who planned on attending the trial asked us to find accommodations for them, Joanne, feared at the local flea market for her negotiating skills, convinced the nearby Marriott Hotel, which normally charged ninety dollars per night for a room, to charge us thirty-five dollars. Joanne's good humor, loyalty, and dedication were a true blessing. Her untimely death from cancer at the age of forty-seven in 1994 was a great loss to her family and to me.

* * *

Of course, we could not have defended Dow without the able assistance of many Dow executives, lawyers, claims personnel, scientists, and paralegals. I must mention three in particular.

Don Frayer, Dow's in-house Claims Manager, supervised the case for the first two years. The terrific working relationship and friendship we developed during the Staten Island explosion case continued during Agent Orange. His photographic memory never ceased to amaze me. He had a keen eye for detail. Frequently he acted as Dow's spokesperson to the media. He was largely responsible for developing Dow's "toxicological cocktail" defense.

Charley Carey, from Dow's Legal Department, took over in 1981 after Don was named a company Vice President. A gracious gentleman and fine attorney, Charley worked with me for four intense years. I ran everything by him; we spoke on the telephone half a dozen times every day. He made me feel at home on all of my numerous trips to Midland. When Charley died after a long illness in 1988, I lost not just a colleague but a dear friend.

Finally, Keith McKennon, Dow's Group Vice President, was the highest ranking corporate officer at Dow who was personally involved in the case. Several steps removed from day to day events, he nevertheless had a full grasp of the issues and facts. His wise assistance and support, particularly during the final days, were instrumental in the ultimate disposition of the case.

Millions of Dollars in Legal Fees: Approximately eighty-nine individual attorneys, law firms, and law professors who represented the class plaintiffs were awarded approximately $10.7 million in legal fees and expenses by the court.[45]

Although no exact figures are available, it has been estimated that defense costs and expenses exceeded $100 million.[46]

Hundreds of Millions of Dollars in Government Expenditures: Aside from the enormous amount of man hours expended by government attorneys defending the United States in the lawsuit and by other government employees, both civilian and military, searching for documents and testifying at depositions, the United States spent hundreds of millions of dollars as a consequence of the Agent Orange controversy, including $70 million per year to treat veterans at VA hospitals and another $150 million on research.[47]

Not Enough Hours in the Day: With so much at stake in such a vast, complex case, there were not enough hours in the day or days in the week for all of the work that had to be done.

We reviewed millions of pages of documents collected and produced by Dow, our co-defendants, and the United States government. The documents were coded, and the information was computerized, at a cost to the defendants of well over a million dollars. But in the words of an attorney for one of our co-defendants, "I'm not going to lose my job because I spent too much money winning the Agent Orange case."

We conducted hundreds of interviews with present and former employees of Dow, present and former employees of the government, scientists, physicians, and other potential fact and expert witnesses.

We obtained one thousand reels of microfilm containing plaintiffs' medical records.

We wrote thousands of letters and internal office memoranda.

We made so many long distance telephone calls that we installed a toll free phone line just for the Agent Orange case.

We attended hundreds of depositions, sometimes as many as five in one day.

We reviewed thousands of scientific papers.

We attended hundreds of meetings and court appearances.

We traveled to nearly every state in the union for interviews, depositions, meetings, and court appearances. We also traveled to Australia, Austria, Canada, England, Germany, Italy, New Zealand, and Sweden in search of expert witnesses.

We researched hundreds of legal, factual, and procedural issues.

We wrote and submitted hundreds of briefs arguing complex legal and factual issues to the trial court, the Second Circuit Court of Appeals, and the Supreme Court of the United States, very often working around the clock right up to the filing deadline.

Like the time we moved for summary judgment on the government contract defense. Our brief and supporting exhibits had to be filed at the clerk's office at the courthouse on Wednesday afternoon by 5 p.m. We finished our eighty-seven page brief late Tuesday evening. We then collected the two hundred supporting exhibits, such as documents and excerpts from deposition transcripts, arranged them in order, and tagged each one with its exhibit number. The stack of exhibits was so high that we compiled two volumes. Volume I contained Exhibits 1 through 100; Volume II contained Exhibits 101 through 200.

Then the fun began. We needed fifty copies of the brief, three for filing at the clerk's office, forty for mailing to the attorneys on the case service list, and the rest for our files, Dow, and Fireman's Fund. That was not going to be a problem. But we also needed fifty copies of the exhibits. In other words, we needed to make fifty copies of Volume I and fifty copies of Volume II, each copy had to contain the exhibits in order, and each exhibit had to be properly tagged. A monumental task.

Steve Brock and a team of paralegals went into one room to make fifty copies of Volume I. Bill Cavanaugh and a team of paralegals went into another room to make fifty copies of Volume II. The two teams worked all Tuesday night and into Wednesday copying, arranging, tagging.

At around 4:45 Wednesday afternoon, fifteen minutes before the filing deadline, after the last staple had been put into the last copy of the last exhibit, Bill Cavanaugh hurriedly stuffed three copies of the brief and exhibit volumes into a cardboard box, raced to the elevator, rode down to the parking lot, raced to his car, stuffed the boxes in the trunk, and sped off to the courthouse, which was ten minutes away. He filed the papers at 4:59, beating the deadline with one minute to spare.

*   *   *

Or the time we filed a brief in the Supreme Court in opposition to plaintiffs' petition for a writ of certiorari. Incidentally, this was the very first brief I had ever filed in the Supreme Court. In their petition, plaintiffs asked the Court to review a November 1980 decision by the Second Circuit Court of Appeals in which the court held that the veterans' claims against the chemical companies did not arise under federal common law. In our brief, we argued that the Second Circuit's decision was consistent with prior Supreme Court rulings and that Supreme Court review was therefore unnecessary.

We worked long and hard on the brief and then sent it to the printing company, which prepared it in final form, served a copy on all parties, and filed the requisite number of copies in the Supreme Court. On the day the brief was due in Washington, the printing company hand delivered our copies to us in Garden City. I opened the package and was shocked to find a stack of briefs with bright orange covers. I blew my top.

"Is this somebody's idea of a joke?" I yelled.

Jeff Silberfeld quickly pulled out a copy of the Supreme Court rules.

"Calm down, Len," he said after finding the appropriate subsection. "The covers of all briefs in opposition to petitions for certiorari must be colored orange. Agent Orange had has nothing to do with it."

*   *   *

The Agent Orange case generated so much paperwork that I had to abandon my customary habit of reading every document. Instead, I instructed the attorneys and paralegals to prepare summaries. But then I found that I did not have enough time to read the summaries, so my staff began to summarize the summaries for me.

I also had to abandon my custom of drafting and forwarding detailed weekly report letters to the client. I simply did not have the time to write about all that was going on. Instead, I assigned the task to

Marge Mintzer, who, as my second-in-command in charge of all aspects of the case except causation, already had more than enough to do. But she accepted the assignment and actually devised a shortcut. Instead of reporting weekly, she reported monthly. And instead of preparing detailed report letters, she simply sent the client a "cover" letter and a stack of documents. Marge's typical cover letter was seven single spaced pages and forwarded more than one hundred enclosures, including deposition summaries, court submissions, pretrial orders, and transcripts of court appearances, a pile of material several feet high.

Very often the senior attorneys on my staff would plead for me to hire more help. "We are stretched to our capacity," they would complain. The amount of work they had to do was "staggering."

Then there were the Saturday meetings. Since the members of our defense team traveled so much during the week, the only day we could all meet to discuss the case was Saturday. The team dreaded these meetings. Each attorney would bring everyone else up to date on his or her particular area of responsibility, and then I would give assignments that were usually due two days later, on Monday. The attorneys sitting around the conference table would sink down in their chairs hoping that I would not see them and therefore not assign them a project.

On one occasion, I gave an assignment at a Saturday meeting to Joe Ortego, who worked in the firm library until 9:30 p.m. When he got home, he walked into a houseful of guests. He was two hours late for a surprise birthday party his wife was throwing for him. Joe was so tired from work that he poured himself a drink, sat down in his favorite easy chair, and promptly fell asleep. Four of the people his wife had invited were on the Agent Orange defense team, but none of them showed up because they also worked that night.

Another time, Les Bennett was in Arizona all week taking depositions. He called me late Friday afternoon to tell me he was flying home on the red-eye and would probably miss the Saturday meeting. "Don't worry," I reassured him. "We'll start the meeting an hour later. That will give you plenty of time to freshen up before you get here." When Les showed up in time for the meeting, he looked exhausted. "You okay?" I asked. "I'm fine," he snapped. He did not say much else that morning, and I spared him a weekend assignment.

There were also my December "vacations." Some vacations. I went to Florida for two weeks, not the usual four, and instead of packing my fishing rod I packed litigation bags filled with Agent Orange documents. I sat on my boat at the dock reading, not fishing. I called the office and the client in Midland a dozen times every day. When I wanted to assign some work to an attorney in the office, I told my secretary Joanne to tell the attorney that I was using my ship to shore radio to phone in, which allowed me to speak to the person I was calling but the person could not speak to me. I wanted to avoid listening to the attorneys' complaints. Most of the time my scheme worked, although a few times I heard some muttering that was definitely not intended for my ears.

Plaintiffs' attorneys worked as hard as we did. In April of 1980, for example, when the case was less than two years old, the judge chastised Victor Yannacone for repeatedly missing filing deadlines. Yannacone explained:

> MR. YANNACONE: You might be doing us all a favor by relieving us of the obligation of representing the plaintiffs at this stage. The case has grown considerably beyond what we expected when we filed it originally, and the organizational problems of converting what amounts to be a country law practice to a lawpractice that looks like the defense attorneys' operations in the city have placed strains on us that we did not expect.[48]

Of course, although the Agent Orange case involved an extraordinary amount of toil and sweat, it was not all work and no play. There was an occasional light moment.

Like the time Les Bennett had two days of depositions on Thursday and Friday in Daytona Beach, Florida, and two more days of depositions the following Monday and Tuesday in Tampa. He flew down with his wife and two children, who spent six days at Disneyworld. He joined them over the weekend.

Or the time our Stan Pierce went to Washington to interview a government witness. The witness agreed to meet Stan for lunch, but when Stan arrived the witness told him that he wanted to go to the National Gallery to see an exhibit of paintings by the Dutch Masters, which was closing that night. So Stan accompanied the witness to the museum and spent three enjoyable hours chatting about art and Agent Orange.

One Hundred Reported Decisions: The case generated paperwork not only by the attorneys but also by the judges, who published nearly one hundred opinions during the course of the litigation. In addition to the many trial court opinions written by Judge Pratt and Judge Weinstein, the Second Circuit Court of Appeals wrote nearly two dozen opinions deciding appeals, motions for leave to appeal, and petitions for writs of mandamus. The United States Supreme

Court also wrote one opinion and ruled upon more than one dozen petitions for writs of certiorari.

Dozens of Legal Issues: In addition to interviewing hundreds of potential fact and expert witnesses, producing and reviewing millions of pages of documents, conducting and defending hundreds of depositions, studying thousands of scientific and technical articles, attending meetings, making phone calls, writing letters and memos, and traveling around the country and the world, the attorneys involved in the Agent Orange litigation spent thousands of hours researching, analyzing, discussing, negotiating, briefing, and arguing in court dozens of important, cutting-edge legal issues, both substantive and procedural, including the following:

Whether the Judicial Panel on Multidistrict Litigation should consolidate all Agent Orange cases for all pretrial purposes in one federal court;

Whether the claims against the manufacturers were governed by state law or by federal common law;

Whether there was a right under the United States Constitution to a safe and healthful environment;

Whether to certify the Agent Orange litigation as a class action;

Whether the manufacturers of Agent Orange owed money damages to veterans and members of their families who were not yet injured or sick as a result of exposure to Agent Orange but who were allegedly "at risk" of becoming sick or injured in the future;

Whether a veteran should be allowed to recover if he is unable to prove which company manufactured the specific batch of Agent Orange to which that veteran was exposed;

Whether to require a veteran to prove causation using scientific studies linking exposure to Agent Orange to his particular illness or allow that veteran to prove causation using only statistical data;

Whether the veterans' claims were barred by the statute of limitations;

Whether the manufacturers were immune from liability because of the government contract defense;

Whether the United States government was immune from tort liability for the veterans' alleged injuries;

Whether to allow thousands of veterans to file lawsuits against the government under the Federal Tort Claims Act without requiring them to first exhaust their administrative remedies;

Whether decisions by the Veterans' Administration denying benefits for Agent Orange related injuries were subject to judicial review;

Whether to impute knowledge about herbicides and dioxin from one government agency to another;

Whether to prohibit government attorneys from advising former government employees not to talk to Dow attorneys about the case;

Whether to enjoin thousands of government offices from destroying documents pursuant to the government's regular document retention program to avoid the possibility of inadvertently destroying documents relevant to the Agent Orange case;

Whether the court could prohibit attorneys from speaking to reporters about the case;

Whether to allow the media to have access to documents produced in discovery;

Whether to allow the parties to videotape the depositions of terminally ill veterans;

Whether to require the manufacturers to produce documents in discovery containing confidential business information;

Whether to conduct a series of mini-trials, each limited to one issue, or one mega-trial addressing every issue; and

Whether to strike plaintiffs' jury demand and conduct a bench trial because of the complexity of the case.

A Ton of Pressure: With so much at stake, so many complex issues, so much work, and so little time, the attorneys in the Agent Orange litigation worked under enormous pressure. Moreover, we worked in a fish bowl, not just before our clients, our adversaries, other attorneys, and the court, but thanks to all the publicity the case generated before the entire world. No wonder we sometimes lost our tempers, spent a sleepless night or two, or needed a hit of Alka Seltzer before bedtime.

In one instance, the consequences of the intense pressure were far more tragic.

On April 5, 1984, one month before the class action trial was scheduled to begin, three defense attorneys, including Monsanto's lead trial counsel, asked Judge Weinstein for an adjournment. The attorney for Thompson Chemical made an impassioned plea for more time, explaining that attorneys were working too hard and some were getting sick.

Judge Weinstein denied the request.

Three weeks later, one week before the trial date, Monsanto's lead trial attorney suffered a nervous breakdown.

Monsanto immediately made a motion for a six month adjournment, which Judge Weinstein denied. The court transcripts relating to Monsanto's request were sealed, but according to one commentator Judge Weinstein told Monsanto's lawyers, "You have a large firm. Get someone else [to try the case]."[49] In Judge Weinstein's defense, it was obvious to me that he was saddened by the news and felt deeply for the stricken attorney and the attorney's family. Nevertheless, the MDL proceedings had been pending for nearly five years. On more than one occasion, the judge had made it crystal clear to all of us that he would not tolerate any further delays. It has been suggested that the judge's strategy was not necessarily to get the case tried but to keep the pressure on all of the parties to induce them to settle.[50] In any event, the message was clear: no adjournment, no matter what the reason.

All of the attorneys left the courthouse that afternoon in a very somber mood. What had happened to Monsanto's lead trial counsel could have happened to any one of us. But, at least for me, this mood did not last very long. Within the hour, I was back at my desk looking at a stack of unanswered phone messages, a pile of unread mail, and a line outside my door of anxious attorneys and paralegals waiting to see me. Business as usual.

*   *   *

This description of the Agent Orange litigation, focusing on the publicity, the related legislative and administrative activity, and the numbers, paints a vivid picture but not a complete one. Having described the outward characteristics of the lawsuit, my next task is to tell you what actually happened, how the case was litigated, and how it was resolved. I begin that task in the next chapter, in which I provide a behind-the-scenes look at Dow's litigation strategy and how that strategy shaped the course of the lawsuit.

CHAPTER TEN

Litigation Strategy

In July 1978, when the first Agent Orange lawsuit was filed, you didn't have to be a genius to recognize that defending Dow Chemical in the Agent Orange litigation was not going to be easy.

This was a case that was likely to be resolved more on the basis of emotion than fact.

Paul Reutershan was the first Agent Orange plaintiff, but we expected thousands if not hundreds of thousands more. Veterans of the Vietnam War, their spouses, and their children. Many suffering from fatal forms of cancer or grievous birth defects. Many of the veterans unemployed and having great difficulty readjusting to civilian life. Perceived by themselves and the public as unknowing victims of chemical toxins. Spurned by the VA. Portrayed heroically in the press and on television.

It would have been hard to imagine a more sympathetic group of plaintiffs.

Their opponent: Dow Chemical, the napalm company. Vilified for the fires that destroyed Vietnamese villages and slaughtered innocent Vietnamese women and children. A war contractor. A long-standing member of the military industrial complex. A company charged with putting profit ahead of the health and safety of American soldiers. In the words of Victor Yannacone, a "soulless stateless multinational conglomerate chemical empire."

It would have been hard to imagine a less sympathetic defendant.

Then there was the jury, to be selected from the general population. Registered voters. People whom the media was bombarding with powerful images of dying veterans and crippled children. People who, upon seeing those images, may have felt guilty about the anti-war movement and the cool reception afforded the veterans upon their return from Vietnam. People who associated Dow with napalm but not much else. People who were likely to look for some way to make it up to the veterans for their sacrifices and suffering. If that had to be done at Dow's expense, so be it.

Under those circumstances, what were the odds of Dow trying the case before a fair and impartial jury.

On the facts, Dow's defenses were strong. In particular, existing scientific data provided virtually no support for the veterans' claims that exposure to Agent Orange caused their various illnesses and injuries.

But would a jury be able to disregard the publicity, put aside its guilt and sympathy for the veterans, and find in favor of the hated Dow Chemical Company solely on the basis of dry, technical, mostly unintelligible scientific data?

We had our doubts.

Accordingly, we had to come up with a strategy. We had to level the playing field. There was no way we were ever going to make the veterans less sympathetic, so we had to find some way to make Dow more sympathetic, or at least to deflect some of the anti-Dow sentiment toward someone or something else.

To me, the answer was obvious.

The "bad guy" in the Agent Orange controversy was not Dow Chemical. It was the United States government.

* * *

Dow's Government Strategy

Having identified the government as the bad guy, our next step was to figure out how to involve the government in the litigation in ways that would strengthen Dow's defensive position. We devised a two-pronged approach. First, we asserted the government contract defense. Second, we commenced a third-party action for contribution or indemnification against the United States government under the Federal Tort Claims Act.

As it turned out, both of these strategies worked to Dow's great advantage in that they did, in fact, shift the focus of the litigation away from Dow's conduct and toward the government's.

They also created the need for substantial additional discovery and raised a host of complex legal and factual issues. Although this dramatically increased the cost of litigating the case, Dow was more than willing to pay that price it if increased Dow's chances of mounting a successful defense.

Finally, Dow's third-party action had an additional impact all its own. It recast the role of the government in the Agent Orange litigation from non-party to third-party defendant. This was hugely significant. As a non-party, the government's only obligation was to produce witnesses and documents. It faced relatively minor litigation expenses and no risk of tort liability. In contrast, as a third-party defendant, not only was the government obligated to produce witnesses and documents, it also had to defend itself against charges of negligence in a multi-billion dollar class action. As such, it faced enormous litigation expenses and a substantial risk of a staggering adverse judgment.

*   *   *

The Government Contract Defense: This was the defense that inspired Victor Yannacone to liken the manufacturers of Agent Orange to Nazi war criminals. "It was not a good defense at Nuremberg," he told a reporter in 1980, "and the veterans we represent feel it's not a good defense here in the United States."[1]

Coming from Yannacone, this inflammatory reference to Nazis and Nuremberg did not surprise us. Later, however, I nearly fell out of my seat when Judge Weinstein, normally dispassionate about the parties' claims and defenses, made the following observation during his first pretrial conference:

> THE COURT: I understand that there is a substantial question here because this is a national defense problem and we can't have manufacturers all over the country telling the government they don't want to manufacture things. The country can't go forward and have a national defense establishment on that basis.
>
> On the other hand, we do have the Nuremberg defense problem, and neither individual soldiers nor manufacturers are free to just operate on the basis that they were ordered to do something and, therefore, they are not responsible for any damages.

Notwithstanding these rather unflattering characterizations, by the late 1970s the government contract defense was well established under American law, having had its origins in a 1940 decision by the United States Supreme Court.[2] The first cases to apply the defense, which was an extension of the doctrine of sovereign immunity, involved companies that had performed government construction contracts, such as a contract to dredge a river[3] or build a road.[4] Although the precise elements of the defense varied slightly from one case to the next, they generally held that even though the work of a government contractor caused damages to another party, the contractor was entitled to the same immunity from liability for those damages as the government if the contractor performed the work in strict compliance with government specifications.[5]

The rationale for sustaining the government contract defense in these early construction cases was purely economic. As one court reasoned:

> To impose liability on the contractor [when it complies with government specifications] would render the Government's immunity...meaningless, for if the contractor was held liable, contract prices to the Government would be increased to cover the contractor's risk of loss."[6]

Later cases, more directly on point to Agent Orange, applied the government contract defense to companies that had contracted to manufacture or produce a product for use by the military. Once again, the dispositive factor was whether the product complied with government specifications. In one case, for example, Ford Motor Company was immune from liability for injuries sustained in an accident involving a Jeep manufactured for the Army in compliance with government specifications without seatbelts or a roll bar.[7] In another, a manufacturer of a dough mixer for use in Army field kitchens was immune from liability for injuries caused by exposed blades when the product as made complied with government specifications.[8]

The rationale for sustaining the defense in these cases was a concern for the government's ability to wage war and protect the national security. In the Jeep case, the court concluded that to impose tort liability upon the manufacturers of military equipment "would seriously impair the government's ability to formulate policy and make judgments pursuant to its war powers."[9] Similarly, in the dough mixer case, the court explained:

> The supplier to the military in time of war has a right to rely upon such specifications and is not obligated to withhold from the United States armed forces material believed by the latter to be necessary because the manufacturer considers the design to be imprudent or even dangerous. His conformance, under such circumstances, to the specifications provided to him should be, and is, a complete defense.[10]

Based on all of this precedent, Dow pleaded a version of the government contract defense that required Dow to prove two elements: that the government established the specifications for Agent Orange, and that the Agent Orange manufactured by Dow complied with those specifications in all material respects.

Later, Judge Pratt added a third element, which required Dow to prove that the government knew as much as or more than Dow about the hazards to people, if any, that accompanied the use of Agent Orange.[11]

Why the third element? Judge Pratt explained that he agreed with the general proposition that compliance with government specifications should be a defense in cases involving the procurement of weapons in time of war. But he believed that it should only apply in those cases where a fully informed government has had the "opportunity to fairly balance the...risks and benefits"[12] of the weapon in question. The judge elaborated:

Courts should not require suppliers of ordnance to question the military's needs or specifications for weapons during wartime. Whether to use a particular weapon that creates a risk to third parties, whether the risk could be avoided at additional cost, whether the weapon could be made safer if a longer manufacturing time were allowed, indeed, whether the weapon involves any risk at all, are all proper concerns of the military which selects, buys and uses the weapon. But they are not sources of liability which should be thrust upon a supplier, nor are they decisions that are properly made by a court.

Public policy does require, however, that the military's decisions on those vital questions should at least be made on the basis of the readily available information. A supplier should not be insulated from liability for damages that would never have occurred if the military had been apprised of hazards known to the supplier. A supplier, therefore, has a duty to inform the military of known risks attendant to a particular weapon that it supplies, so as to provide the military with at least an opportunity to fairly balance the weapon's risks and benefits.

This principle would not impose upon a supplier any duty of testing that was not included in the specifications. It merely would require the supplier to share with the military the extent of the supplier's knowledge about the hazards of the product being purchased. If this knowledge level between supplier and the military is at least in balance, the supplier is then shielded by the government contract defense from liability for damages resulting from use of a product supplied pursuant to and in compliance with government contract specifications.[13]

The two-element version of the defense, as pleaded by Dow, focused to some extent on government conduct because it required the parties to examine the government specification process. When Judge Pratt added the relative knowledge element, government conduct became one of the central issues in the case.

*   *   *

Dow's Third-Party Action: In its third-party action, Dow sued the government for contribution and indemnity. In a carefully worded third-party complaint, Dow emphatically denied that it was liable for any of the veterans' injuries, charged the government with specific acts of negligence relating to its use of Agent Orange in Vietnam, and alleged that if the veterans somehow managed to obtain a judgment against Dow, then Dow would be entitled to recover from the government some or all of that judgment.

Dow's third-party action reflected its strong belief that if anybody was to blame for the veterans' health problems, the United States government was far more culpable than the manufacturers of Agent Orange under any standard of analysis. After all, the government made the decision to use herbicides in Vietnam, after experimenting and testing herbicides for military uses for twenty years. The government unilaterally decided which herbicides to use in Vietnam and determined the exact chemical composition and makeup of those herbicides. In order to guarantee that it received adequate quantities, the government compelled Dow and the other defendants to produce and deliver herbicides to the military pursuant to the mandatory provisions of the Defense Production Act. The government unilaterally controlled the use of deployment of herbicides in Vietnam. Evidence suggested that the government failed to adequately train its soldiers on the safe and proper use of herbicides. The government sprayed herbicides in Vietnam in far greater amounts and concentrations than had ever been done commercially. Finally, the government exposed its servicemen to the herbicides even though the government knew that the herbicides contained trace amounts of the highly toxic chemical impurity known as dioxin.

The belief that most if not all of the fault lay with the government was not Dow's alone. Indeed, so widespread was this belief that Judge Pratt made the following observation in one of his opinions addressing the issue of government liability:

> Overarching the entire dispute is a feeling on both sides that whatever existing law and procedures may technically require,

fairness, justice and equity in this unprecedented controversy demand that the government assume responsibility for the harm caused our soldiers and their families by its use of Agent Orange in southeast Asia.[14]

While there may have been a consensus that Dow's third-party action was strong on the facts, we nevertheless faced some serious legal obstacles in our effort to hold the government accountable.

Dow's asserted its third-party claims against the United States under the Federal Tort Claims Act ("FTCA"),[15] the statutory waiver of the government's traditional sovereign immunity from tort lawsuits. My firm was well familiar with the pitfalls of litigating under the FTCA, having spent nearly four years prosecuting FTCA claims against the government in the Franklin National Bank case. Franklin introduced us to many of the FTCA's troublesome statutory defenses but did little to prepare us for what turned out to be the biggest obstacle to the successful prosecution of Dow's third-party claims: the infamous *Feres* doctrine, which was not even articulated in the language of the statute but was entirely judge made.

The *Feres* doctrine, which took its name from the Supreme Court decision that first applied it,[16] provided that the government could not be liable under the FTCA for injuries sustained by a serviceman "incident"[17] to his military service. The doctrine barred not only direct suits against the government by the injured serviceman but also third-party actions for contribution or indemnity.[18] The term "incident to service" was broadly construed and not limited to injuries sustained during actual combat or other military type operations. Instead, "incident to service" extended to any situation where there was a "rational connection between [the serviceman's] claim or loss and his status as a member of the armed forces."[19] As one court explained it, "It is the status of the claimant as a serviceman rather than the legal theory of his claim which governs."[20] Thus, the doctrine barred a claim by an off duty serviceman injured before he left his military base;[21] it barred a claim by an off duty serviceman injured while flying home on a military aircraft;[22] it barred a claim by a serviceman who died in a fire caused by a defective heating unit while sleeping in his barracks;[23] and it barred a claim by a serviceman injured while riding a horse rented from a Marine Corps stable.[24]

Significantly, the Feres doctrine barred FTCA claims against the government no matter how egregious or outrageous the government's misconduct turned out to be. Indeed, one judge aptly summed up the scope and breadth of the *Feres* doctrine in the following comments addressed to a government attorney during oral argument of a motion to dismiss on *Feres* grounds: "As I read the law, it doesn't matter if they stood up there and said, 'One, two, left, right, left,' and marched them over a cliff...You'd be protected under Feres..."[25]

If the government could not be liable for marching its soldiers over a cliff, certainly Dow was not going to have an easy time imposing liability on the government for spraying its soldiers with Agent Orange.

Dow's response to the *Feres* doctrine was to argue that the rule should be limited to cases the size and scope of the original *Feres* decision, which involved relatively minor claims for damages by three servicemen injured in three unrelated incidents:

> Surely the Supreme Court did not intend to insulate the United States from tort liability in every case involving servicemen without regard to the number of servicemen involved, the extent of their alleged injuries, the amount of damages claimed, the relative culpability of the United States for those injuries, and the potentially disastrous effects of such a rule on parties who do business with the United States in good faith and, as in the case at bar, under the mandate of the Defense Production Act.

We also attempted a rather clever end run. The Agent Orange case involved claims not only by injured veterans but also by wives who had suffered miscarriages and children with birth defects. As many courts held over the years, it was the status of the claimant as a serviceman and not the legal theory of the claim which controls whether the Feres rule applies. Since the wives and children were civilians, and not servicemen, end of discussion.

*   *   *

Other Important Defenses

In addition to raising defenses and asserting third-party claims raising government related issues, the defendants pleaded other affirmative defenses which significantly impacted the flow and focus of the lawsuit. Two of those defenses are summarized below.

Product Identification: We alleged that no veteran could recover from Dow unless that veteran could establish that Dow manufactured the particular batch of Agent Orange to which that veteran was exposed. Each of the other defendants pleaded a similar product identification defense. In most instances, such proof simply did not exist. Seven companies, including Dow, manufactured Agent Orange, which was shipped to Vietnam in fifty-five-gallon drums. Each drum was labeled with a contract number to enable the government to identify the manufacturer. However, once the drums arrived in Vietnam their contents were randomly mixed together in large tanks. The government kept no records indicating which drums were emptied into which tanks and which tanks were utilized on which spray missions. Accordingly, since most veterans were allegedly exposed to Agent Orange during or after spray missions, most likely there would be no way for an individual veteran to connect the particular batch of Agent Orange to which he was exposed to Dow or any other defendant.

Product identification was a strong defense as long as the court applied traditional products liability principles, which recognized product identification as an essential element of plaintiff's case. But new theories, such as "enterprise liability," "alternative liability," and "market share liability,"[26] were gaining acceptance in cases like Agent Orange where, through no fault of the plaintiff, product identification was impossible. These theories shifted the burden of proof on product identification from plaintiff to defendants. In other words, rather than require plaintiff to prove which of several defendants manufactured the product at issue, the new theories imposed liability on all defendants except those which could prove that they did not manufacture the product. Obviously, application of one or more of these new theories in the Agent Orange case would have considerably weakened the defendants' product identification defenses.

Lack of Causation: The defendants alleged that exposure to Agent Orange was not the cause of the veterans' alleged injuries. There were actually several aspects to this lack of causation defense. First, we contended that existing medical and scientific studies and data offered virtually no support for the veterans' claims that exposure to Agent Orange caused various types of cancers, birth defects, and other serious and debilitating illnesses and conditions. Second, we contended that the veterans' exposure to Agent Orange in Vietnam was, at most, minimal and insignificant. Third, we contended that industrial and occupational accidents, in which civilians were exposed to 2,4,5-T, 2,4-D, TCP, or dioxin, offered no data regarding the health of the exposed civilians that supported the veterans' causation claims. Fourth, we alleged that the veterans' injuries were just as likely caused by exposure to other potentially toxic chemicals, drugs, and other agents in Vietnam and also back home in the United States. Fifth, we claimed that Vietnam veterans as a group were suffering from the same incidence of cancers and birth defects as the general population as a whole. Finally, unlike in cases involving asbestos or DES, where the victims were suffering from diseases unique to exposure to those products, the veterans were suffering from diseases that occurred in the general population. Thus, a serious problem would be how to distinguish those diseases caused by Agent Orange from those that would have occurred anyway.

From the outset right up until the end of the case, lack of causation was clearly one of our strongest, most persuasive defenses.

*   *   *

Two Key Issues Raised by the Veterans

The government related issues raised by Dow dominated the case, but the veterans also raised two important issues which demanded a significant amount of attention from the parties and the court.

Federal Common Law: Originally the brainchild of Victor Yannacone, federal common law was an unproven, unprecedented jurisdictional and choice of law theory which the parties litigated for five years before Judges Pratt and Weinstein, in the Second Circuit Court of Appeals, and in the United States Supreme Court.

Stripped of all of its bells and whistles, the Agent Orange litigation was in essence a products liability action which would ordinarily be governed by state products liability law. But Yannacone urged the court to disregard state law and instead apply federal law to the veterans' claims. Since there was no federal law of products liability, Yannacone's theory would require the court to create one. He argued that this was permissible because of the court's power in certain cases to formulate and apply federal common law, that is, to "fashion the governing rules of law according to its own standards.[27]

But why bother? Wasn't state law sufficient to govern the veterans' claims? Not according to Yannacone. Federal common law was needed, he argued, to assure that all veterans would have access to federal court and receive the same treatment under a uniform federal standard. Absent federal common law, uniformity of treatment would be impossible, since products liability law differed significantly from state to state.

In addition, Yannacone urged the application of federal common law to the veterans' claims to avoid the possible application of the New York Statute of Limitations, which prior to its amendment in 1981 may have provided the defendants with a complete defense.

Yannacone was persistent and passionate in advocating his novel federal common law theory. Indeed, many times in open court he stood up, waved his arms, pounded the table, and shouted, "Soldiers fighting shoulder to shoulder in the same foxhole should have their claims governed by the same federal law and not by different state law."

What was the defendants' position on this issue? Just as passionately as Yannacone argued in favor of federal common law, we opposed it. Our concern was that a judge formulating new law on an entirely clean slate would likely fashion a remedy far more favorable to the veterans than to the defendants. We were more than willing to take our chances under existing state principles.

Class Certification: This hotly contested issue took nearly ten years to resolve, beginning in August 1979, when the veterans moved the court for an order certifying the Agent Orange litigation as a class action, a proceeding in which one or more named plaintiffs sue not only on their own behalf but also on behalf of the members of a large group with similar claims. Here, the large group as defined by the named plaintiffs consisted of all 2.4 million Vietnam veterans and their wives, widows, children, parents, and other relatives. Amazingly, with respect to the children of the veterans, plaintiffs defined the class to include children "not only of this generation but of those generations yet to come." As if the Agent Orange litigation were not complicated enough, plaintiffs apparently envisioned a scenario in which the Agent Orange claims of every Vietnam veteran and family member, including those not yet even born, would be litigated and resolved in one massive class action trial.

Needless to say, the veterans were not going to have an easy time litigating a class action the size, scope, and complexity of the Agent Orange case, which posed problems later described by Judge Weinstein as "almost insurmountable." Among other things, the law required plaintiffs to bear the entire cost of identifying members of the class and notifying them in writing of the pendency of the class action. In the Agent Orange case, this expense could total hundreds of thousands of dollars and require thousands of man hours. In addition, plaintiffs would have to undertake the massive task of determining and maintaining records of the particulars of each veteran's claim. They would also have to marshal separate proof for each veteran's claim and present that proof at trial in an orderly and understandable manner. They would be required to brief and argue class related legal issues and submit to class related discovery. The overall scope of discovery would necessarily be broader in a class action than in individual lawsuits. These and other factors were likely to substantially prolong the pretrial process, create the need for an almost unimaginably complicated trial, and delay possibly for years the ultimate resolution of the dispute.

In spite of these problems, the veterans made the strategic decision to pursue one class action as opposed to thousands of individual lawsuits in state and federal courts throughout the country for several reasons: they believed that soldiers fighting shoulder to shoulder in the same foxhole should have their claims resolved in a uniform manner, and that this was more likely to happen in one class action than in an endless series of individual lawsuits in different courts; they believed that the burden of litigating one massive class action was less than the burden of litigating an endless series of mostly duplicative trials; they believed that the veterans would have a greater chance of success pooling their resources against the corporate defendants in one forum rather than taking them on in a piecemeal fashion in dozens of forums one veteran at a time; and they believed that an early disposition in favor of the veterans of certain important issues on a class wide basis, such as the government contract defense, might lead to an early favorable class wide settlement.

These litigation concerns aside, the veterans also sought class certification of the Agent Orange case to further important social and political goals. Remember, to many of the veterans and their attorneys, the Agent Orange case was more than a lawsuit; it was the centerpiece of a campaign by the veterans for answers, assistance, and respect. What better way to focus the eyes of the President, Congress, and the nation as a whole on the plight of the veterans than to concentrate all Agent Orange claims in a single forum in an unprecedented, emotionally charged, highly publicized class action lawsuit.

As vigorously as the veterans supported class treatment of the Agent Orange case, we opposed it for one simple reason. "The numbers game," was how I expressed it. As the number of Agent Orange claimants increased, so did the defendants' potential exposure. We believed that we would face thousands more claimants, perhaps hundreds of thousands or even millions more, in a class action as compared to individual lawsuits.

Judge Pratt understood our position: "Mr. Rivkin says it is a numbers game. If you have a class action, notices go out, more people get involved, and the potential damages go up."

Not just up, way up. If a class were certified, Dow's potential exposure was likely to increase from several million to several billion dollars.

*   *   *

Four issues thus dominated the Agent Orange proceedings almost from day one: the government contract defense, government liability, class certification, and federal common law. In the next chapter, presented in the form of a chronology, we explain how the parties litigated those issues and how the courts resolved them. The chronology also includes a handful of events unrelated to the four key issues to help put matters in context. As such, the chronology should paint a vivid and compelling picture of what it was like for me and the other attorneys on the front line to actually litigate the Agent Orange lawsuit.

CHAPTER ELEVEN

Litigation Chronology

The first eighteen months can best be characterized as the pleading stage. Victor Yannacone files a series of complaints, the Judicial Panel on Multidistrict Litigation transfers the cases to Judge Pratt in Westbury, the defendants make two motions to strike and dismiss, the veterans move for class certification, Judge Pratt rules that federal common law applies to the veterans claims, and the defendants assert the government contract defense in their answers and commence third-party actions for contribution and indemnity against the government. No discovery takes place during these first eighteen months. The reasons: the parties are more concerned with addressing threshold legal and procedural issues, and the judge is proceeding cautiously as he ponders the formulation of an efficient case management plan.

July 20, 1978: Paul Reutershan files the first Agent Orange complaint in state court in New York City. The complaint does not seek class certification. Nor does it allege claims arising under federal common law.

August 3, 1978: I fly to Midland for my first meeting, an all day session, with in-house Dow attorneys, claims personnel, and scientists. Among other items, we discuss the possibility of suing the United States government under the Federal Tort Claims Act and asserting the government contract defense.

October 10, 1978: Another all day meeting in Midland. By this time, the Reutershan case has been removed to federal court in Manhattan. Not much else has happened. To our surprise, no other veterans have filed Agent Orange actions. Based upon our initial research on the viability of suing the United States, I report, somewhat optimistically, that we have a "one in three chance" of arguing around the *Feres* doctrine. The Dow claims supervisor tells us that he wants better odds before giving us the okay to proceed.

January 8, 1979: With Victor Yannacone as his new attorney, Reutershan files a 163-page amended complaint in federal court in Manhattan. The complaint alleges that jurisdiction exists because the claims arise under the United States Constitution and various federal environmental, anti-trust, trademark, and unfair competition statutes. The complaint also alleges that jurisdiction exists on the basis of diversity of citizenship. There is no mention in the complaint of federal common law. The complaint seeks injunctive relief as well as money damages. It is the first Agent Orange complaint seeking to certify the case as a class action.

April 1979: Yannacone files an Agent Orange case in federal court in Illinois. The complaint in this action is the first Agent Orange complaint to seek recovery for birth defects.

May 8, 1979: The Judicial Panel on Multidistrict Litigation orders all Agent Orange cases transferred to Judge Pratt in the Eastern District of New York in Westbury. At the time, there are a total of thirteen pending Agent Orange cases.[1]

May 17, 1979: Dow files a motion "to strike and dismiss and for a stay" directed at Yannacone's 163-page complaint, which we sarcastically describe in our supporting memorandum as a "work of art." Among other things, we move to strike the more than one hundred pages of incomprehensible and irrelevant allegations about Dow's corporate history and the history of phenoxy herbicides, dismiss all of the veterans' federal constitutional and statutory claims, and stay the veterans' claims for injunctive relief. We also ask the court to strike the allegations in the complaint seeking class certification as inadequately pleaded.

May 18, 1979: Judge Pratt issues the first of the hundreds of pretrial orders in the case. Among other things, he orders a stay of all discovery. Although it has been nearly one year since the first Agent Orange action was filed, there has been no movement in the case except for multidistrict consolidation and Dow's motion to strike.

June 4, 1979: Dow is so anxious to avoid a class action that they authorize us to negotiate with Yannacone to get him to withdraw his class action allegations. We offer to toll the statute of limitations and not oppose Yannacone's efforts to intervene in the EPA proceedings seeking to ban the domestic use of 2,4,5-T. We remind him of how difficult and costly it will be to litigate a class proceeding. We tell him that a class action will not necessarily increase the amount of his legal fees. The negotiations get nowhere.

June 20, 1979: Yannacone files another amended complaint. This is the first Agent Orange complaint to allege that jurisdiction exists on the basis of federal common law. The complaint alleges in the alternative that jurisdiction exists based upon diversity of citizenship.

July 2, 1979: We meet with the attorneys for our co-defendants to share views regarding the *Feres* doctrine. Everyone is very pessimistic until we report our "off-the- wall" theory regarding the birth defect and miscarriage claims. Everyone agrees that our theory merits further consideration.

August 14, 1979: Judge Pratt grants most of the relief we requested in our motion to dismiss and strike and for a stay, except that he denies as moot our request to strike the veterans' class action allegations.[2] In an amended complaint filed while the motion was pending, Yannacone has repleaded those allegations with more specificity as required by the Federal Rules.

September 1979: Yannacone files a new lead complaint in which the only basis of jurisdiction is federal common law. Yannacone is now one hundred percent committed to his unproven federal common law theory. Later, in court, when Judge Pratt questions the wisdom of this approach, Yannacone responds:

> MR. YANNACONE: Well, Judge, all of the plaintiffs we represent, and that's a substantial number at this time, have been apprised of the choice we have made, that we are relying exclusively on federal common law, because our research effectively indicates that a large number of plaintiffs would be barred under the presently applicable statute of limitations anyway if we proceeded under diversity. The veterans are committed to that position. They are committed to it morally. They are committed to it philosophically. And they are willing to run whatever risk might be involved.[3]

September 16, 1979: The defendants file a joint motion to dismiss the veterans' federal common law claims. Our argument in support of the motion is strong in precedent but dry, technical, and filled with legalese. For example, we contend that the application of federal common law in the Agent Orange litigation would constitute "not only an unwarranted intrusion upon an area traditionally governed by state law, it [would] also amount to an interference with the legislative prerogative of Congress." In contrast, Yannacone's argument in support of the application of federal common law is weak in precedent but extremely strong in emotion and common sense. His theory, which we nickname the "shoulder-to-shoulder" theory, is that all of the veterans should have access to federal court, receive the same treatment, and have the same federal law applied to their claims. He first expresses this theory in his opposing memorandum:

In the end, granting the defendants' motion would lead to the spectre of young servicemen who fought a difficult war shoulder-to-shoulder and were exposed to virtually identical risks coming home to widely varying systems of compensation for their injuries under different systems of jurisprudence and before disparate forums.

One of Yannacone's colleagues will elaborate on this theory at oral argument:

> COUNSEL FOR PLAINTIFFS: The defendants would have this court rule that the servicemen who served for two years or more on behalf of the United States in a foreign war, who spent those two years, essentially, in a federal state, having their entire lives dictated by the federal government, from what they ate in the morning, to where they slept, to what kind of uniforms they wore, to what kind of materials they used, these federal servicemen were, during that period in their lives, not protected by the laws of the United States.

September 26, 1979: In response to a formal motion by the veterans to certify the Agent Orange litigation as a class action, we file on Dow's behalf a forty-seven-page memorandum in opposition to class certification. Later, in October, we file a thirty-four-page reply memorandum.

November 20, 1979: Judge Pratt denies the defendants' motion to dismiss the veterans' federal common law claims, ruling that the court can properly exercise jurisdiction over the veterans' claims on the basis of federal common law.[4] The court concedes that its decision is "unprecedented, certainly without any direct precedent"[5] and that there is "merit to many of the defendants' contentions."[6] Nevertheless, Yannacone's shoulder-to-shoulder argument apparently carries the day. Judge Pratt explains:

> Application of varying state laws [to this litigation] would...be unfair in that essentially similar claims, involving veterans and war contractors identically situated in all relevant respects, would be treated differently under different state laws.[7]

The defendants will appeal that decision to the Second Circuit Court of Appeals.

December 10, 1979: Finally, eighteen months after the filing of the first Agent Orange complaint, Dow files its very first answer, which includes several affirmative defenses based upon compliance with government specifications.

January 4, 1980: Dow files and serves a third-party complaint for contribution and indemnity against the United States government. The third-party complaint contains separate counts for recovery based upon claims for miscarriages and birth defects.

* * *

The second stage of the litigation lasts for one year, until the end of December 1980. During this period, the parties and the judge focus primarily on case management issues, including class certification and discovery, the government contract defense, and government liability. The Second Circuit reverses Judge Pratt and rules that federal common law does not apply to the veterans' claims. At the end of December, Judge Pratt hands down a major ruling.

February 1, 1980: At a pretrial conference, Judge Pratt takes the extraordinary step of ordering the defendants to move for summary judgment on the basis of the government contract defense. Judges typically establish schedules and deadlines for motion practice but rarely order parties to make a particular motion. Whether to move for certain relief is a strategy decision best left to the attorneys. Moreover, parties ordinarily do not move for summary judgment in complex cases until at or near the end of discovery, in order to present the court with a full and complete factual and evidentiary record. In the Agent Orange case, as of February 1980 discovery has not yet even begun.

But Judge Pratt believes that this is the best way to proceed. The judge understands that the case will ultimately require an enormous amount of discovery. He is searching for ways to minimize this discovery burden and streamline the litigation. Here is a potentially dispositive defense which appears to raise only a few discrete issues. Why not focus on this defense first? If the defendants prevail, all of the cases would be dismissed.

"This might save a lot of work," the judge says, taking the art of understatement to new extremes.

February 5, 1980: Judge Pratt issues a pretrial order continuing the stay of discovery, which has been in effect since May 1979, "except that parties may conduct voluntary discovery by agreement among themselves."[8]

February 26, 1980: The first complaint by Australian veterans is filed in the United States and is assigned to Judge Pratt.

March 10, 1980: As expected, the United States moves to dismiss all third-party actions filed by Dow and the other defendants. In its supporting memorandum, the government relies almost exclusively on the *Feres* doctrine.

March 14, 1980: The defendants file a fifty-two-page law review quality brief in the Second Circuit Court of Appeals. In that brief, we ask the Second Circuit to reverse Judge Pratt's decision that sustained the veterans' federal common law claims. Two months later, the company that printed the briefs and record on appeal sends the defendants a bill for $45,000.

March 28, 1980: Culminating a hectic month of research and writing, we file an eighty-two-page memorandum of law in opposition to the government's motion to dismiss. We also file a motion for summary judgment, supported by a forty-two-page memorandum of law, based on the government contract defense. In support of the summary judgment motion, we argue that the court should dismiss all of the veterans' claims because Dow manufactured Agent Orange in "rigid compliance" with government specifications. In opposition to the motion, the veterans argue that questions of fact exist regarding whether the specifications were "government" specifications and whether Agent Orange complied. They also suggest that the court hold a hearing, or "mini-trial," to resolve these factual questions and dispose of the government contract defense one way or the other once and for all.

April 2, 1980: A federal district court in Arizona releases an opinion ruling that the *Feres* doctrine does not bar FTCA claims against the government for birth defects based upon the father's exposure to radiation while in the armed forces.[9] This is the first case directly on point in support of Dow's argument regarding birth defect claims against the government based upon the father's exposure to Agent Orange. We learn of this decision after filing our memorandum of law in opposition to the government's motion to dismiss, but will submit a copy of the decision to Judge Pratt in our surreply memorandum.

April 24, 1980: The parties appear in court to argue the defendants' summary judgment motions and the government's motion to dismiss, but Judge Pratt does not want to discuss the case law, the evidence, or the underlying facts. Instead, ever sensitive to issues of case management, the judge only wants to talk about mini-trials. Plaintiffs' proposal has apparently struck a very responsive chord. Not only does the judge specifically request the parties' views on whether a mini-trial on the government contract defense is permissible, he also asks whether there are other issues suitable for mini-trial treatment, such as whether Agent Orange was a defective product, whether it could cause the injuries complained of, and whether the manufacturers or the government had knowledge of health hazzards associated with the use of the product.

July 2, 1980: We appear in court for oral argument in support of a motion we filed to lift the stay of discovery for the limited purpose of allowing Dow to take the depositions of the Australian plaintiffs. We want to take those depositions because we believe that we can establish that the Australians were not exposed to Agent Orange. We make the motion after reading statements attributed to Australian veterans about their involvement in the spraying operation. The statements are filled with inaccuracies about the size of the Agent Orange drums, how the contents of the drums were mixed together, and what materials were used. One veteran even said that "they threw in a pinch of dioxin here and there if they wanted to make the Agent Orange stronger." Of course, even Victor Yannacone knows that you didn't season Agent Orange with dioxin, as you might season a steak with salt or pepper. The truth is that the presence of trace amounts of dioxin in Agent Orange was the inevitable result of the manufacturing process.

July 11, 1980: Dow files a memorandum in opposition to the veterans' suggestion for a mini-trial. Dow's position is that maybe mini-trials will prove to be an efficient way of litigating the case, but it is premature to make that decision or to try to identify issues suitable for mini-trial resolution. First things first. We need to learn more about the facts of the case. This can be achieved only through an extensive discovery program aimed primarily at government documents and witnesses.

July 16, 1980: At a second court hearing to discuss mini-trials, in the midst of a rather bland discussion about how much discovery will be required to separately try the government contract defense, the following compelling exchange occurs:

> MR. YANNACONE: Dow tells us that they want to take all the time necessary to read through all the government documents, with a whole staff of lawyers, two and a half million documents, praying before they open each document that somewhere in that document is an exculpatory statement so that they can run back into court and say, "See, we are out of the case, it is the government's fault."

JUDGE PRATT: Isn't that what lawyers always do?

Mr. YANNACONE: Lawyers who are on a straight time basis for clients like Dow. But not plaintiffs lawyers who are forced to litigate on a contingent fee basis. There is a fundamental split in the profession between those two groups, and they have different ways of trying cases.

JUDGE PRATT: You mean to tell me when you are on a deposition and somebody reluctantly hands over to you a document you don't feel a butterfly or two that this may be it, I'd better read it carefully?

MR. YANNACONE: But when you have gone through two million nine hundred and ninety-nine thousand nine hundred and ninety-nine documents, the butterfly has lost a lot of its energy.

JUDGE PRATT: I do not agree.[10]

Yannacone is half correct. There is a certain amount of tedium involved in litigating major cases. But Judge Pratt hits the nail directly on the head. For me, too, the butterflies never lose any of their energy. Those exciting moments, though they may have been few and far between, and though they may not always turn out in your favor, are what major litigation is all about.

November 20, 1980: One year after Judge Pratt's decision sustaining the veterans' federal common law claims, the Second Circuit reverses.[11] In a sharply divided two-to-one opinion, the court rules that federal common law does not apply to the veterans' claims. In flatly rejecting Yannacone's shoulder-to-shoulder argument, the two judge majority reasons that there is "no federal interest in uniformity for its own sake"[12] in the Agent Orange case and that the use of state law to resolve the dispute poses no threat to an "identifiable"[13] federal policy. The Chief Judge disagrees, saying in his dissent:

> If the laws of 30 or 40 state jurisdictions are separately applied, veterans' recoveries for Agent Orange injuries will vary widely despite the fact that these soldiers fought shoulder to shoulder, without regard to state citizenship, in a national endeavor abroad.[14]

December 1980: Shortly after the Thanksgiving holiday, the attorneys for the defendants meet in New York City to discuss the Second Circuit's opinion and celebrate their victory. We sit around a large rectangular table in a posh conference room on Wall Street and take turns expressing our views. Nearly two years have passed since we first faced the federal common law issue, and much has changed. As each attorney speaks, the mood in the room becomes gloomier and gloomier.

"Whatever chance we had of keeping the government in the case is gone now that there's no federal common law," the first attorney says.

"I don't think the absence of federal common law strengthens our argument all that much against class certification," the second attorney says.

"It looks like the legislature is going to amend the New York statute of limitations, so we're going to lose that defense anyway," the third attorney says.

"Now that there's no federal common law, we won't be able to remove and transfer a lot of state court cases," I say. "So it looks like we'll be defending the Agent Orange litigation all over the country."

After everyone has spoken, the attorney who is hosting the meeting and did most of the work on our appellate briefs looks up and asks quietly, "Is anybody here glad that we won?"

December 29, 1980: A Major Decision: Sixteen months after plaintiffs moved for class certification, and nine months after the government moved to dismiss and the defendants moved for summary judgment, Judge Pratt hands down a thirty-seven-page decision deciding all major outstanding motions.[15] We can only speculate that the judge has taken so long to decide these issues because of their complexity, the closeness of the questions raised, and his great concern for managing the litigation as efficiently as possible. His decision resolves the issues as follows:

Class Certification: Judge Pratt grants the veterans' motion to certify the Agent Orange litigation as a class action on behalf of all members of the armed forces of the United States, Australia, and New Zealand and their wives, parents, and children injured as a result of exposure to Agent Orange in Vietnam. Estimates regarding the size of the class range from 600,000 to 2.4 million.

In granting plaintiffs' motion for class certification, Judge Pratt makes two key findings.

First, he rules that "questions of law and fact common to the members of the class predominate over questions of law or fact affecting only individual members."[16] In making this determination, the judge engages in a qualitative rather than a quantitative analysis. In other words, he concludes that a lesser number of common questions predominate over a greater number of individual ones.

The individual questions include: (1) what was the date of exposure (herbicides were sprayed in Vietnam for nine years); (2) where did the exposure take place (herbicides were sprayed over 6 million acres of the Vietnamese countryside); (3) how many times was the veteran exposed and for how long (dosage arguably affected toxicity); (4) how did the exposure occur (ingestion, inhalation, or absorption through the skin, each of which arguably had different toxic potential); (5) what herbicide was it (over the nine year period different herbicides were used, and different manufacturing processes resulted in differences in the same herbicide); (6) what was the state of the art regarding herbicides at the time of exposure (it was constantly changing); (7) what was the extent of the defendants' knowledge of any health hazards associated with the use of the herbicide at the time of exposure; (8) what was the extent of the knowledge of the government at the time of exposure; and (9) did the exposure cause the veteran's particular illness or disease, taking into account his own unique medical, family, and environmental history.

The common questions include: (1) whether Agent Orange was a defective product; (2) whether the manufacturers of Agent Orange were negligent; (3) whether Agent Orange was capable of causing any of the veterans' illnesses; and (4) whether the veterans' claims are barred by the government contract defense.

Second, Judge Pratt rules that an Agent Orange class action is "superior to any other available method for the fair and efficient adjudication of the controversy,"[17] in that it gives the court "the greatest flexibility and the greatest opportunity for judicial efficiency and economy of time and money."[18] For example, in a class action the judge can identify issues common to the class, such as the government contract defense, and resolve those issues, either by motion or trial, in a manner that would bind all class members as well as the defendants. In contrast, in separate trials in federal and state courts around the country, these common issues, including the government contract defense, would be litigated over and over again.

Summary Judgment: Judge Pratt denies the defendants' motions for summary judgment on the basis of the government contract defense because of the need to resolve disputed questions of fact:

> In short, whatever the minimum showing necessary to support a finding for defendants on the government contract defense may be, allegations with respect to their contract performance and relationship with the government present issues of fact requiring trial.[19]

Even though the judge denies the defendants' motion, we consider this aspect of the decision to be an important victory for the defendants because it unequivocally legitimizes the government contract defense and its potential applicability to the Agent Orange case. Thus, the judge concludes that he is "satisfied that a government contract defense exists and has possible application to the facts at bar."[20] He stresses that the need for the defense is particularly compelling in a case, such as Agent Orange, which involves contracts "with manufacturers of military ordnance in time of war."[21] He reasons that the defense is vital in order to assure the free flow of military supplies to the government:

> Without the government contract defense a manufacturer capable of producing military goods for government use would face the untenable position of choosing between severe penalties for failing to supply products necessary to conduct a war, and producing what the government requires but at a contract price that makes no provision for the need to insure against potential liability.[22]

Judge Pratt may have been satisfied that the defense existed, but he is not satisfied that the parties have accurately stated the elements of the defense, that is, exactly what the defendants must prove in order to establish the defense in the context of the Agent Orange litigation. Accordingly, the judge orders the parties to submit additional briefs and proposed special verdicts addressing this concern.

Mini-Trials: Having determined that a trial is needed to resolve factual issues raised by the government contract defense, Judge Pratt decides to conduct a mini trial, which he terms Phase I, for that very purpose. This Phase I trial, limited exclusively to the government contract defense, would determine at the outset "whether the defendants have a complete defense to the claims asserted against them."[23] The judge explains that the government contract defense is particularly well suited for a separate, preliminary trial, since it raises "discrete" and "narrow" issues "separate and part from the issues of liability, causation and damages."[24] The judge rules that, depending upon the outcome of Phase I, he would conduct other phased trials to resolve other equally separable issues, such as whether the defendants were negligent, whether Agent Orange was a defective product, and whether Agent Orange could cause the veterans' injuries.

Judge Pratt justifies his decision to conduct the Phase I trial, and possibly other phased trials, based upon case management considerations:

Although justice is always served by the efficient management of any action, this is especially true in this case where any other procedure adopted might subject the parties to years of discovery and trial only to have later generations of judges, lawyers and litigants discover that an early trial of the government contract defense might have preempted the need for almost all of the discovery undertaken and saved thousands or person-hours and millions of dollars associated with those unnecessary efforts.[25]

Dow reacts to Judge Pratt's Phase I decision with mixed emotions. On the one hand, although we are generally opposed to the concept of mini-trials, we are not that unhappy about the prospect of a Phase I trial limited to the government contract defense. Potentially, we have much to gain from such a trial and little to lose. First, at a Phase I trial limited to the government contract defense, the jury would not need to hear evidence about the actual injuries sustained by the veterans and their family members. Thus, at that trial the sympathy factor would be all but eliminated. Second, if we win a Phase I trial, and we think we have a reasonably good chance, the case would be over. Third, even if we lose, each individual plaintiff would still have to prove liability, causation, and damages and overcome other potentially viable affirmative defenses, such as the statute of limitations, before there could be any recovery.

On the other hand, we are very unhappy about the prospect of litigating the Phase I trial as a class action. Our major concern is still "the numbers game." Thus, even though there is a tremendous potential upside if we win a Phase I class action trial, we believe that there is also a tremendous potential downside if we lose, in that Dow's ultimate exposure would obviously be far greater in a class action than in individual lawsuits.

Discovery: Judge Pratt's decision lifts the stay of discovery, which has been in effect for more than eighteen months, and orders the parties to commence discovery limited solely to issues raised by the government contract defense.

Government Liability: Finally, Judge Pratt's December 29 decision deals Dow a crushing but not totally unexpected blow by dismissing all of Dow's third-party claims against the United States. He rules that all of the claims, including those relating to miscarriages and birth defects, are barred by the *Feres* doctrine. The judge concedes that the wives and children are civilians suing for their own personal injuries. Nevertheless, disregarding the Arizona radiation case cited in our surreply memorandum, he concludes that the injuries to the wives and children resulted from the veterans' exposure to Agent Orange and that this exposure occurred "incident to service."

* * *

During the next stage of the litigation, which lasts from January 1981 through April 1983, the parties focus almost exclusively on the government contract defense and the Phase I trial. Discovery begins. The parties produce millions of pages of documents and take hundreds of depositions. Judge Pratt defines the three elements of the government contract defense. The Supreme Court refuses to consider the federal common law issue.

January 23, 1981: In response to Judge Pratt's order, the defendants submit a joint memorandum of law setting forth their views as to the specific elements of the government contract defense, that is, exactly what we have to prove in order to sustain it. In that memorandum, the defendants argue that "under the circumstances of this action" the government contract defense consists of but two elements: the government set the specifications for Agent Orange, and the product manufactured by the defendants complied with those specifications.

Plaintiffs' view of the defense, as set forth in their memorandum filed simultaneously with ours, is considerably broader. They argue that the defense consists of no less than six elements, as follows: 1) the defendants had no direct or indirect role in establishing the specifications for Agent Orange; 2) the government had sufficient expertise to assess the potential toxicity of the dioxin content in Agent Orange; 3) the defendants were obligated to warn the government if the specifications called for a defective or dangerous product; 4) the defendants exercised no discretion in selecting the manufacturing process of Agent Orange; 5) the defendants complied with the "spirit and intent" of the specifications; and 6) the defendants were guilty of no wrong-doing in carrying out their contractual obligations.

January 23, 1981: Still primarily motivated by "the numbers game," we decide to persist in our opposition to class action treatment of the Agent Orange litigation notwithstanding the potential upside of a class action Phase I trial limited to the government contract defense. Accordingly, the defendants file a joint memorandum of law setting forth our position on class notification. The position we take in that memorandum is a calculated gamble. We argue that the named plaintiffs are required to bear the entire cost of examining voluminous government records, compiling from those records a list of the names and addresses of as many Vietnam era veterans as possible, and then notifying each veteran individually by mail of the pendency of the class action. This uncompromising argument is entirely consistent with existing case law, including decisions by the United States Supreme Court. The concern in those decisions is to protect to the greatest extent possible the rights of absent class members, including the right to opt out of the proceedings to avoid the potentially binding impact of a judgment for the defendants. That right and other rights would be compromised or lost unless every effort is made to identify and notify all absent class members.

The risk we are taking in making this argument is that plaintiffs, on their own or pursuant to court order, will roll up their sleeves, pore through volumes of government documents in dimly lit basements, compile a list of hundreds of thousands if not millions of names and addresses, and mail appropriate notice letters. In that event, our worst fears regarding "the numbers game" would then become a nightmarish reality.

We are betting otherwise. In our view, plaintiffs will be unwilling or unable to undertake such a huge expenditure of time and money. In that event, the law is clear. The class action would have to be dismissed.

May 1981: The veterans file a petition for a writ of certiorari in the United States Supreme Court. They ask the Court to review and reverse the Second Circuit's decision dismissing the veterans' federal common law claims.

May 15, 1981: Jeff Silberfeld flies to San Francisco to argue in federal court in opposition to a motion to remand. The motion was made in an Agent Orange case that plaintiff originally filed in state court in San Francisco. Dow removed the case to federal court in order to obtain a transfer order from the Multidistrict Panel. As Jeff stands up to make his argument, the judge observes that diversity of citizenship does not exist in the case and states his intention to sign the remand order. Jeff replies that federal jurisdiction exists, and removal was proper, on the basis of federal common law. The judge is not convinced, so Jeff becomes Victor Yannacone. He stands up, waves his arms, pounds the table, and shouts, "Soldiers fighting shoulder to shoulder in the same foxhole should have their claims governed by the same federal law and not by different state law." The judge has his doubts but finally decides to reserve decision on the motion to remand pending a decision by the Multidistrict Panel on whether to transfer the case to New York. After the Panel transfers the case, Judge Pratt hears the remand motion and denies it.

December 14, 1981: The Supreme Court denies the veterans' petition for a writ of certiorari.[26] Therefore, the Second Circuit's decision striking down the veterans' federal common law claims becomes the law of the case.

February 24, 1982: Thirteen months after the parties briefed the issue, Judge Pratt releases an opinion setting forth the elements of the government contract defense.[27] In that opinion, Judge Pratt finds a middle ground between the extreme positions urged by the veterans and the defendants and rules that the government contract defense consists of three elements: (1) the government set the specifications for Agent Orange; (2) the defendants' products complied with those specifications "in all material respects"; and (3) the government "knew as much as or more than the defendants about the hazards to people that accompanied the use of Agent Orange."[28] Judge Pratt characterizes the third element, which relates to the relative knowledge of the defendants and the government, as the "central question for the Phase I trial."[29]

We are quite excited by Judge Pratt's decision for several reasons. First, we have been confident from the outset that we could prove that the government established the specifications for Agent Orange and that Dow's product complied with those specifications. Otherwise, we never would have pushed so hard to include those elements as part of the defense. Second, the inclusion of the relative knowledge element does not trouble us at all, since we believe that we can also prove that the government knew as much or more than Dow about the health hazards, if any, associated with the use of Agent Orange. And third, we are thankful that the judge's definition of the defense does not include any broad, all encompassing issues such as whether Agent Orange was a defective product, whether the defendants were negligent, and whether Agent Orange was the cause of plaintiffs' injuries. We like the idea of litigating one narrowly drawn defense, leaving the resolution of other important, potentially dispositive issues for another day.

March 11, 1982: I hold a team meeting with the six lawyers and eight paralegals at my firm assigned to the Agent Orange case. At the time, Stan Pierce is working almost exclusively on the issue of causation. In light of how Judge Pratt defines the government contract defense, I ask Stan to shift gears and concentrate full time on the issue of government knowledge. I assign two lawyers and two paralegals to assist him.

April 29, 1982: Judge Pratt gives the parties the green light to commence full blown Phase I discovery under the supervision of a Special

Master appointed by the court. The judge takes the unusual step of appointing a Special Master because of

> the magnitude of the case, the complexity of the anticipated discovery problems, the sheer volume of documents to be reviewed, many of which are subject to claims of privilege, the number of witnesses to be deposed, [and] the need for a speedy processing of all discovery problems.[30]

The Special Master, Sol Schreiber, is a former United States Magistrate and current partner at a prominent New York City law firm, who is not undertaking a pro bono assignment but will receive compensation at a rate of $180 per hour.

In the same order appointing the Special Master, Judge Pratt sets a June 13, 1983 Phase I trial date.

May 1982: During the course of our investigation into the question of government knowledge, we locate two witnesses, former government employees, who provide us with startling information. They tell us that in the 1960's the Army Chemical Corps Chemical Warfare Laboratories was considering the use of dioxin as a chemical warfare agent! In other words, the government believed that dioxin was so toxic that it was worth studying as a potential chemical weapon! Nevertheless, the government used Agent Orange in Vietnam knowing full well that it contained trace amounts of that highly toxic chemical.

June 8, 1982: Nearly four years after the filing of the first Agent Orange complaint, the parties finally get to depose their first government witnesses: the author of the Ranch Hand Study, which analyzed the health of those servicemen who conducted the spraying operation and therefore had the greatest chance of exposure to Agent Orange; and an Air Force officer who was involved in the procurement of Agent Orange for the government. I complain to Charley Carey that my staff and I worked so hard preparing for those depositions that "we were forced to give up our afternoon naps." Ultimately, the parties depose more than two hundred government witnesses, including soldiers, scientists, physicians, bureaucrats, administrators, and policy makers such as General Westmoreland, the Commander-in-Chief of the American forces in Vietnam, and Henry Kissinger, the former Secretary of State.

July 11, 1982: Marge Mintzer, my second-in-command, appears in court to argue in opposition to a motion by Uniroyal to file a third-party complaint against Dow-Canada, a Dow subsidiary. Marge reports to Charley Carey that "Len says if we win the motion, it's due to his coaching, and if we lose, it's due to my argument!"

August 14, 1982: A Deputy Attorney General from Hawaii comes all the way to Westbury to argue in support of a summary judgment motion in a case that originated in Hawaii but was transferred to New York. "I hope you had other reasons to come to the East Coast," Judge Pratt tells him. "I do have friends here, Your Honor," the attorney replies.

October 1982: Plaintiffs' attorneys submit a list of present and former Dow employees whom plaintiffs intend to depose. The list is four single spaced pages long.

October 14, 1982: Jeff Silberfeld appears before Judge Pratt to argue in support of Dow's motion for an injunction to prohibit the New York State Dioxin Commission from disseminating throughout the state what Dow believes is inaccurate and prejudicial information about Agent Orange and dioxin in the form of posters, transit slips, magazine inserts, and informational brochures. We know that the motion has very little chance of success and that the proceedings are likely to generate a media circus but proceed anyway because we are afraid that the information will prejudice Dow's ability to select a fair and impartial jury.

Our fears regarding a media circus turn out to be well founded. In attendance are reporters from all of the local newspapers and television stations. Since cameras are not allowed in the courtroom, the TV reporters are accompanied by their courtroom sketch artists. Cameramen and sound men lurk in the corridor.

After listening to argument for one hour, Judge Pratt, as expected, denies Dow's motion, saying, "I have found no difficulty in the past finding jurors who can put aside all kinds of publicity barrages, all kinds of false information."

With that, the proceedings end. Jeff lingers for a moment as the attorneys for the Dioxin Commission and the reporters leave the together and gather together in the corridor. When Jeff leaves the courtroom, he notices that reporters and cameramen have surrounded the Commission's attorneys and are asking questions and shooting videotape. Jeff heads for the exit. At that moment, one of the reporters sees Jeff and shouts, "There he is!"

Jeff turns around, half expecting to see a celebrity of some sort, maybe a convicted murderer. Then he realizes the reporters are talking about him. He continues on his way.

About half of the reporters, including one television journalist and his cameraman, pursue Jeff into the parking lot. "I have nothing to add to what was in our papers and stated in court," he tells them, which satisfies everyone but the television reporter and cameraman. They keep after him, all the while the reporter firing questions and the cameraman cursing his equipment because he cannot get it to work. When they reach Jeff's car, Jeff has to stop and unlock it.

The cameraman runs up and thrusts his camera into Jeff's face. Jeff wants to duck behind his briefcase but thinks better of it. "I have nothing else to say," he repeats one final time. Then he gets into his car and drives away.

For the rest of the day, Jeff frets over how he will be portrayed on the nightly news. He expects that they will show him with his back to the camera walking across the parking lot, with the reporter saying something like, "After unsuccessfully trying to stamp out the First Amendment rights of the citizens of New York, the attorney for Dow refused to comment on the proceedings and then skulked away."

The stories on television that night and in the press the next day are not quite that bad, but they are clearly pro-Commission/anti-Dow.

About the only good thing happens to any of us as a result of the proceedings is that a well known sketch artist from one of the television networks gives Jeff one of the drawings she made of him during his argument.

November 17, 1982: Two years have passed since Judge Pratt certified the case as a class action, yet plaintiffs have taken no meaningful steps to satisfy their obligation to provide notice of the class action to absent class members. Accordingly, the defendants file a joint supplemental memorandum asking Judge Pratt to reconsider his class action decision and deny class certification. The defendants argue that plaintiffs' unwillingness or inability to proceed constitutes the best proof yet that an Agent Orange class action is totally unworkable.

April 6, 1983: Although Judge Pratt does not grant the defendants' request, he appears to waiver a bit in his determination to proceed with a class action. At a pretrial hearing, the judge announces his intention to defer a final decision on the troublesome class notice issue until after the Phase I trial. This means that the Phase I trial will not be litigated as a class action. But to assure that the result of that trial will bind as many veterans as is reasonably possible under the circumstances, the judge orders all known Agent Orange claimants, approximately seventeen thousand persons, to formally intervene as party plaintiffs in the Phase I proceedings.

* * *

The next stage of the litigation lasts only two months. In April 1983, seven defendants, including Dow, file motions for summary judgment based on the government contract defense. The motions are supported by thousands of pages of documents and deposition transcripts. Judge Pratt hears oral argument on May 5. On May 12, in one of the most memorable days I have ever spent in court, Judge Pratt reads his decision from the bench in open court.

April 20, 1983: A Major Motion: On the eve of the scheduled Phase I trial, after eleven months of intensive discovery, seven of the nine defendants in the case, including Dow, file motions for summary judgment on the basis of the government contract defense. Unlike the first summary judgment motions, which were filed before the parties had taken any meaningful discovery and therefore lacked substantial evidentiary support, the second summary judgment motions are backed by thousands of pages of documentary and testimonial exhibits. Our strategy in making this second motion is to lay all of our government contract defense cards on the table. We make this motion not simply to educate the judge but because we think we can win it.

Establishing the first two elements of the government contract defense is relatively easy. Evidence that the government established the specifications for Agent Orange and that Dow's product complied with those specifications is virtually undisputed.

Focusing on the relative knowledge of Dow and the government is a bit more complicated.

Dow's Knowledge: Our position is that during the relevant period Dow had no knowledge of any health hazards associated with the use of Agent Orange in Vietnam. For government contract defense purposes, the relevant period begins in 1948, when Dow first manufactured 2,4,5-T, one of the two herbicides combined to make Agent Orange, and ends in 1970, when the last Ranch Hand Agent Orange mission was flown. We reach this conclusion about Dow's lack of knowledge after interviewing scores of Dow employees, reviewing box loads of relevant scientific literature from Dow's corporate files, analyzing the results of toxicological studies conducted by Dow scientists as well as impartial experts, and confirming twenty years of safe commercial use in the United States of herbicides containing 2,4,5-T.

But that does not end our analysis. As everyone involved in the case well knows, Agent Orange contained trace amounts of a chemical impurity known as dioxin, frequently described by Victor Yannacone as "the most toxic chemical known to man." According to Yannacone,

Dow knew that Agent Orange contained dioxin and therefore knew that Agent Orange was potentially toxic. We decide that we have to deal with the dioxin issue head on if we are to have any chance of prevailing on the relative knowledge issue.

We handle the dioxin issue as follows: We admit that Dow knew that dioxin was created during the manufacturing process of TCP, a precursor chemical to 2,4,5-T; that at times it was present in the waste stream in high concentrations; that the presence of high concentrations of dioxin in the waste stream could and did create occupational health hazards at Dow's plants and elsewhere; and that workers at Dow's plants and elsewhere exposed to high concentrations of dioxin in the waste stream could and did contract chloracne, a skin condition. But we explain that well before Dow sold Agent Orange to the government, Dow utilized a manufacturing process that minimized the amount of dioxin produced during the manufacture of TCP; that Dow developed a method of testing for the presence of dioxin in the waste stream as well as in the finished product; that using this methodology Dow could detect the presence of dioxin at levels as small as one part per million ("ppm"); that when tests indicated no detectable dioxin, meaning that it was present, if at all, at levels of less than one ppm, no chloracnegenic response occurred; that Dow tested all TCP and 2,4,5-T that was used to make Agent Orange, and in every instance the tests showed no detectable dioxin, in other words, the finished product was not a chloracnegen or otherwise toxic; and that, therefore, Dow correctly believed that the Agent Orange that it shipped to the government, even though it may have contained minute, undetectable traces of dioxin, was safe for use.

Government Knowledge: We first contend that the question of government knowledge is irrelevant; since Dow had no knowledge that Agent Orange posed any health hazards to end users, it does not matter what the government knew. At best, the government also had no knowledge. In that event, Dow's knowledge and the government's knowledge would be the same and Dow would prevail.

We next argue that the question of Dow's knowledge of potential occupational health hazards associated with the production of Agent Orange is similarly irrelevant, since the government contract defense, as defined by the court, is only concerned with knowledge of hazards to end users of the product and not with manufacturing hazards.

As tempting as it may have been to make these two brief points, we nevertheless submit nearly two hundred exhibits establishing not only that the government, like Dow, had substantial knowledge of potential occupational health hazards resulting from the creation of dioxin during the production of Agent Orange, but also that the government possessed information, unknown to Dow, suggesting that Agent Orange may have been hazardous to end users of that product.

Just to summarize some of that evidence:[31]

Occupational Health Hazards: We submit documents and deposition testimony demonstrating that government physicians, scientists, and military personnel at the following agencies and departments knew as early as 1949 about potential and actual occupational health hazards associated with the production of TCP and 2,4,5-T: the Crops Division, Army Biological Laboratory, Army Chemical Corps, at Fort Detrick, Maryland, responsible for researching and developing herbicides for military purposes; the Army Chemical Laboratories, Army Chemical Corps, at Edgewood Arsenal, responsible for evaluating the toxicity of the herbicides selected by the Crops Division; the Environmental Health Laboratory, Air Force Logistics Command, responsible for evaluating the environmental impact of chemicals, including herbicides, used by the Air Force; the Joint Technical Coordinating Group/Subcommittee on Defoliants, United States Air Force, responsible for coordinating the military's defoliation and anticrop programs; the Defense Supply Agency of the Department of Defense, responsible for overseeing military's procurement of Agent Orange; and the Public Health Service, which during the relevant period was actively studying occupational health hazards associated with the production of TCP and 2,4,5-T as well as hazards to end users of products containing 2,4,5-T.

The evidence demonstrates that government employees at these and other agencies and departments had actual knowledge of the following incidents of occupational health problems associated with the production of 2,4,5-T: in 1949, there was an outbreak of chloracne among workers following an explosion at a Monsanto 2,4,5-T plant in Nitro, West Virginia; in 1955, a German company, C. H. Boehringer Sohn, halted the production of TCP at two plants after workers came down with serious cases of chloracne; in 1959, two hundred workers at 2,4,5-T plant owned by Diamond Alkali contracted chloracne; and in 1964 there was an outbreak of chloracne among workers at a TCP plant owned by Dow.

In addition, in 1966, the government, concerned that suppliers could not meet its demand for Agent Orange, considered constructing its own 2,4,5-T manufacturing plant. When Dow learned of the government's plans, Dow sent the government no less than four letters warning about a "serious potential health hazard to workers involved in the production of 2,4,5-T." The letters made specific references to the potential chloracne problem.

Hazards to End Users: While Dow had no knowledge of any health hazards associated with the use of any Dow product containing 2,4,5-T, including herbicides used commercially in the United States since the late 1940's as well as Agent Orange, the government apparently had knowledge that some products containing 2,4,5-T, including Agent Orange, may have involved dangers to end users. For example, in 1962 the Institute for Defense Analysis prepared a report on military uses of herbicides containing the following conclusion:

> Military requirements dictate the application of over-kill concentrations (lbs/acre) with possible toxicological or cosmetic effects on the exposed population and their domestic animals.

In addition, in 1963 the Public Health Service learned of at least two episodes where forestry workers contracted chloracne after using commercially available 2,4,5-T; also in 1963, a physician at the Public Health Service contracted chloracne on his forearm after applying samples of 2,4,5-T three times per week for three weeks; in 1966 the Army Surgeon learned that there had been instances where end users of products containing 2,4,5-T had come down with chloracne; and in 1968 the Army Environmental Hygiene Agency, Army Surgeon General's Office, recommended attaching a precautionary label on the drums containing Agent Orange stating: "CAUTION! MAY CAUSE SKIN IRRITATION. Avoid contact with eyes, skin and clothing."

Other Government Knowledge: We also submit evidence demonstrating that, as early as 1959, the government believed that dioxin was an extremely toxic substance and knew that dioxin was present in finished products containing 2,4,5-T, including Agent Orange.

The most dramatic evidence is the so-called "Hoffman Trip Report." Dr. Hoffman was the Chief of the Agents Research Branch of the Army Chemical Warfare Laboratories at Edgewood Arsenal. In 1959, he attended a conference of industrial hygienists and toxicologists in Europe. His assignment was to search for potential chemical warfare agents. At the conference, Dr. Hoffman learned that dioxin was an extremely toxic contaminant of a chlorinated hydrocarbon used as a wood preservative. He also learned that several workers at a plant that produced the preservative had died. In his report, Dr. Hoffman described this information as "startling" and concluded that dioxin could cause severe and even fatal liver damage. Although 2,4,5-

T was not involved in the production of the wood preservative, Dr. Hoffman's report noted a 1957 article by Drs. Kimmig and Schulz, who had studied the chloracne outbreak at the C.H. Boehringer Sohn plant and concluded that dioxin was the contaminant in TCP that had caused the workers' health problems. The Hoffman Trip Report was widely circulated among Edgewood Arsenal personnel.

Cancer, Miscarriages, and Birth Defects: Without intending to demean the significance of the issue, most of the evidence submitted by Dow and by plaintiffs on the issue of Dow and government knowledge sounded like much ado about nothing. Chloracne among factory workers was a serious concern, but many veterans were suffering from various forms of cancer and other debilitating and possibly fatal diseases, many of their wives had suffered miscarriages, and many of their children were suffering from crippling birth defects. Where was evidence regarding Dow and government knowledge of these potential health hazards?

The parties did not overlook this evidence; for the most part it simply did not exist. The one exception was the 1969 Bionetics report, which concluded that 2,4,5-T could cause birth defects in mice when administered in high doses to the mothers during pregnancy. The Bionetics study was commissioned in 1963 by the National Institute of Health, a government agency. The government may have learned of the results of the Bionetics study in 1968 or even earlier. Dow did not learn of the report until it was published one year later. Significantly, Dow made its last shipment of Agent Orange to the government in 1968.

That constituted all of the existing evidence regarding birth defects. During and before the time that the government sprayed Agent Orange in Vietnam, there were no studies or reports linking exposure to 2,4,5-T or dioxin to cancer or miscarriages.

One Last Point: Having established that the government's knowledge of the health risks associated with the production and use of Agent Orange was equal to or greater than Dow's knowledge, we make one final point in support of Dow's summary judgment motion. We argue that the government's decision to use Agent Orange notwithstanding the known health risks made perfect sense in light of the military's great need for the herbicide program.

At the time, a fully informed government apparently drew the reasonable conclusion that the known health risks were minimal. In contrast, the benefits to the military from the use of Agent Orange were enormous. Those benefits were succinctly stated in a 1970 memorandum from the Chairman of the Joint Chiefs of Staff to the Secretary of Defense:

> The existence of an effective herbicide operation in Vietnam has improved allied military capabilities; has substantially reduced costs of allied military operations in terms of manpower, equipment, munitions, and losses of civilian property; and has saved the lives of allied personnel as well as Vietnamese civilians.

In its decision setting forth the elements of the government contract defense, the court stressed that one purpose of the defense was to provide a fully informed government with the "opportunity to fairly balance the...risks and benefits"[32] of a particular weapon. With respect to Agent Orange, the government did just that. Under the circumstances, it would have been unfair, unjust, and an interference with the government's power to wage war to hold the manufacturers liable.

*   *   *

April 25, 1983: The "Smoking Gun": The memorandum of law we submitted in support of our summary judgment motion focused almost exclusively on the knowledge of "middle level" government employees responsible for developing the Army's herbicide program and evaluating its safety. Although the court's interpretation of the government contract defense did not require us to prove that high level government policy and decision makers possessed actual knowledge about the risks of using Agent Orange, establishing that such knowledge existed at the highest levels of government would certainly have helped.

Then, at a deposition conducted shortly after we filed the summary judgment motion, a former White House science official gives testimony which we later describe in a report letter to Dow as "the most exciting to come along in a long time." It is the "smoking gun," the irrefutably damning evidence regarding government knowledge, for which we have been painstakingly searching since the beginning of the lawsuit.

The witness had been a member of the President's Science Advisory Committee ("PSAC") during the 1960's. At the time, the PSAC was one of two organizations within the White House charged with reviewing the government's scientific and technological programs, including the defoliation program in Vietnam. To that end, members of the PSAC received periodic reports from the Army Corps of Engineers and the Office of Defense Research of the Department of Defense. The PSAC was empowered to make recommendations and give advice regarding the herbicide program to the President's Science Advisor, who in turn was responsible for communicating the recommendations and advice to the President.

At the PSAC member's deposition, the more than one dozen attorneys who are present sit in rapt silence as the witness testifies about discussions at the White House, the absolute highest level of government, regarding the presence of dioxin in the 2,4,5-T component of Agent Orange and dioxin's potential as a health hazard to humans:

Q: Did there come a time, Doctor, when you became aware that herbicides or defoliants were being used in Vietnam?

A: Yes.

Q: When did you first become aware of that?

A: To the best of my recollection, some time in the March through April time period in association with my work for the PSAC.

Q. What year?

A. 1965.

Q. Did there come a time when you became aware that one of the constituents of the herbicide being used in Vietnam or defoliants being used in Vietnam was a chemical called 2,4,5-T?

A: Yes.

Q: Would you describe the circumstances in which you became aware that 2,4,5-T was a constituent of herbicides or defoliants being used in Vietnam?

A: To the best of my recollection, there was a subgroup of PSAC concerned with biological chemical warfare. In the deliberations of that group, the issue of the use of herbicides and the presence of dioxin in the herbicides was discussed. It was brought before the full committee for informal discussion during the period April, 1965, through, I would say, June or July. I do not recall the exact date, nor do I have the record.

Q: To the best of your recollection, Doctor, what was said in these discussion, and by whom, about the subject of the potential toxicity of 2,4,5-T?

A: The question of whether the material was potentially toxic was discussed, and the evidence relating to the potential toxicity was discussed.

Q: To the best of your recollection, Doctor, what was said in these discussions, and by whom, about the presence of dioxin in 2,4,5-T?

A: As I recall, there was discussion between two PSAC members about dioxin, what was known about the chemical, the chemistry of dioxin and its potential toxicity.

Q: What was said by the two PSAC members about the potential toxicity of dioxin?

A: Yes, sir. There was a discussion about the evidence, as I recall. Both felt that the evidence was fragmentary and inconclusive, but that it was a subject that deserved continuing attention.

Q: Was it discussed that dioxin was an impurity that was present in 2,4,5-T?

A: Yes.

Q: Do you recall whether the subject of human health effects was discussed?

A: Human health effects were discussed.

Significantly, the former PSAC member also testifies that late in 1965 he attended a meeting with representatives of the Defense Department, including Secretary of Defense MacNamara, where the subjects of discussion included the military effectiveness of the herbicide program in Vietnam and the presence of dioxin in those herbicides.

May 2, 1983: Dow files a reply memorandum in support of its summary judgment motion summarizing the above testimony.

May 5, 1983: Oral Argument: Judge Pratt listens to oral argument on the defendants' summary judgment motions in early May. He begins by assuring the parties that he has spent "most of my waking hours" reading the briefs and affidavits and warning us not to repeat arguments "everyone else has already read."

"Now, who wants to go first?" the judge asks. "Does somebody want to flip a coin?"

I stand up. "Dow is the first named defendant so I suppose I will lead off."

The "Conspiracy of Silence": Notwithstanding Judge Pratt's admonition against repeating what was in our briefs, I am determined to address one topic which we covered at length in our reply memorandum: plaintiffs' "conspiracy of silence" theory.

In 1964, there was an outbreak of chloracne at the Dow plant in Midland where Dow was manufacturing TCP. Dow determined that the outbreak resulted from the workers' exposure to high concentrations of dioxin in the waste stream. Dow solved the problem by implementing rigid manufacturing standards and by testing both the waste stream and the finished product for dioxin content with newly developed, highly sensitive technology. Dow determined that if the product contained non-detectable levels of dioxin, in other words, less than one part per million, there was no risk of chloracne and the product was safe for use.

In 1965, Dow hosted a meeting of its competitors to discuss the incident and Dow's reaction to it. In their opposing papers, plaintiffs charge that at this 1965 meeting the companies embarked upon a "conspiracy of silence" to conceal the potential dioxin problem from the federal government. In support of this charge, plaintiffs cite an internal Dow memorandum in which a Dow scientist expressed his desire to avoid "restrictive legislation or regulatory activities."

Even though the alleged "conspiracy of silence" was anything but, plaintiffs' theory, which receives wide coverage in the press and on television, makes us very nervous. It is the kind of sexy allegation that can easily sway public opinion, not to mention the jury. Therefore, I want to recite in open court all of the steps Dow took to report the incident, not conceal it, as follows:

In 1964, Dow reported the incident to the Michigan Department of Health, the agency with lead responsibility for dealing with occupational health issues. Under then existing protocol, the Michigan Department of Health, and not Dow, was responsible for reporting the incident to interested federal agencies, such as the Public Health Service.

In 1965, the same Dow scientist who was concerned about "restrictive legislation" discussed the incident with the Chief Toxicologist at the Division of Public Health, United States Public Health Service.

Dow reported the incident to a Professor of Dermatology at nearby Wayne State University College of Medicine who, along with 10 other dermatologists from around the country, visited Dow's Midland plant shortly thereafter for an on-site inspection.

Dow reported the incident to the Institute for Industrial Health at the University of Michigan College of Medicine. As a result, the incident was reported to and discussed with physicians from government agencies, such as the Navy and the Atomic Energy Commission; private industry, such as General Motors and Ford Motor Company; and foreign countries, including Canada, the Netherlands, England, and Russia.

Dow reported the incident to the Manufacturing Chemists Association, its customers, and it competitors.

Finally, the reason that Dow did not report the incident to the Defense Department was quite simple: at the time of the incident, Dow had not yet contracted with the federal government to produce Agent Orange. When Dow began producing Agent Orange, there was no need to tell the government about the chloracne outbreak since the problem had been cured. But in 1966, when the government was considering opening its own Agent Orange manufacturing facility, Dow wrote no less than four letters warning the government about potential occupational health hazards.

But Judge Pratt cuts me off almost the instant I get started:

> JUDGE PRATT: Mr. Rivkin, I read your reply brief while I was eating my sandwich at lunch and I went through all the people you notified in this country and elsewhere.
>
> I wonder really why you ever address yourself to the so-called conspiracy. I think it detracts from the plaintiffs' position, since the issue is a comparison of the degree of knowledge possessed by the manufacturers and the government, and how the government got its knowledge does not seem to me to be particularly relevant. All the oratory about conspiracy I found to be something of a turn-off and I had to fight my way through the words in order to get down to what few facts I could find.

So much for that theory.

Hercules Scores Points for Dow: I finish the rest of my argument and then listen as attorneys for each of the other moving defendants make brief presentations. Bill Krohley, the attorney for Hercules, is especially persuasive. He addresses the issue of the dioxin content of his client's product. According to Krohley, Hercules used the same technology as Dow to test for dioxin, technology that could detect levels as low as one part per million. Using this technology, Hercules tested all of the Agent Orange it shipped to the government and, with one minor exception, found no detectable dioxin in any of its shipments. Krohley continues:

> MR. KROHLEY: Now, can I tell you that Hercules had no dioxin in its product? Well, I do not know. I can certainly say,

you could not find it there. At the level of sensitivity that one could test, you could not find it there.

You can conclude one of two things. Either too small to measure, or not there at all.

The punch line: since Hercules could not find any dioxin in its product, Hercules had every reason to believe that its product was safe for use.

Hercules's argument applied with equal force to Dow, which, like Hercules, had tested all of the Agent Orange it shipped to the government. Moreover, like Hercules, with only minor exceptions Dow found no measurable dioxin in its product. Accordingly, like Hercules, Dow had every reason to believe that its product was safe.

I Don't Read Footnotes: Toward the end of the proceedings, Judge Pratt compliments the parties on their written presentations:

> JUDGE PRATT: I find that the papers have been so well prepared, so thoroughly prepared and well documented that it is not easy to find answers to the questions presented. That remark, by the way, is one that my law clerk said I should mention for the benefit of those associates who have not had any sleep in the last two weeks. I think without exception all of the motion papers and opposing papers have been extremely well done.

As much as Judge Pratt's compliments pleases the attorneys in my office who had actually prepared our briefs, a later comment by the judge upsets them greatly:

> MR. RIVKIN: Can we touch on one subject which was bothering you earlier? I'll read something to Your Honor, since it is not that long, on page 28 of our reply brief, the second footnote. I think you must have finished your sandwich by then.
>
> JUDGE PRATT: I don't read footnotes. I make it a point of honor that I never read footnotes. I hope all of the lawyers are listening. Don't submit briefs with footnotes.

It is inconceivable to the attorneys on my staff, who are conscientious legal scholars, that the judge, himself a legal scholar, does not read footnotes. A brief without footnotes is like a trial without attorneys. Nevertheless, following the judge's comments, we resolve to eliminate footnotes from all future briefs, or at least keep the number to an absolute bare minimum.

May 12, 1983: The Decision: On May 12, 1983, eight days after hearing oral argument on the defendants' summary judgment motions, Judge Pratt reads his decision from the bench in open court.

As I enter the crowded courtroom that afternoon, I sense more excitement and tension by far than at any other time in the case. After nearly four years of intense litigation, it is entirely possible that Judge Pratt is going to grant the motions and dismiss all claims against seven of the nine defendants, including the lead defendant, Dow Chemical, my client.

A few days earlier, when I learned of the judge's intention to announce his decision, I called Charley Carey and Keith McKennon at Dow and urged them to attend in person. As crazy as it may sound, I had a good feeling about the motion, thought we might actually win it, and wanted Charley and Keith to be there when it happened. Getting a major client dismissed from a billion dollar lawsuit was not an every day occurrence.

The judge sits behind his large mahogany desk, which is located on a platform in front of the courtroom several steps above ground level. Even sitting, the judge appears to tower over the rest of us. Every seat, including those in the jury box, is occupied. People stand in every aisle and around the side and back walls. Two court stenographers sit in front of and below the judge, fingers poised over their transcribing machines. Seventeen attorneys sit at plaintiffs' counsel table. Thirty four attorneys sit at defendants' counsel table and on benches in the area normally reserved for spectators. Two attorneys for the government are present. A dozen reporters. Dozens of veterans in combat fatigues, including the flag bearer who, as usual, stands at attention in the back of the room. Wives and children, some with obvious birth defects, including one confined to a wheelchair, and other curious onlookers.

When Judge Pratt begins to speak, the room becomes absolutely quiet and still.

After summarizing the events leading up to the defendants' motions, Judge Pratt states that "the central issue in the government contract defense focuses on its third element, that is, whether the government knew as much as or more than the defendants about the hazards to people that accompanied the use of Agent Orange." To resolve this issue, it is necessary to focus on dioxin. Specifically, it is necessary "to compare what knowledge the government had about dioxin and about its contamination of Agent Orange with what knowledge each of the moving defendants had about these matters."

Judge Pratt then undertakes a lengthy discussion of "the knowledge of the government." To me, it sounds like the judge is reading directly from Dow's supporting briefs. He covers everything: the government's experiments with herbicides beginning in the 1940s; the chloracne outbreak in Nitro, West Virgina; the chloracne outbreak at the C.H. Bohringer Sohn plant in Germany; the Hoffman trip report; the Kimmig and Schulz article; Edgewood Arsenal; the chloracne outbreak at the Diamond Alkali plant; the Public Health Service physician who applied 2,4,5-T to his forearm and developed chloracne; the report by the Institute for Defense Analysis; the President's Science Advisory Committee; and the Bionetics Report. He cites evidence that during the relevant period the government knew that dioxin was toxic. He also cites evidence that the government knew that dioxin was present as an impurity in 2,4,5-T.

According to Judge Pratt, the evidence of government knowledge submitted by the defendants is "almost entirely uncontradicted and undisputed." He notes that "most of the government's knowledge was classified and not shared with the defendants." His conclusion: the evidence "reveals that the government and the military possessed rather extensive knowledge tending to show that its use of Agent Orange in Vietnam created significant although undetermined risks of harm to our military personnel."

When the judge pauses after making that last statement, I glance over at the row of plaintiffs' attorneys sitting at counsel table. They do not look happy. At that moment, Charley Carey, who is sitting next to me, leans over and whispers into my ear, "So far, so good."

Judge Pratt then turns his attention to the knowledge of the defendants, beginning with Dow. He says nothing to stunt my growing optimism. According to the judge, Dow knew that chloracne was an industrial health hazard associated with the production of TCP. So did the government. Dow knew about the explosion in Nitro, West Virginia. So did the government. Dow possessed a copy of the Kimmig and Shulz article. So did the government. Dow knew about the incident at the Diamond Alkali plant. So did the government.

Judge Pratt then discusses Dow's response to the 1964 chloracne outbreak at the Dow plant in Midland. His discussion portrays Dow as nothing less than a highly responsible corporate citizen: it reported the incident to the Michigan Department of Health, it determined the cause of the workers' chloracne and how to eliminate the problem, it developed a test to detect dioxin at levels as low as one ppm, it instituted procedures to assure that no TCP or 2,4,5-T left its manufacturing facilities with a dioxin level above one ppm, it warned its competitors of the potential occupational health hazards associated with the production of TCP, and when it learned that the government was considering opening its own 2,4,5-T plant, it warned the government as well.

At that point, I am absolutely certain that Judge Pratt is going to grant our motion. The government's knowledge, as summarized by the judge, is not equal to Dow's knowledge, it is greater! I hold my breath and wait for the judge to continue.

"If there is a real difference of the level of knowledge between Dow and the government," Judge Pratt says, "it focuses upon Dow's discovery in 1964 that dioxin was the chloracnegen in 2,4,5-T, its development of a test to determine dioxin levels, and its development of techniques to reduce the dioxin levels during the manufacturing process."

This statement does not trouble me. This knowledge relates to an occupational health hazard, not to a health threat to end users of the product.

But then the bombshell.

Judge Pratt continues: "One question of fact..."

Question of fact?! Those are not the words I want to hear. They mean that the motion is denied. I am stunned.

"...is whether this knowledge, if disclosed to the government, would have made a difference in the government's decision making process about the use of Agent Orange."

Of course it would not have made a difference. Even before the Dow chloracne incident, the government knew all about the presence of dioxin in 2,4,5-T and ways to reduce or eliminate it by changing the manufacturing process.

"Related questions of fact..."

I can't believe my ears! More reasons to deny our motion?

"...are the actual dioxin levels in Dow's product and the actual hazards involved in the use of the products at different levels of dioxin. A lot of this boils down to whether or not one ppm is or was safe."

I want to jump up and object. Those purported questions of fact have nothing to do with the government contract defense. As defined by Judge Pratt himself, the defense is concerned with known hazards, not actual hazards; with whether Dow believed its product was safe, not whether it was actually safe; with what Dow's tests showed the dioxin content to be, not the actual dioxin content. To my dismay, Judge Pratt seems to be changing the rules in the middle of the game.

The judge then turns his attention to the knowledge of the other defendants. I am so upset with what I have just heard that I barely listen. I feel someone tapping my arm. It's Charley Carey. I have forgotten that he is there. I look at him. "What on earth is he doing?" Charley whispers, nodding in the direction of the judge. I shake my head.

"Issues of fact," Judge Pratt repeats. I realize that he has just denied the motions of two more defendants: Thompson-Hayward and Uniroyal. The judge then grants the motions of four defendants: Riverdale, Hoffman-Taff, Thompson Chemical, and Hercules. The first two were such small players that their motions were unopposed. With respect to the third, Judge Pratt concludes, and I cannot disagree, that "without question the government's knowledge greatly exceeded that of Thompson Chemical.

But Judge Pratt's ruling in favor of Hercules is puzzling. According to the judge, Hercules attended the 1965 meeting hosted by Dow to discuss Dow's response to the chloracne outbreak at its Midland manufacturing facility. Following that meeting, Hercules implemented the same new manufacturing technology as Dow to reduce the amount of dioxin created in the production of 2,4,5-T. Hercules also began using the same analytical method as Dow to test the dioxin content of its product. Those tests indicated that Hercules' product contained no measurable dioxin. Judge Pratt's conclusion: "Since the Agent Orange produced by Hercules was free of dioxin contamination, there were no dioxin-related hazards accompanying the use of its product about which Hercules could have had knowledge."

But didn't the same reasoning apply to Dow? Dow's product, like Hercules's, contained no measurable dioxin. Therefore, there were no dioxin-related hazards accompanying the use of Dow's product about which Dow could have had knowledge.

I begin to get angry. Why did Judge Pratt treat Dow and Hercules differently? Why change the rules in the middle of the game for one defendant but not any of the others?

Judge Pratt drones on, and again I barely listen, but then he says something that makes me sit up in my seat: "The problem is illuminated by comparing the situation of Hercules with that of Dow." This should be interesting, I think. Their situations are exactly the same.

"Beginning January 1966," explains the judge, "the 2,4,5-T produced by Hercules was, with one minor exception, free of any detectable dioxin." True. "This meant that if dioxin was present, it was there is concentrations of less than one tenth of one part per million."

Not true. In 1966, existing technology was capable of detecting levels of dioxin as small as one part per million but not any smaller. Thus, if dioxin was present, it was there in concentrations of less than one part per million. "Under all these circumstances Hercules had no knowledge of harm from dioxin contamination caused by its product, because its product was free of such contamination." Or so Hercules believed.

"Dow took a different approach," Judge Pratt continues. Not true. Dow's approach was exactly the same as Hercules's. "Instead of producing a dioxin-free product, it adopted a self-imposed contamination standard of one ppm for its 2,4,5-T." Not true. Dow's standard, like Hercules's standard, was no detectable dioxin. "It may eventually appear that the one ppm standard was safe. If so, then Dow could succeed in its government contract defense, just as Hercules has now done by showing the safety of its product." But Hercules did no such thing. All Hercules established was that it believed that its product, with no detectable dioxin, was safe. Just as Dow believed that its product, with no detectable dioxin, was also safe.

As one incorrect statement by Judge Pratt leads to another, I grow angrier and angrier. I can feel myself actually getting hot under the collar. Later, back at the office, Les Bennett, who was sitting directly behind me in court, says to me, "Len, toward the end of the judge's decision, I could actually see the back of your neck and your ears turning red."

Judge Pratt reads on, talking about the interrelationship between the knowledge element of the government contract defense and other issues in the case, such as whether the product was defective and whether it could and did cause plaintiffs' injuries. But by this time, I cannot focus at all. Our motion has been denied. By all rights, applying the very criteria previously established by Judge Pratt himself, it should have been granted.

When the judge finishes reading his decision, the proceedings are adjourned. He does not give any party the opportunity to speak. I stand up and glance around the courtroom. Plaintiffs' attorneys look relieved. At least five defendants remain in the case: the three whose motions were denied and the two non-moving defendants, Monsanto and Diamond Shamrock. Many of the veterans in the gallery are smiling and quietly celebrating what they apparently perceive as a major victory. Most of the defense attorneys seem stunned by the decision. Bill Krohley, Hercules's attorney, looks like the proverbial cat who swallowed the canary and got away with it.

Outside the courtroom, I go over to where Bill Krohley is standing. "Congratulations," I say. "That was a nice victory."

"Thanks, Len. I thought you guys were going to win, too."

"Maybe you can explain to me how Hercules got out and Dow didn't."

"I'm not going to touch that one."

"We may have to go after you."

"I understand. Do what you think is best."

On the way back to the office, Charley and Keith console me. "Len, the office did a great job," says Charley, who read every draft of our briefs and made numerous helpful suggestions. He also read every supporting exhibit. "There's no way you could have predicted that the judge would backtrack the way he did."

"I agree," says Keith. "You proved all the elements of the defense. But it would have been a pretty gutsy move letting Dow out of the case on a motion for summary judgment. I guess the judge just wasn't up to it."

"Len," Charley continues, "I know you want to go back to the office and have a team meeting to consider our options. But I have a suggestion. Let's go have a few drinks and a leisurely dinner at a nice restaurant and try to talk about something else. Tomorrow morning is soon enough to get back to work."

Charley knows me only too well. Of course I want to call an immediate team meeting. But Charley is the client. If he wants a few drinks and a good meal, so be it.

"I'll try to talk about something else," I tell him, " but I can't promise it."

* * *

The next stage of the litigation lasts until October 1983, when Judge Pratt withdraws from the case. The focus here is on the expansion of the Phase I trial, which Dow opposes, to include not only the government contract defense but also liability and causation.

May 26, 1983: One week after Judge Pratt announced his summary judgment decision from the bench, he releases a written opinion which is virtually identical to his oral ruling.[33] We analyze every word, every punctuation mark, and the more we examine it the more it perplexes us. I have always had the utmost respect for Judge Pratt, and if I didn't always agree with his decisions I could at least see the logic in them. But in this instance we conclude that he simply made a mistake. There is no rational basis for treating Dow and Hercules differently, for granting Hercules's motion and denying Dow's. Accordingly, we decide to make a motion for reargument.

The theme of the motion is first articulated by Stan Pierce. "Dow and Hercules stand in the same shoes," he explains. "The very same shoes. If Hercules is out of the case, we should be, too."

Stan wants Jeff Silberfeld, who is in charge of drafting the supporting memorandum, to repeat that phrase on every page. "The same shoes!" Stan screams. "The very same shoes!"

Jeff thinks it is a good phrase, but believes that sometimes less is more. To tweak Stan, Jeff first insists that he isn't going to use the phrase at all. Ultimately, he uses it once.

The memorandum, which contains no footnotes, attempts to convince the judge that Dow and Hercules do, in fact, stand in the same shoes. It focuses on Judge Pratt's conclusion that "Dow took a different approach" from Hercules in response to the choracne problem. According to the judge, Hercules adopted a standard no detectable dioxin, while Dow adopted a standard of one part per million. This is simply not true. Dow's standard, like that of Hercules, was no detectable dioxin. To support this contention, our memorandum quotes from documents already in the record that unambiguously describe the Dow standard as "zero" or "nil amounts" or "no detectable dioxin." We speculate that Judge Pratt either overlooked this undisputed evidence or misinterpreted it. What may have confused the judge was that each time Dow referred to its "zero" standard, it always included the caveat that its analytical method was "sensitive to 1 ppm." Moreover, Dow occasionally referred to its standard solely in terms of the sensitivity of the measuring technology. Thus, some Dow documents referred to the standard as "<1 ppm," or simply "1 ppm." But these technological references did not change the unalterable fact that Dow's standard, like Hercules's standard, was "zero," that Dow applied this standard to each and every batch of Agent Orange that it shipped to the government, and that Dow never found any detectable dioxin in any such shipment.

As certain as I was that Judge Pratt would grant our summary judgment motion, I am doubly certain that he will grant our motion for reargument. The Agent Orange team has never written anything more persuasive than the supporting memorandum. The judge has made obvious, inexplicable mistakes. The evidence in support of Dow's contentions is undisputed. The law is clearly in Dow's favor. There is no rational way to justify granting Hercules's motion and denying Dow's.

The motion for reargument is fully briefed by June 13. Judge Pratt does not request oral argument. One week later, he will issue a terse, one paragraph decision. Without even mentioning, let alone discussing, any of the issues raised by Dow's motion, Judge Pratt rules as follows: "After careful consideration of all of the materials submitted, the motion is denied."[34]

June 24, 1983: As if we do not have enough reason to be extremely unhappy and concerned about Judge Pratt's decision denying Dow's summary judgment motion, in that decision he makes yet another startling pronouncement. Specifically, the judge unexpectedly rules that although he plans on proceeding with a Phase I trial involving the five remaining defendants, that trial will no longer be limited to the government contract defense. Instead, the trial will be expanded to include the issues of "liability and general causation." The judge explains that, in the early stages of the case, it appeared that the government contract defense raised discrete issues "uniquely suited to separate adjudication." Now, however, after wrestling with the defendants' summary judgment motions, the judge concludes that the issues raised by the government contract defense "no longer remain discrete or separate." On the contrary, it now appears that those issues have "merged" with liability issues, such as whether the defendants negligently failed to provide warnings about health risks associated with the use of Agent Orange, and causation issues, such as whether and at what levels dioxin contamination of Agent Orange was potentially hazardous. Considerations of judicial economy and fairness require that these issues all be tried together.[35]

Since his decision has significantly expanded the scope of the Phase I trial, the judge adjourns the June 27, 1983, Phase I trial date. No new date is set.

Dow's reaction to the proposed expansion of the Phase I trial is swift and decisive. On June 24, we submit a memorandum setting forth our opposition in no uncertain terms. Among other things, we argue that the expansion will cause unnecessary delay, confusion, and prejudice. The parties will require much additional discovery. The trial will have to be postponed indefinitely. The evidence will confuse and overwhelm the jury. Notwithstanding the court's determination that questions of fact exist, those questions can be separately and expeditiously resolved. If resolved in the defendants' favor, the case will be over, resulting in an enormous savings of judicial resources. In contrast, the issue of "general causation,"although arguably discrete, is meaningless. So what if plaintiffs prove that exposure to Agent Orange "could cause" cancer or birth defects. Such a finding will not materially advance the litigation. Each individual plaintiff will still have to prove that his exposure to Agent Orange caused his injuries. The same evidence will still have to be offered by each plaintiff over and over again.

As persuasive as these legal and procedural objections are, the tactical reason Dow opposes any expansion of the Phase I trial beyond the government contract defense is not even mentioned in our memorandum. Simply put, we think Dow is likely to win a Phase I trial limited to the government contract defense. After all, Dow should have won the summary judgment motion. But if the Phase I trial includes liability and causation issues, an outright Dow victory is possible but far less likely.

July 7, 1983: We hear nothing from Judge Pratt in response to our memorandum of law objecting to the expansion of the Phase I trial. Accordingly, we have no choice but to broaden the scope of our already intense trial preparation program to include not only government knowledge but also areas relating to liability and causation.

The causation issue is vitally important, one of our two strongest defenses, along with the government contract defense. To assure that the causation issue is properly developed, I take Stan Pierce off of government knowledge and put him back on causation. I put him in charge of a newly form "causation" team, consisting of two attorneys and three paralegals. The other attorney on the team is Jim Ruger, the licensed pharmacist. I "borrow" Jim from the firm's medical malpractice department, where he has been working for less than one year.

The tasks facing the causation team are formidable: locate and interview potential expert witnesses; review a staggering number of documents relating to causation, including those produced by the government and our co-defendants, internal Dow documents, and scientific publications on 2,4,5-T and dioxin; prepare for and conduct the depositions of government and co-defendant fact and expert causation witnesses; prepare for and defend the depositions of Dow fact and expert causation witnesses; and explore alternative theories of causation based on exposure to other toxic substances in Vietnam and in the United States and on individual medical and family histories.

What about the other eight attorneys in my office, including me, who are working on the case in the summer of 1983 on a full time or near full time basis?

In contrast to Stan and Jim, who now function as causation specialists, the rest of the attorneys on my staff are generalists. Not only do they continue to develop Dow's government contract defense, they also expand their trial preparation efforts to include failure to warn, negligence, and other liability-related issues. But each of the generalist attorneys also has specialized roles. Marge Mintzer, my second-in-command, attends meetings of the co-defendants' trial committee, handles appearances before the Special Master, conducts depositions of government witnesses, prepares for and defends the depositions of Dow witnesses, and coordinates all aspects of Dow's trial preparation except for causation. Les Bennett and Steve Brock write most of the court briefs. Les, who worked on the massive GAF vs. Kodak antitrust litigation before he joined our firm, also supervises Dow's document production and is responsible for preparing our trial book, which basically is an annotated outline of all of Dow's defenses. Steve, with a degree in computer science, is heavily involved in the creation and utilization of the Dow and government data bases. Bill Cavanaugh is responsible for removing Agent Orange cases from state to federal court and for procuring transfer orders from the Judicial Panel on Multidistrict Litigation. Bill also prepares Dow witnesses for depositions and conducts depositions of government witnesses. The younger associates on the case do the grunt work: legal research, document review, etc. My job is to try to stay abreast of everything that is going on; keep in constant touch with Charley Carey about all aspects of the case; provide leadership and guidance to the attorneys on my staff; keep morale as high as possible notwithstanding the grueling working conditions, long hours, and intense pressure; make important decisions regarding strategy and tactics; conduct and defend the depositions of crucial witnesses; argue all motions and appeals; and otherwise handle any matter that, for one reason or another, requires the personal attention of the senior partner on the case.

August 1983: In the midst of our hectic preparation for the expanded Phase I trial, Special Master Schreiber conveys to the defendants a proposal from Judge Pratt that takes us completely by surprise: if the defendants would waive their objections to class certification, the Phase I trial would once again be limited to the government contract defense!

We can only conclude that the judge has finally read our memorandum opposing the expanded Phase I trial and has taken our objections to heart.

When Judge Pratt made his proposal, he knew very well that the defendants remained steadfast in their opposition to class certification. But Judge Pratt was just as steadfast in his belief that a class action was the fairest, most efficient method for resolving the Agent Orange dispute. He also must have concluded that the only way to efficiently litigate a class action was with the defendants' full support. Thus, his offer: give me the class action I want, and I'll give you the Phase I trial you want.

The judge's offer sparks a heated debate among the defendants. We do a complete about face and recommend that the defendants agree to litigate a Phase I trial as a class action, so long as the trial is limited solely to the government contract defense. Although we are still greatly concerned about "the numbers game," it appears to us that the judge is ultimately going to proceed with a class action one way or the other. Therefore, if he wants to give us the opportunity to separately litigate at the outset a defense we think we can win, we should grab it. Other defendants are not convinced. They feel that causation is our strongest defense and that it will be seriously undermined if we try and lose the government contract defense first in the context of a class action.

October 1983: The defendants wrestle long and hard with Judge Pratt's offer but never have the opportunity to respond to it. In October 1983, the judge withdraws from the Agent Orange litigation to devote his full time and energy to his duties as a newly appointed member of the Second Circuit Court of Appeals. Shortly thereafter, the Agent Orange litigation is reassigned to Judge Weinstein in Brooklyn.

Many consider that reassignment to be the pivotal event of the entire lawsuit.

* * *

The next stage begins on October 21, 1983, the parties' first conference with Judge Weinstein, and ends on May 7, 1984, the first day of the trial. During this stage, the pace of the litigation intensifies dramatically. The parties engage in frantic last minute discovery and trial preparation. Judge Weinstein keeps himself almost as busy as the attorneys, holding numerous court hearings and writing dozens of opinions. The judge revisits the four key issues in the case: class certification, federal common law, the government contract defense, and government liability. He abandons the concept of a phased or mini-trial and orders one massive class action trial of every claim, every issue, and every defense. He redefines the government contract defense. He rules that the veterans' claims will be governed by a "national" common law. He re-

considers and denies the government's motion to dismiss as it applies to the claims for miscarriages and birth defects.

October 21, 1983: At the time of the reassignment to Judge Weinstein, although the Agent Orange litigation is proceeding at a frenetic pace, with as many as five depositions on a single day, an endless series of motions and appeals, daily meetings or conference calls with the Special Master, co-defendants' meetings, in-house strategy sessions, and the like, the case seems to be going nowhere, like a rudderless ship, lost at sea. Nearly four years have passed since Judge Pratt granted plaintiffs' motion for class certification, but no formal certification order has been entered. No notice has been provided to absent class members. No suitable class representatives have been designated. Plaintiffs do not appear to be pressing the issue. The defendants are wavering in their opposition to class certification. Judge Pratt also scheduled a June 1983 Phase I trial limited to the government contract defense. That trial never took place. Instead, the judge expanded the scope of the Phase I trial to include liability and general causation. No new trial date was set. Then Judge Pratt appeared to change his mind again and offered to limit the Phase I trial to government contract defense issues. The defendants are now divided on how to respond to the judge's offer.

Judge Weinstein quickly takes control.

On October 21, he meets with all counsel in his chambers at the federal courthouse in Brooklyn. Thirty attorneys sit elbow to elbow around the judge's small conference table. The judge sits behind his desk wearing a business suit, not his robes. Often in court he wears only a business suit. He likes to keep things informal.

"I thought it would be useful," Judge Weinstein begins, "to see everybody and let you see me, perhaps to go over some aspects of the case." He apologizes for the crowded conditions. "My secretary prepared all of this, thinking there would be half a dozen lawyers." He offers us refreshments. "Just take whatever you wish. Anyway, it's my anniversary, so just help yourselves, really. I know it's tedious to be in these cases."

In spite of Judge Weinstein's efforts to place us all at ease, I am very apprehensive and know that others feel exactly as I do. This is a judge whom we all know very well. He is the Chief Judge of the Eastern District, a respected scholar, a skilled trial judge, very active, not afraid of taking controversial action or rendering a controversial decision, one who likes to keep things moving and wrap things up as quickly as possible.

I know the judge particularly well from prior litigation. He took over the Franklin National Bank case in March of 1979, after the case had been pending for nearly four years. Seven months later, the case settled.

After his opening pleasantries, Judge Weinstein gets down to business. "What I want to do is go around the room, briefly, tell me who you are. I'll promptly forget because I have a very bad memory, I'm sorry, but I'll remember what you say. Please indicate what you think, if you can, in a few sentences, what we ought to do with this case."

Imagine that. What should happen in the Agent Orange litigation in twenty-five words or less.

The responses vary.

Counsel for Monsanto: "I would have great difficulty selecting one or two things I could say in thirty seconds, and I would just as soon pass."

Counsel for Thompson-Hayward: "I would like to ask you to dismiss the case against my client, but that wouldn't get the proper response from plaintiffs' attorneys so I won't ask that."

Counsel for Diamond Shamrock: "We would favor a separate trial on the government contract defense and a final resolution of the class action issue."

Counsel for Thompson Chemical: "My client has been granted summary judgment, but judgment in our favor has not yet been entered. The judge said he wanted to resolve all class action issues before entering any judgments. We ask that you simply reaffirm the granting of summary judgment in our favor."

Counsel for plaintiffs: "We would like the earliest possible trial date."

Counsel for Hercules: "We also won a summary judgment motion. We would like judgment entered in our favor as soon as possible."

Co-counsel for plaintiffs: "As Long Island attorneys, we wonder if you could hold your court sessions in Uniondale as opposed to Brooklyn."

Mr. Rivkin: "I represent Dow Chemical, only peripherally involved. I have only one associate here with me today, proving we're only peripherally involved. I would urge that you hold an expeditious trial of the government contract defense and finally resolve the class action issue."

Judge Weinstein waits patiently for each attorney to have his say. Then, he begins to speak. It is clear almost immediately that notwithstanding what any of the attorneys say that afternoon, the judge has already made up his mind as to how the lawsuit should proceed.

Moreover, it is also clear almost from the start that nobody is going to be one hundred percent happy with the judge's proposals and views. First, Judge Weinstein sets a trial date:

> JUDGE WEINSTEIN: I've read some of the papers you've previously submitted and it obviously is a very difficult case. Somebody mentioned it's been pending for four years. We have a general policy in the court that any case over three years is to be promptly disposed of. This case will be promptly disposed of.
>
> The dates I'm giving you now may shock some of you and they are not frozen, of course. They depend on my calendar. We are a very heavily loaded court. We just don't have enough judges and as a result, I've got to run on a tight schedule.
>
> I have tentatively filled in, based on my other needs here, a trial to start on Monday, May 7, when the jury would be selected. Then I have available to you from May 7 until the middle of September for trial.
>
> I know that is a tight schedule, but for a case that has been running four years, it seems to me you ought to be about ready to try it.

I would have been very pleased with a May 7 Phase I trial limited to the government contract. But from Judge Weinstein's remark that the "case" will be promptly disposed of, I assume that the May 7 trial will include everything: liability, causation, affirmative defenses, and damages. This is apparently what the plaintiffs want, but certainly not the defendants.

Judge Weinstein then comments on some of the more difficult substantive and procedural issues facing the parties and the court.

Regarding causation, the judge's comments must worry the attorneys for the plaintiffs. The judge says that plaintiffs will most likely attempt to prove causation using "statistical analysis" and that an early trial "disadvantages plaintiffs from that point of view." He explains:

> JUDGE WEINSTEIN: An early trial date doesn't allow sufficient time for a lot of the statistical material to develop. Some of the statistical material on carcinogens takes many years to develop, as we know from other cases we have tried. Nevertheless, plaintiffs brought the case, and I am prepared to move

ahead and if they can't prove causation, and if in ten or fifteen years it turns out that the jury made a mistake, we can't help it. That is the way we have to proceed in a court of law.

But the judge's comments on class certification should have made the plaintiffs very happy. Although he expresses a willingness "to entertain motions" on the class issue, he makes it abundantly clear that the litigation will proceed one way or the other as a class action. He states his preference for one big class as opposed to fifty subclasses, with the claims of all class members governed by a uniform federal law. He also states his preference for the type of class that does not allow members to opt out and pursue their claims individually, creating the possibility that the entire litigation could be disposed of "in one fell swoop."

The class action envisioned by Judge Weinstein, that is, one big non opt-out class where all claims were governed by a uniform federal law, is exactly what plaintiffs have desired almost from the beginning of the lawsuit. Nevertheless, I think I detect a few frowns among the members of the plaintiffs' bar sitting at the judge's conference table. Maybe they want one big non-opt out class action, but maybe they don't want a May 1984 trial date. So much to do to get such a massive class action ready for trial, so little time.

Regarding the government contract defense, Judge Weinstein's comments concern the defendants very much. "I, myself, don't think very much of that as a dispositive defense," he explains. "I have some question about whether a manufacturer is free to produce a product under contract if the manufacturer knows that the product will cause damages." To our chagrin, he even goes so far as to refer to it as "Nuremberg" defense, stating that "neither soldiers nor manufacturers are free to just operate on the basis that they were ordered to do something and, therefore, they are not responsible for any damages."

The defendants who have won summary judgment motions on the basis of the government contract defense are particularly shaken by Judge Weinstein's comments on that issue:

JUDGE WEINSTEIN: I have no intention of signing a judgment dismissing at this point any of these defendants. It would create a substantial problem, it seems to me, to start lopping off defendants when, as I understand it, it is not clear who produced what. So I am going to be very careful before I enter any judgments.

The judge's next comments must have jolted the attorneys for the government, who are there merely to observe, since the government's motion to dismiss was granted back in December 1980:

JUDGE WEINSTEIN: My general view is that everybody stays in until the litigation is over, unless there is a very good reason to let them out. At the moment, I am just not convinced anybody gets out and that includes the United States. I may want the United States in here, if not as a party defendant, certainly as an amicus.

He then makes the defendants happy by suggesting that, one way or the other, the defendants would likely be allowed to shift a portion of the liability to the government.

JUDGE WEINSTEIN: It seems to me a little unfair to start off with a case where because the government may be immune from suit, the manufacturers may have to bear the entire burden where they were not totally at fault. It will be very difficult to ask the jury to fix percentages of liability without the government having the opportunity to introduce witnesses and cross-examine.

Some of the defendants are considering whether to move to request that the case be tried non-jury, on the grounds that the issues are too numerous and complex for a jury to competently handle. The defendants' real concern here is that any jury would naturally be strongly biased in favor of the veterans. But Judge Weinstein's next observations essentially foreclose any likelihood of a non-jury trial:

JUDGE WEINSTEIN: I know the problems, and I'll be happy to entertain a motion if you want to make the case non-jury. But this seems to me to be the kind of case where the community is going to have to be heard. We're going to get twelve people from the community. We're going to try it in accordance with the law and the facts and community standards. They're going to tell the world what the answers are on all of these technical problems.

Finally, the judge brings up the possibility of settlement. There have been half-hearted settlement efforts among the parties from time to time during the lawsuit, but they went nowhere. Unaware of these efforts, Judge Weinstein nevertheless tells us: "You know my general view, that is, that cases are better settled than tried. If it can be settled, let's. If I can help you, I will." He continues:

JUDGE WEINSTEIN: It would be very difficult to settle this without the other two pieces of the puzzle, the Executive and the Legislature. How that can be handled, I don't know. It creates a very difficult problem. I don't know of any theoretical way of bringing the VA or the Executive Branch into the picture which would, of course, be an intelligent way to handle it, but we can't do that because of limited jurisdiction.

The intelligent way to handle this case if there is any liability is to have the manufacturers make a lump sum donation to help defray some of the VA's costs in paying claims attributable to Agent Orange. I don't know how that could be handled. You can give it some thought. Obviously we can't make the Vice President of the United States or anybody from the House of Representatives a party to these proceedings. You'll have to think about it and I will, too.

"Are there any comments?" the judge asks.

Silence. Nobody knows quite what to say. Several attorneys cautiously raise some housekeeping matters. The judge deals with them. Then he excuses himself to deal with another matter that has suddenly arisen. "I'll be back in a few minutes," the judge says. "Excuse me. I'm serious about these refreshments. I'll be disappointed if you don't try them."

Hardly anyone speaks as we sit around the judge's conference table waiting for his return. A few attorneys, fearing possible judicial reprisals, help themselves to some cider and doughnuts. The judge returns in less than five minutes.

A couple of attorneys raise some more housekeeping matters. Then, as the session is drawing to a close, the attorney for Hercules, which won its summary judgment motion only to hear that Judge Weinstein was not going to enter an order of dismissal, makes the comment of the afternoon: "Up until this very moment I thought I hit a home run a while back, winning the motion for summary judgment on the basis of the government contract defense. From your remarks today, I gather I've struck out."

Judge Weinstein then brings the session to a close. "Thank you very much for coming in and helping me celebrate my anniversary," he says, smiling. "Have a good weekend."

October 22, 1983: I telephone Charley Carey to report on what happened at the previous day's conference. Needless to say, Charley is particularly troubled by Judge Weinstein's negative opinion of the government contract defense, which Charley considers one of Dow's strongest.

"I've been thinking about what the judge said," I tell Charley. "I think he was just posturing. He took pot shots at everybody, trying to make us all nervous about the strengths and weaknesses of our claims and defenses. He thinks that's the way to get the parties to reach a settlement. He did the same thing in the Franklin case. And you know what? It worked. We settled."

"I think this case is going to be a lot tougher to settle than Franklin," Charley replies. "But I hope you're right."

"Meanwhile," I remind him, "we've got a lot of work to do in the next seven months. I don't think we're looking at a Phase I trial limited to one or two issues. I think we're looking at a massive class action trial of the entire lawsuit."

"So why are you wasting your time talking to me?" asks Charley. "Get to work!"

November 7, 1983: Judge Weinstein holds a court hearing to address all unresolved class action issues. To no one's surprise, he quickly demonstrates that he has become totally familiar with the facts and issues in less than one month, notwithstanding his modest and humorous protestations to the contrary:

COUNSEL FOR PLAINTIFFS: Forgive me for suggesting...

JUDGE WEINSTEIN: You don't have to ask my pardon. I understand practically nothing about anything as you will soon find out. You might as well talk to me as you would a kindergarten child.

As he did at his initial meeting with counsel, the judge stresses that his main concern is to get the case to trial as quickly as possible: "I want this case tried and disposed of, and I want it tried fast. Therefore, any attempt to make it more difficult is not going to appeal to me."

The judge also removes any doubt about how he intends to proceed. Unlike Judge Pratt, Judge Weinstein has no intention of struggling to identify issues common to the class for the purpose of separately resolving those issues in a series of mini-trials. Instead, Judge Weinstein is going to try the whole thing, every claim, every issue, every defense, as a class action all at once:

MR. SILBERFELD: What issues will you certify for class treatment? We submitted a brief on Friday which discusses the problem that you have in trying to pick out issues for class treatment.

JUDGE WEINSTEIN: No. We will certify the whole thing. I am going to try the whole case. We will try all the issues to a jury over a long period of time, and every issue will be presented to them, so we can clean out the case as quickly as possible. It will be certified for all purposes. As far as I can see, there is no point in conducting a whole series of trials that will run over the course of our lifetimes. Let's get rid of the litigation.

MR. SILBERFELD: The problem with that procedure is that there are no issues common to the members of the class.

JUDGE WEINSTEIN: We haven't decided that yet. You may be surprised, you may all be surprised.

November 18, 1983: As a result of Judge Weinstein's first rulings, we have but six months, from mid-November to early May, to prepare for a massive class action trial of the entire Agent Orange case. Needless to say, during those six months, I experience the most frantic, intense period of my entire legal career. It is insanity. There is more to do than ever before. More pressure. Shorter deadlines. Depositions. Interviews. Witness preparation. Document review. Staff meetings. Meetings with co-defendants. Meetings with experts. Trips to Midland. Appearances in court and before the Special Master. Motions. Appeals. We work eighteen hour days and sometimes longer. Seven days a week. We lose weight. We don't sleep. Our family lives all but disappear.

Just to illustrate how much we are doing, on November 18 Marge Mintzer writes a report letter to Charley Carey. The letter describes all the firm's activities during the previous month. It is seven single spaced pages and includes 106 enclosures: twenty-six deposition summaries, forty-one court submissions, seven pretrial orders, the transcripts of eight hearings before the Special Master, and twenty-four letters and memos regarding various aspects of our ongoing trial preparation efforts. All from the previous month.

And November's workload is relatively light!

November 21, 1983: Judge Weinstein holds a hearing to discuss whether he can apply federal common law to the veterans' Agent Orange claims. We are perplexed. In a decision binding upon Judge Weinstein, the Second Circuit answered this question with an emphatic "No!" When we remind Judge Weinstein about the Second Circuit's ruling, he tells us, "I would prefer to use the term 'national' common law rather than 'federal' common law...I wouldn't think of trying to create federal common law." He continues:

> JUDGE WEINSTEIN: I know we don't have [federal common law] here because two of the three judges of the Court of Appeals told us that. And there's nothing more firm or fixed in my mind than that proposition. I absolutely accept it. I dream of it. And there's nothing further in my mind. We do not have a federal cause of action here. And I accept that fully.

Then what does the Judge mean by "national common law"? Because of the "national nature of this problem," he says, courts in New York and every other state would probably "look to some kind of national law" to resolve it.

Speaking on behalf of all defendants, counsel for Diamond Shamrock protests:

> COUNSEL FOR DIAMOND SHAMROCK: But, Your Honor, not only can this Court not create federal common law, but in creating a uniform national law or looking to a uniform national law, what we're afraid of is that the court would be doing an end run around the Second Circuit's decision.

Judge Weinstein nods in a way which tells us that an end run around the Second Circuit is exactly what he intends but reserves decision.

During that same court hearing, Judge Weinstein also hears oral argument on a motion by the plaintiffs for reconsideration of Judge Pratt's decision granting summary judgment to Hercules. Plaintiffs contend that the motion should have been denied because questions of fact exist regarding the dioxin content of the Agent Orange manufactured by Hercules as well as Hercules' knowledge regarding the hazards posed by the use of its product.

During the course of the proceedings, Judge Weinstein refers to Dow's earlier, unsuccessful motion for reargument:

> JUDGE WEINSTEIN: And Dow said that the judge misunderstood the information and that Dow's standards were exactly the same as Hercules's standards. Zero dioxin with a possible error of one part per million. So that the judge's suggestion that Hercules had a higher standard than Dow was mistaken. And I find Dow's argument highly persuasive on that point.
>
> MR. KROHLEY: Your Honor, plaintiffs' argument is different...

JUDGE WEINSTEIN: It's all related.

MR. KROHLEY: In 1969...

JUDGE WEINSTEIN: Dow would love to have you back.

MR. KROHLEY: They would love to have me back.

JUDGE WEINSTEIN: Yes. They have grown to love you. They want you in the case.

MR. KROHLEY: Your Honor, this issue...

JUDGE WEINSTEIN: As we all do.

Later in the proceedings, Judge Weinstein announces that he is modifying the applicable definition of the government contract defense in two respects. First, he expands the scope of inquiry to include not only what the manufacturer knew about the hazards associated with the use of Agent Orange but also what the manufacturer should have known. Second, he adds the following caveat to the defense: that it would apply "unless the likely hazard to people was so great that under the circumstances no reasonable manufacturer would have supplied the product."

Toward the end of the proceedings, the judge asks me if Dow is taking a position on plaintiffs' motion for reconsideration:

MR. RIVKIN: I take no position, for or against the motion. I would simply call the Court's attention to the fact that Dow's product was as dioxin free as Hercules's product.

The judge then hands down his ruling: "The motion of Hercules for summary judgment is denied."

December 12, 1983: Judge Weinstein holds a hearing on a wide variety of issues. Among other things, the discussion focuses on whether the government can be made a party to the proceedings. The judge concludes: "Unless we can come up with something, we may be in the position of putting on Hamlet without Hamlet."

December 16, 1983: Judge Weinstein releases a twenty-page opinion reaffirming Judge Pratt's earlier decision certifying the Agent Orange case as a class action.[36] But rather than certify the case for the limited purpose of resolving one or more narrow issues, he certifies it "for all issues."[37]

The opinion contains a lengthy explanation of why and how the case satisfies the statutory criteria for class certification. But the judge also cites three factors, not mentioned in the federal class action statute, that support his decision.

The first factor is the size of the potential class, which numbers "in the tens of thousands." If all of these similar claims are separately tried, the result might be "a tedium of repetition lasting well into the next century."[38]

The second factor is "the need to assure that the financial burden [of Agent Orange] will ultimately fall on the party which...should as a matter of fairness bear it." That party, the judge suggests, is the federal government. He explains:

> A single class-wide determination on the issue of causation will focus the attention of Congress, the Executive branch and the Veterans Administration on their responsibility, if any, in this case. By contrast, possibly conflicting determinations made over many years by different juries make it less likely that appropriate authorities and the parties will arrive at a fair allocation of the financial burden, if any.[39]

The third factor is that "certification may encourage settlement." According to the judge:

> In a situation where there are potentially tens of thousands of plaintiffs, the defendants may naturally be reluctant to settle with individual plaintiffs on the piecemeal basis.[40]

December 30, 1983: The case involves cutting edge substantive and procedural issues but also some interesting side issues. To illustrate, on December 30 we file a memorandum objecting to the production of medical records maintained by Dow in its Corporate Medical Department.

January 9, 1984: We love it whenever Judge Weinstein makes a gratuitous comment about the weakness of plaintiffs' claims or the strength our defenses. At a January 9 hearing, the judge makes us smile when he says, in the course of denying a routine pretrial motion: "I think it's going to be very difficult, if not impossible, for the plaintiffs to prove anything against anybody."

At the same hearing, Judge Weinstein announces that the clerk will summon five hundred potential jurors from which the parties will select their six person jury.

January 15, 1984: Since there is not going to be a Phase I trial limited to the government contract defense, Dow and the other defendants are once again resolute in their opposition to class certification. On this date, we file a petition for a writ of mandamus in the Supreme Court of the United States asking that Court to reverse the ruling certifying the Agent Orange class.

January 16, 1984: Dow files a motion, supported by 132-page memorandum of law, for an order dismissing all claims based on product identification grounds. We argue that we are entitled to the requested relief because no veteran will be able to prove that he was exposed to Agent Orange manufactured by Dow.

January 17, 1984: We ask Dow to send us a check for $36,760, representing two months rent for six apartments located across the street from the United Nations. Rather than make the long trek home to Long Island after each day of trial, the trial team plans on staying overnight in nearby midtown Manhattan.

February 16, 1984: In response to a motion for reconsideration by Dow, Judge Weinstein rules that the *Feres* doctrine does not bar FTCA claims by children with birth defects or by wives who have suffered miscarriages allegedly caused by their fathers' or husbands' exposure to Agent Orange in Vietnam.[41] This is an enormous victory for the defendants. The government, which has been sitting on the sidelines for more than two years, is back in the ball game facing an enormous exposure, with the trial less than three months away.

February 17, 1984: During the course of the litigation we never lose sight of the importance of favorable public relations. On this date, an associate from our office flies to Midland and accompanies two Dow scientists to a meeting of the local American Legion, where the scientists make a presentation about Agent Orange.

February 21, 1984: Judge Weinstein releases another twenty-page opinion. In this one, he rules that the Agent Orange lawsuit, including the government contract defense, will be governed by "either federal or national common law."[42] He reaches this decision even though, three years earlier, the Second Circuit rejected plaintiffs' federal common law theory.

How does Judge Weinstein explain his decision in light of the Second Circuit's ruling? He does so by treating the issue as one of state law. Since federal jurisdiction in the Agent Orange case is based on diversity of citizenship, a federal court in New York is bound to apply New York state law, including New York's choice of law rules, to the veterans' claims. In other words, the New York federal court is bound to act like a New York state court. The issue is: what law would a New York state court apply to the Agent Orange case. Would it apply New York law to the claim of a New York veteran? Illinois law to the claim of an Illinois veteran? Or perhaps the law of the state or states where Agent Orange was manufactured? Or the law of the state of states where each defendant had its principal place of business? Or the law of Vietnam, where exposure to Agent Orange occurred? None of these choices, according to Judge Weinstein, make any sense. In light of the national and even international nature of the dispute, the judge concludes that a New York state court, and state courts from every other state, would probably look to some sort of national consensus products liability law to govern the Agent Orange litigation.

Judge Weinstein argues that his ruling is entirely consistent with the Second Circuit's decision, which does nothing more than rule that the court does not have jurisdiction over the Agent Orange litigation on the basis of federal common law. According to Judge Weinstein, nothing in the Second Circuit's decision forecloses the application of a uniform national rule based upon a state choice of law analysis.

Several years later, a commentator will conclude otherwise and characterize Judge Weinstein's reasoning as combining "prestidigitation and rank insubordination."[43] Nevertheless, the decision is the the new law of the case; federal rules do not allow us to take an immediate appeal.

March 5, 1984: We write a letter to Charley Carey outlining the "visual display materials" needed for the trial. The first item mentioned is a magnetic board large enough to hold 125 magnetized slabs. On each slab, we plan to write with a black magic marker the name of a key witness or document relevant to the question of government knowledge. We want each slab to be large enough to contain writing capable of being read from a distance of twenty feet. The magnetic board will be divided into eleven sections, one for each branch of government that possessed relevant knowledge. Those branches are the Air Force, Army, Navy, Department of Defense, Department of State, HEW, Commerce, Agriculture, the Office of Science and Technology, the President's Science Advisory Committee, and the President. We plan on placing the board in the courtroom during the trial near the jury box. As each witness testifies and each document is offered into evidence, we will attach the corresponding slab to the board in the appropriate section. The idea is to build our case regarding government knowledge in front of the jury not just with pieces of paper and words but with an actual expanding physical model. Ultimately, the board will contain all 125 magnetized slabs.

The letter also speaks of placard enlargements of key documents, enlarged scientific and technical diagrams, looseleaf volumes for each juror containing deposition excerpts and documents, an easel with flip paper for use by expert witnesses, and an overhead projector and screen.

March 9, 1984: On this day, two months before the scheduled trial date, the clerk of the court mails notice of the class action to more than 200,000 persons. Notice is also published in newspapers and broadcast on television and radio throughout the United States, Australia, and New Zealand. For Dow, this is one of the low points of the litigation. One of our worst fears in the case is "the numbers game." The more claimants, the greater Dow's exposure. Our thinking is that class notice was likely to generate thousands if not hundreds of thousands of additional Agent Orange claimants.

March 19, 1984: We receive a seventeen volume work entitled "Agent Orange Science and Medicine Series." The volumes were compiled by a team of fifteen scientists and contained over four thousand articles on Agent Orange and dioxin.

March 26, 1984: The defendants submit to the court a list of 167 "fact witnesses whose deposition testimony may be introduced by defendants at trial." The defendants also submit a list of five fact witnesses who will offer live testimony. I always preferred to offer live testimony as opposed to deposition transcripts. But in this case, the sheer number of witnesses makes it impossible to offer as much live testimony as I would have liked. But remember, this is a list of fact witnesses only. Most of our experts, and we plan on using several dozen, will actually testify in court.

April 5, 1984: Three defense attorneys, including Monsanto's lead trial counsel, ask Judge Weinstein to adjourn the trial date. The attorney for Thompson Chemical makes an impassioned plea for more time, explaining that attorneys are working too hard and some are getting sick. The judge denies the request. Three weeks later, Monsanto's attorney will suffer a nervous breakdown.

April 18. 1984: Dow's local counsel in Houston sends us a copy of promotional material for a recently released documentary on Agent Orange. The film is called "The Secret Agent." According to the material, the film was shown at the New York Film Festival, the Mannheim Film Festival, and the National Association of Environmental Education Film Festival. It is described as "the first comprehensive look at...Agent Orange," focusing on "the tragic legacy of the American spray program [in Vietnam]..." The film was put together "using rare archival and striking war footage in support of interviews with veterans, scientists, attorneys, and representatives of the U.S. Air Force, Veterans Administration, and Dow Chemical." The New York *Times* describes the film as "...excellent...a tough, angry look at the consequences of exposure to Agent Orange...a chilling issue that is effectively addressed here." A copy of the film can be rented for one hundred dollars or purchased for $850.

April 23, 1984: Defense counsel meet with a private investigator who has been hired to develop information regarding the medical histories of the representative plaintiffs. At the meeting, the investigator reports that he has discovered startling information which, if true, deals a near fatal blow to the claims of one of the representative plaintiffs. That plaintiff, an infant, has a deformed hand, which he contends was caused by his father's exposure to Agent Orange in Vietnam. Tragically, several of plaintiff's brothers and sisters suffer from the same deformity, which appears to buttress plaintiff's position. But the investigator reports that he has found a physician who is certain that plaintiff's cousin also suffers from the same deformity and that the cousin's father is not a Vietnam veteran. In our view, it is highly unlikely that exposure to Agent Orange caused a birth defect that has otherwise appeared in the veteran's immediate family.

April 25, 1984: We mail to Charley Carey a final draft of Dow's Pretrial Order, which contains an outline of all of the issues in the case, all of Dow's contentions, and all of Dow's supporting evidence. Ordinarily, pretrial orders in civil cases in federal court are no longer than ten or fifteen pages. Dow's pretrial order fills three volumes and is ten inches thick. The supporting exhibits fill three large cartons.

May 3, 1984: The defendants file a memorandum setting forth their opposition to videotaping the trial.

May 6, 1984 (Sunday): The trial is scheduled to begin the next day. Our office is humming with activity. Two attorneys are putting the finishing touches on my opening statement to the jury. A team of paralegals is making last minute entries into our trial book. Two lawyers are preparing all of our visual display materials for delivery to the courthouse. Another lawyer is working on a last minute evidentiary motion. A lawyer and paralegal are double checking our information on the representative plaintiffs. The causation team is preparing for cross examination of plaintiffs' experts. Everyone works late into the evening and early morning. The last attorney leaves the building at 4 a.m. He goes home, showers, changes his clothes, and without even attempting to sleep drives directly to the federal courthouse in Brooklyn. He waits in his car for two hours for the courthouse doors to open.

May 7, 1984: The first day of the trial. By 9:00 a.m., the courtroom and surrounding corridors are packed with lawyers, veterans, reporters, and other interested persons. The attorney from my office who waited in his car sits nervously in the first row of the gallery directly behind the defendants' counsel table. At 9:45, his nervousness begins to give way to panic. Looking around the courtroom, he notices that there are dozens of young associates present, and one or two junior partners, but no senior partners, no lead trial attorneys. What's going on, he thinks. Where is everybody? Do they expect me to try this case all by myself?

At 10:00 a.m., Judge Weinstein enters the courtroom and solemnly sits down behind his bench. As usual, he is wearing only a business suit. As soon as he sits down, the room becomes eerily silent.

"Ladies and Gentlemen," the judge begins, "I have an announcement."

CHAPTER TWELVE

Settlement

Way back when my office was still in Freeport and I was spending most of my time representing defendants in automobile accident cases, I heard a story about an attorney from neighboring Suffolk County who spent virtually all of his time representing plaintiffs in automobile accident cases. There was a certain sameness to our respective practices. Regardless of which side you were on, the cases tended to be very fact oriented. The issues were: what happened, whose fault was it, and what were the damages. Very rarely did an auto case involve an exotic or novel legal question. Most auto cases were settled. Relatively few went to trial.

One day, the attorney found himself representing one of two plaintiffs who were suing six defendants in federal court for violating a newly enacted federal statute. Plaintiffs were seeking over one million dollars in damages. The crucial issue in the case was one of statutory interpretation. Treating the case no differently than the typical auto accident case, the attorney first tried to negotiate a settlement. Unable to do so, he went to trial and won a sizable verdict, but the defendants appealed, first to the Second Circuit Court of Appeals and then, amazingly, all the way up to the United States Supreme Court.

The attorney filed a brief in the Supreme Court and appeared for oral argument, even though he did not intend to speak. Statutory interpretation was not his strong point. Four different attorneys made presentations on behalf of the defendants, followed by the attorney for the other plaintiff. Each attorney had his own view on how the Court should interpret the statute. The Justices posed questions to each attorney, and there were several lively but respectful exchanges.

When the plaintiff's attorney finished his argument, he sat down. For a moment, the courtroom was silent. Then, the Chief Justice looked at my friend from Suffolk County, the only attorney sitting at counsel table who had not yet spoken.

"Well, counselor, everyone else has his opinion on what should happen in this case. What do you think should happen?"

The attorney rose and, without batting an eye, told the Chief Justice, "I think it should settle."

Which was almost exactly what Judge Weinstein said during his first meeting with all counsel in the Agent Orange case: "You know my general view, that is, that cases are better settled than tried. If it can be settled, let's. If I can help you, I will."

Easier said than done. Settling the Agent Orange litigation involved problems nearly as complex as trying it, which Judge Weinstein himself ultimately recognized. In fact, so troublesome were these problems that six months after offering to help us settle the case, the judge told us that he doubted that we would succeed, saying, "There are just too many unresolved issues."

*   *   *

Settlement Issues

How Much is the Case Really Worth: Ordinarily, a defendant would never seriously consider settling a products liability lawsuit without concrete information regarding the nature and seriousness of plaintiffs' alleged injuries. In the Agent Orange case, we never had a sufficient handle, even on the eve of trial, on the number of claimants and the nature and seriousness of their damages. How could we put a value on the case missing this vital information? Using statistics, we could predict the number of cancers, birth defects, miscarriages, and other serious illnesses suffered by the veterans and their family members. But would it be reasonable for the defendants to pay huge sums of money to settle the case based upon statistical probabilities as opposed to hard facts?

How to Allocate Settlement Dollars Among the Seven Defendants: Even more difficult than getting a dollar figure we could live with from the plaintiffs was getting the defendants to agree on their respective shares of any settlement. At times, the defendants' negotiations among themselves were more bitter than their negotiations with the plaintiffs.

What were the alternatives?

From the very beginning of the lawsuit, many participants, both plaintiffs and defendants, assumed that any settlement would be allocated among the defendants based upon each defendant's share of the Agent Orange market. This method of allocation, which had been utilized previously in mass tort cases involving asbestos and DES, was superficially appealing. The company that produced the most Agent Orange should pay the largest settlement share. That company happened to be Dow, which produced as much as thirty-one percent of the Agent Orange used in Vietnam. Under a market share approach, Monsanto would pay approximately twenty-eight percent, Hercules would pay roughly nineteen percent, and the remaining four defendants would each pay eight percent or less.

Almost immediately, I let it be known to our co-defendants that market share allocation was totally unacceptable to Dow. The very first time this happened was at a meeting of all defense counsel at our office in June of 1979, one week prior to our first appearance before Judge Pratt. During the meeting, several of the attorneys made it perfectly clear that they considered Dow the major player in the litigation and would look to Dow to shoulder the greatest burden. "Not so fast," I shot back. "Don't go looking to Dow just because we made the most Agent Orange. After all is said and done, we may end up allocating responsibility based upon the amount of dioxin in the product, not the amount of the product."

I knew that my comments about dioxin content were potentially very divisive. All of the attorneys believed that the defendants should put up a united front against the veterans. One thing we didn't want was to have the defendants pointing their fingers at each other in ways that would strengthen plaintiffs' case. By making an issue of dioxin content, I may have been doing just that. But certain of the defendants had far more to fear from this issue than Dow. So I said what I had to say to protect Dow's interests.

As divisive as my suggestion on allocation may have been, in my view allocating responsibility among the defendants based upon dioxin content was far more reasonable than allocating responsibility based upon market share. This was because the veterans claimed that it was the dioxin in Agent Orange which caused their various illnesses and injuries. Thus, the company that shipped the most dioxin to Vietnam should pay the largest share. Of course, it didn't hurt that this method of allocation happened to be very favorable to Dow, which produced Agent Orange that was virtually dioxin free. Relying on documents produced by the government during discovery, we ultimately contended that Dow's settlement share based upon dioxin content was 1.3 percent. In contrast, those same government documents suggested that Monsanto's share based upon dioxin content was seventy-five percent (compared to its twenty-eight percent market share), and that Diamond Shamrock's share was twenty-two percent (compared to its five percent market share).

Naturally, the defendants who produced Agent Orange with high levels of dioxin needed a fall back position. They came up with an "equal shares" approach. Under that theory of allocation, each defendant would pay an equal fourteen percent share. But the smaller companies whose market shares were well under fourteen percent vigorously opposed an equal share allocation.

Depending on which allocation approach was used, each defendant's potential share varied by an enormous amount, as set forth in the following chart. Not all of the defendants agreed with Dow that government documents unequivocally established the dioxin content of each defendant's product. Moreover, not all of the defendants agreed with Dow on the precise formula for calculating each company's dioxin share. Accordingly, the last column of the chart contains ranges of numbers rather than set figures:

Defendant	Equal	Agent Orange	Dioxin
Dow	14%	31%	1.3% to 14%
Monsanto	14	28	51 to 79
Hercules	14	19	0.3 to 9
Thompson-Hayward	14	8	1
Diamond Shamrock	14	5	17.5 to 22
Uniroyal	14	5	0.4 to 2
Thompson	14	3	0.1 to 1

*   *   *

Buying Our Peace: Then there was the problem of buying our peace. Ordinarily, when a defendant settled a lawsuit, he expected to buy his peace, in other words, there would be no further litigation of any similar or related claims. But how could we accomplish that in the Agent Orange case? Was there a way to reach a class action settlement that would bind every veteran and family member? What about veterans who claimed they never received notice of the class action? What about veterans who chose to opt-out of the class? What about birth deformed children born after the last settlement dollar was paid? What about American civilians and Vietnamese citizens? What about veterans from Australia and New Zealand? Regardless of how broadly we drew the settlement agreement, it appeared that there was likely to be a large number of claimants who would press on with the litigation.

Going It Alone: Another problem: what if less than all the defendants settled? How would the settling defendants feel about financing the veterans' case against the non-settling defendants? Moreover, would the non-settling defendants have the right to sue the settling defendants for contribution or indemnity?

The Need for Court Approval: And another: class action settlements required court approval. What if we settled, and the settlement was widely publicized, but the court rejected it, or it was rejected on appeal? No matter how many disclaimers the settlement agreement contained, many people would conclude that it was an admission of liability by the defendants. If we then had to go to trial, how could we possibly hope to find an impartial jury?

Insurance Considerations: Then there were insurance considerations. Some of the defendants' insurance companies had denied or reserved their rights on coverage. Any settlement agreement had to avoid prejudicing whatever rights each defendant may have had against its insurers.

The Dow Factor: One final, hugely significant obstacle to settling the Agent Orange litigation was that Dow was one of the major defendants. This was a problem for three reasons.

First, although Dow was usually willing to sit down with any adversary to discuss the possibility of settling a lawsuit, many people at Dow believed that this would be an exercise in futility in the Agent Orange litigation. In their view, this was a case that simply could not be settled. Plaintiffs' demands would be way too high. They wouldn't provide sufficient medical backup. The defendants would never agree on a fair method of allocation. Dow would not be able to buy a sufficient amount of peace. Opt-outs and other parties would press on with the litigation. As long as this widespread pessimism persisted, settlement was a longshot. Dow's belief that the case could not be settled was likely to become a self-fulfilling prophecy.

Second, although no one ever came out and told me this, I sensed that many people at Dow were opposed to the idea of settling the Agent Orange case as a matter of principle and did not even want the company to participate in settlement talks. These people had great faith in the integrity and safety of the product. They genuinely believed that Agent Orange could not possibly have caused the veterans' health problems. This belief was supported by the absence of any reputable scientific data to support the veterans' claims and by the fact that prior to the Vietnam War herbicides containing 2,4,5-T had been widely applied to rangeland, pastureland, and rights-of-way in the United States for more than twenty years without any claims of injuries to end users. Under these circumstances, if the product was safe, why pay anything at all? The general public and the veterans would surely interpret even a nominal payment by Dow as an admission of fault and responsibility. Why make such an admission if Dow did nothing wrong? The company recognized the huge financial risk in trying the case and was sensitive to the enormous amount of sympathy the veterans were generating. Nevertheless, many people at Dow had high expectations that the jury would be able to put its feelings of sympathy aside and decide the case on the basis of hard evidence in Dow's favor.

Third, almost everyone at Dow believed that if anyone should be paying for the veterans' health problems, via settlement, judgement, or otherwise, it was the United States government, which made the unilateral decision to use Agent Orange in Vietnam and exercised exclusive control over the spraying operation. Thus, it was the government, and not Dow, which was morally if not legally at fault. Under these circumstance, why should Dow even consider settling the veterans' claims unless and until the government took the first step.

Not that Dow expected the government to stand up and assume responsibility. Dow's history with the government suggested otherwise. The government had done nothing to deflect the public outrage that had been directed at Dow over the use of napalm. The government appeared to be doing the same thing with respect to Agent Orange. As a consequence, anti-government feeling ran very deeply in some quarters at Dow. In fact, one senior executive told me that if the government were to ask Dow to supply it with water, "We wouldn't say 'no,' we'd say 'hell, no.'"

*   *   *

Early Settlement Efforts

Plaintiffs first approached the defendants to explore settlement possibilities in August 1982, when the litigation was four years old, shortly after the parties had commenced full blown Phase I discovery. Over the next year, plaintiffs made several settlement overtures to the defendants as a group and to Dow separately.

The first group meeting was held at the offices of Monstanto's attorneys in midtown Manhattan. After expressing a certain amount of reluctance and reservations, Dow authorized me to attend. At the start of the meeting, Ed Gorman, a member of Yannacone & Associates, plaintiffs' lead counsel, stood at the head of a long, rectangular table in a elegantly furnished conference room and gave an impassioned speech about why the parties should try to settle the case. It was almost as if he were making an opening statement to a jury, except that this time his audience consisted of eight skeptical defense attorneys.

"No matter how the jury resolves this matter," Gorman explained, "the verdict could be catastrophic for all concerned. If plaintiffs win, the financial impact on the defendants could be enormous, possibly leading to bankruptcy. In addition, because of the expanding reality of tort liability, chemical and drug companies would cease developing new products, and the whole country would be negatively affected. On the other hand, if the defendants win, the morale of the country would suffer and the people's faith in big business and big government would be severely shaken. Therefore, it makes a great deal of sense for both sides to seriously pursue an out-of-court resolution. If we do, we could then pool our efforts and use our enormous combined influence to convince Congress to pass legislation providing for government funds to augment the settlement."

In spite of Gorman's passionate plea, the group negotiations, as Dow fully expected, went nowhere. To the extent there was a high point, it occurred in December 1982, when plaintiffs' attorneys presented the defendants with a detailed breakdown of their existing cases and the value of those cases. Out of a total of twenty thousand claimants, there were one thousand deaths, one thousand living veterans with cancer, one thousand living veterans with other life threatening illnesses, and five hundred catastrophic birth defects. The potential verdict value of just these 3,500 serious cases, according to plaintiffs' attorneys, was $2.5 billion, an average of about $750,000 per case.

Although plaintiffs did not specifically propose a $2.5 billion settlement, their presentation gave us some idea of the figure we would be bidding against. That figure, in our view, was way out of line. Moreover, we had no way of verifying plaintiffs' data. Nevertheless, the defendants expressed their willingness to continue to evaluate plaintiffs' claims, requested medical documentation for some of the more serious matters, and agreed to another meeting in January. The documentation never arrived, and the meeting never took place.

What did take place in January was that Ed Gorman contacted us to ask whether Dow would be interested in negotiating its own, separate deal. Dow's views about settlement hadn't changed, but having nothing to lose, the company authorized us to meet with Gorman. The meeting occurred at our offices on January 6. At the meeting, Gorman demanded $100 million from Dow to settle the litigation. At a second meeting one week later, Gorman indicated that the $100 million could be "structured," meaning that Dow could pay the money over time, making small initial payments and larger payments at the end. According to Gorman, if the settlement were structured over twenty years, Dow's actual out-of-pocket costs would be no greater than $45 million.

I thought that Gorman's demand was too high, but Dow's reaction surprised me. I thought they would reject Gorman's demand out-of-hand. Instead, Wayne Hancock, Dow's general counsel, told me that he wanted to meet with me and Bob Buell, Fireman's Fund's Senior Vice President in Charge of Claims, to discuss settlement issues in general and Gorman's demand in particular.

At Bob's suggestion, we agreed to meet on Tuesday, February 7, at the Silverado County Club, located in the heart of the Napa Valley, where Fireman's Fund maintained two corporate apartments.

I arrived at San Francisco airport Monday evening, the day before the meeting, where I met Wayne Hancock, Charley Carey, and Don Frayer. We rented a car and then drove north for one hour to Silverado. On the way, Charley, Don, and I brought Wayne up to date on the status of the litigation and the details of plaintiffs' settlement demand. We had a dinner and drinks at the club that evening and then retired to the club's guest quarters.

The next morning, at 7:30 a.m., Bob Buell met us for breakfast. At 8:30, we left the restaurant and walked about three quarters of a mile to one of the Fireman's Fund apartments, where the meeting would take place. As usual, Bob walked briskly, taking long, easy strides. Don Frayer, who was several inches taller than Bob, had no trouble keeping up. Wayne, Charley, and I didn't even bother to try. We strolled behind them at our own leisurely pace.

Visiting places like Silverado was one of the perks of doing business with companies like Fireman's Fund. Even though I did not play golf, I certainly appreciated the luxurious surroundings. The complex contained two impeccably maintained eighteen-hole championship courses, numerous swimming pools, a tennis complex, and many attractive residences spaciously placed along the fairways. "Johnny Miller, the famous golfer, has a house in here somewhere," Bob had told us at breakfast, "although I don't think he's the resident pro."

The Fireman's Fund apartment was on the ground floor. Its most outstanding feature was a large outdoor patio which was adjacent to a creek that zigzagged through the entire complex. Jim Haines, Dow's assistant general counsel, met us at the apartment, as did two of Bob Buell's assistants. Jim explained that he had planned on arriving in time for breakfast but got lost driving up from his hotel in San Francisco.

From the patio, we had an excellent view of one of the courses. Several foursomes passed by the apartment during the day. "I should have brought my clubs," Jim Haines said.

At the time, Fireman's Fund and Dow were in the midst of disputing just how much insurance coverage was available to Dow for the Agent Orange case. Fireman's Fund had agreed to pay Dow's defense costs, but had not yet agreed to pay any judgment or settlement. Nevertheless, instead of treating each other as adversaries during the meeting, the Fireman's Fund and Dow people were cooperative, reasonably collegial, candid, and constructive. Perhaps the posh surroundings helped put everyone in the proper frame of mind.

For the next nine hours, the eight of us discussed plaintiffs' latest demand and analyzed the pros and cons of settlement from every possible angle. Each person at the meeting had his own idea about what Dow's response to Gorman should be. Most of us felt that the demand was too high. A few wanted me to tell Gorman to take a hike. Others, including Bob Buell and myself, urged Dow to continue to negotiate.

At the end of the meeting, Wayne Hancock said that he wanted to go back to Midland and reflect for a few days on all that was said.

Friday morning, Wayne telephoned me in my office. He told me that $45 million sounded like a fair figure when he went to sleep Tuesday evening but not when he woke up Wednesday morning. "In good conscience," he said, "I just can't recommend settling for so many megabucks. I think we have good defenses. I don't think they can prove causation. I'm not sure what peace the settlement will buy us. And I don't like the idea of financing plaintiffs' case against our co-defendants. We still do business with them, you know. We don't want to antagonize them."

Wayne concluded our phone conversation by instructing me to tell Gorman that Dow was just not interested in negotiating with the plaintiffs at this time. On Monday morning, I did just that. Gorman and another attorney came to my office, and when I gave them the news they tried to keep straight faces, but I could detect their disappointment and fully expected that they would get back in touch with me.

Which they did, four months later, in June 1983, shortly after the court denied Dow's summary judgment motion and expanded the scope of the Phase I trial. They presented me with a new proposal just for Dow and not any other defendant: $40 million, payable over two years in two installments.

In terms of out-of-pocket costs to Dow, this new proposal was slightly better than the first one, but I suspected that it was still too high for Dow's liking, and I was right. "We may have lost the summary judgment motion," Wayne Hancock told me, "but they're still asking for too much money. I still like our defenses. And I'm still troubled by all of the unresolved procedural issues we discussed last time. So tell Mr. Gorman that we're still not interested."

Which I did, in a phone conversation with Gorman the next day. Once again, Gorman could barely hide his disappointment. Once again, I suspected that he would get back in touch with me.

But that never happened. Instead, early in September, Yannacone & Associates filed a motion asking to be relieved of their lead counsel responsibilities. The reason: Yannacone explained that he and his associates were no longer able "to absorb the enormous expense that continued prosecution of the litigation will inevitably entail."[1] The court granted Yannacone's motion and, at the same time, designated new lead counsel: Stephen Schlegel of Chicago, Benton Musselwhite of Houston, and Thomas Henderson of Pittsburgh,[2] three attorneys with substantial mass tort experience.

*   *   *

The Turning Points

Dow greeted the departure of Yannacone & Associates, as far as settlement was concerned, with a shrug. Dow hadn't been very optimistic about settling the case when Yannacone was in charge. Nor had Dow shown much inclination to actively negotiate; it merely listened to Gorman's demands and then rejected them. Yannacone's departure did nothing to alter Dow's anti-settlement posture.

But then, two things happened which changed everything.

The New Judge: In October 1983, when Judge Pratt withdrew from the case to concentrate full time on his duties as a member of the Second Circuit Court of Appeals, the case was reassigned to Judge Weinstein in Brooklyn, who immediately suggested that the case should be settled rather than tried and offered his help. This was not an empty gesture on the judge's part. If anyone could resolve this enormously complicated dispute, Judge Weinstein was the man. He didn't preside over his cases, he directed them. When he wanted the parties to negotiate, they negotiated. When there were open issues hindering the negotiations, he resolved them. When someone needed persuading, he persuaded them. If the case needed a creative solution, he created one.

At least, that was my opinion, and it was based not upon reputation or speculation but upon experience. Judge Weinstein had taken over the complex, multi-party Franklin National Bank case after the case had been pending for four years. Before his arrival, settlement discussions had gotten nowhere. He settled the case in six months.

When I told all of this to the people at Dow, they softened their anti-settlement position somewhat. To the extent that Dow had been even remotely interested in trying to settle the case, the company was concerned not only with how much money it would have to pay but also with the so-called "procedural" issues, such as how much peace the settlement would buy, allocating the settlement among the defendants, insurance considerations, the need for court approval, and the like. With my encouragement, Dow began to believe that Judge Weinstein offered them the best opportunity to fashion a settlement that would resolve these procedural issues in a way that protected Dow's interests to the greatest extent possible.

The Jury Poll: Late in 1983, Dow hired a consultant, the head of a well- known California think tank, which also provided litigation support services, to conduct a jury poll. This was a relatively new concept. The consultant would randomly select people from the same population from which the jury was to be selected and present those people with a mock trial. The people would then render their "verdict." Thereafter, the consultant would question the people to determine why the reached the result they did and what the client could do to strengthen his case.

After the poll was completed, Jeff Silberfeld and I flew to Midland to hear the consultant present his conclusions to Keith McKennon, Wayne Hancock, Jim Haines, Charley Carey, and other members of Dow's in-house litigation team. We met in a rather sparsely furnished conference room dominated by a large, plain, rectangular table. The consultant stood at the head of the table next to an overhead slide projector. The mood in the room was rather up-beat. The trial was scheduled to start in less than six months, and the government contract defense and the lack of causation defense appeared stronger than ever.

But then the consultant started to speak. After some introductory comments, he stated his ultimate conclusion: "I don't care if Jesus Christ himself takes the stand and testifies that Agent Orange is as harmless as water and that there is no possible way that exposure to Agent Orange caused the veterans' injuries. No matter who you pick to sit on the jury and what evidence you present, the jury is going to find for the veterans. And it's going to award the veterans a huge sum of money."

Those of us who had been sitting back comfortably in our seats suddenly sat straight up. I looked at the faces of the Dow people in the room. Their expressions had changed from complacency to total shock and disbelief. I assumed that my expression had undergone a similar transformation.

"But why?" I asked. "Is it napalm? Is it that people just don't like the name Dow Chemical?"

"That's not it at all," the consultant explained. "It's Vietnam. People still feel guilty about what the veterans have gone through. The defendant could be Walt Disney. It doesn't matter. The jury is going to nail whoever happens to be sitting in the courtroom."

Maybe the consultant's conclusions should not have come as a complete surprise, but they did. We always knew that the veterans generated a substantial amount of sympathy, but not to that extreme degree. We figured that the trial would be difficult but not unwinnable.

But the consultant told us otherwise, and Dow took his words directly to heart. Before meeting with the consultant, Dow had never really been all that interested in making a serious effort to settle the Agent Orange case. After the meeting, settlement became a major priority.

And, once settlement discussions resumed, my job became all the more difficult. I had to participate in the negotiations without tipping my hand, that is, without revealing to anyone—the veterans, the co-defendants, or the judge—just how urgent, at least from Dow's perspective, the settlement issue had become.

*   *   *

Settlement Chronology

March 12, 1984: In October 1983, when Judge Weinstein first offered to help the parties settle the case, I fully expected that the plaintiffs' attorneys would jump at the chance of getting the judge involved in settlement efforts. The judge had just established a firm May 1984 trial date. To complete discovery in time and try the case would cost plaintiffs' attorneys a small fortune. They had to know that they did not have an open and shut case. They must have known about earlier efforts to settle the litigation without the judge's involvement, which went nowhere. They had to believe that the judge's participation in the settlement process could only help.

To my surprise, however, plaintiffs did not approach the judge, at least as far as I knew, for nearly six months. During that period, ever mindful of Dow's new attitude toward settlement, I came close on several occasions to approaching the judge myself, but I never did. Dow may have wanted me to settle the case, but I certainly did not want to be the one to make the first move.

Then, out of the blue, at a March 12, 1984, pretrial conference, just as the day's proceedings were winding down and attorneys were shuffling their papers and closing their briefcases, Steven Schlegel, one of plaintiffs' lead attorneys, stood up and asked the judge to get involved.

Schlegel believed, based upon past experience, that settling the Agent Orange case would require more than simply paying money to the veterans. In his view, the parties would have to establish a fund and thereafter devise a plan for distributing the fund to the tens of thousands of veterans claiming injury from exposure to Agent Orange. Schlegel wanted the judge's help in formulating that plan, or "structure," as he sometimes called it.

"We believe," he explained, "that talking about structure, plans, and ideas is a prerequisite to the possibility of a practical resolution of this case."

April 6, 1984: The judge took Schlegel's request for input on settlement plans to heart. Early in April, he asked for and received everyone's consent to distribute to each of the defendants and the government a lengthy "Settlement Memorandum" which discussed in detail three comprehensive plans for resolving the Agent Orange dispute.

Each of the plans involved three basic functions: medical examinations, claims resolution, and paying benefits. The three functions would be performed either by the Veterans Administration, or private non-governmental agencies, or some combination of both. Each plan required extensive government involvement and/or financing. Each plan required the defendants to establish a trust fund. Two of the plans required the government to contribute to the fund. Each plan had its own rules for determining eligibility and related issues such as medical causation, degree of disability, and the amount of the cash award. Each plan based the amount the award on the then existing VA disability benefit schedule.

Regarding the defendants' potential financial exposure under each plan, the memorandum concluded that it would be impossible to make that calculation without more hard data regarding the number of veterans claiming Agent Orange related health problems and the nature of those problems. The same California think tank which had conducted our jury poll studied the proposals, made some assumptions about the number of veterans and the nature of their injuries, and concluded that depending upon which plan was implemented, the defendants' exposure ranged from approximately $800 million to more than $1 billion and possibly many times higher than that.

Regarding the difficult issue of how to allocate the cost of the plans among the seven defendants, the memorandum concluded that allocation should be computed using a formula factoring in both Agent Orange market share and dioxin content. The memorandum did not attempt to compute each defendant's actual settlement share. Instead, using made up market share and dioxin numbers and fictitious defendants, the memorandum included a table which illustrated hypothetically how the formula worked. It was a simple task for us to apply the formula to the actual market share and dioxin numbers of the actual defendants, which we did. According to our calculations, the "Settlement Memorandum" allocated each defendant's settlement share, as compared to its market share, as follows:

Company	Market Share	Settlement Share
Dow	31%	10
Monsanto	28	66
Hercules	19	6
Thompson-Hayward	8	3
Diamond Shamrock	5	13
Uniroyal	5	2
Thompson	3	1

Obviously, any allocation formula that factored in dioxin content was hugely beneficial to Dow. In this instance, it reduced Dow's share by more than two-thirds, from thirty-one percent to ten percent. Settlement may have become a major priority for Dow, but I still wanted to get the company the best deal possible. The allocation formula set forth in the "Settlement Memorandum" provided me with an excellent starting point.

April 18, 1984: Less than three weeks before the scheduled trial date, the defense attorneys met with Judge Weinstein in chambers to discuss the "Settlement Memorandum." We were very noncommital but on behalf of Dow I did express two main concerns: first, since all three of the settlement plans required substantial government expenditures, I wanted to know whether the government would be willing to participate in the settlement talks; and second, I complained that it was difficult if not impossible to assess the defendants' exposure under the three plans and stressed that I would need more certainty before committing to any settlement.

Regarding my first concern, the judge agreed that the government should be contacted. Regarding my second concern, the judge off-handedly commented that in his opinion the defendants could probably settle the case for between $150 million and $200 million. "I haven't really given it much thought," he told the group. "These figures are just based on some reading I've done, some articles, a study by the Rand Corporation, some asbestos-related papers, things like that."

As soon as I got back to my office, I telephoned Charley Carey.

"This judge does nothing by the seat of his pants," I told Charley. "He is very thoughtful, and I believe there is a purpose to everything he says. He didn't just pick $150 million to $200 million out of the air. They may not be plaintiffs' numbers, but I'll bet they're the judge's."

Based on these numbers, Charley and I established worst-case, best-case settlement scenarios. The worst case scenario was the judge's high figure, $200 million, allocated on the basis of Agent Orange market share. Under that scenario, Dow's share would be thirty-one percent of $200 million, or approximately $62 million. The best case scenario was the judge's low figure, $150 million, allocated on the basis of the dioxin content formula set forth in the "Settlement Memorandum." Under this scenario, Dow's share would be ten percent of $150 million, or $15 million.

Eight months earlier, Dow had flatly rejected a $40 million settlement demand from Ed Gorman. But Charley told me that now, in light of the jury poll, he thought that $62 million was well under the amount that Dow would be willing to pay to settle the case. This was great news. Charley was implying that Dow would consider me a hero if I could settle the case for $62 million. Based on our initial settlement meeting with the judge, I knew I could do substantially better.

*   *   *

Following the April 18 meeting in chambers, the pace of the negotiations picked up dramatically.

Friday April 20: Judge Weinstein's law clerk phoned me mid-morning to advise that the judge wanted all defense counsel in chambers that very afternoon.

"The judge is going to appoint three Special Masters to oversee the settlement process under his supervision," the clerk told me. "He wants the defense attorneys to meet them. Please call the others and let them know."

At the courthouse later that afternoon, I had the opportunity to talk briefly with the other defense counsel before our meeting with the judge. The judge's decision to appoint Special Masters had taken all of us completely by surprise. We did not think he would take such an extraordinary step unless he felt optimistic about the chances of reaching a settlement. We were all at a loss to figure out what we may have said or done at the April 18 meeting to make him feel that way.

In chambers, the judge introduced us to two of the Special Masters, Kenneth Feinberg and David Shapiro. Both were partners in Washington, D.C., law firms. In addition, Feinberg was a former Administrative Assistant to Senator Edward Kennedy. The third Special Master, who was not in court that day, was Leonard Garment, one of Shapiro's law partners and a former Special Consultant and Acting Counsel to the President of the United States.

Since none of the defendants objected to the appointment of the Special Masters, the judge suggested that he leave the room and we meet with the Masters privately, which we did. Feinberg quickly demonstrated that he was quite knowledgeable about the case and confided that he had ghostwritten the judge's "Settlement Memorandum." We all agreed that the first order of business would be for the Masters to contact the government to inquire about its willingness to participate in the settlement talks. Feinberg told us that they would go directly to the White House. Garment would attempt to make an appointment to see James Baker, President Reagan's Chief of Staff.

Since it appeared from the way they were talking that the Special Masters would be with us for a while, I decided that now was as good a time as any to raise two important points.

First, I told the Special Masters that the defendants would only consider a settlement that closed out the entire case. In other words, we wanted the settlement to buy our peace. "Our biggest concern is opt-outs," I said. "Why should we settle the class action, only to find that thousands of opt-outs are continuing with their lawsuits?"

Second, I raised the issue of allocating any settlement among the seven defendants. Feinberg was surprised to hear that even though Dow's market share of Agent Orange was thirty-one percent, using the allocation formula set forth in his "Settlement Memorandum" Dow's settlement share would only be ten percent. In contrast, while Monsanto's market share was twenty-eight percent, its settlement share according to the "Settlement Memorandum" would be sixty-six percent. Feinberg was surprised because he may not have appreciated the extent to which each company's dioxin content would alter the settlement equation. I told Feinberg in no uncertain terms that Dow would not even consider a settlement unless it factored in dioxin content. One of the attorneys in the room, just as emphatically, insisted that factoring in dioxin content was unacceptable to his client. This was the first of many heated exchanges among the defendants and the Special Masters relating to this very sensitive issue.

Monday April 23: Three days later, two weeks before the scheduled trial date, the attorneys for the defendants met to discuss their settlement strategy in light of the involvement of the Special Masters. We decided that before Garment approached Baker, it was essential for us to educate all three Special Masters about the role of the government in the Agent Orange controversy and why the government should participate in the settlement. We discussed the likelihood that plaintiffs would attempt to negotiate a separate settlement with one defendant and use the money to finance their case against the others. Although the consensus was that the defendants should stick together and negotiate as a group, we all recognized that this might not be possible because of our differing views on allocation. A more likely scenario, according to some, was that the defendants would end up splitting into two groups: those companies that produced Agent Orange with relatively low levels of dioxin; and those companies that produced Agent Orange with relatively high levels of dioxin. For my part, I said Dow would be pleased to negotiate with the group as a whole but suggested that if certain defendants took unreasonable positions on allocation, I would not hesitate to deal with plaintiffs on my own or together with the other so-called "clean" companies.

Tuesday April 24: The next day, we met with Feinberg and Shapiro in New York City. We spent the first part of the meeting discussing the legal and moral reasons for the government to participate in any Agent Orange settlement. At one point, I read from Dow's summary judgment papers the testimony of members of the President's Science Advisory Committee regarding their knowledge of the presence of dioxin in Agent Orange and dioxin's potential toxicity. In the midst of my reading of that testimony, Dave Shapiro blurted out, "Stop. I've heard enough." Later, Ken Feinberg assured us that he and Shapiro felt that we were right to go after the government and that "we could not champion a cause we didn't believe in."

Feinberg also told us that he and Shapiro had met with plaintiffs' lead attorneys, and that the judge was very unhappy because the attorneys have thus far failed to provide the judge with adequate data regarding the number of claimants and the nature of their injuries. "If this continues," Feinberg said, "the judge would not hesitate hitting plaintiffs over the head to get them to accept a lower settlement package." This was the first but certainly not the last time the judge threatened to use his considerable powers of persuasion on one of the parties.

Thursday April 26: I flew to Midland to brief Dow's senior management on trial preparation and settlement issues.

Friday Afternoon April 27: Today, ten days before the trial date, defense counsel met with all three Special Masters in a conference room at Dave Shapiro's offices in Washington. The Special Masters began the meeting by reporting that the government had responded with an emphatic "no" to Garment's inquiries about participating in the settlement. The government's position was that its sole obligation to veterans exposed to Agent Orange was to provide them with medical and other benefits under a newly enacted federal statute. Moreover, the government told Garment that, pursuant to the statute, the government had already expended almost $150 million.

After giving us the bad news, the Special Masters urged the defendants to continue negotiating on their own notwithstanding the government's unwillingness to participate. "It makes sense for you to settle even without the government," Shapiro told us. "No matter how strong your defenses are, you have an enormous exposure. Why go to trial and take such a huge risk. You can probably end up settling the case for what you would ultimately have to pay just to defend it."

Feinberg then presented the defendants with a new settlement proposal under which the defendants but not the government would contribute to a settlement fund. In order to recover from the fund, a veteran or family member would be required to prove that the veteran was exposed to Agent Orange and that the veteran or family member was suffering from an illness or injury specified on a list of covered conditions. The claimant would not be required to prove that Agent Orange caused the illness or injury. Medical examinations would be conducted either by the VA or a private physician. The fund would make a lump sum payment of $100,000 or less, depending on the severity of the condition, to each qualifying claimant. There would be special provisions to provide compensation for wives and children and for veterans whose diseases had not yet manifested themselves by the time of the settlement. There would also be a provision for the payment from the fund of plaintiffs' attorneys fees and expenses.

Based upon certain assumptions Feinberg made about the number of claimants to the fund and the nature of their injuries, Feinberg estimated that his proposal would cost the defendants a one-time up front payment of just under $200 million.

I was not surprised when I heard Feinberg's dollar figure. Ten days earlier, Judge Weinstein had "off-handedly" thrown out the exact same number.

For the next two hours, the defense attorneys and the Special Masters discussed every single aspect of Feinberg's proposal in great detail. During this discussion, it became clear that each Special Master had a unique role to play in the negotiations. Garment's role, because of his high-level connections, was to contact the government. When he ran into a dead end, his involvement in the talks basically ended. Feinberg and Shapiro both did the heavy negotiating, with Feinberg acting as the "idea" man. He was the charmer, like the good cop. His job was to devise the proposals. In contrast, Shapiro acted as the "muscle" man. He was the tough guy, like the bad cop. His job was to convince the parties that Feinberg's proposals were reasonable and that we should accept them.

Then there was the judge. He wasn't even in the room with us, but he was clearly the dominant moving force behind the negotiations. "Dave and I are in constant touch with the judge," Feinberg told us. "He is really pushing hard for a settlement. In fact, I have to say I've never seen a more aggressive judge when it comes to settlement. He couldn't care less about the details. He just wants us to get it done."

Shapiro told us, "Don't worry about what plaintiffs are demanding, worry about what the judge is demanding."

"If you have a counterproposal," Shapiro added, "and it's too low, I won't take it directly to the plaintiffs, but I will take it to the judge. He may want to deal with the plaintiffs in his own way. Or if he doesn't like your offer, he may club you a bit to get you to accept a more reasonable proposal."

In case we were wondering what the judge might do to us, Shapiro noted that some time ago the judge decided not to allow plaintiffs to sue for punitive damages. "The judge told me," Shapiro said, "that he is thinking of reconsidering."

The Special Masters asked us to get back to them no later than no later than Tuesday of next week.

Friday Evening April 27: As the meeting was breaking up, the wall at one end of the conference room, which was actually a sliding panel, was opened up to reveal another conference room containing an elegantly set table. Shapiro, the muscle man, had arranged to serve the defense attorneys dinner. The Special Masters did not join us, preferring to give us the opportunity to discuss the day's events in private.

The general consensus was that $200 million was not a firm demand and that plaintiffs, or the judge, might accept $150 million. It was suggested that we come back with an offer of $100 million.

"But we can't really come back with anything," one of the attorneys said, "until we know what each of the parties is willing to put up."

The talk then turned to allocation. I was the loudest proponent of allocating settlement shares based upon dioxin content. The "equal shares" companies argued just as loudly but, in my mind, not nearly as persuasively. One attorney suggested that even though Dow was a clean company, it may have to come up with more than its dioxin share "because of its name and up front involvement."

Nothing was resolved. We agreed to meet Monday morning.

Sunday Night April 29: At 11 p.m., Feinberg telephoned Monsanto's attorney to report that he and Shapiro had spent most of the day on the phone with plaintiffs' attorneys and the judge. "The number on the table is now $180 million," Feinberg said. "Plaintiffs have come down from $260 million."

Monday Morning April 30: The defense attorneys met in New York City. The total dollar figure looked attractive enough for us to begin discussing in detail what terms and conditions to include in the settlement agreement to best protect the defendants from future liability. Remember how passionately the defendants opposed class certification? Now that a settlement seemed within the realm of possibility, suddenly the defendants wanted to certify as broad a class as possible, so that most if not all Vietnam veterans would be bound by the settlement. We talked about the need for Circuit Court approval of the class and the settlement. We talked about including a statement of no causation in the settlement agreement. We talked about how to deal with opt-outs.

We also talked about allocation. When someone suggested equal shares, the attorney for Thompson-Hayward, a former state court judge with an impeccable demeanor, got visibly angry. As everyone there knew, Thompson-Hayward's Agent Orange market share was a meager three percent. "Please understand," the attorney said, "that there will simply not be equal apportionment."

An attorney for one of the other parties, equally soft spoken, shot back, "But no one should expect to get out of this lawsuit for a *de minimus* amount."

"I couldn't agree with you more," I said, "but the bottom line, as far as I'm concerned, is how much Monsanto and Diamond Shamrock are willing to pay."

Finally, we talked about recommending to our clients that they respond to the latest demand by offering $100 million. "It makes no sense to offer anything less than that," Thompson-Hayward's attorney argued. Everyone agreed, with one exception. "I can't do anything," that attorney told us, "until I know how the settlement is going to be allocated."

We scheduled a meeting for the following afternoon.

Monday Night April 30: Monsanto's attorney called Feinberg to report that the defendants were still trying to reach a consensus about how to respond to the Special Master's latest proposal. The Special Master told the attorney that the judge wanted the defendants to get back to the Special Master as quickly as possible with a counteroffer.

Tuesday Morning May 1: Six days before the scheduled trial date, Ken Feinberg called my office at 7:25 a.m. He just missed me. I arrived at work that morning at 7:40. When I called Feinberg back, he told me about his phone conversation the night before with Monsanto's attorney. "I think I'm making a mistake," Feinberg told me. "I've been speaking to the wolf instead of the lamb." I took this to mean that Feinberg had concluded that dioxin content had to be a factor in any settlement allocation and that Monsanto's opposition was holding things up. Feinberg also told me that if the defendants came back with a figure of $100 million, "it would be a problem." I mentioned $135 million, and he said, "that would be an excellent idea."

Tuesday Afternoon May 1: Defense counsel met in New York City. It was now unanimous that even though there was not yet a consensus on allocation, we would respond to the Special Masters with a $100 million counterproposal.

The good feeling that this generated was quickly dispelled as once again the group addressed the allocation issue.

I listened patiently to yet another plea for equal shares. "We're not settling this case because we believe that Agent Orange caused plaintiffs' damages," the attorney explained. "So market share or amount of dioxin should have nothing to do with how we allocate. The only fair way is to divide the settlement equally."

"That's nonsense," I responded. "We're settling this case because each of us has an exposure based upon the possibility of causation. The more dioxin in the product, the greater that possibility, and the greater the exposure. So dioxin share has everything to do with why we're settling and how we should allocate."

When the attorney persisted, I told him, "Look, you really have no choice. What happens if we go to trial? I put Dow scientists on the stand who say they implemented quality controls to assure that Dow's 2,4,5-T contained no detectable dioxin. Plaintiffs ask them why they did that. They testify that if there were high levels of dioxin in the product, more than one ppm, the product was potentially toxic. That testimony would be devastating to some of you sitting around this table. Like Monsanto, for instance. That company's product had more than seven ppm. How would Monsanto deal with that?"

Someone spoke up in Monsanto's defense. "You know, Len," the attorney began, "some of us have serious reservations about the Gulfport dioxin numbers." This was a reference to the results of tests conducted by the government in Gulfport, Mississippi, on sample batches of each defendant's Agent Orange. Dow's position was that allocation based on dioxin content should use the Gulfport test results as the final word on the dioxin levels of each company's product.

The attorney continued, "We're thinking of making a motion to strike the Gulfport numbers as non-representative and inaccurate. We may have some other figures we'd like to offer."

"You may be looking for trouble," I warned. "There may be test results out there that are better for you than Gulfport, but I've seen test results that are worse. The more rummaging around you do, the more you may be helping plaintiffs' case. So please be careful."

"I'm always careful," he said cooly.

With that, another attorney quickly chimed in, "Maybe the Special Masters can help us work this out."

Wednesday May 2: The defense attorneys met with Feinberg and Shapiro in New York City at the offices of Monsanto's attorney. We reported that the defendants had reached a consensus that $100 million was a reasonable figure but were as far away as ever on the issue of allocation. The Special Masters responded that our figure was too low. Shapiro suggested that we come back at $150 million. We were noncommittal, but did say that we would consider moving up from our figure if plaintiffs came down from theirs.

There was very little talk about how the settlement money was to be administered or distributed. The defendants had decided that if the money was acceptable, we would leave it to the plaintiffs to work out those issues.

Instead, we talked at length about the defendants' concern that we would only agree to a settlement that would "buy our peace." Speaking for the group, I presented the Special Masters with a list of settlement conditions designed to give the defendants as much protection from future litigation as possible, including:

1. The settlement must not allow persons to opt out or it must give the defendants the right to walk away from the settlement if too many claimants opt out.
2. The settlement must provide for children born after the case settles.
3. The settlement must provide for Australian and New Zealand veterans, American and Vietnamese civilians, and spouses and children.
4. The settlement agreement must include a statement of no causation.
5. Counsel fees must be low so as to discourage others from commencing dioxin litigation.
6. Plaintiffs must return or destroy all of the defendants' documents they obtained during discovery.
7. Claims for punitive damages must be dismissed.
8. The fund would indemnify the defendants for any liability to any Agent Orange claimant who did not participate in the settlement.

I also insisted on two conditions designed to protect the defendants if the settlement fell through:

1. The settlement agreement must be approved by an appellate court before any money is paid.
2. Plaintiffs must agree to waive a jury trial if the settlement is overturned in court and the case must be tried.

Finally, I insisted that the settlement must protect the defendants' right to insurance coverage for their Agent Orange exposure.

The Special Masters assured us that they would discuss our conditions with the plaintiffs' attorneys and the judge.

We then turned our attention to the allocation problem and asked the Special Masters for some help on this troublesome issue. They suggested that they meet separately with each defendant. Monsanto went first, followed by Thompson-Hayward, followed by Dow.

To my surprise, Feinberg began our separate meeting by suggesting that Dow should pay the largest share of any settlement because it produced thirty-one percent of the Agent Orange used in Vietnam, more than any other defendant. This certainly was at odds with how I read Feinberg during our May 1 phone conversation. My reaction: I blew my top. I went through all of the reasons why allocation should be based on dioxin content, not market share or even equal shares. I told them that Monsanto, because of the dioxin content of its product, and not Dow, was the target defendant. I told them of all the problems Monsanto would have trying the case. I told them that I wasn't completely happy with the judge's allocation proposal, that I thought ten percent for Dow was too high. But I thought that Monsanto's sixty-six percent share was reasonable, and no way would I agree to pick up any portion of that. "I'm in the cat bird seat," I said. "I've got nothing to lose by waiting them out. My product was clean. I'm not afraid of trying this case."

"I'm sorry," I concluded. "That's my position. I see no reason to change."

Thursday May 3: The Special Masters met with plaintiffs' attorneys in Washington. The judge issued an order directing all attorneys to appear in court on Saturday and Sunday for all day meetings. The order also directed that each defendant be represented by a "person or agent with authority to settle the case."

Saturday May 5: At 10:30 this morning, two days before the start of the trial, I arrived at the federal courthouse in Brooklyn accompanied by Keith McKennon, Wayne Hancock, Charley Carey, and Ron Davis of Dow, Otis Hess of Fireman's Fund, who had taken over for Bob Buell, and two of my partners.

It was an incredible scene. Two adjacent courtrooms were open. In one, jury selection was taking place. Prospective jurors sat in the jury box. At least two dozen attorneys and their consultants sat at counsel table reviewing questionnaires, posing questions, and exercising challenges. The spectator area was about one-half full. In the other, where the negotiations would take place, attorneys, corporate executives, and insurance people sat together in groups of ten or twelve, talking quietly, waiting for things to get started. For the most part, the defendants' representatives sat on one side of the room, and plaintiffs' representatives sat on the other. The defendants talked to each other but not to plaintiffs, other than to exchange pleasantries if they happened to bump into each other in the corridor or the men's room. There was a steady flow of people in and out of both courtrooms, which emptied into a common corridor, where a handful of people paced nervously up and down, back and forth, like expectant fathers in a hospital waiting room.

The judge came into the settlement courtroom at about 11:00 a.m. He began by giving a rousing pep talk, urging all of us to be reasonable and to get the deal done. Then he walked plaintiffs' attorneys out of the courtroom and down the corridor to a jury room, so called because juries used it for their deliberations. There, the judge met alone with plaintiffs' attorneys for nearly two hours.

The defendants took that opportunity to meet privately to attempt to make some progress on the allocation issue. We got nowhere. Keith McKennon, who sat in on the discussions, got so frustrated that he took me aside and said, "Len, I'm going to find out the names and telephone numbers of the presidents of each of the co-defendants. I'll call Paul Oreffice, Dow's president, tell him what's going on, and ask him to call the others and urge some movement." These were the days before cellular phones, so Keith spent a good portion of the next two hours in a phone booth in the corridor. Later, he told me that Mr. Oreffice, after hearing Keith's description of what was going on in court that morning, had agreed to make the calls. To this day, Keith believes that Mr. Oreffice's efforts played a significant role in bringing the defendants closer together over that last weekend.

After lunch, the judge met alone with the defendants. The discussion that afternoon was not about money. Instead, we spent nearly three hours discussing the defendants' list of settlement conditions which we had presented to the Special Masters on May 2. The judge said yes to some but no to others. Plaintiffs had made some demands of their own. We came out of the meeting hopeful but not altogether certain that we could resolve these issues to our reasonable satisfaction.

While we were meeting with Judge Weinstein, Otis Hess spent some time in the adjacent courtroom watching the jury selection process. Attorneys for the veterans and for the manufacturers were questioning potential jurors to determine their impartiality. As Otis sat down in the gallery, an attorney for one of the defendants was questioning a stout, balding, middle aged man wearing a union tee shirt and several day's growth of whiskers. The attorney asked, "If you heard uncontradicted expert testimony that Agent Orange did not cause any of the veterans' injuries, would you be able to put your feelings of sympathy toward the veterans aside and find for the defendants?"

To which the man replied, in his best Brooklynese, "Quit joikin' 'em around. Give 'em da money."

Otis immediately ran to find Keith McKennon. "Guess what," Otis told him. "Our jury consultant was right."

* * *

Later Saturday afternoon, at about 4:30, Judge Weinstein summoned the defendants back to the conference room and presented us with a revised allocation formula. Each defendant's share under the judge's new proposal, compared to its market, is set forth on the following chart:

Company	Market Share	Settlement Share
Dow	31%	19.5
Monsanto	28	45.5
Hercules	19	10
Thompson-Hayward	8	6
Diamond Shamrock	5	12
Uniroyal	5	5
Thompson	3	2

Each of Dow's co-defendants reacted to the judge's proposal exactly as expected. Monsanto, whose 45.5% settlement share was more than twice as large as any other company's, and Diamond Shamrock, whose twelve percent settlement share was more than twice its market share, complained the loudest. Thompson Chemical, whose settlement share was a mere two percent percent, cheered the loudest. Hercules, who believed that its ten percent settlement share should have been even lower than that, groaned. Thompson-Hayward, at six percent, and Uniroyal, at five percent, breathed sighs of relief.

For my part, I tried not to react outwardly at all. But inside I was very pleased. Plaintiffs' current settlement demand was $180 million. Dow's 19.9% share of that would be $35.1 million. That number was well below the worst-case settlement scenario which Charley Carey and I had devised two weeks earlier.

The defendants then caucused privately to discuss the judge's proposal and thereafter with the Special Masters, who once again suggested that they meet privately with each defendant. This time, Dow went first. I told the Special Masters that Dow would agree to pay 19.5% of a $150 million settlement, or approximately $29 million. Then I waited in the courtroom until 9:30 p.m. while the Special Masters met separately with each of the other defendants. At 9:45, Ken Feinberg came into the courtroom, where all of the defendants had gathered, and told us that five of the seven defendants had committed to a $150 million settlement based on the judge's allocation formula. When Feinberg then left the room, everyone wanted to know who had given that commitment. It turned out that only three defendants had done so. At that point, we threw up our hands, decided that it was useless to go on, and agreed to meet back in court first thing in the morning.

Very Early Sunday Morning May 6: Keith McKennon got back to his hotel around 2:00 a.m. Sunday morning. He tried to sleep, but could not. So he showered and, at 5:00 a.m., headed back to the courthouse. He arrived at 6:00 a.m. The door was open. He went upstairs to the courtroom, which was locked. He wandered down the corridor in the direction of the judge's chambers and noticed that the conference room door was open. He entered. The room was in shambles. Cigarette butts and coffee cups were on the floor. A waste basket had been knocked over. Keith started to straighten up. Suddenly, another man entered the room carrying two shopping bags filled with doughnuts. The two men finished cleaning up, made fresh coffee, and put out the doughnuts.

The man who helped Keith prepare the room for the day's events was none other than Judge Weinstein himself.

Sunday Morning: By 8:00 am, all of the attorneys and executives were back in court. The defendants spent the entire morning trying to work out the allocation issue. The attorneys for Monsanto and Diamond Shamrock made one final effort to convince the rest of us to allocate based upon Agent Orange market share. They did not succeed. I urged them to compromise. I pointed out that the other five defendants were lined up squarely against them, that they would be the target defendants at the trial because of the high levels of dioxin in their product, and that we would consider making a separate deal with the plaintiffs, thus forcing them to try the case by themselves. Finally, at noon, they relented, and we reached an agreement on allocation that factored in dioxin content. Since the final settlement allocation was placed under seal, I cannot disclose it, but I will say that Dow's share was well under our worst-case settlement scenario and was de minimus when compared to Dow's original assessment of its potential exposure. We summoned the Special Masters and told them that the defendants had agreed on how to allocate a $150 million settlement so long as the agreement included the conditions we had previously discussed.

Sunday Afternoon: The judge met all afternoon with the plaintiffs. At 4:00, Feinberg reported to the defendants that plaintiffs' dollar demand was a firm $200 million. This came as a great surprise, since in a phone conversation with Monsanto's attorney one week earlier Feinberg said that plaintiffs' number was $180 million. Feinberg also reported plaintiffs' position on the defendants' conditions. There were just two potential problems: plaintiffs did not want to waive a jury if the settlement fell through, and they wanted to limit the amount that the settlement fund had to indemnify the defendants for any future Agent Orange liability.

The defendants huddled and then, at 5:00 p.m., told Feinberg that we were sticking firm at $150 million. We also made some counter proposals regarding the conditions.

Sunday Night: By 7:15, there had been no movement, so we went out for dinner. We returned to the courthouse at 8:30. At 9:00, the judge called us into the conference room and told us that if the defendants came up with $180 million the case would settle. At 10:00, we reported directly to the judge that the defendants would agree to $180 million depending on the conditions. The judge was very pleased, but the deal was not yet done. Plaintiffs' attorneys still needed some convincing.

The judge met with plaintiffs' attorneys for the next three hours. Remember, I was not present when the judge or the Special Masters met separately with the plaintiffs, so I do not have first hand knowledge of what the judge said at this particular meeting or at other meetings over the weekend to persuade plaintiffs to soften their demands. But according to one commentator, the judge "exploited whatever leverage he could muster over the lawyers. While not actually threatening retribution if they refused to settle, he did use the ambiguity of his roles — as mediator and as ultimate decision maker — to play upon their fears, magnify the risks, and whittle down their resistance."[3]

That same commentator quoted the recollection of Benton Musselwhite, one of plaintiffs' lead attorneys, regarding the judge's tactics, as follows:

He would say: "Now, I am not going to hold it against you if you don't settle. I am not going to penalize you. I am going to conduct this trial on a fair basis to everybody....But I have carried you plaintiffs all this time. I have decided a lot of questions in your favor that I could have decided the other way. And I want you to know that at nine o'clock Monday morning I am through carrying you. You are on your own. I will do my duty as a judge."

Then a little conversation would take place and then he would come back and say: "You know, remember, I just don't think you have got a case on medical causation. I don't think you have a case on punitive damages."[4]

Musselwhite also described the effect that the judge's around the clock, eleventh hour negotiating sessions had on plaintiffs' lead counsel:

Not only were you tired and not your usual self in terms of resistance, of having control, you know, of what was going on, but it made you feel a kind of helplessness. I mean, you are there and you have got to stay in the negotiations...I could see how psychologically it was affecting all the members of the [plaintiffs' management] committee, particularly the ones who were going to have to try the case, to get to be ready to go on Monday. So many things that we had to do, and here we were down at the courthouse negotiating this settlement on an around-the-clock basis...the judge wore us all down with that tactic...the judge made us negotiate around the clock knowing that we had a difficult time being ready for trial, we were thin on manpower, and we were working night and day to get ready, and to lose the last 48 to 72 hours just before the trial was going to adversely affect us, and we knew it. You had to be dumb not to know that. Plus the fact that it tired us and made us less resistant to pressure, and he knew that, I think.[5]

Very Early Monday Morning May 7: At 1:00 a.m. Monday morning, the day the trial was scheduled to begin, the judge reported to the defense attorneys who were gathered in his courtroom that plaintiffs had finally agreed to defendants' $180 million counter-offer. More work was needed, however, on the conditions.

An hour later, the judge reentered the courtroom. Attorneys for both sides were present. Many attorneys and other representatives had long since gone home. Only Keith McKennon, Wayne Hancock, and I remained from Dow's contingent. The judge looked as tired as the rest of us felt. He announced with a great deal of satisfaction that the case had settled for $180 million. He then read the list of conditions that both sides had agreed upon:

1. Interest on the $180 million would run from May 7.
2. The fund would advance money to pay the cost of notifying the class of the settlement and other administrative expenses.
3. No money would be distributed until the last appeal has been exhausted.
4. The fund would indemnify the defendants for any state court Agent Orange judgments up to a limit of $10 million.
5. The class would include those serviceman and family members whose injuries have not yet manifested themselves.
6. Plaintiffs could keep the defendants' documents for purposes of suing the government.
7. All parties reserved their rights to sue the government.
8. The defendants denied liability.
9. The defendants could terminate the settlement if too many claimants opted out of the class.
10. Any class member who opted out would have a reasonable time to opt back in.
11. The defendants could apply to have what remains of the fund returned to them after twenty-five years.
12. The court would hold fairness hearings as required by the federal class action statute.
13. The fund would provide for afterborn children.
14. The court would retain jurisdiction over the case until the fund is disposed of.

The lead attorneys for plaintiffs and defendants signed some papers hastily prepared by the judge and the Special Masters. There was no celebration. The judge did not invite us into chambers for a champagne toast, as he did after he settled the Franklin case. He must have assumed that we all just wanted to go home and get some sleep after a weekend more strenuous than any I have ever experienced, before or since.

Downstairs, Keith McKennon was ecstatic. "Len," he said, "you did a great job. Dow is going to be so pleased with the final deal. It was a pleasure watching you work. I certainly think that you were the focal point of the negotiations, as far as the defendants were concerned. There were a lot of high priced lawyers running around the courthouse this weekend. I think they all took their cues from you."

Monday Morning May 7: At 10:00 a.m., Judge Weinstein was back in court.

"Ladies and gentlemen," he announced to the crowd that had filled every available seat, nook, and cranny, "I have an announcement." He picked up a piece of paper and began to read a statement prepared by Special Master Feinberg:

> JUDGE WEINSTEIN: The parties in the Agent Orange litigation have agreed to a settlement of the case. The settlement agreement is expected to result in payments to members of the defined class of over ¼ billion dollars over the next six years. Payments by the seven defendants to the settlement trust fund will total $180 million plus interest from today. Funds from the settlement trust fund will be available over a twenty-five year period to assure benefits for members of the class, including spouses and afterborns of Vietnam veterans (as defined in the class).
>
> The plaintiffs and defendants reserve all rights and claims that they may have against the United States.
>
> The Court will hold public hearings concerning the terms of the proposed settlement pursuant to Rule 23 of the Federal Rules of Civil Procedure. Any person or organization requesting information or input into the specific terms of the settlement agreement should contact the Plaintiffs' Management Committee.

Since the people in court that morning were unaware of the marathon settlement talks that had taken place over the weekend, the reaction to Judge Weinstein's announcement was one of total and complete shock. When the judge mentioned the dollar amount of the settlement, more than a handful of veterans and their supporters shouted out in protest. As the judge continued to read, the shouts died down to a low, unhappy murmur. When the judge finished reading, he stood up and walked out of the courtroom.

* * *

Back at our office, word of the settlement spread quickly. The mood among the dozens of attorneys and paralegals who had been working on the case was one of surprise and bewilderment. Surprise, because many did not even know that the settlement talks had taken place. Bewilderment, because many wondered if they would still have their jobs.

At around 9:30 a.m., Jim Rigano arrived at the office. Jim was a young associate whom we had hired two weeks earlier to work in the firm's general litigation department. As Jim walked down the corridor toward his office, he noticed a group of about twenty Agent Orange attorneys and paralegals just milling about, talking quietly, looking rather dazed.

"What happened?" Jim asked, thinking someone had died.

"The case settled last night," one of the attorneys told Jim. "I think we've become obsolete."

Far from it. Agent Orange may have been our biggest case, but it was not our only case. Within days, every single attorney and paralegal who was no longer needed for Agent Orange was reassigned to other matters.

Years later, after Jim had left our firm to form his own, he told me that he was amazed that no one lost his job as a result of the settlement. "There were a lot of impressive things about the firm in those days," he said, "but nothing impressed me more than that. The Agent Orange case settled, and the firm didn't miss a beat."

*   *   *

Monday morning, while Judge Weinstein was announcing the settlement in court, Otis Hess was flying back to California. He was exhausted, but when he arrived at San Francisco airport in the early afternoon he decided to drive to the office, one hour north in Novato. When he got there, he was surprised to find a huge party taking place on the sprawling front lawn of the Fireman's Fund building, complete with music, a speaker's platform, the works. Then he remembered: Fireman's Fund was celebrating its 121st birthday. Otis parked his car and joined the festivities. To his surprise, the talk of the party was the Agent Orange settlement. Everyone was thrilled. All of a sudden, Otis heard someone calling his name over a loudspeaker. He looked up at the speaker's platform. The man who had called his name was Sandy Weill, who was President of American Express, the parent company of Fireman's Fund. Sandy called Otis up onto the stage, congratulated him on the settlement in front of the entire party, gave him a big hug, and kissed him on the cheek.

*   *   *

Settled But Not Over

The Agent Orange litigation did not come to a sudden and screeching halt as a result of Sandy Weill's kiss. The parties may have agreed to a settlement in the wee small hours of the morning, but we had much work to do to finalize the terms of the agreement and obtain court approval. Moreover, the settlement left many issues unresolved, such as the rights of the opt-outs and the question of government liability. These and other issues took years to resolve. In fact, fifteen years after the parties shook hands in Judge Weinstein's court, my firm was still actively litigating Agent Orange cases.

Here is a brief chronology of some of the major events, mostly court decisions, that occurred during that fifteen year period.

June 11, 1984: After a month of drafting and redrafting, quibbling over words and phrases, and soliciting input from dozens of outside and in-house attorneys, the parties finally produce a nineteen-page written settlement agreement. On June 11, they sign the agreement, and Judge Weinstein marks it "so ordered." The agreement requires the defendants to pay $180 million into a fund "to be established, maintained, and administered by the Court." The agreement does not disclose each defendant's share of the payment. Nor does it disclose how the money in the fund is to be distributed. Nineteen separately numbered paragraphs in the agreement address some but not all of the defendants' procedural concerns.

July 24, 1984: The defendants file a motion for summary judgment seeking an order dismissing all claims by the more than two thousand persons who have opted out of the Agent Orange settlement class. We argue that we are entitled to summary judgment for three reasons: no plaintiff can prove that his or her injuries were caused by exposure to Agent Orange; no individual plaintiff can identify the manufacturer of the Agent Orange to which he was exposed; and all of the claims by all of the plaintiffs are barred by the government contract defense.

August 8, 1984: Judge Weinstein presides over the first "fairness" hearing in Brooklyn. The hearing lasts for three days. Later, Judge Weinstein conducts fairness hearings in Chicago on August 13-14, in Houston on August 16-17, in Atlanta on August 20-21, and in San Francisco on August 23-24.

Under the Federal Rules of Civil Procedure, all class action settlements must be approved by the court. Court approval is required to assure that the interests of all class members are adequately protected by the settlement. The standard for approval is that the court must determine that the settlement is fair, reasonable, and adequate. Judge Weinstein feels that he cannot make this determination without providing veterans, their family members, and other interested parties with the opportunity to comment on the proposed settlement and voice their support or opposition.

More than one thousand class members testify in person at the fairness hearings or submit their written comments. The speakers include American veterans, wives, and parents; Red Cross volunteers and other American civilians who had been in Vietnam; representatives of veterans' organizations such as the Agent Orange Children's Fund, Agent Orange Victims International, Vietnam Veterans of America, the Veterans of Foreign Wars, Vietnam Veterans Against the War, and Black Veterans for Social Justice; representatives of several state Agent Orange Commissions; representatives of local self-help organizations; and veteran leaders from Australia and New Zealand.

In a subsequent written opinion, Judge Weinstein will comment at length on the "moving sights and sounds of the hearings":

> . . . broken hearted young widows who have seen their strapping young husbands die of cancer, wives who must live with husbands wracked with pain and in deep depressions, mothers whose children suffer from multiple birth defects and require almost saint-like daily care, the strong men who have tears welling up in their eyes as they tell of fear that their families will be left without support because of their imminent death, the man whose mind is so clouded he must be prompted by his wife standing by with his defective child in her arms to go on with his speech, the veterans trying to control the rage that wells up within them...

> Just a few years ago these veterans were healthy and handsome youths in their teens and early twenties who bravely went to war because their leaders asked them to. And it is clear from what they said and did in court that they are sincere when many of them say they would volunteer their broken bodies and worn spirits once again if their country called. Some are understandably bitter that their government and its people have shunned them instead of embracing them as heroes....They remind us, as we enjoy the fruits of our power and wealth, to remember those men and women who struggle each

day with disastrous medical problems they attribute to service in Vietnam.[6]

The judge will also conclude that although the class members who testified at the hearings shared common problems and sought common goals, there was a "sharp split of opinion"[7] among them as to whether the settlement was, in fact, fair, adequate, and reasonable.

August 24, 1984: On the date of the last fairness hearing, the defendants file a 289-page brief in support of the proposed settlement. The theme of the brief is that even though the veterans cannot establish the defendants' liability, and even though there is no causal connection between exposure to Agent Orange and the veterans' alleged injuries, the defendants were motivated to settle the case, and the settlement should be approved, because "of the uncertainties and extraordinary costs of litigation—and particularly this litigation which aroused much heated controversy and adverse publicity despite the lack of evidence to support plaintiffs' claims."

September 25, 1984: One month after the last fairness hearing, Judge Weinstein releases a 122-page opinion, which reads like an encyclopedic treatise, tentatively approving the settlement.[8] In the opinion, the judge discusses at length the fairness hearings, the use of Agent Orange in Vietnam, the procedural history of the class action, the factual problems with plaintiffs' claims, the legal problems, the issue of government liability, and plans and suggestions for distributing the settlement fund. His conclusion:

> Based upon all the information presently available, the procedural posture of the litigation, the difficulty any plaintiff would have in establishing a case against any one or more of the defendants, the uncertainties associated with a trial, and the unacceptable burdens on plaintiffs' and defendants' legal staffs and the courts, the proposed settlement appears to be reasonable.[9]

January 7, 1985: Judge Weinstein releases an opinion awarding eighty-nine individual attorneys, law firms, and law professors who represented the class approximately $10.7 million in legal fees and expenses.[10]

May 8, 1985: In a monumentally significant decision, Judge Weinstein grants the defendants' motion for summary judgment and dismisses all claims by all opt-outs on two grounds: lack of causation, and the government contract defense.[11]

Thus, in one fell swoop Judge Weinstein vindicates what Dow has been saying from the very beginning of the litigation: based upon existing scientific and medical evidence, Agent Orange did not cause plaintiffs' injuries; and the government contract defense barred plaintiffs' claims.

Lack of Causation: The opt-outs offered two categories of proof to support their causation argument: epidemiological studies, which rely on "statistical methods to detect abnormally high incidences of diseases in a study population and to associate these incidences with unusual exposure to suspect environmental factors,"[12] and experts affidavits.

Regarding the epidemiological studies, including studies conducted by or on behalf of the United States Air Force, the Centers for Disease Control ("CDC"), a subdivision of the United States Public Health Service, the Australian Ministry for Veterans' Affairs, various state health agencies, and private physicians in the United States and Australia, Judge Weinstein concludes that they have been "negative or inconclusive"[13] as to whether exposure to Agent Orange caused the injuries and illnesses sustained by the veterans. He also states that the studies contain "no epidemiological evidence that paternal exposure to Agent Orange causes birth defects and miscarriages."[14]

Just to cite a few examples: After studying the health of veterans who served in Operation Ranch Hand, in other words, those veterans who participated in the spraying operation and thus had the greatest chance of significant exposure to Agent Orange, the United States Air Force concluded: "There is insufficient evidence to support a cause and effect relationship between herbicide exposure and adverse health in the Ranch Hand group at this time."[15] The study conducted for the Australian Ministry for Veterans' Affairs determined that the death rate among Australian veterans who served in Vietnam from cancer and other illnesses attributed by the veterans to Agent Orange was "statistically significantly lower than expected for Australian males, taking age and calendar year into account."[16] The CDC examined ninety-six categories of birth defects which occurred among children of veterans who served in Vietnam and concluded: "This study provides strong evidence that Vietnam veterans, in general, have not been at increased risk of fathering babies with the aggregate of the types of defects studied here."[17] Finally, the Australian study similarly concluded: "There is no evidence that Army service in Vietnam increases the risk of fathering children with anomalies diagnosed at birth."[18]

Regarding the expert affidavits, Judge Weinstein finds them deficient under the Federal Rules of Evidence and refuses to consider them.

Government Contract Defense: After discussing the causation issue for thirty-five pages, Judge Weinstein adds three paragraphs at the end of the decision, almost as an afterthought, in which he rules that the opt-outs "are unable to overcome defendants' government contract defense." The judge concludes:

> It is clear from the record, in light of all the information received to date, that the government knew as much as, or more than, the defendant chemical companies about the possible adverse health effects of Agent Orange as it was used in Vietnam. The information available makes it clear that the government would have concluded that the beneficial saving of American soldiers' lives by defoliating the Vietnamese jungles far outweighed any minimal risks to our own or allied troops posed by exposure to Agent Orange.[19]

Two Other Grounds: Again almost as an afterthought, Judge Weinstein inserts a fourth short paragraph at the end of his decision in which he sets forth two additional grounds for the dismissal: since all of the veterans' alleged injuries occur in the general population, each opt-out will be unable to link his disease to Agent Orange exposure as opposed to some other cause; and no claimant will be able to identify the manufacturer of the Agent Orange to which he may have been exposed.

May 9, 1985: Judge Weinstein dismisses the last remaining third-party claims against the government under the Federal Tort Claims Act.[20] In those claims, the defendants sought to recover from the government some or all of the money the defendants paid to settle the class action. Judge Weinstein explains that the government can be compelled to contribute to the settlement only if there is a legal basis for finding that the government is liable to the class members for their alleged injuries. But there is no such basis because, as both the defendants and the government agree, "Agent Orange cannot be shown to have caused any injury to any member of the class."[21]

During the course of the litigation, many people, including Judge Weinstein, criticized the government for its failure to fulfill its moral if not legal obligation to respond to the needs of the veterans. In this opinion, even though he dismisses the claims against the government, Judge Weinstein takes the government to task yet again. After conceding that "the government was and is within its legal rights in refusing to contribute to the settlement," the judge accuses the government of cruelty and shortsightedness:

That the position of the Department of Justice of benign detachment from this aftermath of the Vietnam War may be cruel to the veterans who served their country and feel that the government has turned its back on them in this litigation is besides the point. That the government may be short-sighted in its refusal to assist contractors who voluntarily produced at government request what amounted to critical war supplies during a foreign crisis is equally irrelevant. Undoubtedly, the United States will pay a high price for its present position. In the future many contractors will require indemnification and increased insurance costs will be added to the price of the goods the government purchases. There will be lingering resentment by veterans and their families who believe that the government has let them down. These matters of good faith and equity are not, however, considerations that the court may take into account under the Federal Tort Claims Act.[22]

May 28, 1985: Judge Weinstein releases an opinion approving a plan for the distribution of the settlement fund to the class members.[23] There are two parts to the plan. In the first part, Judge Weinstein sets aside $150 million, plus interest, for the payment of disability benefits to Vietnam veterans who suffer from long-term total disability and death benefits to the surviving spouses and children of deceased Vietnam veterans. Payments will be made regardless of what disease caused the disability or death, except that no payments will be made in cases where the death or disability resulted from trauma. Each claimant will be required to prove exposure to Agent Orange by comparing his service record to the "HERBS" tapes, a military data base of the dates and locations of Agent Orange spray missions in Vietnam. The payout program will run for ten years. No payments will be made until the last appeal of the last Agent Orange decision has been exhausted.

The second part of Judge Weinstein payment plan sets aside $45 million, plus interest, for the establishment of a class assistance foundation to fund projects and services that will benefit the class as a whole as opposed to individual veterans. He directs that children with birth defects born to Vietnam veterans should receive special priority from the foundation. He declares that the foundation will have a lifetime of twenty five years.

September 11, 1985: Judge Weinstein releases an opinion earmarking approximately $4 million from the settlement fund for the establishment of two private trusts for the benefit of Vietnam veterans from Australia and New Zealand.[24]

April 21, 1987: An incredible day. The Second Circuit Court of Appeals releases ten opinions disposing of all outstanding Agent Orange appeals. The highlights: the Second Circuit affirms Judge Weinstein's decision approving the reasonableness and fairness of the class settlement;[25] it affirms Judge Weinstein's distribution plan insofar as it provides for the payment of death and disability payments to individual veterans but reverses the plan insofar as it establishes a class assistance foundation, the problem being that Judge Weinstein delegated the management of the foundation to an outside board of directors rather than retain control over the foundation either himself or through a court-appointed special master;[26] it affirms Judge Weinstein's dismissal of the defendants' third-party claims for contribution and indemnity against the government;[27] it affirms in part and reverses in part Judge Weinstein's decision regarding the distribution of plaintiffs' attorneys fees from the settlement fund;[28] and it affirms the decision granting the defendants' motion for summary judgment against the opt-outs.[29]

The last decision is the most interesting, in that the Second Circuit expressly declines to rule on causation grounds, essentially ignoring an issue to which Judge Weinstein devoted thirty-five pages. Instead, the Second Circuit affirms the dismissal of all claims by all opt-outs solely on the basis of the government contract defense, an issue to which Judge Weinstein devoted three short paragraphs.

Members of the class unhappy with the Second Circuit for affirming that portion of Judge Weinstein's settlement plan covering the payment of death and disability payments will file a petition for a writ of certiorari in the United States Supreme Court. Opt-outs unhappy with the Second Circuit's ruling sustaining the government contract defense will also seek Supreme Court review.

December 1987: By the end of 1987, the VA has denied compensation claims by more than thirty-one thousand Vietnam veterans alleging injury as a result of exposure to Agent Orange. The VA is still taking the position that chloracne is the only disease caused by exposure to Agent Orange.[30]

June 1988: Opt-outs are not the only category of Agent Orange claimants prosecuting lawsuits against Dow following the class settlement. On this date, a class action is commenced in state court in Texas by veterans who claim that their injuries from exposure to Agent Orange did not manifest themselves until after the May 7, 1984 settlement.[31] Thus, these veterans argue that they are not members of the class and are not bound by the settlement. Dow will eventually remove this case to Texas federal court, and the Judicial Panel on Multidistrict will transfer it to Judge Weinstein, who will deny plaintiffs' motion for remand back to Texas state court. Later, Judge Weinstein will grant Dow's motion for summary judgment and dismiss the claims, ruling that even though the veterans' injuries manifested themselves after the settlement, the veterans are nevertheless members of the class and thus the settlement fund is their only remedy.

Two years later, the Second Circuit will affirm Judge Weinstein's ruling.[32] Thereafter, plaintiffs will file a petition for a writ of certiorari in the United States Supreme Court. Amazingly, the Attorneys General from all fifty states will file amicus curiae briefs in support of plaintiffs' position. The Clerk of the Supreme Court will tell Steve Brock that never before have all fifty Attorneys General filed briefs in the Supreme Court in the same case. In spite of this overwhelming show of support for the veterans, on February 22, 1994, the Supreme Court denies certiorari, thus establishing once and for all that the settlement is binding even on those veterans whose injuries manifested themselves after the settlement date.[33]

June 27, 1988: While the opt-outs' petition for Supreme Court review of the government contract defense is still pending, the Supreme Court decides *Boyle v. United Technologies*,[34] a case in which a marine pilot was killed in a helicopter crash. The pilot's estate sued United Technologies, claiming that the company had defectively designed the helicopter's emergency escape hatch system. The company defends on the basis of the government contract defense, and the issue goes all the way up to the Supreme Court. In a five-to-four decision, the Court sustains the defense, ruling that under federal law a military contractor is immune from tort liability when the government approves the specifications for the product, the product conforms to those specifications, and the supplier warned the government about hazards associated with the use of the product unknown to the government. The elements of the defense as defined by the Supreme Court are virtually identical to the elements as defined by Judge Pratt six years earlier.

June 30, 1988: Three days after deciding the *Boyle* case, the Supreme Court denies the opt-outs' petition for a writ of certiorari in the Agent Orange case, thus allowing the Second Circuit's ruling sustaining the government contract defense to stand.[35] We are thrilled by the decision and let out a huge, collective sigh of relief. Remember, the *Boyle* case was decided five-to-four. If one Justice in the five Justice majority had voted the other way, and the defense had been rejected in *Boyle*, undoubtedly the Supreme Court would have heard our case and, most likely, reversed. Then what? The case would have gone back to the Second Circuit for a ruling on causation. What if the Second Circuit reversed and ordered us to go to trial? Imagine that nightmare. Fortunately, five Justices in the *Boyle* case reached the right result.

Also on June 30, the Supreme Court refuses to hear the class members' appeal from the Second Circuit's decision sustaining Judge Weinstein's death and disability payment program.[36]

July 5, 1988: Following the Supreme Court's denial of certiorari, Judge Weinstein publishes his final settlement plan. He retains most of the elements of the death and disability payout program. He replaces the class assistance foundation, which was to be independently administered, with a class assistance program to be administered by the court.[37]

February 1989: The first disability and death payments are made from the settlement fund to veterans and surviving family members.[38]

March 1989: The first grants are awarded from the settlement fund by the class assistance program.

May 7, 1990: Having failed in its efforts to obtain tort-based contribution from the government under the Federal Tort Claims Act, Thompson Chemical Company commences an action against the government in the Court of Claims for implied contractual indemnification. One month later, Hercules commences a similar lawsuit.[39] Dow assesses the strengths and weaknesses of such a strategy and concludes that the claims are not likely to succeed.

October 26, 1990: The VA issues a regulation authorizing the payment of disability benefits to veterans suffering from non-Hodgkin's lymphoma, a rare type of cancer, allegedly as a result of exposure to Agent Orange.[40] The VA takes this step not because it concludes that exposure to Agent Orange causes non-Hodgkin's lymphoma but because it finds a "statistically significant association" between exposure to Agent Orange and the disease.[41] This is only the second Agent Orange related disease, after chloracne, recognized as "service connected" by the VA. One year later, in October 1991, the VA issues another regulation authorizing disability payments for soft tissue sarcoma, also a rare form of cancer.[42] By 1996, the VA has agreed to compensate Vietnam veterans for the following additional diseases: Hodgkin's disease, porphyria cutanea tarda (a liver condition), multiple myeloma, respiratory cancers (including cancers of the lung, larynx, trachea, and bronchus), prostrate cancer, and peripheral neuropathy.[43] Although Dow disputes the VA's findings that there is a "statistically significant association" or any other connection between exposure to Agent Orange and any of the above diseases, Dow applauds the VA for finally assuming some responsibility to the ailing Vietnam veterans.

August 1993: Opt-outs and veterans with injuries that manifested themselves after the date of the class settlement are not the only categories of Agent Orange claimants with ongoing lawsuits against Dow. In August 1993, a suit is commenced in Texas state court by a woman who served as a civilian nurse in Vietnam working for the United States Agency for International Relief. As a civilian, the nurse was not a member of the class, which included only Vietnam veterans and their family members. Dow will remove the case to Texas federal court, and the Judicial Panel on Multidistrict Litigation will transfer the case to Judge Weinstein, who will transfer the case back to federal court in Texas because of his lack of familiarity with Texas law. Ultimately, the federal judge in Texas will dismiss the case on the ground that the claims are barred by the two-year Texas statute of limitations.[44]

March 4, 1996: Thompson and Hercules never get to take their claims against the government for implied contractual indemnity to trial. On this date, the Supreme Court affirms the lower court decision granting the government's motion for summary judgment.[45]

June 1997: The last disability and death payments are made from the settlement fund.

September 1997: The last class assistance grants are awarded from the settlement fund.

September 24, 1997: The Special Master releases his final report on the distribution of the Agent Orange settlement fund. According to the report, 85,110 veterans filed disability claims, and 38,296 of those claims were approved. In addition, 20,653 surviving family members filed death claims, and 13,920 of those claims were approved. The fund paid a total of $196,595,084 to the 52,216 successful disability and death claimants, an average of just under four thousand dollars per claimant.

In addition, the class assistance program distributed $71,306,758 in grants to fund seventy-six programs in all fifty states which ultimately benefitted 239,000 class members. A listing of the first eight organization to receive grants provides a good cross section of the scope and breadth of the class assistance program: American Red Cross Mid Rio Grande Chapter in Albuquerque, New Mexico; Family Service Association of Brown County in Green Bay, Wisconsin; Federation for Children with Special Needs in Boston, Massachusetts; National Handicapped Sports & Recreation Association in Bethesda, Maryland; Occupational Center of Essex in Orange, New Jersey; Paralyzed Veterans of America in Washington, D.C.; Swords to Plowshares in San Francisco, California; and Team of Advocates for Special Kids in Fountain Valley, California.

The fund also paid $692,834 to the New Zealand Agent Orange Trust and $7,086,684 to the Australian Vietnam War Veterans Trust.

*   *   *

Looking Back

The Agent Orange litigation did not end with the final payout from the class settlement fund. There are still some Agent Orange claims pending in various courts around the country.

But, finally, most of the Agent Orange litigation is behind us now, and looking back I can only add the following observations:

First, without a doubt, the case was far and away high point of my legal career. The size, scope, complexity, duration, publicity, and intensity were unmatched. At times, it was hell to go through, but I wouldn't have missed it for the world.

Second, as much ego as attorneys have, we still like to hear people, especially clients, tell us that we did a good job. Thankfully, all of the supervisors at Dow and Fireman's Fund—Keith McKennon, Wayne Hancock, Charley Carey, Don Frayer, Bob Buell, and Otis Hess—went out of their way to let me and all of the attorneys on my staff know that they were extremely pleased with our work and the result. In fact, shortly after Sandy Weill, the President of American Express, kissed Otis Hess on the cheek, he invited me to his office in New York City to congratulate me personally.

Perhaps the nicest thank you I received was from Charley Carey. In August 1985, one year after the class action settlement, I invited Charley, Keith McKennon, Wayne Hancock, and several others from Dow to Montauk Point for a day of fishing on my boat. We spent the night at the Montauk Yacht Club and then, the next evening, Dow hosted a dinner party at the Garden City Hotel for everyone at Dow and Rikvin, Radler—lawyers, paralegals, secretaries, and other support people—who worked on the Agent Orange case. Two months later, Charley sent me a beautiful album filled with photographs from the fishing trip and the dinner party. "I hope you will enjoy the photo album for many years to come," Charley wrote in his cover letter, "especially because you have brought so much enjoyment to those around you, including your clients. The warm relationship between you and the people at Dow is a tribute to the excellence that you and the people in your law firm have demonstrated so often. May it improve with age!"

Finally, it's a rare case where your adversary pays you the ultimate compliment, let alone any compliment. But years after the case settled, Victor Yannacone complimented me for handling a very difficult task, that is, defending Dow in the Agent Orange litigation, with "grace, charm, and class."

Of course, over the years I came to recognize that Victor said a lot of things he didn't mean. Hopefully, this time he did, and I was most appreciative.

PART FOUR

New Partner, New Offices

CHAPTER THIRTEEN

Garden City: Transformation, Emergence, and Growth

In October 1975, the firm moved its Long Island office from Freeport to 100 Garden City Plaza in Garden City, adjacent to the very spot from which Charles Lindbergh took off on his solo flight across the Atlantic. At the time of the move, the firm consisted of sixteen attorneys, including Stu Sherman, the managing partner; Phil Weinberg, who was concentrating on real estate and bank work; one attorney who was helping me wrap up the Staten Island explosion case; and twelve other attorneys who handled the firm's general liability caseload.

We stayed in Garden City for just over ten years. During that time, we changed in ways I never could have imagined, even in my wildest fantasies.

First, we became involved, one after another, in an incredible series of increasingly complex cases: Franklin in 1975, Agent Orange in 1978, asbestos in 1981, and hazardous waste in 1984. These cases transformed us from a law firm capable of litigating only routine general liability matters to a firm capable of litigating virtually anything.

Second, we litigated complex, major cases in courtrooms not just on Long Island and in New York City but all over the country, in nearly every state, from Maine to Florida to California and even to Hawaii. Moreover, several of our cases, most notably Agent Orange, received massive amounts of national publicity. As a consequence, our small town, purely local law firm emerged as a national powerhouse.

Third, we grew, or I should say we exploded. In October 1975, when we moved to Garden City, we had sixteen attorneys; by December 1985, sixteen had grown to 166. That's a tenfold increase. Once again, we were bursting at the seams, occupying not only most of the first and fifth floors of 100 Garden City Plaza but also most of the third floor of the 200 Garden City Plaza, directly across the courtyard. And that was just in Garden City. By the end of 1985, we also had an office in Chicago with twenty-nine attorneys and another in Washington, D.C., with ten, for a total of 205 lawyers nationwide. No wonder that in 1985 the National Law Journal dubbed us one of the ten fastest growing law firms in the country. We had become, according to The New York *Times*, the largest suburban law firm in the United States.[1]

*   *   *

Transformation, emergence, and growth. These were the themes of our ten years in Garden City. In this chapter, we describe how it all came about.

*   *   *

General Liability

When the firm moved to Garden City, the twelve attorneys doing general liability defense work were responsible for approximately three thousand separate lawsuits. By Long Island standards, both the number of attorneys and number of cases were huge. By New York City standards, twelve attorneys was small potatoes.

Most of the general liability cases involved auto accidents, slip and fall incidents, construction site accidents, injuries caused by defective products, and a wide variety of other matters involving claims for personal injuries or wrongful death. But we also represented defendants in cases where the alleged losses were purely economic, including attorneys charged with legal malpractice and insurance brokers charged with negligently failing to secure adequate coverage.

Most of the cases were pending in state court in Nassau County, Suffolk County, Brooklyn, and Manhattan, although we also appeared in state court in Queens, the Bronx, Staten Island, and Westchester County and in federal court in Manhattan and Brooklyn. Typically, we had three or four men in court every day trying cases, another two or three arguing motions, and another two or three conducting depositions. The attorneys who stayed in the office drafted pleadings, motions, and discovery requests.

Virtually all of this business was referred to us by our four biggest insurance company clients: Fireman's Fund, Allstate, GEICO, and General Accident.

*   *   *

Phil Weinberg

Phil joined the firm in March 1975, when we were still in Freeport. I knew Phil because when I was a teenager, I dated his older sister. We fell out of touch for more than twenty years, but reconnected in the 1960s, when Phil was working as Appointments Secretary to Governor Nelson Rockefeller. He later held the same position with Governor Malcolm Wilson. In 1974, when the Democrats finally succeeded in electing a governor, and Phil was out of a job, I called him and offered him a partnership, which he immediately accepted.

As expected, Phil came to the firm with incredible political and business connections. But even more important than his political and business acumen was his personality. He was probably the most genuinely likeable person I have ever known. Most people who knew him felt the same way. Thus, when Phil informed his political and business friends that he was now in private practice, many of those friends quickly decided that Phil and his new firm were just what the doctor ordered.

For example, Phil knew the Chief Executives of the Dime Savings Bank, Chemical Bank, and Bank Leumi, an Israeli bank doing business in New York City. As a result, the Dime and Bank Leumi sent us residential real estate closings. This was the first significant business for the firm in an area other than litigation and was the beginning of the firm's real estate department. At first, Phil hired one lawyer who spent about half his time handling this business. Within five years, we had five lawyers and five paralegals doing residential real estate closings full time. Ultimately, the firm's real estate business changed from mostly residential matters to mostly commercial, including sales, leases, and financing. All of this important business flowed from Phil's initial efforts.

Chemical Bank did not send us real estate closings, but it did send us some litigation involving the Uniform Commercial Code and other banking statutes. One Chemical case we handled even made it all the way up to the New York State Court of Appeals. (We lost.)[2] This was the beginning of the firm's commercial litigation department, which expanded slowly but surely during our Garden City years to nearly a dozen lawyers.

Phil also knew the head of the New York State Liquidation Bureau, a state entity which was funded by contributions from every insurance company that did business in New York State. If one of those companies became insolvent or was otherwise unable to honor its policy obligations, the Liquidation Bureau would assume insurance coverage responsibility for that company's policyholders. Thus, if a policyholder was in an auto accident and was sued, the Liquidation Bureau would pay defense costs and any judgment or settlement, up to a statutory maximum.

Shortly after we moved to Garden City, the Liquidation Bureau began sending us a steady stream of auto accident lawsuits to defend. Within six months, we had to hire another general liability attorney in order to handle the growing caseload.

*   *   *

Franklin National Bank

Toward the end of October 1975, Bob Buell asked me to represent Fireman's Fund in the Franklin National Bank case. Even though I had no experience in fidelity and surety law, Bob was satisfied with my handling of the Staten Island explosion case and other products liability matters and thought I could do just as well in fidelity and surety. Bob liked our aggressive, counterpunching style and the fact that we were not afraid to try untested or unproven theories and approaches.

The Franklin case involved the largest bank failure in American history. Chief among the reasons for Franklin's collapse was that the bank had lost more than $100 million trading foreign currencies, government securities, and corporate bonds. The FDIC, as receiver of the insolvent bank, and the Trustee in Bankruptcy of the bank's parent corporation were seeking to recover these losses under fidelity insurance policies issued by Fireman's Fund, Aetna, and INA.

After Bob filled me in on the scope and breadth of the case, I realized that I needed to hire a young attorney to back me up. After interviewing several candidates, I hired Jeff Silberfeld, who had graduated from Hofstra Law School the previous June. After graduating, Jeff prepared himself for the rigors of practicing law by teaching tennis. He told me that he accepted my offer because he made the mistake of telling his mother about it and then didn't want to disappoint her by turning it down. He started the Monday before Thanksgiving; thus, he had two days off his very first week on the job.

The case lasted four years. When it settled, in October 1979, we had four lawyers and five paralegals working on it full time.

Franklin was enormously important to the firm's growth and development for several reasons: it cemented my relationship with Bob Buell and Fireman's Fund; it was my first major commercial case; it was my first experience litigating with and against New York City's most prestigious law firms; and it paved the way for the acquisition of important new business, including Agent Orange, asbestos, and hazardous waste.

*   *   *

Lexis

The mid-1970s was a cutting edge period for computerized legal research and litigation support. Shortly after the Franklin case began, we decided to take advantage of the emerging technology and acquired a Lexis computer terminal, which served two purposes. First, Lexis databases contained the full text of reported judicial decisions and federal and state statutes. These databases could be searched in their entirety almost instantaneously. Legal research projects that would have taken hours to complete manually in the law library took minutes to complete using the computer. Second, together with the attorneys for co-defendants Aetna and INA, we created our own litigation support database which contained the full text of all Franklin deposition transcripts. Our adversaries had to search these transcripts manually when attempting to marshal evidence or prepare for future depositions. We could search them in seconds using Lexis.

Computerized legal research and litigation support was so new at the time that we were actually the first law firm on Long Island to use a Lexis terminal. This was reported in *Newsday*, the local Long Island newspaper. After the article appeared, lawyers from all over Long Island called to ask if they could come in for a demonstration or if we would do some research for them. They offered to pay for the research, of course, but we did a lot for free, to build up some good will. In addition, we gave Lexis demonstrations on several occasions to students from local law schools, including Hofstra and St. John's.

*   *   *

The Hofstra Law School Civil Litigation Clinic

Shortly after the firm moved to Garden City, the Dean of Hofstra Law School invited me to lunch. He asked me if I would be interested in teaching a clinical program on civil litigation for second and third year law students. I readily agreed. In my mind, law schools had always put too much emphasis on legal theories and not enough on legal practicalities and realities. I would attempt to devise a program that would get the students out of the classroom and into the courtroom. I would give them the opportunity to experience the law rather than just study it.

As the program was ultimately set up, each student was assigned to a trial lawyer in my office. The students accompanied the lawyers to court, to depositions, and to meetings. Once a week, on Saturday morning, I lectured the students on a specific aspect of civil litigation, such as pretrial discovery, motion practice, depositions, expert witnesses, selecting a jury, opening statements, direct and cross examinations, introducing documentary evidence, and closing statements. During the Saturday morning sessions, the students and I also discussed what they had seen and heard in court the previous week.

I continued the program until around 1978, when I simply got too busy winding up Franklin and starting Agent Orange. I think that both the students and the university benefitted from the program, and the firm did, too. It gave us a presence at the law school, which was extremely helpful to our recruiting and hiring efforts.

*   *   *

Agent Orange

In July 1978, Bob Buell of Fireman's Fund and Don Frayer of Dow assigned me the Agent Orange litigation. Bob knew me from the Staten Island case and Franklin; Don knew me from Staten Island and a handful of other products liability matters we were handling for Dow. The fact that they chose me and my firm for Agent Orange simply confirmed what I had believed almost from the day I started practicing law: treat your clients fairly, keep them informed, do the best you can, get them good results, and they will reward you with more business.

The timing of the Agent Orange assignment couldn't have been better. Franklin was winding down just as Agent Orange was heating up. Thinking that nothing could top his Franklin experience, Jeff Silberfeld was threatening to resume his tennis teaching career. I put an end to that nonsense by putting him on my Agent Orange team.

Originally, that team consisted of four attorneys. By 1983, we had twelve attorneys working on the case full time, including five partners.

It is impossible to overstate the significance of the Agent Orange case to the firm's growth and development. As big as Franklin was, it was essentially a New York case. In contrast, Agent Orange was a national case. In Franklin, we performed on a local stage. In Agent Orange, we performed in front of the entire world.

* * *

Daughter Janet

In June 1975, my daughter Janet graduated from Cornell University with a degree in Psychology. I was thrilled when she decided to attend law school. She enrolled at Hofstra in September of that same year.

As a young child, Janet frequently went with me to the office in Freeport. She played in the library while I worked on files. Very often, at the dinner table, I talked about a case or a trial. My hope was to spark Janet's interest. Much later, Janet told me that she enjoyed hearing my stories but usually had no idea what I was talking about. She also told me that her most vivid childhood memories of my law practice were of a huge black and white mural on the library wall, a life sized skeleton in the corner of my office, and the shock of Victor Leff's death.

Janet went to law school not knowing whether she would ever practice. She did it partly to please her parents and partly because she felt that a law degree would help her no matter what career path she ultimately chose.

After graduation, I was thrilled again when Janet accepted my offer to work at the firm. We both recognized that it was not going to be easy for her. She was the boss's daughter and our first and at the time only woman attorney. We decided that the best way to handle the situation would be for me to keep my distance and for her to work exclusively for Stu in the general liability department. She started out drafting pleadings and motions. Within a year, Stu began sending her to court.

Unlike her father, however, Janet was not turned on by trial work, even after she won her first jury verdict. In fact, after a few years she began to have serious doubts not only about her future in litigation but also about her future as a lawyer.

Finally, in 1984, Janet made a very courageous decision. Having given it her best shot, she realized that the practice of law just wasn't for her. Accordingly, she quit her job and enrolled in the doctoral program in Clinical Psychology at Adelphi University. She got her doctorate in 1991. Now she's a practicing clinical psychologist in Westchester County and loving every minute of it.

When Janet told me back in 1984 that she was going back to school, I thought she was crazy, probably just like my father thought I was crazy when I told him I didn't want to be a doctor. But I was also very proud of her for taking a stand and for choosing what she wanted as opposed to what others may have wanted for her.

In July of 1984, just prior to starting at Adelphi, Janet married Joe Zuckerman, an orthopedic surgeon whom even my father would have loved notwithstanding the fact that Joe had an x-ray machine in his office. Janet and Joe have two energetic sons. She and her family have been and are one of the great joys of my life.

* * *

Although Janet never worked directly for me while at the firm, we did go to court together once. That occurred in mid-1979, when I acted as her sponsor for admission to the federal bar in the Eastern District of New York. As it happened, Judge Pratt was swearing in the candidates that day. I had appeared before Judge Pratt many times, in the Agent Orange case and in other products liability matters.

Judge Pratt opened the swearing in ceremony by calling all of the candidates and their sponsors to the bench. He then gave a short speech welcoming us to his court and outlining the candidates' responsibilities as members of the bar. Then he called each candidate by name. When he called Janet's name, he noticed me standing behind her and nodded. Then, much to my surprise and pleasure, he said to Janet, "Ms. Rivkin, if you turn out to be half the attorney that your father is, you'll be a credit to the bar."

I don't think I have ever been paid a higher professional compliment.

* * *

Senator Dunne

John Dunne was bitten by the politics bug when he was elected president of his fourth grade class. That experience, along with stories about his grandfather, who had been a Tammany district leader in Harlem, convinced John at a very early age that someday he would run for political office.

After graduating from Yale Law School in 1954, practicing corporate law in Manhattan for two years, working in the Nassau County court system for nine years as a law assistant and confidential law secretary, becoming active in community activities and the local Bar Association, and supporting local Republican Party candidates as a member and later President of the Nassau County Young Republicans, John achieved his dream in 1965 when he won the Republican nomination for a seat in the New York State Senate.

John won the election by a wide margin and went on to serve in the New York State Senate for twenty-four years with great distinction. Among other things, he was Chairman of the Senate Insurance Committee. In that capacity, he developed a first name relationship with many insurance company Chief Executives and General Counsels. He frequently met with leaders of the insurance industry to get a sense of what the business was all about, what its needs were, and what the role of the legislature should be.

Like many state senators who were also attorneys, John continued to pursue his legal career while in office. In 1966, he became a partner in a prominent Garden City firm which specialized in corporate law. One year later, he was elected President of the Nassau County Bar Association.

In 1979, when it appeared that John's firm was going to break up, he began to look around for another affiliation. As luck would have it, in 1979 John's closest friend was Phil Weinberg. They met years before in Albany, after John's election to the Senate, when Phil was working for Governor Rockefeller. John and Phil began to talk about the possibility of John joining our firm. Then I got involved in the discussions. At first, the idea didn't seem to make sense. As a practicing attorney, John's background was in corporate law. Ours was in litigation. The atmosphere at John's current firm was very patrician, very understated. The atmosphere at our firm was very informal, very high energy. But the more we talked, the more the marriage began to make sense. After all, as a result of his senatorial responsibilities, John was locked into the insurance industry. Aside from Dow Chemical, our biggest clients were insurance companies.

So the deal was done. In June 1979, John became a senior partner at Rivkin, Leff & Sherman, as the firm was then called. This was one of the signal events in the firm's history. By that time, four years after the move, because of Franklin, Phil's real estate business, Agent Orange, and a moderate but steady increase in our general liability caseload, we had grown to twenty-four attorneys. We were well known on Long Island and, because of Agent Orange, were gaining recognition around the state and even around the country. But we were primarily litigators, and in many circles litigation was still a dirty word. With his corporate and legislative background, John Dunne gave the firm instant state-wide respectability and stature.

Aside from his professional assets, John Dunne has always been a man of impeccable character and integrity. It has been my privilege to work with him and to know him for upwards of forty years.

* * *

A Boatload of New Clients

John Dunne joined our law firm with the understanding that he would exercise his best efforts to expand the firm's insurance company client base. He went to work on this project immediately. His efforts proved to be stunningly successful.

Typically, John picked up the phone and called the Chief Executive or General Counsel of an insurance company, someone he knew on a first name basis from his days in Albany. The purpose of the call was not to discuss legislative concerns. In fact, although John was still a state senator, he was no longer Chairman or even a member of the Senate Insurance Committee, having resigned those positions just prior to joining the firm. Instead, the purpose of John's call was to let the Chief Executive or General Counsel know that John was now a partner at Rivkin, Leff & Sherman. "Can we get together?" John would ask. "I'd like you to meet some of my new partners."

Because John was so highly regarded in insurance company circles, dozens of insurance company Chief Executives and General Counsels readily agreed to meet with John and either me, Stu Sherman, or Phil Weinberg. Of course, it didn't hurt that most of the people John called had heard of Rivkin, Leff & Sherman, because of our work on the Staten Island explosion case, Franklin, and Agent Orange.

At these meetings, we talked politics, insurance, and law. Invariably, someone would mention the ongoing Agent Orange litigation. Then someone else would mention all of the general liability work we were doing for our existing insurance company clients. The seed was planted. Either at that meeting or a subsequent one, the Chief Executive or General Counsel would introduce us to the head of the company's claims department. Maybe the head of claims would arrange to visit our office in Garden City. More often than not, shortly thereafter the company would begin sending us business. At first, a few cases trickled in. But then, the floodgates opened. We were deluged.

Ultimately, as a result of John's contacts, the firm's reputation, and our collective ability to market the firm's talents, we acquired almost one dozen new insurance company clients. These new companies sent us the types of cases we had been defending for years: automobile accidents, slip and falls, construction site accidents, defective products, and the like. But they also sent us cases in areas that were completely new to us: malpractice claims against architects, engineers, accountants, and even veterinarians. In addition, one of the new companies was a major medical malpractice insurer which became our first big client in this highly specialized area.

The flow of new cases into the office was staggering, as many as three hundred per month. It seemed that every time we hired a dozen new attorneys to help us dig out from beneath a mountain of new files, the very next day we needed to hire a dozen more. It was an incredibly exciting and exhilarating period, especially for me, since all of this explosive growth was occurring at the same time that I was up to my eyeballs in the once-in-a lifetime Agent Orange litigation.

*   *   *

Compartmentalization

As the number and variety of our general liability cases increased, we realized that the firm would operate more efficiently and more effectively if we compartmentalized. Accordingly, rather than maintain one huge general liability department, we decided to break that department down into smaller sub-groups, each with its own specialty or area of concentration.

We were receiving so much new medical malpractice business that we formed a "med mal" department which, at its peak, consisted of fifteen attorneys.

We organized a separate department to handle cases involving economic loss as opposed to personal injury and wrongful death, such as malpractice claims against attorneys, insurance brokers, architects, engineers, and accountants.

We set up a separate department, consisting of one attorney and a paralegal, to handle all of the veterinarian malpractice claims.

We created separate departments to handle all cases sent to us by particular insurance companies. CNA had its own department, as did Allstate , Kemper, and Scottish & York.

We also set up a separate department to handle all of the firm's appellate work.

*   *   *

More Cases from Dow

Agent Orange was not the only case we received in Garden City from Dow. Immediately after we settled the Staten Island explosion case, Dow began sending us a whole host of products liability matters involving commercial herbicides, pesticides, chemicals, pharmaceuticals, and other products. Most of these cases were pending in New York, although on occasion Dow asked us to litigate in other jurisdictions, including Maine, Colorado, Texas and Arizona. At first, I personally handled all of the Dow cases. Later, when Agent Orange heated up, I knew I had to make a change.

At the time, Kemper was also sending us a substantial number of products liability cases. The attorney in our office in charge of the Kemper account was a young associate named Bill Savino. Coincidentally, before coming to work for us in 1978, Bill had been counsel to the Senate Insurance Committee under John Dunne. Bill was doing such a terrific job with the Kemper products liability cases that I had no hesitation about asking him to take over all of the Dow cases, except of course Agent Orange. Bill, who never turned down an assignment, enthusiastically agreed.

Bill, who became a partner in the firm in 1982, ran the Kemper/Dow products liability department until 1985, supervising as many as six attorneys and three paralegals. During that time, Bill tried cases involving stoves, gas barbecues, glassware, measles vaccines, three-in-one diphtheria-polio-tetanus vaccines, oven cleaner, dry cleaning chemicals, and industrial solvents.

*   *   *

During his early years at the firm, Bill occasionally handled cases other than for Dow or Kemper. In one such case, he was defending Allstate in a class action by policyholders who were challenging surcharges that Allstate had added to their premium payments. Bill's wife Barbara was a nurse who worked the four to midnight shift on weekends, so Bill ordinarily spent that time at home caring for his one year old daughter. But on this particular weekend Bill had to write a brief for his Allstate case that was due on Monday. So Saturday afternoon, after Barbara went to work, Bill packed his daughter, a playpen, some bottles, and some toys into his car and drove to the office. He set up the playpen in the library, and his daughter played quietly and ultimately fell asleep while Bill worked. He was careful to get his daughter home before midnight so that Barbara wouldn't find out that she had been out gallivanting with her father.

*   *   *

Two that Got Away

Not every potential client that John Dunne introduced to the firm ended up sending us business. For example, one of John's college classmates was on the Board of Directors of General Motors. The board member arranged for John and me to meet with company's general counsel. We had a very cordial meeting in Detroit, but General Motors had a long standing relationship with a law firm in New York City. We came away empty handed.

But the most fun I had with John courting a potential client occurred in England. John knew many of the managing directors and lead underwriters at Lloyd's of London from his days chairing the Senate Insurance Committee. So twice I flew with John on the Concorde to London, where the Lloyd's people treated us like royalty. They arranged for a limousine to pick us up at the airport and take us to our hotel. For three days, we were chauffeured from one meeting to another. We met only with senior managers. They treated us to lunch every day in the board room and took us out to fancy restaurants for dinner. They told us that they knew of the firm from following the Staten Island case, Franklin, and Agent Orange. They couldn't believe we had gotten our clients such good results in such difficult matters. They repeatedly told us that "we want a firm like yours working for us." Then they chauffeured us back to the airport, where we boarded the Concorde and, because of time zones and supersonic travel, arrived in New York before we took off from London. I was certain that it was just a matter of time before Lloyd's started sending us cases. In fact, I told my wife Lenore, "They gave us everything but the files. I'm sure they're going to hire us."

But they never did. John kept telling me that if I really wanted Lloyd's business, two visits just wasn't going to do it. "You have to court these people for a long time," John explained. "Not like here in the United States." But as much fun as I was having flying on the Concorde and being chauffeured around London, with all that was going on in the office I just wasn't able to put in the time. So the Lloyd's business never arrived.

*   *   *

How We Acquired Our Asbestos Defense Work

The asbestos defense work we began receiving from the home office of Commercial Union Insurance Company in Boston in March of 1981 was a major factor not only in the firm's growth but also in its emergence in the national litigation spotlight.

In February 1981, I attended a semi-annual meeting of the Federation of Insurance Counsel. Organized in 1936, the FIC was an association of insurance attorneys and company representatives the purpose of which was to disseminate legal information on insurance topics to its members. I had been a member of the FIC for about five years and enjoyed attending its meetings, which were usually held in five star locations like Scottsdale, Palm Springs, and Palm Beach. These meetings gave me the opportunity to develop personal relationships with some of my insurance company clients.

At this particular meeting, Bill Bailey, whom I had never met, gave a speech about the growing asbestos crisis. At the time, Bill was a Senior Vice President at Commercial Union's home office. He ran the company's Latent Injury Task Force, later renamed the Environmental Issues Task Force. His responsibilities included asbestos.

Bill, a 1968 graduate of Harvard Law School, was the younger brother of F. Lee Bailey, the famous trial lawyer. After working at Hale & Doer, a prominent Boston law firm, for three years and after that for his brother, Bill went to work for Commercial Union in 1978 following a chance encounter with the company's chairman at a Sunday morning church service.

Bill was a brilliant and charismatic speaker. In his speech that December morning, he warned that many asbestos manufacturers and insurance companies were utilizing unwise and wasteful strategies in defending asbestos personal injury lawsuits, which at the time numbered in the tens of thousands. According to Bill, the insurers were too willing to provide coverage, even though the manufacturers were claiming coverage under policies issued as many as twenty years earlier. In many cases, the manufacturers could not produce copies of the policies. In many others, the manufacturers were claiming coverage under questionable legal theories. Bill also warned that many insurance companies and manufacturers were too willing to settle claims with the asbestos claimants. Rather than make the claimants prove the elements of their case, such as product identification and causation, the insurers and the manufacturers were settling large blocks of cases with minimal supporting evidence in the hope that this approach would somehow make the whole asbestos controversy disappear.

Bill's suggestions: make the asbestos manufacturer prove its entitlement to insurance coverage. Deny coverage when it appears that none exists. In addition, make the asbestos claimant prove his case against the defendants. Don't settle claims just to make them go away. Only settle cases that appear to have merit. Defend the others vigorously.

Bill's speech caused his audience some degree of alarm, since many of them were guilty of the very practices Bill was condemning. But I agreed with Bill's theories one hundred percent. Defend aggressively. Take the initiative.

I didn't get the opportunity to meet Bill after his speech. He was always on the run. When he finished, he fielded some questions from the audience and rushed off to the airport. But shortly after I returned to Garden City, I wrote Bill a letter complimenting his presentation.

Years later, Bill told me his reaction to my letter. He knew my name from Franklin and Agent Orange because, as part of his job, he followed cases of importance to the insurance industry. He knew that in both cases we had some degree of success suing the United States for contribution and indemnity. At the time, Bill was helping to develop Commercial Union's asbestos defense strategy, which would ultimately include suing the United States government for contribution. The theory was that since most asbestos claimants were exposed to asbestos while constructing United States Naval vessels, the government was responsible for at least some of those claimants' damages. When Bill read my letter, a light bulb went off. He immediately decided that he wanted my firm on his asbestos defense team to spearhead his litigation campaign against the government.

Bill yelled for Mike Sommerville, his right hand man. Mike is now a partner in his own law firm in Boston. At the time, his title at Commercial Union was Manager of the Special Claim's Unit. While Bill was doing all of the running around on asbestos, Mike was doing all of the work.

"I want you to fly to Garden City and hire Len Rivkin and his law firm," said Bill. "I want them on our team."

Mike rolled his eyes. He didn't know me or my firm. "Bill," he complained, "I don't want to hire some guy I never heard of who writes letters. I need workers."

"Just go and hire this guy," Bill replied. "You won't be sorry."

So Mike called me, told me who he was, and asked for a meeting. Of course, I said yes. The next day, Mike and Len Mirtsching, another of Bill Bailey's right hand men, arrived at our office at 10 a.m. Len Mirtsching was an attorney, a Navy veteran, and an expert on the Federal Tort Claims Act, which had been our vehicle for suing the United States in Franklin and Agent Orange and was the likely vehicle for suing the United States in asbestos litigation. Mike and Len spent the morning with me, John Dunne, and Jeff Silberfeld. We showed them our offices. We told them about Franklin and Agent Orange. They told us about asbestos. Mike suggested that they were going to hire us. Nothing was formalized.

A few days later, Mike and Len Mirtsching telephoned Jeff Silberfeld. "We want to talk to you about the Federal Tort Claims Act," they told him. "What do you see as the obstacles under the Act for suing the United States in the typical asbestos case?"

Even though Jeff was not expecting the phone call, he was more than prepared to answer Mike and Len's question. Because of his role in Franklin and Agent Orange, Jeff knew as much about the Federal Tort Claims Act as anybody and could talk about the Act and all of its catches, traps, and pitfalls at length. The phone call lasted close to two hours. Mike and Len promised to get back in touch.

My letter, the firm's reputation, our physical plant, and Jeff's knowledge of the Federal Tort Claims Act ultimately carried the day. One week later, Bill Bailey himself, along with Mike Sommerville and Len Mirtsching, came to our office and officially hired us as Commercial Union's National Coordinating Counsel for Claims Against the United States in Asbestos Litigation.

*   *   *

Mardi Gras

Our first assignment for Commercial Union was to fly to New Orleans for Mardi Gras.

Actually, Mardi Gras was the fringe benefit. The real reason for our trip to New Orleans in March 1981 was to attend a continuing legal education seminar on asbestos litigation. Bill Bailey wanted all of Commercial Union's attorneys from around the country who were defending asbestos lawsuits or were otherwise involved in the asbestos controversy, including his national and regional law firms, to be present.

Jeff Silberfeld, my wife Lenore, and I arrived in New Orleans the Wednesday before Mardi Gras Tuesday. We stayed at a five star hotel adjacent to the French Quarter. Jeff and I attended two full days of seminars and received a brief but thorough asbestos education. After class, we watched the Mardi Gras parades. In the evening, Bill Bailey treated us to dinner at five star restaurants. One night, Jeff even found the time to take in a college basketball game at the Superdome.

Each morning, many of Bill's attorneys showed up at the seminars bleary eyed from a long night of partying. Not Jeff and I, of course. We toured the French Quarter in the evening but always made it back to the hotel in time for the evening news.

On Saturday afternoon, when everyone else in the world was arriving in New Orleans, Jeff, Lenore, and I boarded a plane for the flight home. We were the only passengers. We each had our own personal flight attendant. Shortly after takeoff, one of the attendants said to us, "You can have as many dinners as you want."

*   *   *

Litigation Asbestos Claims against the United States

Upon our return from New Orleans, we began what turned out to be one of the firm's biggest and most important litigation projects. The first issue we faced was staffing. It was clear that Mike Sommerville and Len Mirtsching wanted Jeff Silberfeld to run the effort, so I had to relieve him of most of his Agent Orange duties and assign him to asbestos nearly full time. Because of my Agent Orange responsibilities, I was only able to get peripherally involved in asbestos. In the beginning, Jeff's asbestos team consisted of three attorneys and one paralegal. Later, the team consisted of eight attorneys and five paralegals, and even then Jeff would complain that the work wasn't getting done.

The project started slowly. In the beginning, Commercial Union was only providing primary insurance coverage to two companies involved in asbestos litigation, Sepco Corporation and Standard Asbestos. This meant that Commercial Union hired the law firms to defend Sepco and Standard and also paid those companies' shares of any judgments or settlements. It also meant that, if it so chose, Commercial Union could institute suits on behalf of Sepco or Standard for contribution against the United States or any other party. It would have been our job to represent Sepco and Standard in any such suit against the United States.

But Sepco and Standard were relatively minor players in asbestos litigation. In most states, each asbestos lawsuit typically involved twenty or more defendants. Those with the biggest share of the market were usually the target defendants. Since Standard and Sepco had such small shares of the market, the injured claimants generally paid them very little attention. So Commercial Union concluded that it would not be fiscally or strategically prudent for Standard and Sepco to sue the United States. Thus, we conducted legal research and factual investigations, formulated our strategy, and waited for just the right moment, just the right case.

Just the right case came our way in June. I should say, thirty thousand cases came our way. What happened was that Pittsburgh Corning Corporation, a major target defendant in asbestos lawsuits throughout the country, exhausted its primary insurance coverage, which had been provided by The Traveler's, and tendered the defense of its asbestos lawsuits to its excess carrier, which just happened to be Commercial Union.

Pittsburgh Corning was a perfect candidate to institute suits for contribution against the government. The company made a product called Unibestos, which was widely utilized as pipe insulation in the construction of United States naval vessels during World War II and after. Most of the suits against Pittsburgh Corning were by former shipyard workers who alleged exposure to asbestos while constructing naval vessels in both privately owned and government owned shipyards. In defense of those suits, Pittsburgh Corning could reasonably contend that since the government knew all about potential health hazards associated with exposure to asbestos and failed to protect the shipyard workers from those hazards, the government should pay a substantial portion of any adverse judgment or settlement.

Armed with this theory of governmental liability, we began a nationwide program of filing third-party complaints on Pittsburgh Corning's behalf for contribution against the government. In addition, Pittsburgh Corning also began to amend its answers to plaintiffs' complaints to include the government contract defense, which was premised upon the same theory, compliance with government specifications, that we had been advocating in the Agent Orange case. Ultimately, Pittsburgh Corning filed third-party actions against the government and asserted the government contract defense in thousands of cases pending in federal courts in thirteen states: Arkansas, California, Connecticut, Florida, Georgia, Hawaii, Maine, Massachusetts, Mississippi, Pennsylvania, Texas, Virginia, and Washington. The jurisdictions where we were most active included Honolulu, Portland, Seattle, Philadelphia, and Norfolk.

As Commercial Union's National Coordinating Counsel, our job was not only to supervise Pittsburgh Corning's government related third-party claims and affirmative defenses but also to actively litigate them. We associated ourselves with Pittsburgh Corning's local counsel in each jurisdiction and worked closely with them on all aspects of the litigation. In addition, we worked closely with other local law firms, as many as twenty in each jurisdiction, that were representing Pittsburgh Corning's co-defendants. Thus, in asbestos we gained a different sort of national exposure than we did in the Agent Orange case. In Agent Orange, most of our national exposure resulted from media coverage of what we were doing on Long Island and in Brooklyn. Only a handful of law firms around the country actually got to work with us in person. In contrast, in asbestos, we worked hand in hand with dozens of the nation's best law firms on their home turf. They didn't just read about us, they sat next to us at the conference table and in court.

Although the firm's asbestos team consisted of as many as eight attorneys, there were never more than three or four in the office on any given day. The attorneys had as much difficulty keeping track of their frequent flyer miles as they did their deposition schedules.

Occasionally, there was some confusion. One time, Jeff and a young associate were scheduled to fly to North Carolina. Grace, the firm's travel agent, brought the tickets to Jeff's office. "Your flight leaves from Kennedy at 4:00 p.m.," she told Jeff, who was in the midst of drafting a letter. Jeff nodded absent mindedly at Grace and waved her out of the room. Later in the day, Jeff and the associate hopped into a taxi. "LaGuardia Airport," said Jeff. When they arrived, Jeff and the associate stood in line at the ticket counter to check in. Jeff scanned the departure board. He didn't see his flight. When it was his turn, the agent looked at his tickets and said, "Sir, this flight leaves from Kennedy." Without batting an eye, Jeff looked at the associate and said, only half in jest, "If you ever tell anyone about this, you're fired."

They caught a later flight.

*   *   *

One of the many things that Jeff learned litigating asbestos cases all over the country was that New York lawyers are a breed apart. The best evidence of this fact is the following incident, which occurred in Seattle. Jeff was there for a defense strategy meeting with about fifteen other lawyers. At noon, they decided to break for lunch. They all went outside together and walked along the main street of downtown Seattle to the restaurant of choice. They came to an intersection. The sign said, "Don't Walk." There were no cars approaching the intersection from any direction. Without hesitating, Jeff continued across the street. It was only when he got to the other side that he realized he was alone. He looked back. All of the other attorneys stood patiently on the corner waiting for the signal to change.

*   *   *

Our asbestos effort on Pittsburgh Corning's behalf lasted four years. Suing the United States and asserting the government contract defense involve many legal and factual obstacles, but we made substantial headway in a number of jurisdictions. For example, in Seattle, relying heavily on Judge Pratt's decision in Agent Orange, the judge granted our motion for a Phase I trial limited to the government contract defense.[3] In Maine,[4] Philadelphia,[5] Connecticut,[6] and Massachusetts,[7] the judges denied motions for Phase I trials but refused to strike the defense, thus allowing Pittsburgh Corning to assert it on a case-by-case basis. In addition, in Maine,[8] Hawaii,[9] and Philadelphia[10] the judges denied motions by the government to dismiss Pittsburgh Corning's third-party claims that charged the government with negligence in its capacity as the owner of the vessels where the asbestos exposure occurred. Following the decision in Maine and a related appeal,[11] we began to gear up full speed ahead for out first trial against the government in federal court in Portland.

But the trial never took place. Early in 1985, Pittsburgh Corning exhausted the Commercial Union excess coverage, just as it had exhausted the Traveler's coverage four years earlier. In four years, Commercial Union spent nearly $100 million defending suits against Pittsburgh Corning, suing the United States, and paying asbestos judgments and settlements. With the Commercial Union policies exhausted, Pittsburgh Corning had no choice but to look to its next level of excess insurance coverage, which just happened to be policies issued by Traveler's. Then, shortly after Traveler's re-entered the picture, Pittsburgh Corning, for reasons of its own, and presumably with Traveler's support or acquiescence, decided to abandon its strategy of suing the United States. Just like that. After four years of incredibly hard work and long hours, on the verge of taking our first case to trial, we were told our services were no longer required.

* * *

John Rivkin

My son John graduated from the University of Virginia Law School in June 1981. Unlike his sister Janet, John never had any doubts about going to law school or practicing law. Moreover, much to my delight, John couldn't start working for his father's law firm soon enough. He took the New York Bar in July and came on board right after Labor Day.

We put John to work in Bill Savino's group, which was defending products liability cases sent to us by Dow and Kemper Insurance. The biggest matter he worked on for Bill was the Stouffer fire case. Thirty-nine people had died in a fire caused by arson at a conference center in Tarrytown, New York. After the criminal proceedings ended, the heirs commenced a civil action against any company having any connection to the site. Dow's connection was that it manufactured a cleaning agent that maintenance people had used on the carpets at the conference center. The allegations against Dow were that the cleaning agent acted as an accelerant. But after years of discovery plaintiffs never came forward with any significant proof for that theory, so Dow made a motion for summary judgment, which was granted.

John also defended Dow in a class action by prisoners who claimed they were exposed to toxic fumes from Dow product used to fumigate the prison. That case involved relatively minor injuries and was ultimately discontinued.

After working for Bill for two years, he spent one year trying general cases liability cases. Then, in March of 1984, I assigned him to the firm's hazardous waste effort, but more on that later.

In 1986, the firm rewarded John for his fine work on hazardous waste and other cases by electing him a partner. None of my achievements as a practicing attorney thrilled or excited me more than watching my son blossom as a lawyer. Today, he is one of the firm's senior partners and a major reason for its continuing success.

*   *   *

Ed Hart

I knew Ed Hart from my early days in Freeport, when we were both up and coming young trial attorneys. At the time, I represented plaintiffs, and Ed represented defendants, but we became close friends anyway. After I began representing defendants, Ed and I talked about the possibility of some day joining forces. But Ed was well established in his own firm, Curtis & Hart, and as his reputation as a trial lawyer in Nassau County grew, the chances of him making a change seemed more and more remote.

Besides the law, Ed's other passion was politics. He started out as a Democrat, but John Dunne liked to say that Ed woke up one morning, saw the light, and became a Republican. He never ran for office, but he became very active in local politics. The local Republican leaders thought so much of Ed that they chose him to defend the party in the famous kick-back trial in the early 1980s.

It was shortly after that trial that Ed began to do a long, slow about face about his professional affiliation. We talked, we were on the verge of a deal, he had second thoughts, we talked some more. Finally, it June 1984, he made his move and came on board as a full partner.

Ed's contributions to the firm over the years were significant. Many of his clients, including insurance companies and major Long Island businesses such as LILCO, the local power company, followed him when he switched firms. Many of our existing insurance company clients, recognizing that we had added another senior trial attorney to our staff, began sending us a greater number of "heavier" cases to try. As the head of our ever expanding general liability section, he trained, supervised, and inspired the younger lawyers on staff. Later, he shifted gears and became the Executive Partner of the Garden City office, responsible for overseeing all aspects of the business side of that office's operation.

Ed stayed with us for seven years. In 1992, he fulfilled a lifelong dream when he became a New York State Supreme Court judge. Later, in recognition of his achievement and ability, the governor appointed him to the Appellate Division in Brooklyn.

We all lost a dear friend and a gifted attorney and jurist when Ed died suddenly in 1996.

*   *   *

The Numbers Tell the Story

Franklin, Agent Orange, and asbestos were the major cases in the Garden City office between 1975 and 1984. They accounted for much of the firm's growth not only in terms of numbers but also in terms of reputation and stature. But "major litigation" was not our only thriving area. The firm's general liability department had grown exponentially. There was also significant growth in medical malpractice, appeals, commercial litigation, and real estate. The numbers best tell the story. We had sixteen lawyers in the Garden City office when we moved there in 1975. Four years later, we had twenty-four. Two years later, we had forty-one. One year later, in December 1982, we had fifty-nine. By December 1983, we had 109. By December 1984, we had 136.

Hard to believe that it all started in the back of Paul Leff's insurance brokerage office.

*   *   *

O.P.M. Leasing Services

Toward the end of 1981, Bob Buell asked us to represent Fireman's Fund in what The New York *Times* described as "one of the largest fraud cases in the nation's history."[12]

The perpetrator of the fraud was O.P.M. Leasing Services, Inc., a company which rose from obscurity to become, by the late 1970s, one of the largest computer leasing firms in the United States. O.P.M. purchased I.B.M. mainframe computers and then leased those computers to some of the largest, most sophisticated corporations in the world, including Rockwell International, American Express, Merrill Lynch,

General Motors, Xerox, Polaroid, and AT&T. In 1979, the company's lease portfolio was worth nearly 400 million dollars.

Supposedly, O.P.M. stood for "Other People's Money," which was an apt description of how the company did business. Rather than purchase the I.B.M. computers with its own money, O.P.M. borrowed the money from banks, insurance companies, and other lending institutions, using the computer leases as collateral.

O.P.M.'s problems began in 1978, when I.B.M. came out with a new line of mainframe computers that were cheaper and faster than existing models. When that happened, many of O.P.M.'s customers decided to exercise a clause in their leases that allowed them to terminate the leases and return the old equipment to O.P.M. As more and more leases were terminated, O.P.M.'s cash flow suffered and it became increasingly difficult for O.P.M. to repay its bank loans. To solve that problem, O.P.M. turned to fraud. To raise money, O.P.M. submitted forged or altered computer leases to potential lenders. For example, O.P.M. submitted a lease with Rockwell International which O.P.M. altered to show monthly payments of $54,000, when in fact the monthly payments were for less than five hundred dollars. O.P.M. altered another Rockwell lease to show equipment valued at $3.1 million when the actual value of the equipment was $30,000. This type of fraudulent conduct continued for nearly three years and raised enough money not only for O.P.M. to meet its loan obligations but also for its two founding partners to enjoy a rather extravagant lifestyle. But then, in 1981, reports began to surface questioning O.P.M.'s financial viability. Later in the year, the company stunned the business world by filing for Chapter 11 bankruptcy.

Shortly thereafter, O.P.M.'s two founding partners pleaded guilty to federal fraud charges and were sentenced to ten- and twelve-year prison terms. At the sentencing proceedings, the judge observed that the defendants had engaged in a "series of frauds which, in length of time and in amounts stolen from victims, are without parallel in the history of this court."[13]

With O.P.M. out of business, the company's customers and lenders faced staggering losses of nearly $190 million. To recover those losses, the customers and lenders sued O.P.M.'s attorneys, accountants, and investment bankers, alleging that the defendants knew or should have known of O.P.M.'s fraudulent conduct and of the forged and altered leases.

Fireman's Fund entered the picture because it had issued primary and excess insurance policies to O.P.M.'s investment banker, one of the leading firms on Wall Street. The policies, in very general terms, covered losses sustained by the investment banker caused by forged or altered documents.

At first, it looked like the investment banker was, in fact, entitled to insurance coverage under the Fireman's Fund policies in the context of the O.P.M. related lawsuits. But then, in the course of investigating the matter, we made a remarkable discovery. We found evidence suggesting that long before the fraud was made public, the investment banker may have known or suspected that O.P.M.'s conduct was not wholly above board. The evidence further suggested that shortly after making that discovery, the investment banker purchased additional insurance coverage from Fireman's Fund without disclosing its suspicions about O.P.M. If true, this would have been a major oversight by the investment banker, whether intentional or otherwise, and would have provided Fireman's Fund with a very strong argument that all of the policies were null and void. Suddenly, in a case where Fireman's Fund faced a multi-million dollar exposure, we may have discovered a complete defense.

This was such an exciting development in the case that I had to tell Bob Buell right away. I called his office, but he was out for the day and could not be reached. So late that evening, I telephoned him at his home. Even though I had known him for ten years and had worked closely with him on major cases, I had never done that before and was a bit nervous. When he answered the phone and realized that it was a business call, he sounded a bit put off. But as I told him the story, he warmed up immediately. I could almost see him smiling from three thousand miles away.

Within a few days we presented our findings to the investment bankers. At first, they disputed our interpretation of the evidence and denied that they had withheld information from Fireman's Fund. But we found their arguments unpersuasive and threatened to disclaim all coverage. Ultimately, they must have seen the logic behind our position because they settled with Fireman's Fund for a nominal amount.

*   *   *

Other Noteworthy Cases

A few other cases from our years in Garden City are worth a brief mention.

We defended the New York Mets in a case in which a fifteen-year-old girl was struck in the eye by a foul ball while attending a game at Shea Stadium. The girl was sitting in the first row of seats directly behind first base. She was looking at the scoreboard in right field when the ball was hit. She never saw it coming. As a result of the accident, she lost most of the sight in her left eye.

Although the Mets vigorously defended the lawsuit, they were not unsympathetic to the injured teenager. Although not legally obligated to do so, they paid her medical expenses. In their view, however, and ours, the case involved an unfortunate accident that was nobody's fault.

The case went all the way up to the New York State Court of Appeals. In a four-to-three decision, the Court ruled in favor of the Mets.[14] According to the Court, the Mets had satisfied their obligation to protect fans from injury from batted balls by screening off the seats directly behind home plate. They were under no obligation to erect screens down the first base line or anywhere else in the stadium.

This case was followed very closely not only by the Mets but also by the Commissioner's office. The fear was that if the Mets lost, baseball teams would be required to screen off additional areas of the grandstand. This would reduce or eliminate one of the great attractions of attending baseball games: the thrill of catching or retrieving a foul ball or home run. Fortunately, this didn't happen.

When we won the case, an executive from the Mets' front office wrote us a letter congratulating us on our victory. "The decision is not only good for the Mets," the executive explained, "it is good for all of Baseball!"

*   *   *

We defended Martina Navratilova in a case by a photographer who claimed that Martina injured his shoulder when she grabbed his camera in anger after a loss at the United States Open. The photographer had hounded Martina for years, and Martina was pretty distraught after her loss, so when the photographer followed her snapping pictures as she left the court, Martina decided that enough was enough. She grabbed the camera, which was strapped around the photographer's shoulder, pulled it away from him, which allegedly caused his injury, exposed the film, and then, fighting her instincts to smash the camera, she placed it gently on the ground and walked away.

The photographer, who was represented by Marvin Mitchelson, the famous California palimony lawyer, sued Martina for personal injuries and for the loss of his pictures. Ed Hart tried the case and lost. But it was a pyrrhic victory for the photographer, since the jury awarded him only fifty dollars. After the verdict, Ed consoled Mitchelson, who undoubtedly was working for a contingent fee, by presenting him with a bottle of champagne. Mitchelson accepted Ed's gift, hopped into a waiting limousine, and drove away.

* * *

Other big clients of the firm during the Garden City years included Merrill Lynch, whom we defended in a huge employment discrimination case, and General Electric, whom we defended in a case involving the pollution of the Hudson River.

We also defended CNA Insurance Company in a suit by the drug company Squibb in which Squibb sought to establish its right to insurance coverage from CNA and two dozen other insurance company defendants for Squibb's multi-million dollar DES liability. CNA hired us when the case was about three years old. On Thursday morning, twenty-five boxes of documents arrived at our office. A status conference was scheduled for ten o'clock the next morning.

Jeff Silberfeld, who was in charge of the case, called my son John into his office. "I want you to go to the status conference tomorrow," said Jeff. "Just skim through the files before you go," he continued, pointing to the twenty-five boxes taking up most of the room. "But don't worry, CNA is a high excess insurer. They're not a major player. Just sit in the back of the courtroom and find out what's going on."

The next morning, after spending about thirty minutes skimming through twenty-five boxes, John went to federal court in Manhattan. The courtroom was packed. There must have been at least thirty attorneys present. John sat down in the far corner of the last row. The judge entered the courtroom. Everyone grew silent. The judge sat down and glanced at some papers on his desk. Then he looked up, cleared his throat, and spoke.

"Mr. Rivkin," the judge began, "perhaps you can take a moment to bring us all up to date on what's been happening in this lawsuit."

John couldn't believe his ears. He knew very generally what the case was about but had no idea about where the matter stood. He could feel little beads of sweat forming on his forehead. He looked around. There was no place he could hide. So he started to stand up, when all of a sudden he noticed that another attorney had approached the bench.

"Good morning, Your Honor," the attorney said. "Bob Rifkin from Cravath, Swaine & Moore. We represent Squibb. Here's what we've been doing the last couple of months."

John breathed a sigh of relief and sank back into his seat.

*   *   *

In another big case, Joe Ortego and I defended Dow Chemical in a suit in federal court in Arizona. Plaintiffs were local residents who claimed that they were injured when they were exposed to a Dow herbicide sprayed in and around the Tonto National Forest by the United States Forest Service.

During the course of the lawsuit, Joe and I made frequent trips to Phoenix, where the case was pending. On most of those trips, we were accompanied by Mike Makulski, Dow's in-house attorney in charge of the matter.

One afternoon, the three of us arrived at Phoenix airport, picked up our mid-sized rental car, and drove to the hotel. After dinner, I went to my room, did some reading, and went to sleep. Joe was just about to do the same when his phone rang. It was Mike Makulski, who wanted to out for a drink and wanted Joe to go with him.

"Lenny doesn't like me to go out when I travel," Joe said. "He says I need my sleep."

But Mike persisted, so Joe relented. After all, he wanted to keep the client happy.

"Just don't tell Lenny," Joe pleaded.

Mike and Joe drove to several bars and then, at around 2:00 a.m., started back to the hotel. Suddenly, the car stopped. They couldn't get it started. So Mike walked to a pay phone and called Avis. Thirty minutes later, an Avis representative drove up in a brand new Cadillac.

"Here, take my car," he told Joe, handing him the keys. "A tow truck is on the way. I'll handle it from here."

So Joe and Mike drove the Cadillac back to the hotel. Joe got about one hour's worth of sleep. He and Mike were very apprehensive about how I would react when I saw the Cadillac. They would have to confess that they were out together the previous night. They knew I would be angry.

The three of us ate breakfast in the hotel restaurant and then walked to the car. Joe was the driver. Mike climbed into the back seat. I sat in the front seat next to Joe. Nobody said a word. As Joe backed out of his parking space, I leaned back in my seat and extended my legs under the dashboard.

"You know," I said, turning to look at Joe, "I didn't notice last night how roomy this car is. This is really great."

I learned fifteen years later how poor my powers of observation could be. Joe finally confessed when we interviewed him for this book.

* * *

Hazardous Waste

In the 1970s and early 1980s, environmental law was an up-and-coming area of practice. I sensed that if a law firm could get in on the ground floor, the opportunities for new business would be endless.

In 1984, because of our long standing relationship with Fireman's Fund, we got in on the ground floor not as environmental litigators but as hazardous waste insurance coverage litigators. In other words, we didn't represent the polluters, we represented the polluters' insurance companies. Fireman's Fund was our first major client in this specialized and demanding area of practice, soon to be followed by Commercial Union, The Hartford, AEGIS, and Allstate. By 1986, when the firm moved to EAB Plaza in Uniondale, we had become the premier hazardous waste insurance coverage law firm in the country. At the peak of our involvement, we employed as many as fifty attorneys in the firms hazardous waste insurance coverage department. We represented nearly one dozen major insurance companies. We litigated cases in more than thirty states. The business has lasted more than fifteen years. As much as or more than Franklin, Agent Orange, and asbestos, hazardous waste insurance coverage litigation enhanced the firm's national reputation and contributed to its explosive growth.

Here's how it all came about.

* * *

In March of 1984, I received a telephone call from Dick Jordan of Fireman's Fund. A 1968 graduate of Dartmouth College, Dick served in the Army for two years. Then, in 1970, after turning down a job as a vacuum cleaner salesman, he went to work for Fireman's Fund as a claims adjuster. By 1984, he had worked his way up from a local office in San Jose to the Home Office in Novato, where he headed the company's environmental operation. That operation included asbestos and hazardous waste.

I had known Dick since early 1983. At that time, Fireman's Fund reassigned some people and asked Dick to assume responsibility for monitoring the Agent Orange litigation. Thereafter, he was a frequent visitor to Garden City for lengthy strategy meetings with me, my staff, and Charley Carey from Dow. During those visits, Dick and I not only developed an excellent working relationship but also became good friends.

During that period, Dick also took a liking to Jeff Silberfeld, not because of Jeff's legal abilities but because he lived right around the corner from a wonderful seafood restaurant with a spectacular water view. While the rest of us typically went out to dinner at a local inland restaurant known for its French cuisine, more often than not Dick and Jeff opted for the all-you-can-eat clambake or the surf and turf.

Dick called me in March of 1984 because Fireman's Fund was in desperate need of legal advice and representation, all because of the federal Superfund statute, formally known as the Comprehensive Environmental Response, Compensation and Liability Act, or CERCLA.[15] Enacted in 1980, CERCLA empowered the Environmental Protection Agency to recover cleanup costs from companies responsible for environmental contamination at hazardous waste disposal sites. In short order, the EPA had identified hundreds of disposal sites in need of cleanup and thousands of companies responsible for the contamination, including companies that had produced or generated the waste, companies that had transported the waste to disposal sites, and the site owners. Cleanup costs were likely to run into the billions of dollars. Faced with such an enormous potential liability, the generators, transporters, and site owners had begun to seek insurance coverage under their general liability insurance policies. At the time of Dick's call, hundreds of companies had submitted formal demands for insurance coverage from Fireman's Fund for cleanup costs. Dozens of companies had actually started declaratory judgment lawsuits against Fireman's Fund for rulings on hazardous waste insurance coverage issues.

Dick was looking for a firm or firms to review the status of the demands for coverage and the coverage lawsuits, to represent Fireman's Fund in negotiations with and litigation against its policyholders, to research the meaning and applicability of the many terms and conditions of the Fireman's Fund policies, and to assure that Fireman's Fund took consistent positions on these troublesome coverage issues from one jurisdiction to the next.

Was I interested?

Of course I was.

"Then send out some people to review our files," Dick said.

I was tied up on Agent Orange and couldn't go myself. So I asked Warren Radler if he would cover for me, and he agreed. Warren was the senior partner in our Chicago office, which had opened in 1981. He brought along Barbara Guibord, a Chicago associate formerly employed by the New York State Department of Environmental Conservation. I also sent Jeff Silberfeld and John Rivkin from Garden City.

I broke the news to John on Sunday night. I telephoned him at his apartment.

"How'd you like to be an environmental insurance coverage lawyer?" I asked him.

"Not really," he answered. At the time, he was happily working on products liability cases for Bill Savino.

"Well, you have no choice," I told him. "You and Jeff are going to California tomorrow."

That week, Warren, Barbara, Jeff, and John spent three days with Dick Jordan in Novato reviewing files and discussing the firm's assignment. When they returned home, they reported that Dick had formally retained Rivkin, Leff, Sherman & Radler, as the firm was then known, to represent Fireman's Fund on all hazardous waste insurance coverage matters as National Coordinating Counsel.

*   *   *

Coverage Issues

Our first assignment as National Coordinating Counsel was to thoroughly research whether and under what circumstances the Fireman's Fund policyholders were entitled to insurance coverage for environmental cleanup costs incurred as a result of the improper generation, storage, or disposal of hazardous waste. For two months, a team of attorneys from the Garden City and Chicago offices analyzed policy language, identified coverage issues, reviewed the case law, and drafted coverage opinions.

The coverage issues that we identified and analyzed were nearly as numerous and complex as the legal issues raised in the Agent Orange litigation. A few examples:

Whether "property damage," defined in the policy as "physical injury to or destruction or tangible property," included environmental pollution.

Whether the policy covered Superfund cleanup costs. Traditionally, the measure of the insurer's liability under the policy was the diminution in value of the damaged property. Thus, if a waste facility was worth $10 million before the pollution occurred and only one million dollars after, the insurer's liability would have been limited to nine million dollars. But Superfund cleanup costs at that same facility may have been as high as $100 million. If those costs were also covered, the insurer would face ten times the financial exposure not just at that facility but at dozens or hundreds of others.

Whether the property damage "occurred during the policy period." In the typical hazardous waste case, policyholders disposed of waste at the site over an extended period of time. Did property damage occur every year that the site was open, triggering coverage under every policy that was issued during that period? Or did property damage occur only at one discrete point in time, such as when the site first became polluted or when the pollution was discovered, thus triggering coverage only under the one policy in effect on that date?

Whether the pollution was caused by an "occurrence," which the policy defined as an accident or continuous event resulting in property damage "neither expected nor intended from the standpoint of the insured."

Whether the case involved one occurrence, which triggered one policy limit, or multiple occurrences, which triggered one policy limit for each occurrence.

Whether the environmental pollution was limited to property "owned, leased, or controlled by the insured." In other words, did the policyholder own or control the groundwater under his land? If so, no coverage was available.

Whether the discharge or dispersal of contaminants into the environment was "sudden and accidental." If not, coverage was disallowed under the policy's so-called "pollution exclusion."

Whether the policy, which obligated the insurer to pay the cost of defending lawsuits against the policyholder, also obligated the insurer to pay the policyholder's cost of defending administrative proceedings.

*   *   *

The Coverage Demands

Our second assignment was to deal with the hundreds of demands by Fireman's Fund policyholders for insurance coverage for Superfund cleanup costs. Fireman's Fund had created a separate file for each such demand. After he retained the firm, Dick Jordan arranged to copy every document in every file and send the duplicate files to Garden City. When the truckload of files arrived, in mid-April, we organized two teams of lawyers, one headed by Jeff Silberfeld and the other by John Rivkin. Their assignment was to thoroughly review each file, request more information from the policyholder if the file was incomplete, monitor the progress of the underlying environmental proceeding against the policyholder, advise Fireman's Fund on whether to accept or deny coverage, and, when appropriate, attempt to negotiate a settlement of all coverage issues. This work has lasted more than fifteen years. As we settled or otherwise disposed of old matters, new ones arrived at an ever increasing rate. Ultimately, when Jeff Silberfeld moved on to other assignments, John Rivkin supervised the entire operation. His "team" consisted of as many as ten attorneys.

*   *   *

The Declaratory Judgment Actions

Our third assignment involved the dozens of declaratory judgment lawsuits against Fireman's Fund. In these actions, which were pending in state and federal courts throughout the country, policyholders were seeking to establish their right to insurance coverage from Fireman's Fund for Superfund cleanup costs.

Our role here was to coordinate and actively litigate these proceedings, with the help of local counsel. We were to draft all pleadings and motions, handle all depositions, and conduct all trials. The teams headed by Jeff Silberfeld and John Rivkin were also responsible for this work, but by the end of the year it became obvious that we needed more help. So in December, I walked into Bill Savino's office and made him the same offer that I had made to my son back in March.

"Bill, how'd you like to be an environmental insurance coverage lawyer?" I asked.

"Not really," he answered, to my great surprise. Bill never said no to any new assignment. "I like doing products liability," he explained.

But Bill knew it was no use. My mind was made up. We needed his trial skills on our Fireman's Fund team. So John kept control of the demands for insurance coverage, and Bill took over the declaratory judgment actions. This work has also lasted more than fifteen years. Bill's declaratory judgment team, which originally numbered four attorneys, grew to more than twenty. They handled some of the biggest cases in the office.

*   *   *

The Hazardous Waste Symposium

Having broken into environmental insurance coverage law in a big way, we continued to explore ways of acquiring other environmental business.

In those days, as today, one way a firm marketed its abilities to prospective clients was to have its attorneys speak at continuing legal education and trade and manufacturing association seminars. John Dunne, Jeff Silberfeld, Bill Savino, and I lectured several times each year, but the problem was that we had to wait for invitations. One morning, I was thinking about how to increase our exposure in this area when all of a sudden it hit me right between the eyes: why not have the firm sponsor a seminar of its own.

We formed an exploratory committee. It recommended that we co-sponsor an environmental seminar with nearby Hofstra University Law School, whose participation would add an aura of intellectual integrity to the undertaking. The Law School readily agreed. After extensive planning, the firm and Hofstra Law School presented the First Annual Hazardous Waste Symposium on September 24 and 25, 1984, at the four-star Garden City Hotel.

The Keynote Speaker at the Symposium was United States Congressman James J. Florio, who wrote the Superfund reauthorization legislation. Florio later became Governor of New Jersey. United States Congress Norman Lent, a member of the House Energy and Commerce Committee, delivered the opening remarks. Other speakers from the public sector included Colonel Alvin L. Young, whose rather impressive title was Senior Policy Analyst for Life Sciences, Office of Science and Technology Policy, The Executive Office of the President; and Courtney Price, the Assistant Administrator for Enforcement and Compliance Monitoring, United States Environmental Protection Agency.

John Dunne, still a New York State Senator and Chairman of the Senate Committee on Environmental Conservation and Recreation, acted as the Symposium's host. Five other partners from the firm gave speeches: Warren Radler, Jeff Silberfeld, Stan Peirce, Barbara Guibord, and me. Eric Schmertz, the Dean of Hofstra Law School, and two Hofstra professors also spoke. Other speakers included representatives from corporate America and the insurance industry.

We invited representative from all of our major clients. We also sent invitations to scores of businesses throughout the metropolitan area with obvious environmental concerns. Nearly two hundred people attended. The Symposium went off without a hitch. It turned out to be a marvelous showcase for the firm. It cemented our relationship with existing clients and attracted dozens of new ones.

The firm and Hofstra co-sponsored a total of four annual hazardous waste symposiums, each one a significant educational and marketing success.

*　　*　　*

Other Major Insurance Company Clients

The Hazardous Waste Symposium helped us acquire numerous corporate clients in need of environmental advice and representation. But this corporate environmental work paled in comparison to the hazardous waste insurance coverage work we were doing for the insurance industry. Fireman's Fund was our first client in this practice area. Other major insurance company clients soon followed.

Commercial Union: Early in 1985, Commercial Union retained us to evaluate demands from their policy holders for insurance coverage for cleanup costs and to represent Commercial Union in declaratory judgment lawsuits. We acquired this business because of the relationship that Jeff Silberfeld had developed with in-house Commercial Union claims supervisors and attorneys during the asbestos litigation and also because of John Dunne's relationship with Commercial Union's senior management.

When Commercial Union decided to hire us, the Vice President in charge of the environmental claims unit told Jeff that he wanted to use the firm on a regional basis and that he would send us all of his New York and New Jersey claims. The next day, Jeff received his first Commercial Union file, which involved a demand for coverage for cleanup costs at a waste facility in Texas. Jeff called Ed Albanese, the Commercial Union supervisor in charge of the matter, to ask if the file was sent to us by mistake.

"No mistake," said Ed, who had worked with Jeff for years on asbestos. "We thought it over and decided that we want you guys to handle everything."

Ultimately, Commercial Union sent us hundreds of files. The Commercial Union work, like the Fireman's Fund work, has lasted more than fifteen years. The firm's Commercial Union team consisted of as many as seven lawyers.

Coincidentally, in 1987, Commercial Union hired Dick Jordan to be its Senior Vice President of Claims. His responsibilities included supervising the environmental insurance coverage unit. What good luck for the firm. Dick knew us well from his days at Fireman's Fund, first supervising Agent Orange and then hazardous waste. Thanks in large part to Dick's confidence in our abilities, our relationship with Commercial Union has continued to this day.

The Hartford: Late in 1985, John Rivkin was defending Fireman's Fund in a declaratory judgment action. As part of his defense, John filed a cross-claim against The Hartford Insurance Company, also a defendant in the action. Several days later, John received a phone call from Rolf Salinger, one of Hartford's in-house claims supervisors.

"I'd like an extension of time to answer your cross-claim," Rolf told John. "I spoke to Victor Leff a couple of days ago, and he said it would be okay."

"If it's okay with Victor Leff," John replied, "it's okay with me. Except I have to tell you that Victor's been dead for almost thirty years."

Nevertheless, John granted the extension.

Several weeks later, John attended a co-defendants meeting in that same case. Rolf Salinger was there representing The Hartford. After the meeting, Rolf took John aside.

"I like the way you guys are handling this matter," said Rolf.

"If you like us so much," John replied, "why not hire us for yourself."

Several days later, Rolf called John to invite him to Hartford's Farmington, Connecticut, home office to talk about doing business. John allowed Jeff Silberfeld and me to accompany him. We met for two hours with Rolf, some of his co-workers, and their boss, who told us that they had decided to retain the firm to represent Hartford in some of the company's biggest hazardous waste declaratory judgment lawsuits.

Jeff ended up supervising the Hartford business. The best part of working for Hartford, he told me, was the three hour drive to and from Farmington. Every trip, Jeff stopped on the way home at the same fruit stand and returned to the office with bushels of fresh apples and gallons of fresh apple cider.

The Hartford business also lasted more than fifteen years and occupied as many as five attorneys.

USF&G: United States Fidelity & Guaranty Insurance Company hired us to represent them in two hazardous waste declaratory judgment actions. We acquired that business in a rather round-about manner.

One day, an in-house attorney from USF&G called his an-house attorney at The Traveler's.

"Do you know any good coverage attorneys?" the USF&G attorney asked. "We need someone to handle an appeal for us in Cincinnati."

The Traveler's attorney was casually acquainted with Bill Savino and Jeff Silberfeld from working on the same hazardous waste cases. "Here are a couple of names," the Traveler's attorney said. "They both do good work."

The next day, the USF&G attorney called Bill, who was out for the day. Rather than wait for Bill to return the call, the attorney asked for Jeff, who was napping at his desk. Jeff spoke to the attorney for an hour and must have said something right, because USF&G sent him not only the Cincinnati case but also another major case pending in Florida.

AEGIS: Associated Electric & Gas Insurance Services, known by the acronym AEGIS, was the largest client we acquired as a result of the Hazardous Waste Symposium. AEGIS was a mutual insurance company, owned by its policyholders, which issued liability insurance only to public utilities, including gas, oil, electric, and pipeline companies. Jim Weinert, a staff attorney at AEGIS, attended our second symposium in 1985. He was very impressed with the firm's presentation and gave a favorable report to Peter Clemente, AEGIS's General Counsel. Peter knew me from the Federation of Insurance Counsel. About one month after the symposium, Peter phoned me. After a series of meetings, he retained the firm to represent AEGIS in a coverage dispute against a major United States pipeline company. More business soon followed. We assigned the account to John Rivkin, who in the late

1980s and 1990s developed AEGIS into one of the biggest, most important clients in the office.

* * *

Major Coverage Cases

The hazardous waste insurance coverage work we were doing for our insurance company clients included some of the biggest cases in the office. A few examples:

In Colorado, we represented Fireman's Fund in a declaratory judgment action by the Shell Oil Company, in which Shell sought insurance coverage for the cost of cleaning up the Rocky Mountain Arsenal disposal site. Estimated cleanup costs at the site: three billion dollars. Shell's first settlement demand against Fireman's Fund was $300 million. The case actually went to trial. Bill Savino and three other attorneys from office essentially moved to Denver for three months. Ultimately, the case settled. The amount of the settlement is subject to a confidentiality order, but Fireman's Fund was more than satisfied.

In Boston, we represented Fireman's Fund in a declaratory judgment action by RTE Corporation, in which RTE sought insurance coverage for the cost of cleaning up the PCB contamination of Boston and New Bedford Harbors. RTE was one of more than fifty companies charged by the EPA with causing the pollution. Estimated cleanup costs: three hundred million dollars.

In Kentucky, we represented Fireman's Fund in a declaratory judgment action by the James Graham Brown company, which sought insurance coverage for the cost of cleaning up its facility used to manufacture telephone poles and railroad ties. Bill Savino took a helicopter tour of the area. He flew over lush green countryside, and then all of a sudden it looked like someone spilled jet black ink on the terrain. Estimated cleanup costs: $50 million to $60 million.

In Michigan, we represented Fireman's Fund in a declaratory judgment action against Ex-Cell-O Corporation, in which Ex-Cell-O sought coverage for the cost of cleaning up twenty-six hazardous waste facilities in ten states. Ex-Cell-O, later acquired by Textron Corporation, manufactured products for the aerospace, defense, automotive, and consumer industries. Fireman's Fund sued Ex-Cell-O and twenty insurance companies in federal court in Detroit. In response, Ex-Cell-O sued Fireman's Fund and twenty other insurance companies in state court in San Rafael, California, in a beautiful courthouse designed by Frank Lloyd Wright. We moved to dismiss the California action. Jeff Silberfeld flew to San Rafael to argue the motion. The courtroom was packed with dozens of attorneys representing all of the other parties to the proceedings. At the start of the proceedings, the judge looked at Jeff and said, "Mr. Silberfeld, you're the first attorney to walk into this courtroom and say he'd rather be in Detroit."

We represented Commercial Union in Boston in a declaratory judgment by W.R. Grace & Co., in which Grace sought insurance coverage for the cost of cleaning up its Woburn manufacturing facility. At the time, Grace had other problems at Woburn besides cleanup costs. Families living near the facility were suing Grace, charging that their children had died of cancer caused by chemicals that emanated from the site and contaminated the area's drinking water. Years later, the best selling book *A Civil Action* would chronicle the efforts of those families to prove their case.

We represented AEGIS in a series of declaratory judgment actions by Texas Eastern Corporation, which owned and operated an oil pipeline that leaked or otherwise caused environmental contamination at eighty-nine sites in fourteen states. Estimated cleanup costs: $750 million. Texas Eastern filed the first action against AEGIS and its other insurance carriers in state court in New Jersey. AEGIS filed a countersuit in federal court in Pennsylvania. Texas Eastern filed a second suit in state court in Texas. The parties spent years arguing over which was the proper forum. Ultimately, AEGIS prevailed and the cases were all consolidated in Pennsylvania. After ten years of pretrial discovery, we moved for summary judgment on late notice grounds. In other words, we argued that Texas Eastern failed to notify AEGIS of its environmental problems in a timely manner. The trial court granted our motion and ruled that Texas Eastern was not entitled to any insurance coverage from AEGIS for any of the pipeline contamination. Texas Eastern appealed to the United States Court of Appeals for the Third Circuit, which affirmed the trial court's decision. Texas Eastern then filed a petition for a writ of certiorari in the United States Supreme Court, which was denied.[16]

In Seattle, we represented The Hartford in a declaratory judgment action by the Boeing Company, in which Boeing sought insurance coverage for the cost of cleaning up the Western Processing waste site. Boeing was one of more than one hundred companies that disposed of waste at the Western Processing facility. Estimated cleanup costs: $100 million.

*   *   *

We also handled an appeal for USF&G in the Sixth Circuit Court of Appeals in Cincinnati. The only issue in the case was the meaning of the term "sudden" as used in the policy's pollution exclusion. The policyholder contended that "sudden" meant "accidental," without regard to the element of time. We contended that "sudden" meant quick or abrupt.

Jeff Silberfeld flew to Cincinnati to argue the appeal. He wanted to come up with a clever way of making the point that "sudden" meant "quick" or "abrupt." Then he remembered a recent National Football League playoff game between the New York Jets and the Cleveland Browns that ended up going into sudden death overtime. What better way to make the point that "sudden" means "quick" or "abrupt." In sudden death overtime, as soon as one team scores, the game quickly and abruptly ends.

The next morning, the Chief Judge of the Sixth Circuit presided over the three judge appellate panel.

"Good morning, Your Honor," Jeff began. "The issue in this case is the meaning of the term 'sudden' in the USF&G insurance policy.

"I'm an attorney from New York, and this is my first visit to Ohio, and isn't it a coincidence that a football team from New York recently visited Ohio for an NFL playoff game. The New York Jets against the Cleveland Browns."

"Counselor!" the Chief Judge interrupted, angrily pounding his gavel down on his desk. Jeff nearly jumped out of his shoes. The courtroom, which was filled with attorneys and spectators, became as silent as a tomb.

Oh no, Jeff thought, I must have violated some rule of decorum about telling folksy stories.

The Chief Judge looked at Jeff sternly. "You're in Cincinnati, Mr. Silberfeld," he said. "and we have rules here. If you've got a story about the Cincinnati Bengals, we'd be happy to listen. But we're not interested in hearing anything about the Cleveland Browns."

PS: Jeff told his Cleveland Browns story anyway, and the court, including the Chief Judge, decided the case unanimously in our favor.[17]

*   *   *

Bursting at the Seams

By the end of 1985, our hazardous waste insurance coverage business was nearly overwhelming us. We had more than forty attorneys working for our various insurance company clients. The rest of the firm's business, which included general liability, medical malpractice, products liability, commercial litigation, and real estate closings, was also booming. In all, our Garden City office had grown to 166 attorneys. We were bursting at the seams. We occupied most of the fifth floor at 100 Garden City Plaza in two non-contiguous wings of the building. We also occupied most of the first floor of that same building and most of the third floor of 200 Garden City Plaza, directly across the courtyard.

But our growth was not confined to Garden City. Early in 1985, we opened a small office on Madison Avenue in New York City. By the end of the year, we had also opened up larger offices in Chicago and Washington, D.C. The Chicago and Washington offices came about as a result of mergers with existing firms. The next chapter tell the story of how those mergers came about.

CHAPTER FOURTEEN

Chicago and Washington

Warren Radler

After graduating from Cornell Law School in 1960, Warren Radler drove a beat up old Plymouth to Washington D.C., where he worked in the Civil Rights Division of the Department of Justice. For two years, he second seated voting rights cases in Louisiana, Alabama, and Mississippi.

In 1962, Warren moved to Buffalo, where he went to work as a trial lawyer for Saperston, McNaughan & Saperston, later known as Saperston, Day & Radler. He stayed at Saperston until 1978, ultimately becoming the firm's managing partner.

Early in his career, Warren tried as many as twenty-five cases per year. He liked to characterize these cases as "rear enders" involving "bump and bruise" injuries. The trials generally lasted no more than three days. Later, he tried more complex tort and commercial matters.

One of Saperston's biggest clients was Fireman's Fund, and Warren handled a lot of the Fireman's Fund work. In 1971, the Buffalo office of Fireman's Fund asked Warren to defend a Fireman's Fund policyholder in a products liability case pending in state court in Manhattan. After accepting the assignment, Warren needed to find a lawyer in the New York City metropolitan area to act as his local counsel. He called the New York City office of Fireman's Fund for a recommendation. The person he spoke to suggested Len Rivkin. Warren and I didn't know each other at the time, and he had never heard of me. Nevertheless, he gave me a call, told me what he was looking for, and asked to meet me.

Two days later, Warren flew to New York. We met for two hours in a conference room at LaGuardia Airport. Warren and I hit it off immediately, probably because of our similar experiences working for insurance companies and trying negligence lawsuits. We also discovered that Fireman's Fund was not our only common client. We both represented Dow Chemical. At the time, I was defending the Staten Island explosion case, and Warren was defending a handful of products liability matters.

As we wrapped up our meeting, Warren asked if I was interested in being his local counsel. Never one to turn down new business, I quickly agreed. I assigned the case to a young attorney in my office, who ended up doing most of the work.

Years later, Warren told me that at our first meeting he found me to be "a Long Island kind of guy." I wasn't sure whether that was a compliment or an insult.

*   *   *

Dole v. Dow

In 1972, Warren represented Dow in a landmark products liability action entitled *Dole v. Dow Chemical*.[1] In that case, an employee died from exposure to fumes while on the job. The employee's widow sued Dow, which had manufactured the chemical causing the fumes. Dow commenced a third-party action for contribution against the deceased's employer, charging that the employer's negligence was the cause of death. Existing law did not permit a suit for contribution under those circumstances. Nevertheless, Warren convinced Dow to pursue the claim in the hope of making new law.

The case went all the way up to the New York State Court of Appeals. Judge Jasen, one of the judges on the Court, was from Buffalo and knew Warren quite well. Each side was allotted twenty minutes for oral argument. Warren went first. After twenty minutes, he said, "Well, I see my time is up." Judge Jasen responded, "No, Mr. Radler, please continue. We're very interested." Warren argued for another forty minutes. Several months later, the Court decided the case in Dow's favor.

Dole v. Dow was hugely significant, in that it essentially created the right of contribution among joint tortfeasors in New York and was the birth of the doctrine of comparative negligence.

As a result of the *Dole* decision, Warren became somewhat of a celebrity in New York tort circles, lecturing all over the state on the impact of the Court's ruling. In addition, Dow rewarded Warren for his good work on the case by sending him more and more business.

*   *   *

The Styrofoam Cases

Shortly after the *Dole* decision, Dow became involved in a growing number of lawsuits around the country involving Styrofoam roofing insulation. Builders had installed this product in factories, warehouses, high rise apartments, office buildings, and other structures. The problem was property damage caused by leakage. The building owners sued Dow, claiming that the insulation was defective. The owners also sued the architects, engineers, and contractors who had worked on the buildings.

At first, Dow hired law firms all over the country to defend the cases. For example, a San Francisco firm defended the cases in California, and a New Hampshire firm defended the cases in New England. But with so many firms involved, Dow found it very difficult to maintain consistent positions from one jurisdiction to the next. To solve that problem, Don Frayer, then with Fireman's Fund, approached Warren, who had no Styrofoam experience at the time, and offered him the position of National Coordinating Counsel for the Styrofoam leakage cases. Warren accepted the assignment, which turned out to be not national in scope but international. Ultimately, Warren defended Dow in more than one hundred Styrofoam cases in the United States, many of which involved buildings located in Europe.

* * *

The Midland Meetings

In the mid-1970s, Dow began to hold quarterly meetings in Midland to review the status of all of its major products liability cases. The meetings were attended by Dow defense attorneys from all over the country. Warren attended because of his involvement in the Styrofoam cases. I attended because of my involvement in the Staten Island explosion litigation. At the meetings, the attorneys discussed tactics, strategy, recent developments, new ideas, and theories.

Warren and I spent a lot of time together at the Midland meetings and got to know each other quite well. More than once I took him aside and said, half in jest, "Warren, you and I are the only New Yorkers here. We've got to stick together."

Aside from providing me with a whole host of helpful ideas regarding substantive and procedural products liability issues, the Midland meetings planted two seeds in my mind which ultimately came to fruition.

First, Warren and I not only developed a personal friendship as a result of the meetings but also a mutual professional respect. He was a rainmaker for his firm as well as an experienced and skillful trial attorney. We had similar practices. I began to speculate about the possibility that someday I could convince him to leave his current firm and join ours.

Second, I learned at the meetings that there were other attorneys besides Warren who were representing Dow in products liability litigation on a national or regional basis. I also learned that Dow was concerned about the possibility of future lawsuits involving other Dow products that might require national oversight. I began to consider how I could put my firm in a position to acquire some of this national business, not just from Dow but from other companies as well. What better way to become a national law firm, I concluded, than to open new offices or merge with existing firms in other states.

*   *   *

Sarabond

Late in 1978, Charley Carey of Dow called Warren, who was busy working on the Styrofoam roofing cases.

"I have some cases for you," Charley told Warren, "that will make the Styrofoam litigation look like kid stuff."

The cases involved a product called Sarabond, which was a chemical added to brick mortar to make it stronger. Since the mortar was stronger, architects and builders could use bricks in the design and construction of high rise buildings in new and exciting ways. For example, Sarabond made it possible to construct brick facades using only a single layer of brick rather than two layers, the traditional method.

Sarabond was used in hundreds of high rise buildings and other structures throughout North America, including offices, hospitals, hotels, department stores, banks, college dormitories, libraries, fire stations, and meeting halls. It was used in the construction of the Eisenhower Memorial Tunnel in Colorado, which cut through the Continental Divide. It was also used in the construction of the giraffe house at the Denver Zoo.

But the problem was that in many of the buildings and structures where Sarabond was used the brick facades cracked and had to be replaced at enormous cost. In rare instances, bricks actually fell from buildings. Fortunately, no one was ever injured by a falling brick. The building owners claimed that the brick facades cracked because Sarabond allegedly corroded the supporting steel framework.

Warren became Dow's National Coordinating Counsel for the Sarabond litigation, which lasted ten years and required as many as twelve attorneys. The cases were so big and so complex that Dow asked Warren on several occasions, "Are you sure you have enough lawyers to handle this litigation?" Ultimately, Warren represented Dow in fifty Sarabond cases in state and federal court in California, Colorado, Indiana, Massachusetts, New York, Ohio, Pennsylvania, and South Dakota. Later, after Warren joined the firm and the Agent Orange case settled, I became involved in the effort, along with several other attorneys in the Garden City office.

One of the cases I handled was in Denver. Because there was so much going on in Garden City at the time, I didn't want to be out of the office any longer than was absolutely necessary. So whenever I had to appear in court in Denver, I left New York on an 8 a.m. flight and, because of the time change, I got to court in plenty of time for the morning calendar call. After court, I usually conferred with local counsel or interviewed a potential witness. Then I caught a 5 p.m. flight back to New York, was home and in bed by midnight, and back at my desk first thing the next morning.

*   *   *

Chicago

Late in 1978, Warren and his close friend Bruce Drucker, who was also a partner in the Saperston law firm, decided to leave Buffalo and move to Chicago. Warren made the move for two reasons: he felt that he had outgrown his Buffalo surroundings, and most of his business, much of it coming from Dow, was located in the midwest.

In Chicago, he and Bruce joined Ruben & Proctor, a law firm with seventy attorneys and a very impressive client list, which included the Chicago Bears, the Chicago Archdiocese, and the Chicago Tribune. Warren became head of the firm's litigation department. Many of his biggest clients, including Dow and Fireman's Fund, followed him to

Ruben & Proctor, where he continued to spend most of his time on the Styrofoam and Sarabond cases.

But Warren was never completely satisfied in his new surroundings. He decided that he would be happier practicing on his own. So in 1980 he left Ruben & Proctor and opened up his own firm. He persuaded Bruce Drucker and one other attorney to join him.

As soon as I learned that Warren had gone out on his own, I picked up the phone. By this time, I had become firmly committed to the idea of becoming a national law firm. I believed that Warren was the perfect candidate and Chicago the perfect location for our first satellite office.

"Why the heck didn't you call me?" I asked. "I have a proposition for you." I told him my idea. "We represent the same clients. Dow, Fireman's Fund, Commercial Union. Now, for the most part, I represent them in New York and you represent them in Chicago. If we joined forces, we could end up representing them all over the country."

Warren needed some persuading. Although he was intrigued by my vision, he was quite happy and successful where he was. In less than one year, his firm had grown from three to seven attorneys. He was his own boss. But I kept at him. "One of your great traits," he told me years later, "is that you're the most persistent guy in the world. You never give up. You never let go of a good idea."

Soon, I stopped trying to persuade him and began negotiating with him. He wanted to a make a certain amount of money. He got it. He wanted to bring Bruce Drucker in as a partner. He got it. He wanted his name in the firm. He got that, too.

We finalized the deal effective October 1981: Warren and Bruce joined the firm as partners, we changed the name of the firm to Rivkin, Leff, Sherman & Radler, and the Chicago office, located inside the famous loop at 39 North La Salle Street, officially opened for business. This was a major milestone not just for us but for the legal profession generally. We were the first New York firm to expand into Chicago. Many others soon followed. On the day of the opening, Rivkin, Leff, Sherman & Radler consisted of forty-two attorneys, thirty-five in Garden City and seven in Chicago.

*   *   *

Highlights

From day one, our Chicago office was a huge success. Some highlights:

The firm expanded almost as rapidly in Chicago as it did in Garden City. Thus, as of December 1982, seventeen months after the merger, Chicago had grown from seven to sixteen lawyers; by December 1983, to eighteen; by December 1984, to twenty-two; and by December 1985 to twenty-nine. That's an increase of approximately four hundred percent. During that same four year period, Garden City grew from thirty-five lawyers to 166, a 475 percent increase.

Having an office in Chicago enabled us to successfully sell ourselves to existing and potential clients as a firm capable of litigating cases anywhere in the country. For example, although we represented Fireman's Fund before the merger in major cases such as Franklin National Bank, we did not become that company's National Coordinating Counsel for hazardous waste insurance coverage matters until after the merger. Similarly, we did not acquire national hazardous waste coverage business from Hartford or Allstate until after the merger. Maybe all of those companies would have hired us anyway if we didn't have the Chicago office, which ultimately did a lot of their work. Thankfully, we never had to face that issue.

The firm's major client in both offices at the time of the merger was Dow. The merger occurred at the height of my involvement in Agent Orange and Warren's involvement in Sarabond. Charley Carey assured me before my deal with Warren was finalized that Dow had no objection to the proposed partnership. In fact, Dow was somewhat reassured that the two lawyers handling Dow's two biggest cases had gotten together. The thinking was that one would be available to back the other up if the need arose.

After the merger, Warren more than lived up to his reputation as a rainmaker. Just to give two examples of how Warren was able to acquire major clients:

In the mid 1980s, hundreds of women who claimed that they had been injured by their use of the Copper Seven intrauterine birth control device commenced lawsuits against G.D. Searle, which had manufactured the product. Searle was looking to retain attorneys to defend the cases on a regional basis. At the time, Warren was very friendly with a former president of the Litigation Section of the American Bar Association. Based on this man's recommendation, Searle hired Warren to defend more than thirty Copper Seven cases in the midwest region.

A junior partner in the Chicago office had a law school classmate who worked for Baxter Health Care (now Baxter International), a large medical supply company. Warren met the classmate, who ultimately retained Warren to defend several major corporate matters. The most interesting case arose from an incident in Australia, where a supplier was improperly marketing Baxter surgical staples. Warren sued the supplier in federal court in the United States, the case went to trial, which resulted in an injunction against the supplier and a substantial damage award for Baxter.

Warren also hired good people, including Barbara Guibord. Barbara was an expert in environmental law, having previously worked for the New York State Department of Environmental Conservation in Albany. Barbara was an excellent attorney but had no experience attracting clients. With Warren's help and guidance, Barbara was able to develop a very successful environmental practice in Chicago. Her clients included General Electric, Browning Ferris, and Waste Management.

*   *   *

These days, Warren is "of counsel" to the firm and continues to try cases and bring in new business, although recently he has been spending fewer and fewer hours in Chicago and more and more hours on golf courses on the west coast of Florida.

Teaming up with Warren was one of the best moves I ever made. Some attorneys can litigate. Some can bring in new business. Some are firm leaders. Some can instruct and inspire. Warren could do it all, and we were lucky to have him.

*   *   *

Birch Bayh

In 1953, two years after graduating from Purdue University with a degree in Agriculture, Birch Bayh decided to run for the Indiana state legislature. At the time, Birch was a farmer in western Indiana, near Terre Haute, with no prior experience in state politics. But he did have a keen interest in local, state, and national politics. He had also been very active in campus politics at Purdue, having been elected President of his senior class.

Birch told his decision to his father, who had been a school teacher in rural Indiana for fifty-five years. His father reacted by wondering what he had done wrong as a parent to cause his son to decide to run for office.

Vigo County, where Birch lived, was controlled by the Democrats, whose strong party organization stood squarely behind the Democratic incumbent. Undeterred, Birch bucked the party leaders, declared his candidacy, and with virtually no campaign war chest toured Terre Haute and the surrounding area with his wife Marvella knocking on doors. A majority of the voters must have been excited by this young newcomer, because Birch upset the incumbent in the primary and went on to win the election against his Republican opponent.

Birch served in the Indiana House of Representatives for eight years, from 1954 through 1962, including four years as Minority Leader and two years as Speaker.

In 1957, Birch left the farm and moved his family to Bloomington, where he entered Indiana University Law School, earning his degree in 1960. After practicing law for about one year, Birch decided to run for the United States Senate. This time, he had the full backing of the Democratic party. In the election, he defeated three term Republican incumbent Homer Capehart in a major upset.

Birch served three terms in the United States Senate, from 1963 to 1981, with great distinction. Among his major achievements, he is the only Senator to author two constitutional amendments: the 25th Amendment, which deals with presidential succession and disability, and the 26th Amendment, which lowers the voting age to eighteen years; he helped to draft much of the civil rights legislation adopted into law in the early 1970s; as a Senate leader in efforts to gain equality for women, he was the primary drafter of Title 9 legislation, which guaranteed equal rights for women in school, on the job, and in other areas; and he was the chief Senate sponsor of the Equal Rights Amendment.

In 1971, Birch sought the Democratic party's nomination for President. The leading Democratic candidate at the time was Senator George McGovern. Birch challenged McGovern because he did not believe that McGovern had wide enough appeal to defeat President Nixon. Birch ran a strong nine month campaign, with most of his support coming from liberals, labor, and young voters, but decided to withdraw in October when his wife had cancer surgery.

Birch sought the Democratic presidential nomination again in 1975, entering the race at the last minute. In the primaries, he finished second to Carter in Iowa and third in New Hampshire, but he ran out of money in Massachusetts and withdrew.

In 1981, Birch's eighteen-year career in the Senate came to an end as a result of the Reagan landslide, which cost about twelve Democratic senators their jobs. Birch was defeated by Dan Quayle, who later served as Vice President under George Bush.

After leaving the Senate, Birch resumed his legal career. He and Don Tabbert, a staunch Republican and former United States Attorney from Indiana, started a firm with eight attorneys in Indianapolis and two, including Birch, in Washington.

Birch and I met for the first time, thanks to our sons, three years later.

* * *

The U. Va. Connection

In September 1978, following in my footsteps, my son John enrolled at the University of Virginia Law School. The day before classes began, John attended an orientation session. He entered the room and took one of the few remaining empty seats. Sitting next to him, purely by coincidence, was Birch's son, Evan Bayh.

After the session ended, John and Evan went to a local pub for lunch and a few beers. As usual, John ordered a well-done hamburger. "Please ask the chef to burn it beyond recognition," John told the waitress. "When he thinks it's done, ask him to cook it for five more minutes."

John and Evan ended up spending the rest of the afternoon at the pub and have been best friends since that day. Very often while in school they talked about the possibility of practicing law together some day. But that didn't happen. After graduation, both boys returned home, Evan to Indiana and John to Long Island. Evan worked for Birch's firm in Indianapolis, and John worked for me in Garden City.

In 1984, after we became Fireman's Fund's National Coordinating Counsel for hazardous waste insurance coverage, one of the Fireman's Fund claims supervisors assigned John an environmental matter in Indiana. John needed to find an attorney in Indiana to defend the Fireman's Fund policyholder, so he called Evan. Evan agreed to take the case.

During one of their many conversations about the matter, Evan happened to tell John that Birch was planning to leave his current law firm and set up his own practice. So John said to Evan, "Look, if we can't practice together, maybe our fathers can. Let's go ask them what they think of the idea of Birch joining our firm and opening up a Washington office."

Birch and I both reacted very favorably to John's suggestion. We agreed to meet in Washington. Almost immediately, I was enormously impressed with the man. He was soft spoken, unassuming, self depre-cating, but very smart, very perceptive. In person, he lived up to every single one of his extraordinary political credentials. Just as John Dunne gave the firm instant statewide respectability when he joined the firm in 1979, I knew that Birch would give us instant national recognition and respectability if only I could convince him to come on board.

A few weeks later, Birch visited our Garden City and Chicago of-fices, looking us over, meeting the people. Then Birch and Evan joined John and me in Florida, where we spent nearly one week together va-cationing on my boat. By this time, Birch and I were both very inter-ested in making a deal. We spent a good portion of the week ironing out the details.

Finally, we reached an agreement. "Len," Birch said to me, "I like your people, your practice, your two offices, the size of your firm, and your drive and vision. But you know what sold me? If two strong per-sonalities like you and me can live together for one week on a boat, I think we can probably practice law together successfully 250 miles apart."

In July 1985, Birch officially opened the Washington D.C. office of Rivkin, Radler, Dunne & Bayh at 1575 Eye Street in downtown Wash-ington. With that opening, the firm consisted of 182 attorneys in three offices: 147 in Garden City, twenty-five in Chicago, and ten in Wash-ington.

Shortly after that opening, Birch hosted a reception at the office to formally announce his new affiliation. All of the New York and Chicago partners attended. Although I wanted the partners to "work the room," that is, mingle with the invited guests, which included clients and potential clients, Jeff Silberfeld spent almost the entire time studying the baseball memorabilia in Birch's office. When Birch was a senator, he met Hank Aaron, who was doing public relations work for Magnavox, which had a plant in Indiana. Hank gave Birch a signed copy of the bat he used to hit his last major league home run. In addi-tion, Birch knew Charley Finley, the owner of the Oakland A's, who owned a farm in northern Indiana. When the A's won their first pen-nant in 1972, Finley gave Birch some bats, rings, and other mementos.

These and other items meant a great deal to Birch, whose ambition early in life was to play professional baseball.

Many of Birch's long time political friends and admirers also attended the Washington office reception, including some present and former United States Senators and former Vice President Walter Mondale. I couldn't help but think how far the firm had come. Here I was at an office function talking about fishing for blues with a man who five years earlier had been a heartbeat away from the Oval Office.

*   *   *

Rivkin, Radler, Dunne & Bayh

When Birch joined the firm, ninety percent of the firm's business in Garden City and Chicago was litigation. We represented major insurance companies, Fortune 500 corporations, mom and pop businesses, and individual defendants in everything from the most complex commercial and products liability litigation to the simplest slip and fall lawsuits. We also did real estate closings and had a small corporate practice, but the essence of our practice, what the firm was known for, was litigation.

Birch's practice in Washington was completely different. His office specialized in regulatory work, lobbying, and other legislative activities. His clients included Chemical Bank, Merrill Lynch, Cummins Diesel, Georgia Pacific, the National Soft Drink Association, and the National Basketball Association. His job was to monitor pending legislation that might impact on the business activities of one or more of his clients and to present his clients' views on that legislation to senate and congressional leaders. Birch had an impeccable reputation for honesty and integrity in Washington, and no senator or congressman ever said "no" when Birch requested a meeting. Birch also represented his clients in rule making and adversarial proceedings before the Federal Communications Commission, the Environmental Protection Agency, the Federal Trade Commission, the Food and Drug Administration, and other regulatory agencies.

Why merge such dramatically different practices? Our hope was that the firm's Garden City and Chicago clients would look to Birch for their regulatory and legislative needs in Washington and that Birch's Washington clients would look to Garden City and Chicago for their litigation needs. In addition, Birch was hoping that the Washington office could capitalize on the firm's reputation and build a litigation practice of its own.

At first, things went reasonably well. There was, indeed, a small amount of cross-pollination. A few of our Garden City and Chicago clients utilized Birch's legislative services. A few of Birch's Washington clients sent us some litigation business. Birch actually hired three litigating attorneys. One handled general liability defense work for GEICO, one of our Garden City clients. The other two assisted Warren on the Copper Seven and Sarabond cases.

As a result of this new business, the Washington office grew slowly but steadily, from ten attorneys at the time of the merger to twenty-seven attorneys in 1990, five years later.

But right from the start we ran into some major obstacles. The Garden City and Chicago clients most likely to require legislative representation in Washington were major insurance companies, which already had longstanding relationships with Washington law firms and lobbying organizations. As impressive as Birch was, none of those companies were willing to make a change. In addition, Birch's existing client list consisted of Fortune 500 companies and other major enterprises, and he was hoping to attract more of the same. But many of these companies were already involved in litigation against the firm's insurance company clients, which objected to our representation of those companies on conflict-of-interest and business grounds.

Then, in 1991, the Federal Savings and Loan Insurance Corporation wanted to retain the Washington office to represent the FSLIC on a national basis in suits to recover the billions of dollars in losses resulting from the savings and loan scandals of the early 1990s. This was a huge piece of business, and Birch saw additional opportunities on the horizon for the litigators in his office. The problem was that in these cases the office would be suing former bank officers and directors, whose potential liability would be covered by fidelity bonds issued by the firm's insurance company clients. In some cases, the office would be suing the insurance companies directly. The potential for a conflict of interest was obvious. Our insurance company clients objected. Not wanting to pass up these opportunities, and recognizing that we were likely to have similar problems in the future, Birch reluctantly concluded that he needed to go his separate way. The Garden City and Chicago partners reluctantly reached the same conclusion. The split, which was completely amicable, occurred on the last day of business in 1991.

Although things didn't pan out in Washington as well as all of us hoped, Birch nevertheless made invaluable contributions to the firm. His affiliation did, indeed, give us instant national recognition and stature. Not many firms can brag that their partners include a former United States Senator who twice ran for president. But Birch Bayh was more than a famous name. He was a superb attorney and, as a member of the firm's Executive Committee, an excellent manager. All of us, partners and associates, benefitted from his experience, wisdom, and insight.

*   *   *

For the entire time that Birch practiced law with us, he flew to New York at least once per month to attend the firm's partnership meetings. Ordinarily, he arrived the night before. The next morning, Jeff Silberfeld would pick Birch up at his hotel at the crack of dawn for some early morning tennis. Birch was an excellent athlete and a good tennis player, but Jeff was a former teaching pro and won their matches quite handily.

"People in public life are always surrounded by well wishers," Birch once told me, "some of whom are sincere but some of whom are just trying to get something from us. They are constantly telling you how good you are. Under those circumstances, it's always good to have someone or something to bring you back down to earth. It's good from the human soul perspective to have someone or something to increase your humility. I always thought that playing tennis with Jeff was almost as good at making me humble as losing the election to Dan Quayle."

*   *   *

Birch's political career may have ended in 1981, but his son Evan is doing an exceptional job of keeping the Bayh name alive. In 1988, after serving for two years as Indiana's Secretary of State, Evan was elected Governor of Indiana. At the time, he was the nation's youngest governor. In 1992, he was reelected by the widest margin of any governor in modern state history. Then, in 1998, he was elected to his father's former seat in the United States Senate.

Naturally, Birch helped out on Evan's various campaigns whenever possible. Once, during the Senate campaign, Birch went to a small county courthouse to drum up some support for his son from the party faithful. He approached a white-haired woman who was working at her desk, stuck out his hand, and said, "Sure hope we can count on your vote this fall."

"Young man," the woman replied, "I want you to know that I worked my ass off for your old man."

"Thanks very much," Birch replied. "But I am the old man."

Another time, Birch, long out of politics, was eating lunch in the Senate dining room. He saw Senator Bob Graham of Florida, an old friend, sitting across the room at a crowded table, so Birch went over to say hello. After all of the introductions were made, an elderly gentleman sitting at Senator Graham's table looked at Birch and said, "Young man, your father was the best United States Senator this country ever had."

To which Birch replied, "Thank you, sir. I'll be sure to tell him when I see him."

CHAPTER FIFTEEN

EAB Plaza

On a brisk wintry morning in February of 1985, my wife Lenore and I drove to EAB Plaza, the future site of the firm's Long Island office. Advertised as the most prestigious business address on Long Island, EAB Plaza was a spectacular new office complex located on Hempstead Turnpike in Uniondale which consisted of two fifteen story glass towers connected by an enormous glass atrium. Directly in front of the building was an outdoor skating rink. The complex also included a multi-level parking garage, acres of outdoor park, and a heliport. Although we were still in the process of ironing out the details, the firm had just reached an agreement in principle with the owner of the building to lease three entire floors, a total of ninety-four thousand square feet, for ten years. Notwithstanding our eagerness to relocate, the move from the Garden City office was still more than one year away.

At the time, Lenore was in the final stages of her battle with cancer. We both knew that she would not live to see the firm move into its new quarters. Nevertheless, Lenore refused to let her deteriorating condition dampen her spirits. When I told her that morning that I planned on visiting the new building, she insisted on going with me and could barely contain her excitement.

We entered one of the towers and rode up in the elevator to the eleventh floor, one of the three floors that the firm would ultimately occupy. All morning, Lenore and I had been having an animated conversation about the new building and the upcoming move. The elevator doors opened, we stepped gingerly out onto the landing, and the conversation stopped. We were both overwhelmed by what we saw. The entire floor, more than thirty thousand square feet, was nothing more than a glass enclosed concrete and steel shell, an open area the size of a football field. There were no walls, no subdivisions. But for the bank of elevators in the middle of the building, we had unobstructed views in every direction.

Hand in hand, Lenore and I walked slowly around the huge expanse of space, from one end to the other. Then we stopped and looked at each other. Lenore spoke first.

"I hope the people responsible for turning this place into a law office know what they're doing."

"You're telling me," I replied.

"Do you really have enough lawyers to fill this entire floor?"

"This floor and most of two others."

"I can't believe that you've come so far, from the back of Paul Leff's insurance brokerage office to this place."

"To tell you the truth," I said, "I can hardly believe it myself."

Lenore died that May. The firm moved into the new building one year later, in April of 1986. I felt great joy on the day of the move but also great sadness. Great joy, because of our glamorous and prestigious new surroundings. Great sadness, because Lenore, who had been with me from the very beginning, through good times and bad, wasn't there to share my most recent good fortune.

*   *   *

A Crowning Moment

The move to EAB Plaza was a crowning moment for Rivkin, Radler, Dunne & Bayh. Recently acclaimed as one of the ten fastest growing law firms in the United States, the firm had a glittering roster of partners, attorneys with impeccable state and national reputations. We had litigated some of the most complex and controversial cases in the country. Our client list included Fortune 500 corporations and major national and international insurance companies. Our attorneys had appeared in court in almost every state from Maine to Florida to California to Hawaii. We had recently opened elegant new offices in Chicago and Washington, two important legal meccas. All that was missing was a home office on Long Island that befit a firm of our stature, a home office worthy of housing Long Island's preeminent law firm. The very first time I visited EAB Plaza, even though it was still under construction and more than two years from completion, I knew that I had found the perfect building and the perfect location, just what the firm was looking for.

We began searching for new quarters in 1984. Early in 1985, after inspecting buildings all over Nassau County, we chose EAB Plaza. This particular decision was a no-brainer. It was by far the most impressive new office building on Long Island. It was conveniently located. And because of the firm's size and growing stature, the owners of EAB Plaza were quite eager to have us.

We formed a move committee, headed by John Dunne. We hired an architect to design our office space, which included an internal spiral staircase connecting all three floors, and a general contractor to oversee the construction. The entire process of negotiating the lease and designing and constructing the office space lasted more than one year. The week before the move, the attorneys and support staff packed all of their books, papers, and files into cardboard boxes. A moving company completed the move over one weekend.

Immediately after the move, office morale was at an all time high. Our new quarters were first class all the way, as impressive as any law office I had ever seen, spacious and efficiently designed. Each practice unit occupied its own area with plenty of room for expansion. We had a state of the art library.

The views were fabulous. My tenth floor office faced westward toward the New York City skyline. Many evenings I had the pleasure of witnessing spectacular sunsets. The view to the south overlooked the tree-lined Meadowbrook Parkway, the route to Jones Beach. On a clear summer day, if you used a pair of high powered binoculars and your imagination, you could actually catch a glimpse of the surf.

To show off our new offices, we threw a gala office reception in the fall after the move. Hundreds of guests attended, including judges, attorneys, law professors, clients, family, friends, and neighbors. The guests toured all three of our floors. A string quartet stationed near the spiral staircase provided the entertainment.

*   *   *

The firm continued to expand in size after the move to EAB, reaching a high of 251 attorneys in 1988. In addition, the firm opened new offices in Los Angeles in 1986 and Newark, New Jersey, in 1994. The Los Angeles office moved to Santa Rosa, California, in 1990.

*   *   *

Partnership Changes

There were great changes in the makeup of the firm's partnership in the years after the move to EAB.

Stu Sherman, who was with me almost from day one, retired in 1985, shortly before the move.

We lost a wonderful managing partner and dear friend in 1987 when Phil Weinberg died. Phil had been with us since 1975.

Jeff Silberfeld, who joined the firm in 1975 and helped litigate the most important cases in the office, including Franklin National Bank, Agent Orange, asbestos, and hazardous waste, retired in 1989 to teach, play tennis, write short stories, get married, and raise a family.

John Dunne, who came to us in 1979 and was largely responsible for attracting more than a dozen major new insurance company clients, left the firm in 1990 to become the Assistant Attorney General at the United States Justice Department in charge of the Civil Rights Division. After leaving the Justice Department, John relocated to upstate New York, near Albany. Today he is of counsel to a prominent Albany law firm and is still very active in government and public affairs.

Ed Hart, who joined us in 1984, relatively late in the game, nevertheless made invaluable contributions as a trial attorney and managing partner. In 1992, Ed became a judge in the New York State Supreme Court, Nassau County. Two years later, he was promoted to the Appellate Division. All of us were saddened by his sudden death in 1996.

Birch Bayh left the firm in 1991 in order to pursue new and exciting litigation opportunities that would have conflicted with some of the firm's existing business.

Finally, Warren Radler, who opened up our Chicago office in 1981, became of counsel to the firm in 1998. He continues to work in that capacity in the Chicago office.

But a host of new young partners quickly rose through the ranks to assume new and greater responsibilities, including Bruce Drucker, who opened the Chicago office with Warren Radler but now works at EAB Plaza as the firm's managing partner; Bill Savino, who now heads a litigation unit specializing in commercial and insurance coverage litigation; and, of course, my son John, who runs one of the firm's environmental insurance coverage practice groups.

In addition, several prominent attorneys joined the firm from the outside. The most notable addition was Jerry Kremer, who became a partner in 1988. Prior to joining the firm, Jerry served in the New

York State Assembly for twenty-three years. He was Chairman of the Ways and Means Committee, a member of the Public Authorities Control Board, and a member of the Metropolitan Transit Authority Capital Review Board. Today, Jerry is one of the senior partners in the firm, now known as Rivkin, Radler & Kremer, and runs the firm's Administrative and Government Affairs Practice Group. Another significant addition was Eric Schmertz, who became of counsel to the firm in 1989. Eric, a former Dean of Hofstra Law School, is one of New York City's most prominent labor attorneys and mediators.

* * *

A Full Service Law Firm

Today, Rivkin, Radler & Kremer is truly a full service law firm. We continue to represent major insurance companies doing our traditional defense and coverage work, but we also represent a broad range of other clients, including trade and business associations, banks, chemical companies, radio and television stations, hospitals, real estate developers, and municipalities. Our clientele includes multinational conglomerates, family owned businesses, and individuals. Our practice areas include appeals, banking, bankruptcy, corporate, employment discrimination, environmental, environmental insurance coverage, general liability, intellectual property insurance coverage, legislative and regulatory, medical, professional liability, real estate, science and technology, tax, and trusts and estates.

* * *

A Good Time to Retire

One day in the summer of 1997, I arrived at my office at EAB Plaza at around 10:00 a.m. In the past, I had always been one of the first to arrive for work. But now, after nearly fifty years of practicing law, at seventy-two years of age, I was more than entitled to sleep a little bit later in the morning.

For me personally, much had changed in the eleven years since the firm moved to its new quarters. For one thing, in 1987 my son John married Nancy Morris. Today, John and Nancy have two beautiful daughters and one splendid son who have one very proud grandfather.

For another, shortly after John's wedding, I married Betty Friedman, a woman I had known for more than forty years. Betty's first husband, who died shortly after Lenore, was Lenore's first cousin. The marriage "extended" the Rivkin family by six: Betty; her two grown sons, Doug and Rob; and Doug's wife Linda and their two children.

Things were different for me professionally as well. In 1988, at the age of sixty-three, I resigned my partnership in the firm and assumed an of counsel position. I continued to work a full time schedule but was no longer involved in managing the firm's business. Then, in July of 1989, I switched to part time, basically working my own hours. At first, I worked full days and weeks, but in short order I began to spend less time in the office and more time at my new home in Jupiter, Florida.

Which brings us to the summer of 1997. I arrived at the office, checked my messages, made a few phone calls, and then went to the men's room. As I stood in front of one of the sinks washing my hands, a gentleman who looked about fifty years old stood at the sink next to mine. I had never seen him before.

"Do you work here?" he asked me.

"Yes," I replied. "Do you?"

"Yes. I work in the file room. I've been here for about three months. What about you?"

"I"ve been here considerably longer than that," I answered.

"Are you an attorney?"

"Yes."

"What's your name?"

"I'm Mr. Rivkin," I said.

The man's eyes lit up.

"So you're John Rivkin! It's nice to finally meet you."

At that moment, I knew that the time had finally come to pass the torch. On January 1, 1998, I resigned as of counsel to the firm and retired from the practice of law once and for all.

*   *   *

One Last Summation

May it please the court:

It would not be easy to sum up my fifty years as an attorney in a few short paragraphs, so I'm not even going to try, other than to say that for someone who was supposed to be a doctor, I had a pretty good run practicing law. That comment aside, I'll just let the preceding four hundred pages speak for themselves.

But I would like to make a few observations about the practice of law in general.

Just as my own professional situation changed dramatically over the years, from solo practitioner to senior partner, from auto accidents to Agent Orange, from local to national prominence, so, too, did the practice of law change dramatically during that same time period. Some of the most striking changes occurred in the last twenty years. Although no one lawyer can change the profession by himself, I believe that, with the help of my partners and my clients, I was an active participant if not in some small way one of the leaders in three emerging law firm trends since the early 1980s.

First, major law firms began to aggressively market their services.

When I was a solo practitioner specializing in negligence litigation, I had to hustle for business just to survive, let alone prosper. So did most of my colleagues and adversaries on Long Island. To us, the law was a profession, but it was also a business, and a very competitive one at that.

Although this entrepreneurial and competitive mentality stayed with me after my firm grew and entered the arena of big time civil litigation, to my great surprise I discovered that many of my new found colleagues and adversaries, New York City's largest, most prestigious law firms, had a completely different attitude. I may have thought that I was lucky to have my clients, but the attitude in New York City was that the clients were lucky to have their lawyers. Nobody hustled. Nobody marketed. Most of the firms relied on their good names and reputations to attract business, and for years that was sufficient.

But things changed in the 1980s. Primarily because of the downturn in the economy, clients began to tighten their belts. Among other things, they started scrutinizing their legal bills and, if dissatisfied, shopping around for firms with better rates. When this happened, firms began courting each other's clients. They also began the practice of raiding star attorneys and even entire departments from rival firms. The once genteel practice of law in New York City became almost as competitive as it had been in the old days on Long Island. So competitive, in fact, that many big name firms failed to survive.

While this change may have made the practice of law more difficult for many attorneys, it was certainly beneficial to clients and potential clients, as it undoubtedly had the effect of lowering legal fees and increasing the efficiency of legal representation.

Second, major law firms began to litigate more aggressively.

Almost from day one, my litigation strategy was to take the initiative. Take control. Instigate, rather than respond, even when representing a defendant. I used this strategy in the early days when I was defending fender bender and slip and fall cases as well as later on in my career when I was defending Fireman's Fund and Dow in Franklin and Agent Orange.

In contrast, the major New York City firms generally litigated in a much more subdued and restrained manner. Don't get me wrong, I'm not criticizing the quality of the representation those firms provided. It was excellent. My problem was one of style. I usually wanted to press forward; the New York City firms generally wanted to bide their time. I was not averse to taking calculated risks; the New York City firms were generally reluctant to bet on anything other than a sure winner.

But once again, by the early 1980s, things began to change. Perhaps as firms began to compete more openly for clients, this new found competitive mentality began to affect their litigation style. Perhaps firms began to litigate more aggressively because more was at stake, not just in terms of how the outcome of the case would affect the client but also how that outcome would affect the law firm. In this new competitive environment, lose the case, and the firm just might find itself losing the client.

Third, law firms began to represent clients in litigation on a national basis.

I first saw this trend developing in the early 1970s, when Dow used regional and national counsel to defend products liability lawsuits. I foresaw that this was just the beginning. Dow was one of many companies marketing drugs, chemicals, and other products on a national basis. It was inevitable that more and more of these products would generate a multitude of lawsuits throughout the country. To me and many others, it made sense to use one firm to defend all lawsuits involving a particular product. That firm would become an expert in the field and could use that expertise to litigate all of the cases in a cost effective and efficient manner. The alternative would be to "reinvent the wheel," that is, to educate a numerous law firms in different jurisdictions. Under that scenario, litigation costs would likely skyrocket, and duplication of efforts would likely occur.

The main reason I wanted to open branch offices in different cities was to position the firm to market its national capabilities. That strategy was successful, as we ultimately embarked upon several national efforts for Dow, Fireman's Fund, Commercial Union, Allstate, and other major clients.

Many other firms adopted the same strategy, expanding into new cities or otherwise positioning themselves to handle national litigation efforts. Incidentally, prior to the 1970s many major firms in New York City and elsewhere did have national capabilities, but generally only for corporate work, not for litigation. And in many of those firms, the corporate attorneys, and not the litigators, were the stars. But by the 1980s, most if not all of the major big city law firms were looking for national litigation assignments. And in many of these firms the litigators were the rising stars.

*   *   *

One final comment. I grew up the son of a doctor, who believed that medicine was not just the most honorable and noble profession, it was the only profession. I feel almost as strongly about the practice of law. They say that the acorn doesn't fall far from the tree, and maybe I did inherit some of my father's extreme tendencies. Nevertheless, having spent fifty challenging and rewarding years as a practicing attorney, I can't imagine having done anything else. No matter what your field, if you're having half as much fun in your job as I had in mine, you're way ahead of the game.

Sources and Footnotes

During the course of our research for *May It Please the Court*, we interviewed dozens of attorneys (colleagues and adversaries), clients, friends, and family members, including Ed Albanese, Steve Arnosky, Bill Bailey, Birch Bayh, Les Bennett, Joan Bernott, Steve Brock, Bob Buell, Ed Cerny, Ron Davis, John Dunne, Bruce Drucker, Les Fagan, Ken Feinberg, Jim Feuerstein, Don Frayer, Ed Hart, Otis Hess, Dick Jordan, John Kirby, Don Koehlinger, Bill Krohley, Keith McKennon, John Morrison, Bruce Nims, Joe Ortego, Stan Pierce, Bill Purcell, Warren Radler, Jim Rigano, John Rivkin, Janet Rivkin, Mary Roach, Bill Savino, Stu Sherman, Frank Skillern, Mike Sommerville, and Victor Yannacone. We are grateful for the information they provided and for their cooperation and patience.

In connection with the chapters and sections on the *Ezagui* case, the Staten Island explosion, Franklin National Bank, Agent Orange, and the O.P.M. case, we reviewed tens of thousands of pages of documents, both hard copy and on microfilm, including pleadings, discovery requests and responses, briefs, affidavits, memos, letters, court and deposition transcripts and exhibits, newspaper and magazine articles, scientific reports, government reports, and corporate and government documents.

In connection with the chapter on the Judicial Inquiry, we reviewed copies of the briefs and appendix filed in the New York State Court of Appeals in *Matter of Rivkin*, 234 N.E.2d 701 (N.Y. 1967), and court records maintained by the New York State Supreme Court, Appellate Division, Second Department.

We also relied upon the following books: Luigi DiFonza, *St. Peter's Banker* (1983); Walter S. Ross, *People's Banker: The Story of Arthur T. Roth and the Franklin National Bank* (1987); Peter H. Schuck, *Agent Orange on Trial: Mass Toxic Disasters in the Courts* (1986); and Nick Tosches, *Power on Earth: Michele Sindona's Explosive Story* (1986).

In the sections that follow, we have footnoted all references to and quotations from written judicial decisions and opinions, all important statutory references, all direct quotations where the source of the quotation is not made clear in the text, and any other direct quotation or factual information where documenting the source seemed necessary or appropriate.

Footnotes to Chapter Four

1. N.Y. Civ. Prac. L. & R . §§ 3041 - 3045 (McKinney 1991).
2. N.Y. Civ. Prac. L. & R. § 3043(b) (McKinney 1991)(effective Sept. 1, 1979).
3. *Matter of Rivkin*, 277 N.Y.S.2d 454, 456 (App. Div.), *rev'd*, 234 N.E.2d 701 (N.Y. 1967).
4. 277 N.Y.S.2d at 457.
5. 277 N.Y.S.2d at 459.
6. *Matter of Rivkin*, 227 N.E.2d 899 (N.Y. 1967).
7. *Matter of Rivkin*, 234 N.E.2d 701 (N.Y. 1967).

Footnotes to Chapter Five

1. N.Y. Ins. Law §§ 5201-5225 (1985).
2. *Application of Motor Vehicle Accident Indemnification Corp.*, 228 N.Y.S.2d 508, 509 (Sup. Ct. 1962), *rev'd sub nom. Motor Vehicle Accident Indemnification Corp. v. Brinson*, 236 N.Y.S.2d 567 (App. Div. 1963).
3. *Application of Motor Vehicle Accident Indemnification Corp.*, 229 N.Y.S.2d 788 (Sup. Ct.), *rev'd*, 234 N.Y.S.2d 152 (App. Div. 1962).
4. The 1965 changes in the statutory scheme regarding uninsured and hit-and-run motorists are described in "Memorandum of American Insurance Association," *New York State Legislative Annual*, at 381-82 (1965); *see also State Wide Ins. Co. v. Curry*, 372 N.E.2d 31 (N.Y. 1977).

Footnotes to Chapter Six

1. The information regarding the development of four-in-one vaccines was taken from *Ezagui v. Dow Chem. Corp.*, 598 F.2d 727, 731 (2d Cir. 1979).
2. *Tinnerholm v. Parke, Davis & Co.*, 411 F.2d 48 (2d Cir. 1969).
3. *Parke-Davis & Co. v. Stromsodt*, 411 F.2d 1390 (8th Cir. 1969).
4. The trial court's collateral estoppel ruling and dismissal orders are discussed in *Ezagui v. Dow Chem. Corp.*, 598 F.2d at 730-31.
5. *Id.* at 730.
6. *Ezagui v. Parke-Davis & Co.*, 69 Civ. 1193 (E.D.N.Y. May 28, 1981).

Footnotes to Chapter Seven

1. Carl Musacchio, "Lessons to be Learned from Staten Island Disaster," *Occupational Hazards*, June 1975, at 31, 33.
2. *Id.*
3. *Liquid Carbonic Corp. v. BASF Wyandotte Corp.*, 468 So. 2d 1225 (La. App. 1985). *See also Kloepfer v. Honda Motor Co.*, 898 F.2d 1452 (10th Cir. 1990)(holding that court properly excluded prior consent order between Honda and Consumer Protection Safety Commission, where consent order entered without litigation or any admission of liability by Honda); *cf. Johnson v. Hugo's Skateway*, 974 F.2d 1408 (4th Cir. 1992)(admitting consent order for limited purpose of determining whether the defendant complied with its terms).

Footnotes to Chapter Eight

1. *See, e.g., FDIC v. Lott*, 460 F.2d 82 (5th Cir. 1972); *Phoenix Sav. & Loan, Inc. v. Aetna Casualty & Sur. Co.*, 427 F.2d 862 (4th Cir. 1970).
2. Sanford Rose, "What Really Went Wrong at Franklin," *Fortune*, Oct. 1974, at 223.
3. *FDIC v. National Sur. Corp.*, 425 F. Supp. 200, 201 (E.D.N.Y. 1977).
4. *Id.* at 204.

5. *Id.*
6. *Id.* at 203.
7. 28 U.S.C.A. § 1346(b) (1993); 28 U.S.C.A. §§ 2671-2680 (1994).
8. *Indian Towing Co. v. United States*, 350 U.S. 61 (1955).
9. *In re Franklin National Bank Sec. Litig.*, 445 F. Supp. 723 (E.D.N.Y. 1978).
10. *Id.* at 733-34.
11. *In re Franklin National Bank Sec. Litig.*, 449 F. Supp. 574 (E.D.N.Y. 1978).
12. Max H. Siegel, "F.B.I. Said to Violate Law on Jury Reports," *N.Y. Times*, July 1, 1978, at 20.
13. Robert J. Cole, "Judge Out in Sindona Bank Suit," *N.Y. Times*, March 29, 1979, at D1.
14. Luigi DiFonzo, *St. Peter's Banker*, at 245 (1983).
15. Wolfgang Saxon, "At the Center of Scandals," *N.Y. Times*, March 23, 1986, at 44.
16. *In re Franklin National Bank Sec. Litig.*, 478 F. Supp. 210, 217 (E.D.N.Y. 1979).
17. *Id.* at 223.
18. *Id.* at 224.
19. *Id.*
20. "Ernst Accountants Paid $4 Million to Satisfy FDIC," *Legal Times of Washington*, Jan. 21, 1980, at 6.

Footnotes to Chapter Nine

1. The information in this and the following paragraphs about the government's use of herbicides in Vietnam comes from my own recollection, court documents, and the following additional sources: *In re Agent Orange Prod. Liab. Litig.*, 597 F. Supp. 740, 775-77 (E.D.N.Y. 1984), *aff'd*, 818 F.2d 145 (2d Cir. 1987), *cert. denied sub nom. Pinkney v. Dow Chem. Co.*, 484 U.S. 1004 (1988); and William A. Buckingham, Jr., *Operation Ranch Hand: Herbicides in Southeast Asia 1961-1971* (1982). *See also* notes 2 and 3, *infra*.

    In the four chapters on the Agent Orange litigation, we cite more than twenty reported decisions captioned *In re Agent Orange Prod. Liab. Litig.* All of those decisions will hereinafter be cited as *Agent Orange*.

2. Alvin L. Young, et al., *The Toxicology, Environmental Fate, and Human Risk of Herbicide Orange and its Associated Dioxin*, (USAF 1978), at. V-13.

3. Don Irish, et al., *Information Manual for Vegetation Control in Southeast Asia* (1969), at 61.

4. *Dow Chem. Co. v. Ruckelshaus*, 477 F.2d 1317, 1318-19 (8th Cir. 1973).

5. Transcript of Proceedings, Jan. 30, 1981, at 217.

6. Adrian Peracchio, "Study of Vietnam Defoliant Urged," *Newsday*, April 18, 1979, at 19.

7. Transcript of Proceedings, Jan. 21, 1979, at 73-74.

8. Sandra Murphy, Note, "A Critique of the Veterans Administration Claims Process," 52 Brooklyn Law Rev. 533, 539 n. 32 (1986).

9. *Id.* at 535 n. 8.

10. *Id.* at 536.

11. Pub. L. No. 96-151, § 307, 93 Stat. 1097 (1979).

12. Pub. L. No. 97-72, § 102, 95 Stat. 1047 (1981).

13. *Agent Orange*, 597 F. Supp. at 852.

14. The data in this section was compiled from articles in *The New York Times* and *New York Magazine*. *See also* Murphy, *supra* note 8, at 538 n. 28.

15. *Nehmer v. United States Veterans' Admin.*, 712 F. Supp. 1404, 1407 (N.D. Cal. 1989).

16. The information in this section on EPA administrative proceedings comes from my own recollection, court documents, and the following additional sources: *Dow Chem. Co. v. Ruckelshaus*, 477 F.2d 1317 (8th Cir. 1973); *Dow Chem. Co. v. Blum*, 469 F. Supp. 892 (E.D. Mich. 1979); and *Citizens Against Toxic Sprays v. Bergland*, 428 F. Supp. 908 (D. Or. 1977).

17. State legislative action in response to the Agent Orange controversy is discussed in John J. Kulewicz, "Agent Orange: The States Fight Back," 44 Ohio St. L.J. 691 (1983). *See also Agent Orange*, 580 F. Supp. 690, 697 (E.D.N.Y. 1984).

18. Conn. Gen. Stat. § 52-577b (1991).

19. Del. Code Ann. tit. 10, § 8131 (Supp. 1998).

20. N.Y. Civ. Prac. L. & R. § 214-b (McKinney 1990).

21. Ohio Rev. Code Ann. § 2305.10 (Anderson 1995).

22. R.I. Gen. Laws § 9-1-14.2 (1997).

23. W. Va. Code § 16-28-10 (1998).

24. Tex. Health & Safety Code Ann. §§ 83.001-83.010 (West 1992).

25. Minn. Stat. §§ 196.19-196.27 (West 1992).
26. Conn. Gen. Stat. §§ 27-140aa to 27-140ee (1990).
27. Mich. Comp. Laws §§ 333.5701-333.5749 (1992).
28. N.Y. Pub. Health Law § 2475 (1993).
29. Ohio Rev. Code Ann. §§ 5903.21-5903.26 (Anderson 1993).
30. Okla. Stat. tit. 72, §§ 350-358 (1995).
31. S.C. Code Ann. §§ 44-40-10 to 44-40-60 (Law Co-op. Supp. 1998).
32. A brief but compelling discussion of numbers that reflect the unprecedented size and scope of the Agent Orange case appears in Peter Schuck, *Agent Orange on Trial*, at 4-6 (1986).
33. The data in this paragraph was compiled from *Agent Orange*, 597 F. Supp. at 750, 756; and Schuck, *supra* note 32, at 4.
34. 28 U.S.C.A. § 1407 (1993).
35. *Agent Orange*, 597 F. Supp. at 751.
36. *Agent Orange*, 100 F.R.D. 718, 729 (E.D.N.Y. 1983), aff'd, 818 F.2d 145 (2d Cir.), *cert, denied sub nom. Pinkney v. Dow Chem. Co.*, 484 U.S. 1004 (1987).
37. *Agent Orange*, 597 F. Supp. at 756.
38. *Id*. at 751.
39. Fed. R. Civ. P. 23(c)(2).
40. The data in this section was compiled from *Agent Orange*, 597 F. Supp. at 756; and *Agent Orange*, 100 F.R.D. at 729-30.
41. Schuck, *supra* note 32, at 5.
42. Adrian Peracchio, "Dow Blames U.S. for Dioxin Use," *Newsday*, Jan. 5, 1980, at 3.
43. *Agent Orange*, 100 F.R.D. at 727.
44. The data in this paragraph was compiled from Schuck, *supra* note 32, at 5; and *Agent Orange*, 611 F. Supp. 1296, 1301, 1302, 1329, 1331-1336 (E.D.N.Y. 1985), *modified*, 818 F.2d 226 (2d Cir 1987).
45. *Agent Orange*, 611 F. Supp. at 1344-46.
46. Schuck, *supra* note 32, at 5.
47. *Agent Orange*, 597 F. Supp. at 750.
48. Transcript of Proceedings, April 4, 1980, at 60.
49. Schuck, *supra* note 32, at 118.
50. *Id*. at 118-119.

Footnotes to Chapter Ten

1. *Sanner v. Ford Motor Co.*, 364 A.2d 43 (N.J. Super. Ct. Law Div. 1976), aff'd, 381 A.2d 805 (App. Div. 1977), cert. denied, 384 A.2d 846 (N.J. 1978).
2. *Casabianca v. Casabianca*, 428 N.Y.S.2d 400 (Sup. Ct. 1980).
3. *Sanner*, 364 A.2d at 47.
4. *Casabianca*, 428 N.Y.S.2d at 402.
5. *Yearsley*, 309 U.S. 18; *Myers*, 323 F.2d 580; *Dolphin Gardens*, 243 F. Supp. 824; *Green v. ICI America, Inc.*, 362 F. Supp. 1263 (E.D. Tenn. 1973).
6. *Dolphin Gardens*, 243 F. Supp. at 827.
7. *Sanner v. Ford Motor Co.*, 364 A.2d 43 (N.J. Super. Ct. Law Div. 1976), *aff'd*, 381 A.2d 805 (App. Div. 1977), *cert. denied*, 384 A.2d 846 (N.J. 1978).
8. *Casabianca v. Casabianca*, 428 N.Y.S.2d 400 (Sup. Ct. 1980).
9. *Sanner*, 364 A.2d at 47.
10. *Casabianca*, 428 N.Y.S.2d at 402.
11. *Agent Orange*, 534 F. Supp. 1046, 1055 (E.D.N.Y 1982).
12. *Id.*
13. *Id.*
14. *Agent Orange*, 506 F. Supp. at 784.
15. 28 U.S.C.A. § 1346(b) (1993); 28 U.S.C.A. §§ 2671-2680 (1994).
16. *Feres v. United States*, 340 U.S. 135 (1950).
17. *Id.* at 146.
18. *Stencel Aero Engineering Corp. v. United States*, 431 U.S. 666 (1977).
19. *Agent Orange*, 506 F. Supp. 762, 775 (E.D.N.Y. 1980).
20. *Rotko v. Abrams*, 338 F. Supp. 46, 47 (D. Conn. 1971).
21. *Watkins v. United States*, 462 F. Supp. 980 (S.D. Ga. 1977).
22. *Archer v. United States*, 217 F.2d 548 (9th Cir. 1954).
23. *Feres v. United States*, 340 U.S. 135 (1950).
24. *Hass v. United States*, 518 F.2d 1138 (4th Cir. 1975).
25. *Jaffee v, United States*, 468 F. Supp. 632, 635 (D.N.J. 1979).
26. These theories are discussed in *Agent Orange*, 597 F. Supp. at 820-828.
27. *Clearfield Trust Co. v. United States*, 318 U.S. 363, 366 (1943).

Footnotes to Chapter Eleven

1. *Agent Orange*, MDL No. 381 (J.P.M.L. May 8, 1979)(transfer order).
2. *Agent Orange*, 475 F. Supp. 928 (E.D.N.Y. 1979).
3. Transcript of Proceedings, Dec. 21, 1979, at 17-20.
4. *Agent Orange*, 506 F. Supp. 737 (E.D.N.Y. 1979), *aff'd*, 635 F.2d 987 (2d Cir. 1980), *cert. denied sub nom. Chapman v. Dow Chem. Co.*, 454 U.S. 1128 (1981).
5. Transcript of Proceedings, Nov. 21, 1979, at 6.
6. *Agent Orange*, 506 F. Supp. at 744.
7. *Id.* at 748.
8. *Id.* at 751.
9. *Jessup v. United States*, Civ. 79-271-TUC-RMB (D. Ariz., April 2, 1980).
10. Transcript of Proceedings, July 16, 1980, at 42-44.
11. *Agent Orange*, 635 F.2d 987 (2d Cir. 1980), *cert. denied sub nom. Chapman v. Dow Chem. Co.*, 454 U.S. 1128 (1981).
12. 635 F.2d at 993.
13. *Id.* at 995.
14. *Id.* at 999.
15. *Agent Orange*, 506 F. Supp. 762.
16. *Id.* at 791.
17. *Id.*
18. *Id.* at 785.
19. *Id.* at 796.
20. *Id.*
21. *Id.* at 794.
22. *Id.*
23. *Id.* at 796.
24. *Id.* at 785.
25. *Id.* at 796.
26. *Chapman v. Dow Chem. Co.*, 454 U.S. 1128 (1981).
27. *Agent Orange*, 534 F. Supp. 1046.
28. *Id.* at 1055.
29. *Id.* at 1057.
30. *Agent Orange*, 94 F.R.D. 173, 174 (E.D.N.Y. 1982).
31. The information in the following paragraphs was complied from the briefs, affidavits, and exhibits Dow submitted in support of its summary judgment motion and from *Agent Orange*, 565 F. Supp. 1263, 1266-68 (E.D.N.Y. 1983).

32. *Agent Orange*, 534 F. Supp. at 1055.
33. *Agent Orange*, 565 F. Supp. 1263.
34. *Id.* at 1278.
35. Transcript of Proceedings, May 12, 1983, at 5128-36.
36. *Agent Orange*, 100 F.R.D. 718.
37. *Id.* at 720.
38. *Id.*
39. *Id.* at 720-21.
40. *Id.* at 721.
41. *Agent Orange*, 580 F. Supp. 1242 (E.D.N.Y.), *appeal dismissed*, 745 F.2d 161 (2d Cir. 1984).
42. *Agent Orange*, 580 F. Supp. 690, 693 (E.D.N.Y. 1984).
43. Peter Schuck, *Agent Orange on Trial*, at 130 (1986).

Footnotes to Chapter Twelve

1. *Agent Orange*, 571 F. Supp. 481, 482 (E.D.N.Y. 1983).
2. *Id.* at 481.
3. Peter Schuck, *Agent Orange on Trial*, at 163 (1986).
4. *Id.* at 160-61.
5. *Id.* at 161.
6. *Agent Orange*, 597 F. Supp. at 764.
7. *Id.* at 775.
8. *Agent Orange*, 597 F. Supp. 740.
9. *Id.* at 858.
10. *Agent Orange*, 611 F. Supp. 1296.
11. *Agent Orange*, 611 F. Supp. 1223 (E.D.N.Y. 1985), *aff'd* 818 F.2d 187 (2d Cir.), *cert. denied sub nom. Krupkin v. Dow Chem. Co.,* 487 U.S. 1234 (1987).
12. 611 F. Supp. at 1231.
13. *Id.* at 1232.
14. *Id.* at 1231.
15. *Id.* at 1232.
16. *Id.* at 1233-34.
17. *Id.* at 1232.
18. *Id.*
19. *Id.* at 1263-1264.
20. *Agent Orange*, 611 F. Supp. 1221 (E.D.N.Y. 1985), *aff'd*, 818 F.2d 204 (2d Cir. 1987).

21. 611 F. Supp. at 1222.

22. *Id.*

23. *Agent Orange*, 611 F. Supp. 1396 (E.D.N.Y. 1985), *modified*, 818 F.2d 179 (2d Cir.), *cert. denied sub nom. Krupkin v. Dow Chem. Co.*, 487 U.S. 1234 (1987).

24. *Agent Orange*, 618 F. Supp. 625 (E.D.N.Y. 1985).

25. *Agent Orange*, 818 F.2d 145 (2d Cir.), *cert. denied sub nom. Pinkney v. Dow Chem. Co.*, 484 U.S. 1004 (1987).

26. *Agent Orange*, 818 F.2d 179 (2d Cir.), *cert. denied sub nom. Krupkin v. Dow Chem. Co.*, 487 U.S. 1234 (1987).

27. *Agent Orange*, 818 F.2d 204 (2d Cir. 1987).

28. *Agent Orange*, 818 F.2d 226 (2d Cir. 1987).

29. *Agent Orange*, 818 F.2d 187 (2d Cir.), *cert. denied sub nom. Krupkin v. Dow Chem. Co.*, 487 U.S. 1234 (1987).

30. *Nehmer v. United States Veterans' Admin.*, 712 F. Supp. 1404, 1408 (N.D. Cal. 1989).

31. *Ryan v. Dow Chem. Co.*, 781 F. Supp. 902, 912 (E.D.N.Y. 1991), *aff'd sub nom. Agent Orange*, 996 F.2d 1425 (2d Cir. 1993), *cert. denied sub nom. Ivy v. Diamond Shamrock Chems. Co.*, 510 U.S. 1140 (1994).

32. *Agent Orange*, 996 F.2d 1425 (2d Cir. 1993), *cert. denied sub nom. Ivy v. Diamond Shamrock Chems. Co.*, 510 U.S. 1140 (1994).

33. *Ivy v. Diamond Shamrock Chems. Co.*, 510 U.S. 1140 (1994).

34. *Boyle v. United Technologies*, 487 U.S. 500 (1988).

35. *Krupkin v. Dow Chem. Co.*, 487 U.S. 1234 (1988).

36. *Id.*

37. *Agent Orange*, 689 F. Supp. 1250 (E.D.N.Y. 1988).

38. All data in this paragraph and the paragraphs that follow regarding payments from the Agent Orange settlement fund were compiled from the *Final Report of the Special Master on the Distribution of the Agent Orange Settlement Fund* (September 1997).

39. *Hercules Inc. v. United States*, 24 F.3d 188 (D.C. Cir. 1994), *aff'd*, 516 U.S. 417 (1996).

40. 38 C.F.R. § 3.313 (1991).

41. 38 C.F.R. § 1.17 (1991); *Nehmer v. United v. United States Veterans' Admin.*, 712 F. Supp. 1404, 1420 (N.D. Cal. 1989); National Veterans Legal Services Project, "Veterans Law Developments," 25 Clearinghouse Review 1268, 1278-79 (Jan. 1990).

42. 38 C.F.R. § 3.311a (1992).

43. 38 C.F.R. § 3.309(e) (1995); 38 C.F.R. 3.309(e)(1996). In 1997,

the VA issued another regulation authorizing benefits for children of Vietnam veterans suffering from spina bifida, a birth defect. 38 C.F.R. 3.814 (1998).

44. *Winters v. Diamond Shamrock Chem. Co.*, 149 F.3d 387 (5th Cir. 1998), *cert. denied*, __ U.S. __, 119 S. Ct. 1286 (1999).

45. *Hercules Inc. v. United States*, 516 U.S. 417 (1996).

Footnotes to Chapter Thirteen

1. Michael Winerip, "The Law Firm that Toxic Waste Built," *N.Y. Times*, Nov. 22, 1985, at B2.

2. *Hechter v. New York Life Ins. Co.*, 385 N.E.2d 551 (N.Y. 1978).

3. *Tefft v. A. C. & S., Inc.*, No. C80-924M (W. D. Wash. Sept. 15, 1982), *aff'd on reh'g*, (W.D. Wash. May 6, 1983), *appeal dismissed*, No. 83-8099 (9th Cir. Aug. 2, 1983).

4. *In re All Maine Asbestos Litigation*, 575 F. Supp. 1375 (D. Me. 1983).

5. *McCrae v. Pittsburgh Corning Corp.*, 97 F.R.D. 490 (E. D. Pa. 1983).

6. *In re General Dynamics Asbestos Cases*, C.M.L. No. 1 (D. Conn. Apr. 22, 1983).

7. *In re: Massachusetts Asbestos Cases*, M.B.L. No. 1 (D. Mass. July 11, 1984).

8. *In re All Maine Asbestos Litigation*, 581 F. Supp. 963, 977 (D. Me. 1984). This case involved claims against the United States arising from work performed on naval vessels at the Bath Iron Works, a privately owned shipyard. In a companion case involving worked performed on naval vessels at the government owned Portsmouth Naval Shipyard, Pittsburgh Corning's third-party claims against the United States were dismissed. *In re All Maine Asbestos Litigation*, 589 F. Supp. 1571 (D. Me. 1984), *aff'd in part and vacated in part*, 772 F.2d 1023 (1st Cir.), *cert. denied sub nom. Eagle-Picher Industries, Inc. v. United States*, 476 U.S. 1126 (1985).

9. *In re All Asbestos Cases*, 603 F. Supp. 599 (D. Ha. 1984).

10. *Colombo v. Johns-Manville Corp.*, 601 F. Supp. 1119 (E. D. Pa. 1984).

11. *See* note 8, *supra*.

12. Arnold H. Lubasch, "Guilty Pleas in O.P.M. Fraud Case," *N.Y.*

Times, Dec. 18, 1981, at D1.

13. Stuart Taylor, Jr., "Two Get Prison in Computer Case," *N.Y. Times*, Dec. 21, 1982, at D1.

14. *Davidoff v. Metropolitan Baseball Club*, 463 N.E.2d 1219 (N.Y. 1984).

15. 42 U.S.C.A. §§ 9601- 9626 (1995).

16. *In re Texas Eastern Transmission Corp. PCB Contamination Ins. Coverage Litig.*, 870 F. Supp. 1293 (E.D. Pa. 1992), *aff'd*, 15 F.3d 1249 (3d cir. 1993), *cert. denied sub nom. Texas Eastern Transmission Corp. v. Fidelity & Cas. Ins. Co. of N.Y.*, 513 U.S. 915 (1994).

17. *United States Fidelity & Guar. Co. v. Star Fire Coals, Inc.*, 856 F.2d 31 (6th Cir. 1988).

Footnotes to Chapter Fourteen

1. *Dole v. Dow Chem. Co.*, 282 N.E.2d 288 (N.Y. 1972).

Index

AEGIS (Associated Electric & Gas
Insurance Company), 3, 377, 387
Clemente, Peter, 385
v. Texas Eastern Corporation (interstate pipeline), 3, 387
Aetna Casualty and Surety Company,
145, 147, 152-154, 197, 199, 352-
353
Agent Orange (case)
class certification, 250, 255-256,
264, 289-290
class action notification, 220, 300
complaints, 247, 248, 249
damages, 221
decisions, 229-230, 276-281
defendants, 220-221
defense attorneys, 221-223
defense strategies, 234-235
government contract defense,
235-238, 253-254, 278, 285,
286, 288, 290, 296, 337, 339,
342
lack of causation, 241-242, 284,
338
product identification defense,
240-241
third-party action, 238-240,
251
Feres Doctrine, 239-240, 247, 249,
252, 258, 298
government liability, 258-259, 286
jury selection, 263, 297, 313-314,
326-327
litigation, 216-232, 247-302
media coverage, 209-212, 220,
263-264
mini-trials, 253, 257-258, 286, 293
motions to dismiss, 249, 252, 291,
298, 341

motions for summary judgment,
252, 296, 335, 337
national common law, 294-295
plaintiffs, 216-217, 219-220
plaintiff strategies, 242-245
Class certification, 243-245
Federal Common Law, 242-243,
286
"Nuremberg" defense, 211, 235, 290
retention of law firm, 207-209, 354-
355
settlement, 291-292, 303-334, 335-
345
settlement issues, 304-308
"Settlement Memorandum," 315-
319
"shoulder-to-shoulder" theory, 249-
250, 260
statute of limitations on, 214
summary judgment, 256-257, 270,
281-282, 283, 292, 337
witnesses, 300
Agent Orange (substance)
"2,4-D," 205, 207, 241
"2,4,5-T," 205, 207, 213-214, 241,
248, 265-269, 271, 277-280, 284,
307, 324
Agent Blue, 205, 207
Agent Green, 205
Agent Pink, 205
Agent Purple, 205
Agent White, 205, 207
chloracne, 213, 267, 269, 273, 277-
278, 341, 343
dioxin (TCDD), 207, 241, 253,
259, 262, 265-266, 269, 271-276,
277, 279-280, 282-284, 295-296,
300, 305-306, 316, 319-320, 322-
325

Hoffman Trip Report, 268-269
Kimmig and Schultz article, 269, 277
manufacturers
  Diamond Shamrock, 221, 280, 288, 295, 305-306, 316, 323, 328-329
  Hercules, 221, 274-275, 279-283, 288, 292, 295-296, 305-306, 316, 328, 343-344
  Hoffman-Taft, 279
  Monsanto, 221, 231-232, 267, 280, 288, 300, 305-306, 308, 316, 323-324, 326, 328-330
  Thompson Chemical, 231, 279, 288, 300, 306, 316, 328, 343, 344
  Thompson-Hayward, 279, 288, 306, 316, 323, 326, 328
  Uniroyal, 221, 262, 279, 306, 316, 328
physical defects allegedly caused by Agent Orange, 203, 208-209, 210-211, 214, 219-220, 240-241, 248, 251, 269, 284, 298, 300, 304, 336, 338, 340
trichlorophenal (TCP), 207, 241, 266-267, 269, 273, 277-278
Agent Orange Advisory Council of Ohio, 215
Agent Orange Plaintiffs' Management Committee, 221
Agent Orange Science and Medicine Series, 300
aflatoxin, 212
Albanese, Ed, 384
Allstate Insurance Company, 71, 78-79, 82, 350, 360, 377, 397
"alter ego" defense (Franklin National Bank case), 148-149, 171-172, 175, 185, 192, 194
American Association for the Advancement of Science, 206
Army Chemical Corps Chemical Warfare Laboratories, 262, 267
  Crops Division, Army Biological Laboratories, 267
Army Corps of Engineers, 270
Army Environmental Hygiene Agency,

Army Surgeon General's Office, 268
asbestos litigation, 362-363, 365-366, 368, 371
  Commercial Union Insurance Company, 362-369
    asbestos defense strategy, 363, 369
    Commercial Union's National Coordinating Counsel, 364, 367
  defendants, 366
  defense strategies, 363, 368
  Federal Tort Claims Act, 364
  Federation of Insurance Counsel (FIC), 362
  government contract defense, 368
  Pittsburgh Corning Corporation, 366-369
  retention of law firm, 362-364
  Sepco Corporation, 366
  settlement, 369
  Standard Asbestos, 366
  Traveler's Insurance Company, The , 366, 369, 385

Bailey, Bill, 362-365
Baker, James, 318-319
Bank Unione, 177
Bayh, Birch, 38, *137*, 398-405, 410
  Chemical Bank, 402
  Cummins Diesel, 402
  Georgia Pacific, 402
  Merrill Lynch, 402
  National Soft Drink Association, 402
  National Basketball Association, 402
Bayh, Evan, 400-401, 404
Beckley, Gilbert Lee, 51
Bennett, Les, 222, 228-229, 280, 285
Bionetics Research Laboratory for the National Institute of Health, 207, 214, 269, 277
Boyle v. United Technologies, 342-343
Brock, Steve, 222, 226, 285, 342
Browning Ferris, 398
Byrnes, Dick, 72
Buell, Bob, 109, 126, 143-145, 147, 149, 154-155, 161, 165, 175, 189-

191, 193, 195, 198-199, 310, 326, 345, 352-354, 371
Bernott, Joan, 162-163, 166
Bunting, Frank, 42
Burdow, Herb, 42
Bush, George, 400

Calabria, Nick, 36
Carey, Charley, 222-223, 225, 262-263, 276-277, 279, 285, 292-294, 299, 301, 310, 313, 317, 326, 329, 345-346, 378, 394, 397
Cavanaugh, Bill, 222, 226-227, 285
Cedarpoint Realty, 29-30
Center for Disease Control (CDC), 213, 338
C.H. Boehringer Sohn, 267, 269, 277
Clemente, Peter, 385
Commerical Union Insurance Company, 362-369, 377, 383-384, 387, 396
   v. W.R. Grace & Co., 387
Compligen, 91-93, 95
Comprehensive Environmental Response, Compensation and Liability Act (CERCLA), 378
Connecticut Vietnam Herbicides Information Commission, 215
Continental Bank of Illinois, 145, 158, 170-171, 184, 199
Copper Seven intrauterine birth control device, 397-398

dapsone, 212
Davis, Ron, 326
Davis, Stu, 42
DDT, 212
Diamond Alkali, 267
Defense Production Act, 238, 240
Department of Agriculture, 207, 299
Department of Defense, 213, 216, 299
Department of Health, Education and Welfare, 207, 216, 299
Department of the Interior, 207
Department of Justice, 340
"Dole Decision" or Dole v. Dow, 392-393
"Dole Doctrine," 123

Dow Chemical, 3, 4, 85, 89-99, 101-128, 203-205, 207-208, 210, 213-215, 219, 221-226, 231-234, 236-237, 239-242, 247-248, 250-253, 258, 260-263, 265-270, 272-275, 277-285, 288, 297-298, 301, 305-311, 313-317, 319-320, 322, 324, 326, 328-330, 341, 343-345, 354, 358, 360-361, 369, 376, 392-394, 396-397
   chloracne outbreak, 273-274
   "conspiracy of silence," 272-273
   Dow-Canada, 262
Drucker, Bruce, 136, 395-396, 412
Dunne, John, 138, 357-360, 370, 382-383, 409, 410

Environmental Health Laboratory, Air Force Logistics Command, 267
environmental insurance, 378-380, 382
Environmental Protection Agency (EPA), 214, 248, 378, 386, 402
Esterman, Pam, 222
European American Bank, 141-142, 182
Ezagui v. Dow, 91-98
   Compligen, 91-93, 95
   Parke-Davis Company, 91-95, 97-98
   Parke-Davis and Company v. Stromsodt, 92, 94-96, 98
   Quadrigen, 91-93, 95-98
   Tinnerholm v. Parke, Davis & Co., 92, 94-98

Federal Communications Commission, 402
Federal Deposit Insurance Corporation (FDIC), 141, 143, 145-150, 153-159, 162, 165, 168, 170-172, 174-176, 182, 184, 189-193, 194-198, 199
Federal Reserve, 141, 150, 158, 162, 168, 174
Federal Reserve Bank of New York, 168
Federal Rules of Civil Procedure, 216, 220, 249, 333, 335
Federal Rules of Evidence, 338
Federal Savings and Loan Insurance Corporation (FSLIC), 403

Federal Tort Claims Act (FTCA), 162, 164-165, 183, 230, 234, 239, 247, 252, 298, 339-340, 343, 364
Federal Trade Commission, 402
Federation of American Scientists, 206
Federation of Insurance Counsel (FIC), 144
Feinberg, Kenneth, 318-324, 326, 329-330, 333
Feres Doctrine, 239-240, 247, 249, 252, 258, 298
fidelity and surety law, 144, 147
Fireman's Fund Insurance Company, 3, 71, 82, 84-85, 89-90, 101, 107-110, 123, 143-199, 153, 155, 158-159, 164-165, 168, 189, 190, 193, 195, 197, 310-311, 326, 334, 345, 350, 354, 371-373, 377-382, 384, 386, 391-392, 396-397
  James Graham Brown company, 386
  National Coordinating Counsel, 379
  Superfund cleanup costs, 380-382
  v. Ex-Cell-O Corporation, 386
    Trextron Corporation, 386
  v. Shell Oil Company (Rocky Mountain Arsenal disposal site), 388
  RTE Corporation, 386
  see also Franklin National Bank
First Annual Hazardous Waste Symposium (Hofstra Law School), 382, 385
Florio, James J., 382
Food and Drug Administration, 402
Fortune 500 clients, 402-403, 408
Franklin National Bank, 3, 4, 85, 141-199, 239, 288, 313, 352
  Aetna Casualty and Surety Company, 145, 147, 152-154, 197, 199, 352-353
  "alter ego" defense, 148-149, 171-172, 175, 185, 192, 194
  Comptroller of the Currency, 147, 149-150, 158-162, 164, 166-167, 174, 181, 189, 196, 198
  Continental Bank of Illinois, 145, 184

European American Bank, 141-142, 182
Federal Deposit Insurance Corporation (FDIC), 141, 143, 145-150, 153-159, 162, 165, 168, 170-172, 174-176, 182, 184, 189-193, 194-198, 199, 352
Federal Reserve, 141, 150, 158, 162, 168, 174
Federal Tort Claims Act (FTCA), 162, 164-165, 183
grand jury secrecy, 152-153
guilty pleas by board members, 148-149
guilty pleas by employees, 152
Insurance Company of North America (INA), 145-146, 153-154, 197-199, 352-353
Lloyd's of London, 151
Manufacturer's Hanover Trust, 145, 150
"one loss" defense, 192
Purchase and Assumption Agreement, 182
retention of law firm, 143-144, 352
Securities and Exchange Commission, 146
settlement, 193, 199
statute of limitations, 162
Talcott National, 149
third-party complaints
  against bank's former directors, 158
  against bank's outside accountants, 158
  against Continental Bank of Illinois, 158, 170-171, 199
  against United States of American, 158
Trustee in Bankruptcy for Franklin New York Corporation, The, 153-159, 170-172, 175-176, 184, 197-198
United States Attorney, 153
Frayer, Don, 89-90, 93, 95, 105-106, 108-109, 121, 123, 125-126, 211-212, 224, 310, 345, 354, 393
Freeport Police Department, 47, 83

"Good Samaritan" theory, 162-164
Garment, Leonard, 318-321
GEICO, 82, 350
General Accident Insurance Company, 350
General Electric, 398
Gorman, Ed, 308-312, 317
Graham, Bob, 405
Gray, L. Patrick, 175
Guibord, Barbara, 381, 385, 398
  Browning Ferris, 398
  General Electric, 398
  Waste Management, 398

Haines, Jim, 310-311, 313
Hancock, Wayne, 310-313, 326, 331, 345
Hart, Edward J., 35, 44, 46-47, *136*, *138*, 370-371, 410
  LILCO, 370
Hartford, The, 377, 384-385, 387, 397
  v. Boeing Company (Western Processing waste site), 387
Hauft, Al, 36
hazardous waste insurance, 380, 382, 383, 386, 389
Health and Human Services, 213
Henderson, Thomas, 312
Hess, Otis, 326-328, 334, 345
hit-and-run accidents/arbitrations, 73, 76, 81-82
Hofstra Law School, 354, 382-383
  First Annual Hazardous Waste Symposium (Hofstra Law School), 382, 385
    speakers
      Florio, James J., 382
      Lent, Norman, 382
      Price, Courtney, 382
      Schmertz, Eric, 383, 411
      Young, Col. Alvin L., 382
  Hofstra Law School Civil Litigation Clinic, The, 354
Indian Towing, 162-164
Institute for Defense Analysis, 268, 277
Insurance Company of North America (INA), 145-146, 153-154, 197-199, 352-353

insurance defense work, 71-79

Jasen, Hon. Matthew, 392
Johnson, Hon. George S., 30
Joint Technical Coordinating Group/Subcommittee on Defoliants, USAF, 267
Jordan, Dick, 377-379, 381, 384
Josefsberg, Irving, 23-26, 29, 31, 66
Judd, Hon. Orin, 155-156
Judicial Panel on Multidistrict Litigation, 217-219, 230, 247-248, 260, 285, 340, 342

Kelly, Bill, 169, 190, 193-194, 196-198
Kemper Insurance Company, 360-361, 369
Kennedy, John F., 206
Kissinger, Henry, 206, 262
Koehlinger, Don, 89-90, 93-95, 101, 108
Kolb, Dan, 163, 169, 184
Kremer, Jerry, *138*, 410
Krohley, Bill, 274, 280-281, 295-296

Lansky, Meyer, 51
Leff, Jack, 27-28
Leff, Paul, 27-28, 33, 371
Leff, Victor, 33-39, 41, *132*, 355, 384
Lent, Norman, 382
Levy, Norman, 42, *137*
LILCO, 370
Lloyd's of London, 151, 360-362
London, Martin, 152, 163-164
  Paul, Rifkind, Wharton & Garrison, 152

Makulski, Mike, 376
Manufacturer's Hanover Trust, 145, 150
McGovern, George, 401
McKennon, Keith, 225, 276, 281, 313, 326-329, 331-332, 345
MacMillan, Don, *136*
Michigan Agent Orange Commission, 215
Miele, Joanne, 224, 229

Mintzer, Marge, 222, 228, 262-263, 285, 294
Mirtsching, Len, 364-365
Mitchelson, Marvin, 375
Mondale, Walter, 402
Motor Vehicle Accident Indemnification Corporation (MVAIC), 72-78, 84
   O'Boyle, Tom, 74-75, 79
Musselwhite, Benton, 330-331

Nassau County Bar Association (NCBA), 32, 55-56, 66-67
   Grievance Committee, 55-56
negligent bank regulation (Franklin National Bank case), 150-151
New York State Association of Trial Lawyers, 67
New York State Dioxin Commission, 215
New York State Medical Society, 72
New York *Times* (articles)
   Franklin case parody/Platt recusal, 180
   Grand Jury leaks, 174
   Growth of law firm, 349-350
   O.P.M. case, 371
   "Secret Agent," 300
   Veterans' illnesses, 210
Newsday
   picture of Rivkin and Gilbert Lee Beckley, 51
   article on Second Department decision, 64

O'Boyle, Tom, 74-75, 79
"of counsel" work, defined, 25
Office of Defense Research, Department of Defense, 270
Oklahoma Agent Orange Outreach Committee, 215
O.P.M. Leasing Services, Inc., 373-375
O'Reagan, Ralph, 85
Oreffice, Paul, 327
Ortega, Joe, 222, 228, 376-377

Phase I Trial (Agent Orange), 255-257, 259-260, 262, 279, 281-285, 286, 291, 295, 306, 309, 368

Pierce, Stan, 222-223, 229, 261, 282, 285, 383
Pittsburgh Corning Corporation, 3, 366-369
Platt, Hon. Thomas, 156-157, 159-161, 164-165, 167-169, 171-173, 179-180, 194
Pratt, Hon. George C., 217-218, 229, 237-238, 242, 245, 247-252, 254-265, 272, 274, 276-279, 281-287, 296, 305, 312, 356, 368
President's Science Advisory Committee (PSAC), 270-272, 277, 299, 320
Price, Courtney, 382
Project Ranch Hand, 206-207, 213, 262, 265, 336
Public Health Service, 267-268, 277
Purcell, Bill, 151-152, 173

Quadrigen, 91-93, 95-98
Quayle, Dan, 400, 404
Quinn, Joe, 85

Radler, Warren, *136*, *138*, 379, 383, 391-398, 403, 410
   Baxter Health Care (Baxter International), 398
   Dole v. Dow Chemical, 392
   Dow's National Coordinating Counsel for the Sarabond litigation, 395
   G.D. Searle, 397-398
      Copper Seven intrauterine birth control device, 397-398, 403
   National Coordinating Counsel for the Styrofoam leakage cases, 393
   Sarabond, 394-395, 397
Rand Corporation, 206, 317
Republican party, 46-47
Reutershan, Paul, 205, 207, 216-217, 233, 247
Richman, Noah, 36
Rigano, Jim, 334
Rivkin & Leff, 34
Rivkin, Leff & Sherman, 358
Rivkin, Leff, Sherman & Radler, 379, 396
Rivkin, Leonard, *129-130*, *132-133*, *136-140*

early career, 4
  Brooklyn office, 4, 24
  Far Rockaway, 13, 18, 23, 46
  Josefsberg, Irving, 23-26, 29, 31, 66
    early in-court experience, 25-26
    personal injury lawyer, 24
    "of counsel" work, 25-26, 32
  Katz, William, 23
  member of New York State Bar (1950), 26
  politics, 46
    Republican Committeeman, Hewlett, 46
  starting own office, 26
  Village Court, Freeport, 4, 7
    Village of Freeport PBA, 47, 83
education
  University of Virginia, 3, 11, 14, 17
    law, 20-21
    pre-med, 19-20
  Woodmere Academy, 14
family
  Feldman, Judy (Rivkin), 13, *130*, *139*
  Rivkin, Betty Friedman, 6, *139-140*, 412
  Rivkin, Hyman, Dr., 6, 11-14, 72, *129-130*
  Rivkin, Nettie, 12-14, 17, *129-130*
  Rivkin, John, 6, *138*, *140*, 369-370, 375, 379, 381-382, 384-385, 400-401, 410
  Rivkin, Lenore, 6, 27, *132*
  Zuckerman, Janet (Rivkin), 6, *140*, 355-356
firms
  Rivkin & Leff, 34
  Rivkin, Leff & Sherman, 358
  Rivkin, Leff, Sherman & Radler, 379, 396
  Rivkin, Radler, Dunne & Bayh, 3, 401, 408
  Rivkin, Radler, & Kremer, 411
military service, 14-17
  capture of German soldiers (Rarin), 16

discharged, 17
Enlisted Reserve Corps (ERC), 15
Grossingers, Catskills Mountains, 18
purple hearts, 15
silver star, 16, 193
judicial inquiry, 56-66, 68-69, 71
  Gulotta, Hon. Frank A., 56-58
  Hanrahan, William F., 56-57, 63, 68
  disciplinary proceedings, 58-59
    bills of particulars, 59-60
  Second Department, 57-58, 63-66
    charges dismissed, 68
  Court of Appeals, 65-67, 71
  Greason, Samuel, 58
  Beasley, William, 58, 60, 69
  Brennan, William R., Jr., 60-64, 66
  Hennefeld, Edmund B., 65-66, 69
  witnesses,
    Affatato, Peter T., 62
    Johnson, Hon. Cortland A., 62
    Meyer, Hon. Bernard S., 62
    Montfort, Frederic, 62
noteworthy cases
  Mets' spectator injury, 374
  Marina Navratilova, 374-375
  Merill Lynch, 375
  CNA Insurance Company, 360, 375
  Squibb, 375-376
offices
  11 West Sunrise Highway, 42, *134*
  16 West Sunrise Highway, 42-45, 50, 52, 54, 74
    "New Case Book," 45, 53
    staff increase, 44
    "tote board," 43
  35 West Merrick Road, Freeport, Long Island, 26, 72, 95, *133*
  39 North LaSalle Street, Chicago, 3, 350, 379, 396
  55 North Ocean Avenue, 54, 80, 196
  100 Garden City Plaza, *135*, 142-143, 349, 370-371, 389
  200 Garden City Plaza, 349, 389

1575 "I" Street, Washington, DC,
3, 350, 389
Century City, Los Angeles, 3
EAB Plaza, Long Island, 3, *135*,
377, 407-409, 411
Madison Avenue, New York, 3, 389
partners
Bayh, Birch, 38, *137*, 398-405,
410
Drucker, Bruce, *136*, 395-396, 410
Dunne, John, *138*, 357-360, 370,
382-383, 409, 410
Hart, Edward J., 35, 44, 46-47,
136, *138*, 370-371, 410
Leff, Victor, 33-39, 41, 194, 355,
384
Radler, Warren, *136*, *138*, 379,
383, 391-398, 403, 410
Savino, Bill, *136*, 360-361, 369,
379, 381-382, 385-386, 410
Sherman, Stuart, 36-39, 41, 47-
49, 54, 60, 68-69, 76, 80, 83-84,
136, *138*, 349, 355, 358, 410
Silberfeld, Jeffrey, 147-148, *136*,
222, 227, 260, 263-264, 282,
293-294, 313, 352, 355, 364-368,
375, 378-379, 381-385, 387-388,
401, 410
Weinberg, Phil, 75-76, 107, *136*,
349, 351-352, 357-358, 410
retirement, 411-412
Rivkin & Leff, 34
Rivkin, Leff & Sherman, 358
Rivkin, Leff, Sherman & Radler, 379,
396
Rivkin, Radler, Dunne & Bayh, 3, 401,
408
Rivkin, Radler, & Kremer, 411
Rockefeller, Nelson, 351
Rose, Howard, 54
Rudes, Nat, 35
Ruger, Jim, 222, 285

Salinger, Rolf, 384
Sarabond, 394-395, 396-397
Savino, Bill, 198, 360-361, 369, 379,
381-382, 385-386, 410
Schlegel, Stephen, 312, 315

Schmertz, Eric, 383, 411
Schreiber, Sol, 262
Scottish & York Insurance Company,
360
Second Circuit Court of Appeals, 208,
217, 226-227, 229, 242, 250-252,
254, 260, 286, 294-295, 299, 303,
312, 341-343
Securities and Exchange Commission,
146
Shapiro, David, 318-322, 324-325
Sherman, Stuart, 36-39, 41, 47-49, 54,
60, 68-69, 76, 80, 83-84, *136*, *138*,
349, 355, 358, 410
"shoulder-to-shoulder" theory, 249-250
Sidona, Michele, 149-150, 171, 173,
175-180, 185-188, 192
Silberfeld, Jeff, 147-148, *136*, 222,
227, 260, 263-264, 282, 293-294,
313, 352, 355, 364-368, 375, 378-
379, 381-385, 387-388, 401, 410
Silberman, Morton, 222
Skillern, Frank, 194-199
Hamilton Bank case (TN), 194
United States National Bank case
(San Diego), 194
Social Security Administration, 216
Sommerville, Mike, 364-365
South Nassau Lawyer's Association
(SNLA), 32, 35, 46
South Carolina Agent Orange Advisory
Council, 215
Special Masters, 318-327, 329-330,
332
Feinberg, Kenneth, 318-324, 326,
329-330, 333
Garment, Leonard, 318-321
Shapiro, David, 318-322, 324-325
Staten Island natural gas tank
explosion, 90, 99-118, 354, 358,
360-361
ABC Documentary, 124-125
American Society for Testing and
Materials (ASTM), 118-119, 124-
125
Battelle Memorial Institute, 101,
108, 111, 114, 119-120, 122, 124,
127-128

Brown & Root, Inc., 101, 111
Bureau of Mines, 105, 125
D'Anna, Sam, 110
Darger, Dick, 108-110, 126
"Dole Doctrine," 123
Federal Trade Commission (FTC), 103-104
    Consent Decree, 103-104
first wrongful death settlement, 123
Occupational Heath and Safety Administration, The (OSHA), 102-103, 122
polyurethane, flammability of, 103, 104, 105, 106, 114, 118-120, 124-125
Sheldahl, Inc., 101
Sinapp Company of Staten Island, 101
Special Subcommittee on Investigations of the House Committee on Interstate and Foreign Commerce, 106-107
Stouffer fire case, 369-370
Styrofoam, 393-394, 396

Talcott National, 149
Texas Eastern Transmission Corporation, 101-102, 104-128
"tote board," 43-44

United States Agency for International Relief, 344
USF&G (United States Fidelity & Guaranty Insurance Company), 385, 388

Veterans Administration, 208-209, 212-213, 216, 220, 230, 233, 292, 297, 300, 314-315, 321, 341, 343-344

Vietnam, 203, 205-206, 208, 211-212, 214, 216, 219-220, 231, 233, 238, 241-242, 255-256, 262, 265, 269-272, 277, 284, 300, 308, 336-340, 344
Allied Forces, 203, 206
Defoliation, 205-206, 238, 271

Washington Post, 206
Waste Management, 398
Weill, Sandy, 334-335, 345
Weinberg, Philip, 75-76, 107, 198, 349, 351-352, 357-358, 410
Bank Leumi, 351
Chemical Bank, Uniform Commercial Code litigation, 351
Dime Savings Bank, 351
New York State Liquidation Bureau, 351-352
Weinstein, Hon. Jack B., 179-182, 184, 188-189, 194, 197-199, 217-218, 229, 231-232, 235, 242, 286-296, 297-301, 304, 312-314, 317-318, 327-343
Weiss, Jerry, 29
Westmoreland, Gen. William, 206, 262
Wilson, Malcolm, 351
Wolff, Lt. Arthur, 47

Yannacone, Victor, 208, 211-212, 216, 218, 221, 229, 233, 235, 242-243, 247-250, 253-254, 260, 265, 346
Yannacone & Associates, 308-309, 312
Young, Col. Alvin L., 382